The Tormented Alliance

The Tormented Alliance

American Servicemen and the
Occupation of China, 1941–1949

· ·

ZACH FREDMAN

The University of North Carolina Press Chapel Hill

The University of North Carolina Press has been a member
of the Green Press Initiative since 2003.

Library of Congress Cataloging-in-Publication Data
Names: Fredman, Zach, author.
Title: The tormented alliance : American servicemen and the occupation
    of China, 1941–1949 / Zach Fredman.
Description: Chapel Hill : University of North Carolina Press, [2022] |
    Includes bibliographical references and index.
Identifiers: LCCN 2022015060 | ISBN 9781469669571 (cloth; alk. paper) |
    ISBN 9781469669588 (paperback; alk. paper) | ISBN 9781469669595
    (ebook)
Subjects: LCSH: World War, 1939-1945—China. | United States—Armed
    Forces—China—History—20th century. | United States—Military
    relations—China. | China—History—1937-1945. | China—History—
    Civil War, 1945-1949. | China—Foreign relations—1912-1949. |
    United States—Foreign relations—1933-1945. | United States—Foreign
    relations—1945-1953. | China—Foreign relations—United States. |
    United States—Foreign relations—China.
Classification: LCC UA26.C58 F74 2022
LC record available at https://lccn.loc.gov/2022015060

Cover illustrations: *Top*, Alfred T. Palmer, *Tank Driver, Ft. Knox, Ky.*, 1942;
bottom, interior of U.S. Army Air Force DC-3 transporting Chinese soldiers,
1943. Both photos courtesy of Farm Security Administration–Office of War
Information collections, Library of Congress Prints and Photographs Division.

Chapter 2 was originally published in a different form as "Lofty Expectations
and Bitter Reality: Chinese Interpreters for the U.S. Army during the Second
World War, 1941–1945," *Frontiers of History in China* 12, no. 4 (September 2017):
566–98. Chapter 5 was originally published in a different form as "GIs and
'Jeep Girls': Sex and American Soldiers in Wartime China," *Journal of Modern
Chinese History* 13, no. 1 (September 2019): 76–101.

To my family

Contents

Figures and Maps, ix

Acknowledgments, xi

Chronology of Wartime Sino-American Relations
and the U.S. Military Presence in China, xv

Introduction, 1

1 Making Our Friends at Home, 21
China's Hostel Program

2 Communicating without Understanding, 48
China's Interpreter Program

3 Unequal Partners, 79
Military-to-Military Relations

4 Living with the U.S. Military, 108
Chinese Civilians

5 GIs and Jeep Girls, 135
Sexual Relations

6 Everything Comes Undone, 163
The Postwar Occupation

Epilogue, 196
The Occupation of China's Long Shadow

Notes, 207

Bibliography, 269

Index, 295

Figures and Maps

Figures

1.1 Huang Renlin towering over Chiang Kai-shek and Brigadier General Frederick McCabe, Ramgarh, India, 1943, 25

1.2 Hostel No. 1, Kunming, 28

1.3 Night soil collector in Chongqing, 33

3.1 Chinese cadets and American instructors at Ramgarh, 89

4.1 AVG blood chit: "This foreigner has come to help China fight. Soldiers and civilians, one and all, rescue him." 110

4.2 Airfield construction in Yunnan, 114

4.3 Three American soldiers and a Chinese traffic officer in Chongqing, 125

5.1 Chinese women and American enlisted men at a badminton exhibition organized for U.S. Army headquarters in Chongqing, 140

5.2 The Nanping Theater on "GI Street," downtown Kunming, 142

5.3 *Lively Jeep Girls*: three images from a larger series titled *Allied Soldiers in Chongqing*, 144

6.1 American marines and their dates in Qingdao, 186

E.1 The U.S. military presence in 1940s China as portrayed during the Resist America and Aid Korea campaign, 1950, 198

E.2 Image of Chiang Kai-shek and an American serviceman as portrayed during the Resist America and Aid Korea campaign, 1950, 199

Maps

China, December 1941, xxv

The U.S. military in Southwest China, xxvi

Chinese retreat from Burma, 1942, 86

North China, 1945, 166

Acknowledgments

I owe a heavy debt of gratitude to my family for their unwavering support over this long project. This book is dedicated to my parents, Gerald Fredman and Carol Rogers Collins, who never gave up on me despite everything I did to test their patience. My sister Rachel let me sleep on her couch for a month when I began research and, along with my brother Ben and sister Rebecca, has always believed in me. My cousin Miles Liss, stepfather Gary Collins, and in-laws Zhou Chang'an and Zhang Mingqing have all been helpful beyond the call of duty. Tom Price deserves mention alongside family for taking me under his wing and convincing me to move to China, setting me on the path that eventually led to this book. There is no way I could have completed this project without the love and support of my wife, Wenjing, who stoically persevered through three transpacific moves to different universities and countries over a two-year stretch. I'm tremendously grateful for every day together, and I can't imagine a better friend, partner, co-parent, and travel companion. Thank you to our daughter Sylvia, for bringing so much joy to our lives.

I feel truly privileged to have attended graduate school at Boston University. Andrew Bacevich is a national treasure and everything one could hope for in an advisor. His mentorship and unflagging support over the past decade helped make this project possible, while his scholarship, teaching, and contributions to public debate in the United States will always be the model I aspire to. While most graduate students would be lucky to have one great advisor, I had two. Brooke Blower always remained steadfast in championing my work. She was also a voice of constant support and encouragement and, to this day, another inspiring model as a thinker, scholar, and person. Joe Fewsmith helped me understand Chinese history and probably treated me to more meals than all my other professors combined. Louis Ferleger was generous with funding, while coursework and conversations with Eugenio Menegon, Jonathan Zatlin, Jon Roberts, Brendan McConville, and William Keylor provided sound advice and helped me craft my work as a historian. David Atkinson, D. J. Cash, Mark Kukis, Sarah Childress, Amy Noel, Aaron Hilter, Anshul Jain, Jeremy Weiss, and Andrew David made my time spent in Boston engaging and festive. I am also grateful to the BU History Department for supporting my semester at the University of Cambridge, where conversations with Arne Westad, Matthew Jones, Andrew Preston, Rana Mitter, and Hans van de Ven helped get this project off the ground.

Fellowships at Nanyang Technological University and Dartmouth College's John Sloan Dickey Center for International Understanding were crucial to this book's development. In Singapore, Masuda Hajimu and Wen-Qing Ngoei taught me how to write a book proposal. K. K. Luke, Chen Song-chuan, Els van Dongen, Uganda Kwan, and Daniel Chua provided valuable feedback on various parts of the manuscript. Lin Ling-Fei was a terrific office mate and friend. I was equally fortunate to spend a year with the fantastic community of professors, staff, and postdocs in Hanover, New Hampshire. Conversations and seminars with William Wohlforth, Jennifer Lind, George Yin, Andrew Bertolli, Andrew Shaver, Sheri Zaks, Stephanie Freeman, and Ore Koren helped me strengthen my arguments. I am especially grateful for the warm welcome, thoughtful advice, and continued friendship offered by Jennifer Miller, Udi Greenberg, and Edward Miller.

As a faculty member in the Division of Arts and Humanities at Duke Kunshan University for the past three years, I have been fortunate to be part of a rigorous, supportive, and fun-loving intellectual community. I am indebted to division chairs James Miller and Kolleen Guy for their generosity with funding, advice, and timely breaks in my teaching schedule. Colleagues at DKU, including Scott MacEachern, Qian Zhu, Nellie Chu, Bryce Beemer, Lincoln Rathnam, Yu Wang, Selina Lai-Henderson, and Ben Schupmann, each read parts of the manuscript and made helpful suggestions. Mengjie Zou tracked down obscure published sources, and research assistants Qi Pan and Sirui Yao helped with various pressing tasks in the last stages of the work.

A few individuals who read and reread this manuscript deserve special mention. Wen-hsin Yeh, Prasenjit Duara, Andrew Bacevich, Edward Miller, Carlos Rojas, and James Miller read the book cover to cover for my manuscript review and helped make it what it is now. Erez Manela, Steven I. Levine, and two anonymous reviewers at the University of North Carolina Press read every chapter and gave me crucial feedback that guided my follow-up research and proved essential to the book's completion. It has been a great pleasure to work with the University of North Carolina Press, and I am particularly grateful to Brandon Proia, who has played an integral role at every stage in the life of this book.

Portions of this book have been presented at a variety of conferences, lectures, and workshops at the Australian National University; Renmin

University; Chongqing University; the University of Hong Kong; Nanyang Technological University; Mississippi State University; the University of Wisconsin, Madison; Merrimack College; the Massachusetts Historical Society; the London School of Economics; Oxford University; the University of Birmingham; the University of Manchester; the Summer Institute China in a Global World War II at the University of Cambridge; the Uneasy Allies conferences at Duke Kunshan; and panels at the annual meetings of the Association for Asian Studies, the American Historical Association, the Chinese Society for Military History (Taipei), and the Society for Historians of American Foreign Relations. I wish to thank a host of scholars who listened patiently and provided feedback: Shuge Wei, Chang Jui-te, Daqing Yang, Seung-joon Lee, Ch'i Hsi-sheng, Joshua Howard, Jonathan Henshaw, Henrietta Harrison, Xu Guoqi, Priscilla Roberts, Jian Chen, Hans van de Ven, Ke Ren, Mary Brazelton, Chi-man Kwong, David Cheng Chang, Linh Vu, Covell Meyskens, Zhiguo Yang, Yanqiu Zheng, Chunmei Du, Mary Louise Roberts, Elisabeth Leake, Aaron O'Connell, Meredith Oyen, Andrew Rotter, Charles Hayford, Guo Haiying, Henry Marr, Jonathan Hunt, Asa McKercher, Zhong Zhong Chen, James Cameron, Chris Capozzola, Daniel Immerwahr, Kristin Hoganson, Jay Sexton, Mary Kathryn Barbier, Alan Marcus, Julia Osman, Barak Kushner, and Lyle Goldstein. The contributions of Jamie Miller and Judd Kinzley to this project have been enormous. Without their support, I would have lost my way long ago.

This project, which involved sustained research in mainland China, Taiwan, the United States, and Myanmar, would not have been possible without the help of many key individuals and institutions. Yao Zexun, Yuan Zujie, Chang Jui-te, Deng Hegang, Tai Chun, Liu Xun, and Mr. and Mrs. S. T. Lung have assisted me in ways too plentiful to enumerate. Archivists and librarians in Kunming, Chongqing, Shanghai, Nanjing, Beijing, Tianjin, and Taipei were unfailingly supportive and understanding, especially those who helped me decipher difficult handwriting or looked the other way when I exceeded daily print quotas. Margaret Wong, Thant Thaw Kaung, and the late Raymond Lum facilitated a fruitful, last-minute visit to the Myanmar National Archives, based on a hot tip from Sergey Radchenko. In the United States, I am indebted to Megan Harris at the Veterans History Project, Kurt Piehler and Mike Kasper at the Institute on World War II and the Human Experience, and Hsiao-ting Lin at the Hoover Institution. I am also grateful to archivists and staff at the National Archives and Records Center, the Wisconsin Veterans Museum, the Harvard University Archives, the U.S. Army Center for Military History, and the Marine Corps

History Division. The research and writing of this project was made possible by grants from Boston University, St. Catherine's College at the University of Cambridge, the Duke Kunshan University Humanities Research Center and Chancellor's Office, the Association for Asian Studies, the American Council of Learned Societies, the Society for Historians of American Foreign Relations, the Institute on World War II and the Human Experience, and the University of Wisconsin, Madison.

An earlier version of chapter 2 was published in the December 2017 issue of *Frontiers of History in China*. An earlier version of chapter 5 was published in the September 2019 issue of the *Journal of Modern Chinese History*. I am grateful to be able to reprint portions of these articles in revised form.

Chronology of Wartime Sino-American Relations and the U.S. Military Presence in China

1937

May 1
: Captain Claire Chennault retires from the U.S. Army Air Corps and departs for China to conduct a confidential survey of the Chinese Air Force for Chiang Kai-shek.

July 7
: The Second Sino-Japanese War begins near Beijing with a clash at the Marco Polo Bridge.

November 15
: The Supreme Defense Council accepts Chiang's proposal to move China's capital from Nanjing to Chongqing. Offices needed to direct the war move to Wuhan, roughly halfway between Shanghai and Chongqing along the Yangzi (Yangtze) River.

December 5
: Chiang announces no peace negotiations until Japanese forces leave China.

December 12
: Japanese naval aircraft sink the USS *Panay*, a U.S. Navy Yangtze Patrol gunboat anchored near Nanjing, killing four Americans.

December 13
: A month after seizing Shanghai, the Japanese take Nanjing and begin a massacre.

1938

January 3
: Chiang Kai-shek and his wife Song Meiling appear on the cover of *Time* magazine as "Man and Wife of the Year," Chiang's sixth *Time* cover appearance.

March 2
: The U.S. Army's Fifteenth Infantry Regiment, stationed in Tianjin since 1912, leaves China. Fifteenth Infantry veterans who will return to China as generals during the war include John Magruder, Joseph Stilwell, Haydon Boatner, Frank Dorn, and Albert Wedemeyer.

August 10
: U.S. ambassador Nelson Johnson arrives in Chongqing with his staff after a journey from Wuhan aboard the Yangtze Patrol gunboats USS *Luzon* and USS *Tutuila*.

| October 25 | The Nationalist government orders the evacuation of Wuhan, and Chiang sends Chennault to Kunming to open an air force training academy. |
| December 13 | The Export-Import Bank of the United States extends a $25 million loan to China. |

1939

May 3–4	Heavy Japanese bombing of Chongqing kills more than five thousand civilians.
May 13	Colonel Joseph Stilwell ends his deployment as U.S. military attaché in Beijing, where he had served in this capacity since June 1935, his third tour in China.
September 1	Germany invades Poland, and the Second World War begins in Europe.
September 15	Japan and the Soviet Union sign a cease-fire after a battle near Nomonhan, on the Mongolian-Manchurian border. Japan now focuses on eliminating Chinese resistance.

1940

March 30	Establishment of Chinese puppet government in Nanjing under Wang Jingwei, Chiang's onetime rival in the Nationalist Party (Guomindang) and former ROC premier.
September 25	Franklin Roosevelt approves another $25 million loan to China, two days after Japanese troops enter Indochina and halt French rail shipments into Kunming.
September 27	Japan, Germany, and Italy sign the Tripartite Pact.
November 25	Chinese Air Force major general Mao Bangchu and Claire Chennault travel to Washington to request five hundred combat aircraft for China. In late December, the Roosevelt administration agrees to provide China with one hundred obsolete Curtiss P-40B aircraft.

1941

| March 31 | Song Ziwen, Chiang's brother-in-law and personal envoy to the United States, presents China's lend-lease requests, including arms to equip thirty army divisions. |

April 15	Roosevelt allows Chennault to begin recruiting American military personnel to fly P-40s for the Chinese Air Force as part of the American Volunteer Group (AVG).
May 6	China becomes eligible for lend-lease aid, but the United States continues to sell oil to Japan.
May 9	Chiang orders War Area Service Corps (WASC) director Huang Renlin to set up hostels for the AVG in Kunming. Huang begins training interpreters for the AVG in July.
July 28	The first group of AVG pilots and ground crew arrive in Rangoon to begin training.
October 10	Brigadier General John Magruder, commander of the American Military Mission to China, arrives in Chongqing to assess ROC military needs. He concludes without foundation that Chiang intends to hoard U.S. aid and use it against the Communists.
December 5	The U.S. Navy's Yangtze Patrol, organized in 1921, is formally dissolved.
December 7–8	The United States and the ROC become formal allies after Japan attacks Pearl Harbor and begins a two-pronged offensive against Southeast Asia. The Nationalists prepare to extend hostel and interpreter services to all U.S. military personnel coming to China.
December 20	The AVG engages in its first battle with the Japanese over the skies of Kunming.
December 22– January 14	Roosevelt and Winston Churchill decide on a "Europe-first" strategy and exclude Chiang from the U.S.-UK Combined Chiefs of Staff.

1942

March 4	Joseph Stilwell, now a lieutenant general, arrives in Chongqing as commander of U.S. forces in the China-Burma-India (CBI) theater and Chiang's chief of staff.
March 7	Stilwell recommends that the War Department procure and ship arms to equip thirty Chinese divisions, making Chinese Army training a central U.S. aim in China.
March 8	Japanese forces seize Rangoon, cutting off the Burma Road, China's last link to the outside world. A week later, the Chinese Expeditionary Force enters Burma following

initial British rejection of Chinese support. Chiang grants Stilwell command over Chinese forces in Burma, but Allied attempts to halt the Japanese advance fail.

March 20   Roosevelt creates the Assam-Burma-China Ferry Command to airlift supplies to China. This dangerous route across the Himalayas will become known as "the Hump."

May 6–20   Stilwell abandons Chinese forces in Burma and walks to India, leading a group of about one hundred people. His actions outrage Chiang, but the American press lionizes him as a hero. The Chinese Army's Twenty-Second and Thirty-Eighth Divisions eventually reach India.

June 11   The U.S. Army's Services of Supply (SOS) is activated in Kunming and charged with receiving, storing, and transshipping war matériel being flown to China.

July 2   Chiang gives Stilwell command of his Twenty-Second and Thirty-Eighth Divisions, now called the Chinese Army in India (CAI).

July 4   The AVG is disbanded and replaced by the Twenty-Third Fighter Group of the China Air Task Force under Chennault, who was recalled to active duty on April 15.

August 26   The U.S. Army's Ramgarh Training Center for Chinese forces is activated in Bihar, India. Airlifts will bring the CAI, also known as X-Force, up to five-division strength.

October 10   The United States and the United Kingdom announce their decision to relinquish extraterritoriality in China.

December 1   The U.S. Army's Air Transport Command takes over the Hump airlift, aiming to fly five thousand tons of supplies to China per month. This goal is not reached until June.

1943

January 19   Stilwell begins training program for Chinese forces in Yunnan, known as Y-Force, under the command of Colonel Frank Dorn. U.S. Army–run infantry and artillery training centers open on April 11 near Kunming.

February   Stilwell directs construction of the Ledo Road toward the India-Burma border.

March 19   The China Air Task Force is dissolved and made part of the newly activated Fourteenth Air Force, with Chennault, now a major general, still in command.

May 20	The U.S. Senate unanimously ratifies the Sino-American New Equal Treaty, relinquishing extraterritorial rights in China; on May 21, however, the U.S. and Chinese governments sign an agreement granting the U.S. military exclusive jurisdiction over U.S. forces in China.
June 18	Stilwell consolidates American organizations working with Y-Force into a single command, with Dorn as chief of staff. In addition to running training programs, Dorn takes charge of distributing lend-lease aid in Yunnan.
July 4	Dai Li signs the Sino-American Cooperative Organization (SACO) agreement, creating a clandestine intelligence partnership between the Juntong—the Guomindang's most powerful secret police agency—and the U.S. Navy. Commodore Milton Miles, a Yangtze Patrol veteran, serves as deputy director under Dai Li. Twenty-five hundred Americans, mostly sailors and marines, will serve with SACO during the war, training guerrilla fighters and secret police in Chongqing and at fourteen field branches around China.
October to November	The Fourteenth Air Force, now operating a string of bases across Yunnan to Guilin and Hengyang in Guangxi and Hunan Provinces, intensifies an anti-shipping campaign and hits ground targets in Xiamen, Hong Kong, Hunan, and Taiwan.
November 1	The U.S. Army opens the Guilin Infantry Training Center.
November 4	Chiang asks Frank Price, a trusted American advisor, to recruit Chinese-speaking American civilians as liaison officers assisting the hostel and interpreter programs.
November 23–26	Chiang attends the Cairo Conference with Churchill and Roosevelt, where plans for the reinvasion of Burma are approved. Chiang demands significant Allied participation, and Roosevelt promises large-scale amphibious operations in the Bay of Bengal. The Cairo Communiqué declares that Manchuria and Taiwan will be returned to the ROC.
November 18–December 1	Roosevelt and Churchill agree to the early invasion of France at the Tehran conference. Days later, and without Chiang present, they decide that operations in Europe prevent deployment of amphibious forces in Burma.
December 17	Congress repeals the Chinese Exclusion Act.

1944

January	The ROC Ministry of Education drafts fourth-year college students for interpreter duty alongside U.S. forces in the CBI theater.
January 10	X-Force goes on the offensive in Burma's Hukawng Valley with support from U.S. Army liaison officers, medical personnel, and aircraft.
January 24– May 10	Chennault's chief engineer, Colonel Henry Byroade, supervises construction of four B-29 airfields near Chengdu, relying on more than 300,000 conscripted laborers.
April 17	Japan begins the Ichigo offensive to establish an overland route to Southeast Asia.
May 11	The Chinese Y-Force goes on the offensive against Japanese-occupied western Yunnan, beginning the Salween campaign. U.S. Army liaison officers, field hospitals, and air force units support Chinese Y-Force operations.
May 17	X-Force, supported by British and U.S. troops, takes the Japanese airfield at Myitkyina. Fighting for the town itself continues until August, after which Myitkyina becomes the main Allied supply center in northern Burma.
June 6	The Allied invasion of Normandy opens a second front in Europe.
June 15	Chengdu-based B-29s raid Japan for the first time as part of Operation Matterhorn. The August capture of airfields in the Marianas renders the Chengdu bases irrelevant to the war.
July 22	The U.S. Army's Dixie Mission arrives at Yan'an to meet with the Chinese Communists.
August 8	Hengyang, site of the Fourteenth Air Force's easternmost major base, falls to the Japanese.
September 19	Roosevelt issues an ultimatum to Chiang, threatening to end U.S. support unless he places Stilwell in unrestricted command of all Chinese forces.
September 25	Chiang asks Roosevelt to withdraw Stilwell and replace him with another general.
October 15	Stalin informs the U.S. military mission in Moscow that he will deploy sixty divisions against Japan beginning three months after Germany's defeat. Combined with U.S.

victory two weeks later in the Battle of Leyte Gulf, this development makes bases in China no longer essential to the U.S. war against Japan.

October 19   Roosevelt relieves Stilwell of his command.

October 31   General Albert Wedemeyer takes up duty as Stilwell's replacement. Wedemeyer's mission is to advise and assist Chiang, carry out air operations, and assist Chinese air and ground forces in operations, training, and logistical support.

November 10   Wang Jingwei dies in Nagoya.

November 11   Japanese occupy Guilin, site of main SOS, Fourteenth Air Force, and U.S. Army training centers for Chinese forces outside Yunnan and Sichuan.

November 17   Wedemeyer regroups U.S. Army liaison teams, service schools, and Y-Force staff into a new organization: the Chinese Training and Combat Command under Brigadier General Frank Dorn.

December 5   Frank Price opens an interpreter training center in Chongqing. The center is staffed by his American liaison officer team, all Chinese-speaking American missionaries.

December   Operation Ichigo ends because of logistical problems, but Japanese forces capture ten major airbases and occupy Henan, Hunan, and Guangxi Provinces.

1945

January 5   The U.S. Tenth Air Force completes transport of China's Ramgarh-trained and battle-tested Fourteenth and Twenty-Second Divisions from Burma to Yunnan.

January 7   To facilitate the buildup of thirty-six Chinese Army divisions, known as ALPHA Force, Wedemeyer splits the Chinese Training and Combat Command into two organizations, the Chinese Combat Command (CCC) and the Chinese Training Center (CTC). The CTC supervises training schools, and the CCC comprises more than three thousand air and ground liaison personnel attached to SOS-supplied Chinese forces.

January 24   The Salween campaign ends victoriously after elements of the CAI and Y-Force link up at the Chinese-Burmese border town of Wanding.

January 27	The Ledo Road connecting Kunming to Assam via northern Burma opens.
February 4	The first truck convoy from Ledo arrives in Kunming. Driver training for Chinese troops at Ramgarh operates around the clock.
February 4–11	Yalta Conference. Stalin agrees to join the war against Japan, with a secret agreement granting the Soviets a naval base at Port Arthur and joint Sino-Soviet control over Manchurian railroads. Chiang is not informed.
May 8	Victory in Europe.
May 8–June 7	Chinese forces supported by CCC liaison officers and the Fourteenth Air Force stage a successful counteroffensive against the Japanese attack near Zhijiang, Hunan Province. U.S. aircraft airlift the Fourteenth, the Twenty-Second, and other seasoned divisions from Yunnan to Zhijiang.
May 20	The Japanese begin withdrawing forces from the Hunan-Guangxi Railroad and consolidating troops in southern China around Wuhan, Guangzhou, and Shanghai.
August 1	Chennault retires and leaves China after eight full years of duty, five with the Chinese Air Force and three with the American Air Forces.
August 6	The *Enola Gay* drops an atomic bomb on Hiroshima.
August 9	Soviet forces begin massive offensive in Manchuria. The United States drops an atomic bomb on Nagasaki.
August 12	The secretary of war approves plan for the III Marine Amphibious Corps to land in northern China to assist the Chinese Nationalists.
August 15	Japan surrenders unconditionally. Harry Truman issues General Order Number One, specifying that all Japanese forces in China surrender to the Chinese Nationalists.
September 2	The formal Japanese surrender takes place on the USS *Missouri*.
September 13	The first U.S. marines land near Tianjin. Within weeks, approximately fifty-three thousand marines are ashore in northern China, tasked with securing key cities and railway junctions for the Nationalists and disarming and repatriating Japanese forces.

September to November	U.S. aircraft and naval vessels ferry some 500,000 Nationalist troops into previously occupied areas along the Chinese coast and in Manchuria.
November 2	The Soviets block U.S. naval vessels from landing Nationalist troops in Manchuria.
December	Wedemeyer sets up a nine-hundred-man-strong military advisory group (MAG) for China, based in Nanjing.
December 20	Truman's envoy George C. Marshall arrives in Chongqing to try to avert a civil war between the Chinese Nationalists and the Communists.

1946

January 10	Marshall persuades the Nationalists and Communists to accept a cease-fire, which each side soon violates in Manchuria.
March 5	Churchill delivers the Iron Curtain speech in Fulton, Missouri.
March 13	Soviets begin their withdrawal from Manchuria, which will be complete by mid-April. They hedge their bets by arming the Chinese Communists as they leave and make further arms deliveries throughout the summer.
July 1	The Chinese Communist Party (CCP) instructs its members to inform the public about "atrocities" committed by American military personnel in China.
August 4	U.S. forces finish repatriating Japanese soldiers. Nearly twenty-four thousand marines remain in China.
September 22	An American sailor beats rickshaw puller Zang Da Erzi to death in Shanghai.
November 4	United States and ROC sign the Sino-American Commercial Treaty to condemnation across party lines in China.
December 24	Marines Warren Pritchard and William Pierson allegedly rape Peking University student Shen Chong in Beijing.
December 30– January 31	An estimated 500,000 people join protest marches across China as part of an anti-American brutality movement, demanding U.S. forces leave China. More than sixteen thousand marines remain in China.

1947

January 8	Marshall ends his mediation mission and leaves China.
January 22	U.S. military court-martial convicts William Pierson of rape.
May	Marines withdraw from the Beijing area but remain in Tianjin, Dagu, and Qingdao.
July 16–September 18	Truman sends Wedemeyer on fact-finding mission to China and Korea.
August 11	The secretary of the navy overturns Pierson's conviction.

1948

November 11	Communist forces under Lin Biao complete the Liao-Shen campaign, driving Nationalist forces from Manchuria. CCP agents incarcerate Angus Ward—the U.S. consul in Shenyang—and his staff for the winter.

1949

January	MAG withdraws from Nanjing.
February 3	Secretary of State Dean Acheson calls for suspension of all aid to the Nationalists.
May 25	Last marines depart Qingdao.
August 5	The Truman administration publishes the *China White Paper*.
October 1	Mao Zedong proclaims the establishment of the People's Republic of China.
December 10	Chiang leaves the mainland and flies to Taiwan.

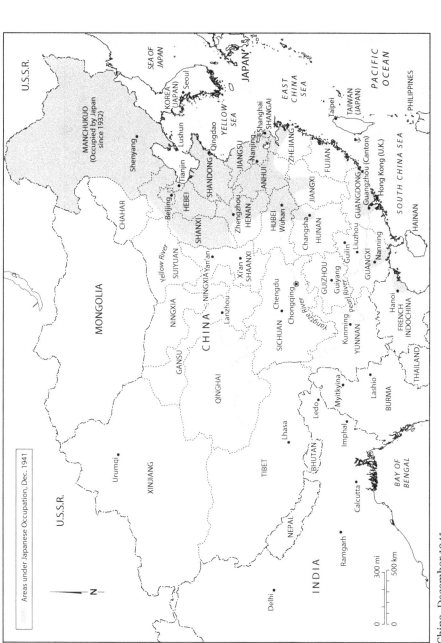

China, December 1941

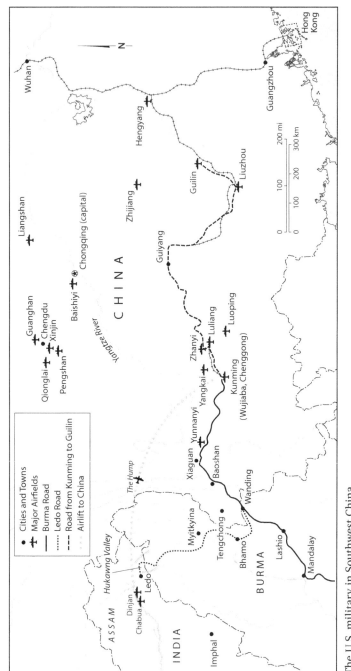

The U.S. military in Southwest China

The Tormented Alliance

Introduction

· ·

A military alliance with the United States means a military occupation by the United States. That is the truth this book uncovers. It is a conclusion that I resisted over the course of my research—after all, the annex to Hague IV of the Hague Regulations of 1907, which remain in force today, defines a territory as occupied only "when it is actually placed under the authority of the hostile army."[1] According to this definition, U.S. military commanders never ruled over Great Britain, Australia, or China during the Second World War, when together these three countries hosted several million American servicemen as allies. But the closer I looked at Chinese history, the harder it was to draw any other conclusion. In the end, nearly a decade of evidence documenting the unraveling of the U.S. alliance with Nationalist (Guomindang [GMD]) Party leader Chiang Kai-shek's Republic of China (ROC) during World War II and the Chinese Civil War left me with no other conclusion. To agree to a U.S. alliance, from the Second World War on, is fundamentally to accede to U.S. occupation.

In China, that occupation exposed gaping flaws in the American way of war. Each side brought to the alliance expectations that the other side was simply unable to meet, resulting in a tormented relationship across all levels of Sino-American engagement. By anchoring larger Sino-American struggles over race, gender, and nation, the U.S. military in China transformed itself into a widely loathed occupation force: an aggressive, resentful, emasculating source of physical danger and compromised sovereignty, and—after Japan's surrender and the spring 1946 withdrawal of Soviet forces from Manchuria—the chief obstacle to consigning foreign imperialism in China irrevocably to the past.

Both countries still benefited from the alliance-cum-occupation, often against massive odds. With last-minute assistance from the Soviets, the two countries beat Japan into submission without invading its main islands or vanquishing Japanese forces in China. While the war raged, the United States bolstered China's ability to tie down Japanese troops, preventing their redeployment in the Pacific at a relatively low cost. U.S. troop strength in wartime China peaked at around seventy thousand men, and the ROC received only 3.2 percent of America's foreign lend-lease aid.[2] Just delivering supplies to China past the Japanese blockade was an enormous logistical challenge, leading to a space-annihilating breakthrough that became a pillar of postwar American power.[3] The Hump air bridge connecting India to Southwest China across the Himalayas proved, according to its commander, that the U.S. military "could fly anything anywhere anytime."[4] American airpower also helped put an end to the Japanese terror bombing of Chinese cities, including the wartime capital of Chongqing, where Chiang's government fled after the Japanese occupied Nanjing in 1937. The ROC carried out its own unprecedented logistical mobilizations—interpreter and hostel programs that overcame the language barrier and kept American personnel in China housed and fed.[5] These efforts enabled the ROC to emerge from the war with an elite corps of U.S.-trained-and-equipped army divisions.

The alliance facilitated Chinese diplomatic and political gains. In 1943 alone, the United States rescinded its extraterritorial rights in China, ended its anti-Chinese immigration policy, and accepted that all Chinese territories lost to Japan since 1895 would be restored to Chinese sovereignty. Two years later, the ROC's great power status was affirmed with a permanent seat on the UN Security Council. But Chiang lost his country in 1949, and the U.S. military presence contributed to his defeat.

In 1942, Chinese welcomed American soldiers as *mengyou*, meaning "allied friends." Unlike U.S. troops stationed in the prewar Chinese treaty ports, these Americans, the Chinese believed, came to China to help crush foreign imperialism, not perpetuate it. Many Chinese elites had aspirations for the alliance beyond Japan's defeat, seeing the U.S. military presence as a means to transform American perceptions of China and uplift the Chinese nation. U.S. officials had a similar vision. President Franklin Roosevelt wanted to make China a pillar of a new, non-imperialist postwar order.[6] Army training material for China-bound personnel emphasized racial equality, and senior American commanders believed in their unique capacity to mentor Chiang's armies and impart effectiveness.

These lofty ambitions still appeared viable in 1943 in light of China's stunning diplomatic achievements, but by mid-1945 they had crashed and burned. Chinese who came into contact with GIs now felt anger and alienation. The Chinese Nationalist government's complicity with the American racism and violent misconduct so blatantly on display in Chinese public life—much of it targeting women—drained Chiang's regime of legitimacy. Most American personnel, for their part, openly dismissed Chinese as thieving, corrupt, ignorant, and filthy "Chinks" and "slopes," unworthy of American tutelage. The tormented alliance staggered on after Japan's surrender with the arrival of fifty-three thousand U.S. marines and sailors, hailed as liberators in formerly Japanese-occupied coastal cities. But wartime patterns of mutually damaging Sino-American engagement continued, only now occurring in an entirely new geopolitical context, allowing Mao Zedong's Communists to harness resentment against the U.S. military presence and deploy it as a powerful tool in their struggle to seize power.

By examining day-to-day interactions between American military personnel and an entire spectrum of Chinese, along with efforts by U.S. and Chinese authorities to manage the U.S. military presence, this book offers a new story about the formation, evolution, and undoing of the U.S.-ROC alliance. It is a tale that has never been told before, and one with implications for the present day.

· · · · · ·

Not long after beginning research, I discovered that the rise and fall of the U.S.-ROC alliance turned upon the actions of a much larger cast of characters than scholars have recognized. More than 121,000 American soldiers, sailors, and marines deployed to China during the 1940s, making this military presence the largest sustained engagement between Americans and Chinese that has ever taken place in China (only ten thousand Americans lived there before the war, and less than seventy-two thousand were living there in 2010).[7] Yet most studies have reduced this encounter to a story about the contentious relationship between Chiang and General Joseph Stilwell, who served until October 1944 as Chiang's chief of staff and commander of U.S. forces in China. Throughout the Cold War and into the early 2000s, popular writers and scholars took Stilwell's disparaging conclusions about Chiang as their starting point, arguing that Chiang's defeat in 1949 resulted from his myopic refusal to follow Stilwell's advice, his corruption and authoritarianism, his unwillingness to fight the Japanese, and his desire to let the Americans win the war for him while he hoarded U.S. aid to fight the Communists.[8] Hans van de Ven's landmark study *War and Nationalism in China, 1925–1945* demolished what he called the "Stilwell myth" by documenting the GMD's undeniable contributions to the joint war effort against Japan and Stilwell's profound flaws as a military commander.[9] Subsequent studies by Rana Mitter and Ch'i Hsi-sheng, among others, have bolstered van de Ven's crucial reappraisal of Stilwell and the Nationalists.[10] My book adds another dimension to this revisionism by revealing how everyday interactions between U.S. forces and an entire spectrum of Chinese contributed to the unraveling of the relationship from the bottom up.

I also learned through my research that it is simply not possible to separate U.S. military support for the ROC during the war against Japan from U.S. military support for the ROC after Japan's surrender. Unlike much of the previous scholarship on wartime Sino-U.S. relations, which takes Japan's August 1945 acceptance of the Allied demand for unconditional surrender as its beginning or end point, this book treats all operations involving or catering to U.S. military personnel in China throughout the decade as an interlocking series of events.[11] President Roosevelt's April 1941 approval of the Chinese government's secret plan to recruit American pilots to defend China's skies as part of the American Volunteer Group (AVG) marked the beginning of U.S. military intervention undertaken to bolster the Nationalists. Within weeks, the ROC established its interpreter and hostel programs, which evolved into the Nationalist government's key alliance-building initiatives after Pearl Harbor. Japan's surrender did not bring the fighting to an end in China (or elsewhere in Asia), nor did it signal the end of U.S. military intervention to shore up the Nationalists, which continued on a large scale through January 1947 and did not fully cease until the last marines departed Qingdao in May 1949. V-J Day made it possible for Americans to regard their job in China as finished, but the transition to peace was not so straightforward.

My search for sources connecting operational and lower-level Sino-American interactions to the alliance's high politics took me across mainland China, Taiwan, and Myanmar. I started in Kunming, where I spent weeks trying to decipher a room full of smudgy, handwritten archival finding aids. I began to doubt that I would ever get my hands on an actual archival file, but the records eventually came, and after three months of transcribing any file that made reference to American soldiers, I departed with a ninety-six-page Microsoft Word document. For the remainder of my time in China, I tried to be more judicious in my transcriptions, scouring local court, city government, social affairs bureau, garrison command, and police records at municipal and provincial archives from all parts of the country where U.S. troops deployed. Most of these have never been used before. I also pored over newspapers, memoirs, alumni newsletters, local gazettes, and oral history transcriptions. Visits to the Academia Historica in Taipei and the Second Historical Archives in Nanjing yielded central government, foreign ministry, and high-level military records. When battlefield diaries pointed beyond the border, I followed them to Yangon and combed through colonial Burmese intelligence reports from Bhamo and Myitkyina.

The making and unmaking of the U.S.-ROC alliance left evidence scattered across the United States, including a surprising amount of Chinese-language material. Senior commanders donated their papers to well-known repositories, such as the Hoover Institution, the U.S. Army Heritage and Education Center, and the U.S. Marine Corps Historical Center. These archives also contained collections from lower-ranked American officers, noncommissioned officers, and senior Chinese officials, including Chiang Kai-shek. Enlisted soldiers, sailors, and marines, meanwhile, make up the lion's share of the nearly five hundred American China theater veterans who contributed interviews, unpublished memoirs, or wartime records to the Library of Congress's Veterans History Project. The largest collections of wartime U.S. military and diplomatic files from China are stored at the National Archives, with many official ROC records mixed in. A summerlong archival slog in College Park, Maryland, yielded sources that, when analyzed alongside Chinese records about the same events and themes, provide some of the book's most important insights on attitudes and interactions between American and Chinese actors.

Many people contributed to the alliance's rise and fall. The American military personnel who served in China came into contact with an eclectic array of Chinese. These included fellow soldiers as well as intellectuals, college students, business owners, rickshaw pullers, police officers, farmers, prostitutes, beggars, smugglers, and thieves. These engagements, and the efforts by ROC and U.S. authorities to manage them, constitute the bulk of the historical record. U.S. forces, too, mirrored the diversity of American society, reflecting the heterogeneity of a citizen army drafted from all regions and walks of life but for two key exceptions: women and African Americans. No more than 150 women in the Army Nurse Corps and Women's Army Corps served in China, making up less than two-tenths of 1 percent of American troop strength.[12] More than twenty thousand Black GIs, on the other hand, served in India and Burma, where they loaded cargo aboard China-bound aircraft and built the Ledo Road from Assam to Yunnan, completed in February 1945.[13] But with the exception of a small number of truck drivers permitted to enter western Yunnan temporarily in spring 1945, Chiang barred Black American personnel from serving in China, which rendered their indispensable contributions to the Sino-U.S. war effort invisible from the perspective of most Chinese.[14] The process of making and remaking race and gender in wartime China was not a one-way street, and decisions by both U.S. and ROC authorities contributed to the almost entirely male, largely white composition of the U.S. military presence.

In the end, my research afforded me more than enough material to write six stories spanning World War II and the Chinese Civil War. The first story begins in May 1941, when Chiang ordered Huang Renlin, the American-educated director of the Nationalists' War Area Service Corps (WASC), to establish a network of Western-style hostels for the AVG in Yunnan. This story is vital, because the Nationalists expanded the program after Pearl Harbor, aiming to prove their commitment to the alliance by housing, feeding, and providing cultural outreach to all American servicemen in China. Equally important, the Nationalists envisioned the program as a nation-building initiative that combined assimilationist and antiracist ideas. By insulating American soldiers from China's poverty, demonstrating their capacity for adhering to American dietary, hygienic, and comfort norms while also showcasing China's cultural achievements, the Nationalists believed they could reshape American perceptions of China and convince their allies to treat them as equals. The program succeeded operationally by keeping U.S. forces housed and fed at Chongqing's expense, thereby crucially contributing to the war effort, but it fell short at the alliance- and state-building levels. Hostels failed to insulate the U.S. Army from China's offenses and affronts to the five senses. Americans interpreted these sensory encounters and other hostel program shortcomings as evidence of Chinese incapacity, corruption, and untrustworthiness. The program thus became grounds for the Americans to deny the Chinese the equal relationship they wanted. This story comprises the book's first chapter.

The effort to operate Western-style hostels was succeeded by another Nationalist initiative that facilitated military success against Japan but failed in its deeper alliance and nation-building aims: the ROC's interpreter program. As chapter 2 details, the Nationalists enabled American soldiers to communicate with other Chinese by cooperating with Chinese intellectuals and Chinese-speaking American missionaries to train more than thirty-three hundred college students and recent graduates to work as military interpreters alongside U.S. forces. But for both Chinese elites and senior U.S. commanders, these interpreters were more than simply a means to facilitate communication; they were also the central figures in realizing their respective visions of how the alliance could and should make China into a modern nation. Both visions were assimilationist, stressing the Chinese interpreter's special role in uplifting the country by introducing American technology and work habits to the Chinese Army. But administering the program proved more difficult than Chongqing expected, which eroded interpreter morale and support for the initiative on college campuses. It also heightened tensions with the U.S. Army and exacerbated the paternalism and covert racist prejudices embedded within the American vision. Interpreters, who had been trained to believe their work would reduce American racism, responded by staging frequent strikes against mistreatment at the hands of American personnel in 1945. The U.S. commanders who had viewed interpreters as agents of Americanization now dismissed them as ungrateful children and pressured the GMD to crack down. By the time of Japan's surrender, the interpreter program had helped turn China's educated youth against the U.S. military and the Nationalists, a development with important implications for the coming civil war.

The third chapter narrates the story of the U.S. military's efforts to improve the fighting efficiency of Chinese armed forces and carry out joint operations during the war against Japan. It shows how the alliance created a system of political and military vassalage, with the Chinese serving as junior partners, even in outfits like the Sino-American Cooperative Organization (SACO)—a secret intelligence partnership with the U.S. Navy that operated under Chinese command. This produced constant tensions and contradictions, culminating in Chiang's fall 1944 showdown with Stilwell. Senior-level military relations improved after Roosevelt relieved Stilwell, but ties among the men in the ranks continued to worsen as Chinese soldiers gained combat experience and became less inclined to play second fiddle to American logistical and support troops (the U.S. military did not deploy ground combat forces in China).[15] Violent confrontations between Chinese and American servicemen increased sharply over the war's final months, even as U.S. Army training programs for Chinese forces and liaison work alongside them on the battlefield convinced both Chiang and Stilwell's replacement, General Albert Wedemeyer, that Sino-American military cooperation had reached new heights. Meanwhile, the self-serving myths Stilwell had popularized in order to justify his chief goal of seizing command over China's armies—that senior ROC military leaders were irredeemably incompetent, while ordinary Chinese soldiers could become capable troops if given proper (read white American) leadership and training—lived on after the general's departure, contributing to widespread American resentment against the Chinese military personnel who resisted such designs for enlightenment.

The contempt most American military personnel felt toward their Chinese allies was also the product of everyday interactions with Chinese civilians, the subject of chapter 4. These engagements took place mostly without the mediation of hostel staff or interpreters. They unfolded across southwestern and central China, at construction sites where conscript laborers built runways for U.S. aircraft, in remote villages where farmers rescued downed aircrews, and, above all, in the cities and towns where American soldiers spent their free time. Because U.S. troop strength in China doubled during the first half of 1945, most interaction occurred after Japan's 1944 Ichigo offensive. The acute economic and refugee crises that followed this devastating campaign enlarged the already immense power disparity between American servicemen and local civilians, influencing their engagements in diverse and often indirect ways as ever more Chinese became dependent on the U.S. military for their livelihoods. Rampant theft, offensive sensory encounters, and banditry led American personnel to racialize Chinese civilians with striking speed and consistency. The increasingly draconian, sometimes deadly measures they employed in response to theft provoked outrage, adding to the cumulative effect of civilian anger over forced dislocations, deadly accidents, and violent crimes caused by GIs, who were emboldened by their exemption from Chinese law. When cross-cultural cooperation did occur, more often than not it involved smuggling and black-market trading, which had a negative effect on military operations. So while a minority of engagements—particularly the power-disparity-inverting aircrew rescues—strengthened Sino-American relations, the majority contributed to the alliance's unraveling.

By spring 1945, the U.S. military had already worn out its welcome in China, but what finally precipitated a violent backlash was public disapproval of sexual relations between American servicemen and Chinese women, the subject of chapter 5. While the preceding chapters cover the entire war against Japan, this one focuses on 1945, when two interrelated, patriarchal narratives about sex emerged in the wake of the Ichigo campaign. Beginning in March, government-backed newspapers began publishing articles and other features criticizing "Jeep girls," an epithet coined to describe the increasing number of women who consorted with American troops. Rumors also circulated that GIs were using Jeeps to kidnap "respectable" women and rape them. Each narrative portrayed women's bodies as territory to be recovered and inextricable from national sovereignty. They resonated widely, making Jeep girls into the catalyst through which all variables causing resentment against the U.S. military intersected and converged. GMD secret police turned a blind eye as Chinese men began attacking GIs and their female companions in mid-April. In speaking to his own troops, Wedemeyer admitted that American misconduct had caused the crisis, but in discussions with Chiang he blamed it on a Chinese newspaper campaign. With little leverage, Chiang was strong-armed into cracking down on Chinese demonstrators and deploying a preposterous Jeep girl counternarrative that tarnished his anti-imperialist bona fides. The way the crisis brought tensions surrounding race, gender, and nation to the fore was also a harbinger of struggles to come after Japan's surrender.

The final story spans the Chinese Civil War, when U.S. Marines occupied formerly Japanese-held areas in eastern and northern China. From the alliance to the GMD, everything came undone. The moment Japan surrendered, political realities shifted both locally and in terms of the broader geostrategic picture. The Chinese Communist Party (CCP), which had grown far more powerful after flooding into areas vacated by the GMD during the Ichigo campaign, hardened its position against the United States. Soviet forces overran Manchuria. American combat veterans of the battle for Okinawa were sent to parts of China where no U.S. forces had been deployed during the war. Tasked with repatriating Japanese forces and helping the Nationalists secure these areas ahead of the CCP, they were being used for completely different purposes from what U.S. forces had done in China before Japan's surrender. Sino-American relations on the ground deteriorated along the same patterns that had emerged during the war against Japan, but the entirely new set of dynamics, especially power dynamics, enabled the CCP to weaponize race, gender, and nationalism against the U.S. military and the GMD, particularly after two intoxicated marines raped a Peking University student on December 24, 1946. Urban public opinion shifted against the Nationalists and the Americans just as U.S. logistical support and military aid facilitated Chiang's ill-advised attempt to recover Manchuria.

Each of these stories amplifies a motif in wartime U.S.-China relations that is reflected in America's militarized present. Today, host country governments and the Pentagon spend upward of $20 billion each year to keep American military personnel and their dependents living comfortably at overseas U.S. military bases.[16] In Iraq and Afghanistan, an estimated fifty thousand local interpreters have worked with U.S. forces since 2001, accompanying them on nearly all missions outside American outposts.[17] Military training programs, meanwhile, remain a bedrock of U.S. military policy— despite nearly two decades and over $100 billion spent in a largely futile effort to build up Iraqi and Afghan security forces.[18] Outside war zones, displacement, crime, deadly accidents, and military prostitution continue to breed resentment against U.S. troops, while status of forces agreements (SOFAs) shield them from host country laws. When American servicemen rape local women, these resentments can coalesce into large-scale protest movements.[19] But the global military base network endures, as U.S. and host country officials have worked together to make it easier for local populations to tolerate the U.S. military presence and easier for American military personnel to live with them.[20]

Thus, while each chapter tells a distinct story that sheds new light on the present, as a whole they reveal something more. Together, these stories inscribe the arc of America's rise to global preeminence and, more broadly, the worldwide shift from a traditional imperial to a postimperial mode of domination and wielding power. The Second World War irrefutably discredited colonialism. The 1941 Atlantic Charter's professed Anglo-American commitment to self-determination for "all peoples" galvanized anticolonial nationalists, but it was Japan's conquest of the U.S., British, and Dutch Pacific empires in a mere three months that broke the old colonial system in Asia.[21] The war also left the United States in a remarkable position, singularly capable of projecting power across the globe without the need for large colonies. As the historian Daniel Immerwahr shows, it possessed more than two thousand overseas military bases, accounted for 60 percent of the industrialized world's economic production, and wielded mastery over an array of technologies—aviation, wireless communication, and synthetics, among others—that provided the benefits of empire without the costs of annexing populated foreign territories.[22] The new Cold War order arose from this reconfiguration of the relationship between imperialism and nationalism.[23] And the alliance the United States formed with China during this 1940s paradigm shift set patterns for ties with U.S.-allied nation-states, particularly non-Western ones, throughout the Cold War and beyond.

· · · · · ·

The United States is an empire. It dominates and wields power, first and foremost through its overseas military bases and alliances with nominally sovereign foreign countries that have varying degrees of clientelist ties to Washington. Historian Prasenjit Duara describes this system as the "imperialism of nation-states," a reinvention of empire emphasizing political and military vassalage with opportunities for client states to move up the developmental ladder by adhering to American "designs for enlightenment."[24] Scholars have documented the paradoxical nature of America's overseas military base network, which underpins U.S. power and creates economic and cultural opportunities in host countries while also harming relations with allies and fostering anti-American blowback.[25] Other studies have looked closely at American client states and the dynamics of legitimacy, stressing the importance of foregrounding agency and investigating how the U.S. military's territorial footholds in other countries intersect with local societies, histories, and cultures.[26] U.S. imperialism has never been a one-sided story of American impact and local response but rather a mutually constitutive and contested process—a delicate balance, as historian Paul Kramer shows, of force and consent.[27] By integrating histories of wartime China and American empire, *The Tormented Alliance* illustrates how the United States' "imperialism of nation-states" unfolded in Asia and first came undone.

When I began researching the U.S. military presence in China, I hoped to do for wartime China what scholars had already done for the U.S. military presence in other allied and occupied countries during World War II: to account for what happened during the war from both top-down and bottom-up perspectives while drawing extensively from non-U.S. sources. Because Chinese archives were closed to scholars for so long and because the history of China's war against Japan became caught up in Cold War wrangling over the politically charged question of Who lost China? recent studies of wartime U.S.-China relations have remained focused on revising our understanding of high-level military and diplomatic relations, rarely incorporating the methodological innovations of the cultural and transnational turns.[28] I set out to correct this lack of transnational and grassroots attentiveness. As I completed my research, I found parallels between the U.S. military presence in China and wartime deployments in other allied countries and American liberty ports, but even more similarities in comparison to the U.S. occupations of Normandy, Germany, and Japan.[29] The sources I discovered also demanded that I expand my methodological horizons beyond the 1940s. Scholarship on prewar American empire in the Caribbean and the Philippines, as well as the postwar military base empire, helped me grapple with what I uncovered.[30] The dynamics of imperialism and its mid-century paradigm shift run through each chapter and bind them together.

Sino-American engagements in wartime China were rooted in the cultures and institutions of empire. Among those institutions were hierarchical relations, which empires produce by racializing and engendering.[31] Notions of race and gender in China were dynamic, contingent, and mutually constitutive—made and remade in the context of ongoing Sino-American interactions. Imperial relations are also mediated by the senses.[32] Chinese and Americans formed perceptions of each other through seeing, hearing, smelling, tasting, and touching. In addition to exceptionalizing difference through race, gender, and bodily encounters, empires reorganize space and extend state power. The U.S. military reordered urban and rural landscapes in China, while the jurisdiction agreement U.S. and ROC officials negotiated after Washington rescinded its extraterritorial rights in 1943 placed all U.S. military personnel outside Chinese legal boundaries, in effect creating another extraterritorial system. Wherever American military personnel traveled in China, their extraterritorial status traveled with them.[33]

Empires are also tutelary, structured around an inclusionary, development-oriented politics in which the dominant power aims to transform the subject population while arrogating for itself the sole right to determine and evaluate said population's progress toward this end. In a prewar colonial context, like that of the Philippines beginning with the establishment of civilian government in 1901, this framework enabled Americans to conduct an extended test of Filipino "capacity" for self-rule, based on American recognition—or denial—of Filipinos' fulfillment of American standards of morality, governance, self-discipline, soldierly conduct, and sensory refinement.[34] Wartime China was a sovereign state, but the U.S.-ROC alliance adhered to the same tutelary logic, with American soldiers defining themselves as judges of the Chinese they engaged with—a population to be improved under American guidance. Self-rule might not have been at stake, though if Chiang had acceded to Stilwell's demand for control over the ROC military, it would have weakened his authority irrevocably, but the alliance was still an extended test of Chinese capacity. U.S. military commanders made judgments about Chinese adherence to American standards that affected the lives of huge numbers of people on the ground in China.

Collaboration is another central component in the construction and dynamics of imperial systems.[35] Chiang welcomed the U.S. military presence in China despite the wrinkles in ROC sovereignty it entailed because U.S. aid, military training, and diplomatic support helped him shore up his own authority.[36] The United States exercised extraordinary leverage over the terms of this collaboration because U.S. scalar power flattened the world. The Hump air bridge was the final leg in the "Fireball Express" flying route that shipped supplies to China from the continental United States via South America, Africa, and India.[37] While U.S. military training programs and diplomatic backing helped Chiang pursue his wartime aims, the air bridge was a truly existential issue for him. After the 1936 Xi'an Incident, when

Chiang was kidnapped by two of his own generals and pressured to enter a truce with the Chinese Communists, he staked the legitimacy of the ROC state on defeating Japan.[38] Once Japan severed the Burma Road in early 1942, the Hump was his sole lifeline.

To be clear, U.S. imperialism in China did not begin with the U.S.-ROC alliance. By the outbreak of the Spanish-American War decades earlier, China already occupied a central place in the fantasies of American businessmen, missionaries, and policy makers, all of whom advocated visions of China transformed under American tutelage. These would-be reformers also shared the conviction that they understood Chinese interests better than the Chinese did. But when assimilation fell short of expectations, or the Chinese failed to display sufficient gratitude, this paternalistic, inclusionary form of racism often gave way to the exclusionary view of the Chinese population as hopelessly inferior—a form of bigotry rooted in scientific racism and expressed in Jim Crow and Chinese exclusion. Yet the American belief in a special tutelary relationship with China persisted into the 1940s, amplified by popular writers like Pearl Buck and the publishing magnate Henry Luce, both of whom grew up as children of American missionaries in China.[39] And while many Americans and American-educated Chinese elites pioneered important innovations in Chinese politics, science, higher education, and other fields before World War II, U.S. policy makers deluded themselves by denying American complicity in the history of foreign imperialism in China since the First Opium War (1839–42).[40] The United States might not have carved out territorial concessions in China, but the most-favored nation clauses in the treaties it negotiated with the Qing Empire ensured that Americans in China enjoyed whatever privileges other powers took at gunpoint.

The United States had plenty of its own firepower in China as well. By the time of Pearl Harbor, U.S. armed forces had spent more than eighty-five years there, and for most of the 1920s and 1930s China hosted the largest U.S. military presence on foreign soil in the world.[41] U.S. Navy gunboats began patrolling the Yangtze River in 1854. In 1900, U.S. ground forces joined troops from seven other countries to march on Beijing during the Boxer Uprising, while the 1901 Boxer Protocol gave the United States the right to station troops in northern China, which enabled all three service branches to build up significant deployments.[42] The Yangtze Patrol protected U.S. property along China's largest river with six modern gunboats. Another gunboat squadron—the South China Patrol—carried out the same mission in the waterways surrounding Guangzhou. Larger oceangoing destroyers often supplemented these gunboats, and during tense periods the U.S. Navy sent dozens of additional vessels to China.[43] China was also home to the U.S. Army's Fifteenth Infantry Regiment, stationed in Tianjin between 1912 and 1938, with troop strength fluctuating between 640 and 1,400 men. The Marine Corps presence was even larger, with as many as 5,600 men stationed in-country at any given time, divided between a legation guard in Beijing, the Fourth Marine Regiment in Shanghai's International Settlement, and other units deployed on shorter missions.[44]

The tutelary and military elements of U.S. imperialism did not intersect in China before Pearl Harbor—as they had in the Caribbean and the Philippines—but these deployments established perceptions of China that would cast a long shadow over the 1940s.[45] Uplift played no part in the U.S. military's mission of protecting American lives and property. Interaction with Chinese armed forces was limited to intelligence gathering, and analyses were clouded by the exclusionary racism rife in the treaty ports. For example, when Joseph Stilwell reported a hostile encounter as a major in 1927, the Fifteenth Infantry's commanding general relayed his findings to the army's chief of staff with a note, adding, "The average mind of the average Chinese, in my opinion, is little above that of one of our five-year-old children, with apologies to our children of that age."[46] Stilwell served three tours in China before Pearl Harbor, including a stint as military attaché, where he and deputy Frank Dorn denigrated the GMD's prosecution of the war against Japan with judgments based on Orientalist views of Chinese civilization.[47] Like Dorn and Stilwell, most senior U.S. military officers who served in China during the 1940s had also served there during the interwar years, as had wartime army chief of staff George C. Marshall, who commanded the Fifteenth Infantry while Stilwell served in China during the mid-1920s. These men believed their service gave them a superior understanding of the Chinese, and they were accustomed to the Chinese treating them as superiors.[48]

While most American servicemen in the prewar treaty ports looked down on the Chinese, they also viewed China as an Orientalist playground. Junior officers could afford to rent large houses for their families and hire a half-dozen servants. Enlisted men also lived far more comfortably than they could have in the United States. As one old Fifteenth Infantry veteran told a new arrival in 1927, "you don't shine your own shoes; you don't fill your own canteen; you don't shave yourself; the chink coolies do it for you."[49] Help from unskilled laborers ~~coolies~~ and servants gave these men ample free time. Unit newspapers devoted much of their space to coverage of interservice sporting competitions, hunting trips, and social events. Other leisure-time activities went largely unmentioned, but medical records show that the Fifteenth Infantry Regiment had the army's highest rates of venereal disease and alcoholism. Navy and Marine Corps personnel in China achieved similar notoriety, with a venereal disease admission rate nearly six times higher than that in the remainder of the navy in 1938. China's legendary reputation for easy living and, according to George C. Marshall, "cheap booze and cheaper women" gave the country an allure unmatched by any other overseas military posting.[50]

Even with the Chinese Revolution in the rearview mirror, the authors of the U.S. Army's three-volume history of the World War II China-Burma-India (CBI) theater described these prewar deployments as "tiny garrisons" maintained in China "as a symbol in support of Chinese nationalism," but Chinese nationalists of all political stripes understood them as imperialist infringements on Chinese sovereignty.[51] Mao Zedong described the navy and Marine Corps presence in the Yangtze Delta region as part of a larger imperialist effort "to completely enslave the Chinese nation."[52] Chiang Kai-shek similarly denounced the "gunboat policy" that allowed the United States and other foreign powers to sail their warships wherever they pleased and "take off the gun covers" whenever a dispute occurred. According to Chiang, the treaties that allowed the U.S. military and other foreign forces to operate in China rendered "China no longer a state" and "the Chinese people no longer a nation."[53] After Pearl Harbor, Chiang's government made the attainment of equality—including equal treatment for Chinese abroad and equal treatment for foreigners and Chinese within China—a central war aim. One did not have to be a GMD member to support this goal. Opposition to foreign imperialism united Chinese across party, class, and regional lines.[54]

But despite the history of U.S. imperialism in China and the centrality of anti-imperialism to Chinese nationalism, the undoing of the U.S.-ROC alliance was not inevitable. For all their differences, Americans and their Chinese counterparts actually had much in common. Chiang wanted to reform the Chinese military along American lines. He also had a track record of effective cooperation with foreign military advisors, to whom he had granted significant authority and responsibility. During the 1930s, German advisors helped transform Chiang's ragtag forces into a real national army, and between 1938 and 1941, the Soviets trained some ninety thousand Chinese soldiers and participated in operational planning for several major military campaigns.[55] If the ROC military could work with Soviet Communists and German Nazis, then surely it could work with the Americans. After all, Chiang had appointed American advisors to senior positions in numerous government ministries, as well as the police and air force, throughout the Nanjing decade (1927–37). Many Chinese elites, for that matter, saw the United States as an icon of modernity. They wanted to emulate American examples beyond the military and government.[56]

A tutelary, development-oriented relationship was possible, but it would require a soft touch, one that accounted for Chinese nationalism and would allow Chinese across the social spectrum to maintain a sense of self-respect in any interaction with American military personnel. Chiang's senior German advisors had walked this line, salvaging a bilateral relationship strained by prior German imperialism and condescension toward the Chinese.[57] President Roosevelt, too, recognized the importance of treating China as an equal despite the country's weaknesses, telling Undersecretary of State Sumner Welles in 1937 that doing so was the best means of preventing "a fundamental cleavage between the West and East in the years to come."[58] After Pearl Harbor, Roosevelt consistently pushed back against British and Soviet objections to his plan for China's inclusion as one of "Four Policemen" responsible for postwar security.[59] U.S. Army higher-ups also understood that American racism played into Japanese hands. "Japan will harp on the color question first, last, and all the time," the army warned in the opening passage of its *Pocket Guide to China*, which also instructed all China-bound military personnel to "show the Chinese that Americans treat the Chinese as we treat any of our allies, and that we respect them as human beings on an equality with ourselves."[60] This was wise advice, an unambiguous rejection of the premises undergirding treaty port racism and Chinese exclusion. But soldiers who came to China would invariably find themselves confronted with frustrations and bodily encounters that would put this lofty aspiration to the test.

The ROC's hostel and interpreter programs attempted to thread the alliance's bundle of contradictions but fell short. On the one hand, the programs reinforced the power disparity between China and the United States by extending extraordinary privileges: freeing American personnel from having to struggle with a foreign language and providing them a standard of living beyond the reach of nearly all Chinese. But this was intentional, as Chongqing understood that the language barrier and logistical challenges of shipping material goods to China offered the opportunity to demonstrate Chinese capacity: the U.S. military *needed* the ROC government to provide housing, food, and translators. The ROC did so, investing a far larger share of its national budget than the U.S. government devoted to supplying lend-lease aid to China. While these programs led to military success against Japan, they nevertheless failed the capacity test before American arbiters, who found interpreters wanting in linguistic proficiency and military masculinity, and hostels deficient in terms of food, hygiene, and comfort. Many GIs also treated interpreters and hostel staff—including senior administrators—as second-class citizens in their own country, while short-comings in the ROC's administration of each program helped convince U.S. commanders that Chongqing was incapable of managing its own affairs. Programs undertaken to raise the status of the country ironically produced relations of hierarchy, thereby damaging GMD legitimacy.

The U.S. military's contributions to the war effort—its tutelary military training and liaison programs—served worthy goals, but the fundamental American dissatisfaction with things as they were in China brought the alliance's vulnerabilities to the surface. Senior commanders failed to implement the *Pocket Guide to China*'s claims that Americans viewed the Chinese as equal to other allies. Despite having no prewar combat command experience, Stilwell enjoyed War Department backing while devoting his tenure in China to wresting control of the ROC's armed forces away from Chiang, something Chiang's battle-tested Soviet and German advisors had never attempted.[61] Stilwell's vision of commanding and remaking China's army—and contempt for ROC officials who challenged his authority—mirrored prewar experiences in the colonial Philippines and U.S.-occupied Haiti, rather than wartime Great Britain or Australia. Making matters worse, Stilwell's views filtered down the ranks, providing a narrative upon which to draw whenever American GIs encountered difficulty in their dealings with their Chinese counterparts. This fueled American arrogance in situations where anti-imperialist nationalism made the Chinese vigilant against any perceived slight or dismissal of China's status. The more tactful and able Wedemeyer earned Chiang's trust while expanding military training and liaison programs, but lower-level military-to-military relations continued to deteriorate under his watch.

The alliance's transformation into an occupation placed great strain on Chinese civilians. Evicted from their homes to make way for military bases, conscripted by the thousands into poorly paid and dangerous airfield construction projects, and forced to go without meat and eggs so that the Americans could eat their fill, civilians' initial gratitude to U.S. forces quickly turned to dismay. Plane crashes, test-firing accidents, and emergency bomb jettisoning claimed the lives of those who lived near airfields, while reckless driving and indiscriminate shooting by American personnel maimed or killed hundreds, including children. American servicemen on liberty (pass) destroyed homes and businesses, committed assault and murder, and harassed and raped women. Most escaped punishment, while civilians or hostel workers who stole from U.S. forces risked lengthy prison terms or worse, as the judge advocate of the CBI theater okayed the shooting of suspected thieves who ignored orders to halt.[62] Few Chinese had protested when the ROC followed the UK and Australia in granting the U.S. Army exclusive jurisdiction over all American military personnel in China in 1943. In spring 1945, however, the threats to Chinese sovereignty and masculinity that this new extraterritorial system facilitated sparked anti-American riots in Chongqing, with tacit support from the Juntong—the GMD's most powerful secret police agency. But when Wedemeyer warned that his men would fight back against angry crowds, Chiang invested his meager political resources in placating his American chief of staff, turning his propaganda apparatuses, police, and paramilitaries against his own people.

The Chinese people recognized that American troops were contributing to the fight against Japan; however, after V-J Day, newly arriving U.S. forces had little purpose beyond occupation and domination. These men, mostly marines, expected to enjoy the spoils of victory in the U.S. military's favorite prewar stomping ground, but they found themselves intervening on behalf of the GMD in a civil struggle they wanted no part of while living among a desperate population. Poverty, theft, military prostitution, and harassment by both Communist and Nationalist forces reinforced their assumptions about Chinese inferiority and ungratefulness. Resentful, arrogant, and frequently drunk, many Americans lashed out. They brawled over price disputes, shot suspected thieves, caused accidents, and committed crimes at even greater frequency than their comrades had during the war. But China and the United States no longer faced a common enemy. Moreover, Chiang's government could no longer claim that the U.S. military presence served nation-building goals, as the hostel, interpreter, and military training programs ended soon after Japan's surrender. ROC and U.S. authorities also failed to articulate a credible justification or withdrawal timeline for the U.S. presence after its ostensible mission—the repatriation of Japanese forces—was completed in mid-1946. There was nothing radically new about the conduct of U.S. forces in China, but the entirely new postwar context enabled Chiang's domestic opponents to turn the Americans' behavior against him with great effect.

By the time U.S. forces withdrew, continued ROC support for the U.S. military presence had become delegitimizing to the Nationalists and contributed substantially to the demise of Chiang's regime. American misconduct and transportation of Nationalist forces aboard U.S. ships and aircraft enabled the CCP to build a persuasive narrative of the U.S. military running rampant over Chinese sovereignty with Chiang's complicity, while also enabling the GMD to wage civil war. Communist newspapers published a constant stream of allegations against U.S. forces, and party activists harnessed anti-American resentment to expand CCP influence on college campuses, making the biggest inroads, ironically, at the universities that had provided the bulk of recruits to the wartime interpreter program. Anti-Americanism resonated widely, becoming a cornerstone of civil war politics. The liberal and independent periodicals that proliferated in the freer publishing atmosphere that followed Japan's surrender devoted substantial space to documenting the social ills, crimes, and accidents caused by U.S. forces. Misconduct had also been rife during the Soviet occupation of Manchuria, but because the Soviets withdrew in spring 1946 and the GMD still hoped to make Moscow more of an ally than an outright enemy, the Soviet presence remained far less visible.[63] The Red Army was long gone in late December 1946, when the rape of a nineteen-year-old student by two marines in Beijing led CCP activists and university students to begin demonstrations that quickly snowballed into the largest protest movement of the Nationalist era, with thousands of people taking to the streets in some twenty-five cities to demand that U.S. forces leave China.

The Anti-Brutality Movement, as it came to be known, resulted from the accumulated grievances of ordinary Chinese since the arrival of U.S. forces in China. It was their collective rejection of U.S. and GMD designs for China's subordinate place in a U.S.-dominated postwar world.[64] The GMD's response—mass arrests, attacks by club-wielding paramilitary thugs, and hackneyed defenses of U.S. military justice in official party organs—simply reinforced the widespread perception that the Americans were imperialists and Chiang's Nationalists their lackeys. The Americans, frustrated with opposition from the Chinese public and the GMD's refusal to implement political reforms, withdrew most troops and withheld supplies from the Nationalists just as the tide began turning against Chiang's forces on the battlefield. In the cruelest twist of fate, from Chiang's perspective, U.S. policy in the region then reoriented toward Japan and its economic recovery.

Like any imperial relationship, the U.S.-ROC alliance was fragile. U.S. efforts to reform the Chinese military and extend American authority fell short of expectations, GMD nation- and alliance-building projects imploded, and the balance of dominance and subordination widened. Setting a pattern that many U.S.-allied autocrats would follow, Chiang had little choice but to make the U.S. military's demands in China his highest priority. Torn between pleasing his American patrons and supporting his own people, he ended up satisfying neither.

In the end, Chiang's fall in the Chinese Revolution of 1949 brought about the very outcome that the U.S. military's intervention in, alliance with, and occupation of China had aimed to prevent. The world's most populous country had fallen under the control of a power hostile toward the United States.

1 Making Our Friends at Home

China's Hostel Program

. . . .

On February 14, 1945, Major General Huang Renlin spoke to reporters in Chongqing about the ROC's efforts to create "a home away from home" for American soldiers. As director-general of the Guomindang National Military Council's War Area Service Corps (WASC), Huang supervised a network of hostels that provided free board, lodging, and cultural outreach to all American troops in China. The American Volunteer Group (AVG) initially paid a nominal fee for these services, but Chiang Kai-shek decided in late 1942 to fund the program for the duration of the war, a decision with crucial implications for the U.S.-ROC alliance. Huang had just returned from Kunming, where half of the nearly forty thousand U.S. Army personnel now deployed in China were stationed. In Kunming alone, Huang said, hostels provided GIs with "fifty cows, eighty pigs, seven-hundred chickens, and eighty thousand" eggs each day, in compliance with U.S. War Department standards that called for a daily ration that included eighteen ounces of fresh meat and twenty ounces of fresh vegetables.[1] In addition to food, WASC supplied fuel, hot water, and laundry service, while its cultural outreach program included banquets, opera performances, educational pamphlets, and a daily English-language news bulletin. The hostels themselves featured Western-style dormitories, latrines, and mess halls.

These facilities and services, which enabled American troops to carry out their missions in China while living with the creature comforts they were accustomed to, were not cheap. ROC government spending to support the U.S. presence, Huang noted, "formed the second-largest item in the total national expenditure."[2]

As reporters listened to Huang describe the privileged existence American personnel enjoyed at Chongqing's expense, the sharply contrasting situation Chinese had to contend with must have weighed heavily on their minds. Operation Ichigo, Japan's largest land offensive of the Second World War, swept Nationalist forces from the provinces of Henan, Hunan, and Guangxi during 1944, triggering acute refugee flight and economic crisis.[3] Like other salaried workers in China, journalists had become destitute as a result of inflation, which reached a wartime high in early 1945.[4] Food prices in Kunming nearly doubled in January, while the Nationalist secret police ruthlessly suppressed antigovernment rice riots in Chongqing in February.[5] Chinese soldiers, meanwhile, suffered from malnourishment and disease.[6] The average GI in China probably consumed more protein each day than did the average Chinese infantry platoon. National collapse appeared a real possibility, but as Huang affirmed, Chongqing remained committed to affording soldiers from the world's wealthiest country a living standard beyond the reach of nearly all Chinese.

When Chiang decided to make hostels free for American soldiers in 1942, he expected the U.S. government to take these services into consideration in any future mutual aid settlement. The governing principle behind mutual aid was "to take advantage of the potentialities of each of the allies," and Japan's blockade created a logistical bottleneck that made it very difficult—if not impossible—for U.S. forces to provide their own food and housing.[7] Chiang understood the hostel program as a crucial alliance-building initiative, and although it would be expensive, he anticipated that everything would balance out in the end: Article VI of the June 2, 1942, U.S.-ROC mutual aid agreement stipulated that "full cognizance shall be taken of all property, services, information, facilities or other benefits" provided to U.S. forces by the ROC government in any "final determination" on mutual aid.[8]

The ROC government did not devote scarce resources to hosting American personnel in China solely to prove its commitment to the Sino-U.S. alliance. Though signaling the government's commitment was an important goal, Chiang, Huang, and other ROC officials saw the hostel program as a solution to a fundamental question of China's search for national rejuvenation: How could they convince Americans to treat Chinese as equals? From their perspectives, part of the answer was the creation of a hostel network and outreach program that would demonstrate their capacity for adhering to American norms while also showcasing China's cultural achievements.

For Chinese authorities, Western-style hostels were key to indicating that they had internalized American sanitary, dietary, comfort, and efficiency standards. American soldiers' sensory perception of China would now be mediated by the hostels. They would be insulated from unwelcome encounters with unsightly poverty, noxious odors, unfamiliar tastes, cacophonous streets, and harmful physical contact. At the same time, displays of high culture—such as Peking opera and well-stocked formal banquets—would reveal the best China had to offer, as would an educational pamphlet series written for Americans by Western-educated intellectuals. The hostel program was one expression of the ROC's larger anti-imperialist nation-building project, which was aimed not only at defeating Japan but also at attaining equal international standing for China as a great power.[9]

The hostel program succeeded in shaping American perceptions, but not in the way ROC officials had intended. In creating privileged spaces cordoned off from surrounding communities, it replicated the unequal Sino-Western relations of the prewar treaty ports. The spaces themselves, meanwhile, fell short of American standards. "The American soldier may live in barracks with a tile roof turned up at the corners like a pie crust," wrote one army sergeant in 1944, "however, his roof is likely to leak when it rains [and] sharing his quarters are spiders, fleas, mosquitos with a two-inch wingspan and fat rats."[10] Western-style hostel food provoked even more complaints. And while soldiers initially enjoyed WASC banquets and performances, they soon came to see cultural outreach as a nuisance. The unmediated sensory experience outside the hostels left an even deeper impression. When striking out on their own, GIs discovered a noisy society full of pitiful, impoverished humanity who consumed disgusting food. The air reeked of human feces, and the proximity to Chinese bodies—perceived as diseased or unclean—often triggered revulsion.

Apprehending China through the senses led American soldiers to racialize and infantilize the Chinese with striking speed and consistency.[11] The common term U.S. troops assigned to hostel staff—men often older than themselves—was "boy," and they referred to ordinary Chinese as "Chinks" or "slopes." American commanders, for their part, understood the program's shortcomings as evidence of the Nationalist elite's incompetence, untrustworthiness, and corruption. Chiang Kai-shek tried to salvage the program in 1944 with the help of a liaison group consisting of Chinese-speaking American missionaries, to no avail.

China's precarious wartime finances quickly rendered Chiang's commitment to funding the hostel program unsustainable, and the ROC would pay a heavy price as a result. The U.S. and ROC governments began reverse lend-lease negotiations in early 1944, but because U.S. officials concluded that the entire program was an elaborate ruse undertaken to cheat the U.S. government, the two sides failed to reach an agreement. This left the beleaguered Chinese Nationalists on the hook for the hostel program's entire 34 billion fabi expenditure (US$1.7 billion at December 1941 exchange rates).[12] American demand on strained resources also accelerated inflation and depleted Yunnan Province's meat and poultry supplies, making life harder for ordinary civilians and exacerbating tensions between Chongqing and longtime Yunnan governor Long Yun's semiautonomous provincial government in Kunming.

The hostel program is crucial to understanding the lofty expectations and bitter realities that poisoned the ROC-U.S. alliance.[13] Guomindang officials imbued the program with internationalist aspirations about brotherhood, which matched President Roosevelt's universalist rhetoric and the U.S. Army's antiracist message in its *Pocket Guide to China*.[14] But instead of fulfilling Huang's ambition, the hostel program became grounds for Americans to deny Chinese the equal relationship that both U.S. and Chinese authorities had deemed essential to the war effort. Rather than showcasing China's achievements, the hostel program undermined the alliance by offending the five senses, reproducing imperialistic treaty-port hierarchies, and demonstrating the purported incapacities of the country's officials.

Huang Renlin's Vision

After Roosevelt approved Chiang's proposal to recruit American pilots for the AVG, Chiang's Office of Personal Attendants, which handled classified party information, recommended Huang Renlin (see figure 1.1) as the "obvious, ideal choice" for accommodating the aviators in China.[15] On May 9, Chiang ordered Huang to establish hostels for the AVG in Yunnan, which gave the WASC director-general the opportunity to fulfill long-standing professional and personal ambitions.[16] Huang's views on the importance of U.S.-China relations had been developing for decades. He also had more than ten years' experience hosting foreign guests, including German and Soviet military advisors. In 1937, he started looking after a retired U.S. Army Air Service aviator who had come to Nanjing to carry out a confidential survey of the Chinese Air Force.[17] This man, Claire Chennault, now commanded the AVG, which is better known by its nickname, the Flying Tigers. Huang was able to capitalize on this mission and endow it with internationalist aims, due to his extensive experience in the transnational spaces linking China and the United States as well as his success in adapting American models to advance Chiang's political goals.

No ROC official embodied the American belief in a special Sino-American relationship—in which the United States served as a benevolent and admired guide in China's search for modernization—quite like Huang. He had enrolled at Vanderbilt in 1922 after converting to Christianity under the influence of an American missionary educator and completing junior college at the American Methodist-run Soochow (Suzhou) University.[18] Out-

FIGURE 1.1 Huang Renlin towering over Chiang Kai-shek and Brigadier General Frederick McCabe during a November 1943 stopover at the U.S. Army's training center for Chinese forces, Ramgarh, India. (William Vandivert/the LIFE Picture Collection/Shutterstock)

going, religious, and massive for a southern Chinese at six feet two and 210 pounds, Huang thrived in Tennessee. As a senior, he won the university's oratory prize for a speech titled "The Sino-American Relationship: The Key to World Peace." In it, he praised the "high Christian ideals" underpinning U.S. China policy but also urged his audience to learn more about China. The headquarters of the Methodist Episcopal Church South in Nashville, where Huang worked part-time, took his message to heart, paying for him and five classmates to perform an original play called *A Pageant of China's Progress* at schools and churches in twenty-eight cities. Huang went on to graduate school at Columbia, took a work-study job at Ford's Highland Park factory, and accepted an offer for a YMCA secretary position in Shanghai.

In October 1926, after six months' training at the Cleveland Y, he returned to China.[19] He credited his time in the United States for enabling him to develop independent thinking skills and a devotion to service; thus, upon his return to Shanghai he made "a secret vow that whenever possible I want in return to show my hospitality and to render any service toward my American friends."[20]

A connection Huang made in Cleveland enabled him to enter government service. While he grew up comfortably in Shanghai's International Settlement and the nearby city of Suzhou as the oldest son of an English-speaking telegraphic superintendent, Huang did not have a powerful patron until he met the wealthy banker Kong Xiangxi (H. H. Kung) in 1926. That summer, Kong returned to his alma mater, Oberlin College, to receive an honorary doctorate. Huang organized the festivities at Oberlin for Kong, who told the young YMCA trainee to "come and see him" after he returned to China.[21] When Huang called on him in 1928, Kong was one of China's most powerful men. He had become Chiang Kai-shek's brother-in-law through marriage and had taken up the post of China's minister of commerce and labor. Kong urged Huang to resign from the YMCA. He told him that he would be the ideal candidate for leading a new movement Chiang wanted to promulgate called the Officers' Moral Endeavor Association (OMEA, *Lizhi she*). Huang agreed, and Chiang appointed him associate secretary-general of the *Lizhi she* with the rank of colonel. He became the full secretary-general a few months later.[22]

As *Lizhi she* director, Huang was charged with "instilling an uplifting moral influence" on Chinese military officers and cadets. He implemented a recreation program modeled on American efforts to create a new fighting man during World War I, when the YMCA collaborated with the U.S. War Department's Commission on Training Camp Activities to halt drinking and prostitution at military camps.[23] OMEA members swore an oath to abstain from alcohol, prostitution, smoking, and gambling. According to Huang, OMEA headquarters in Nanjing became a "center for social gatherings and wholesome entertainment." In addition to introducing American-style Progressive reforms to the Chinese officer corps, the movement helped build Chiang's personality cult by producing and disseminating propaganda.[24] Huang earned high marks, and the OMEA expanded to other cities during the 1930s. In 1934, he earned a promotion, becoming concurrent director of the New Life Movement General Association after Chiang launched the New Life Movement in order to purge China of habits that weakened the nation, such as disorderly public behavior and poor hygiene.[25]

Lizhi she headquarters and branch offices made ideal sites for hosting foreign guests. Designed to enable Chinese officers and cadets to avoid the "demoralizing influences" available at hotels, each site contained dormitories, showers, kitchens, and meeting halls.[26] OMEA headquarters in Nanjing, an expansive compound located down the street from Chiang's presidential palace, was more like a dry country club constructed in the Chinese palatial style. In addition to a sixty-room dormitory, the compound included larger guest suites, reading and game rooms, riding stables, sporting facilities, and an auditorium that could hold a thousand people. Huang hosted the League of Nations' Lytton Commission there in 1932 during its investigation of Japanese aggression in Manchuria. In the mid-1930s, he expanded OMEA services to Chinese combat units with German advisors.[27] After the Resistance War began in July 1937, Chiang rechristened the OMEA as the War Area Service Corps and put Huang in charge of looking after Soviet military advisors and volunteers, including more than four hundred pilots scattered at new WASC hostels around the country.[28] By the late 1930s, Huang had more experience as a practitioner of China's long-standing official hospitality tradition than anyone else in the Nationalist government.[29]

When he received orders from Chiang in May 1941 to prepare hostels for Chennault's Flying Tigers, Huang understood the gravity of his mission. Securing American support against Japan had been Chiang's overriding diplomatic goal since 1938.[30] By granting his blessing to the AVG and earmarking $45 million to initiate China's lend-lease program on April 23, Roosevelt made China and the United States tacit allies.[31] Chiang secured the U.S. president's discreet but undeniable commitment during one of the Resistance War's darkest hours. On April 13, Japan and the Soviet Union signed a neutrality pact. The termination of Soviet military aid gave Japan complete superiority over China's skies. Japanese forces launched the most extensive terror bombing offensive of the entire war, intensifying a campaign that since 1938 had subjected Chongqing to what *Life* photographer Carl Mydans described as "the worst bombing a city has ever received."[32] By the time AVG pilots and ground crewmen began arriving in Rangoon on July 28 to begin training, Huang's preparations were well underway.[33]

Chiang granted Huang unlimited authority to keep the Americans "healthy and happy, irrespective of cost and effort."[34] While WASC had expanded to accommodate Soviet volunteers, preparations for the much smaller AVG contingent dwarfed these efforts, illustrating this group's importance to the Nationalists. Chiang never fully trusted the Soviets, but he had placed Chennault, who retired from active duty at the relatively low

FIGURE 1.2 Hostel No. 1, Kunming. (James B. Hinchliff Collection, Institute on World War II and the Human Experience)

rank of major, in charge of forging a new Chinese air force in 1938.[35] In the summer of 1941, Huang transferred WASC headquarters to Kunming, where the Flying Tigers would be based. Relations between Chiang and Long Yun, the regional militarist who had governed Yunnan since 1927, had always been strained, but Long offered his full cooperation. He granted Huang use of Kunming's Agricultural College as the site for his new headquarters and the AVG's first hostel (see figure 1.2).[36] China's Commission on Aeronautical Affairs, the central government agency in charge of military airfields, turned over buildings at other air bases in Yunnan, Sichuan, Guiyang, and Guangxi Provinces for AVG use. Huang also worked with the China-Burma Transport Administration to refurbish eight service stations for use as hostels along the Burma Road, which connected Kunming to Rangoon. In all, Huang spent 40 million fabi (US$2 million at the official 20:1 exchange rate) turning these facilities into suitable hostels for the American volunteers.[37]

Huang wanted hostels to demonstrate China's capacity for adhering to American standards while insulating his guests from encounters that could lead to negative impressions about the Chinese. "To ensure a speedy and effective administration" that met "American efficiency" norms, Huang divided the far-flung hostels into four districts and provided each regional director with a sizable revolving fund. As his deputy he hired Dr. Ernest K. Moy, a Chinese American newspaper editor who had served as first ROC president Sun Yat-sen's English secretary.[38] He also set up programs, staffed by some of the country's leading intellectuals, to train English-speaking hostel managers and interpreters. Many of the men he hired to cook and clean for the Americans had experience working for Westerners in the prewar treaty ports. Competent English-speaking staff who had internalized American manners would prevent AVG members from seeing the Chinese as inferiors, Huang believed.

Reassuring the American senses was fundamental to Huang's strategy. He understood that bodily encounters would influence how Americans would feel about, and act toward, their Chinese hosts. As OMEA and New Life Movement General Association director, Huang had devoted eleven years to uplifting Chinese soldiers and civilians by reordering the senses along American lines: imposing quiet on city streets, conducting public campaigns against spitting, and teaching Western manners and hygiene practices to young military officers. But the AVG would be stationed in poorer provincial areas that had been outside Nationalist control prior to 1937. Clean, modern, and well-equipped hostels would thus be needed to contrast with the poverty American volunteers would see around them. Spacious hostel facilities, most of them located outside city limits, would shield them from the din of city streets, while Western-style latrines would carry away noxious odors. Huang planned to satisfy the American preference for beef by using water buffalo meat as a substitute. While at banquets, the Flying Tigers could feast on high-end Chinese cuisine. Comfortable bedding, hot water, new towels, and laundry service would provide a familiar touch. Huang even created a newspaper, the *WASC Diary and Bulletin*, that soldiers could read each day. It was edited by the English Department at Southwest Associated University in Kunming, the wartime agglomeration of Peking, Nankai, and Tsinghua Universities and the best institute of higher education in China. A slogan Huang adopted, "Home Away from Home," was posted in every hostel.[39]

Huang also tried to shape American perceptions with an educational pamphlet series that evoked his earlier experience sharing "China's progress" with audiences throughout the American South. Written mostly by Western-educated intellectuals, including the sociologist Fei Xiaotong and the historian Lei Haizong, WASC's Information Pamphlets on China series introduced local culture, history, law, current affairs, and other topics to Huang's American guests. Each pamphlet was around twenty to thirty pages long and contained a Chinese-English glossary. As a whole, the five-pamphlet series portrayed China as a civilization that had a rich history but that had just begun to emerge from centuries of decline. But like the monthly journal *Filipino People*, published by Filipino Nacionalista Party leader Manuel Quezon in Washington, D.C., before World War II, these pamphlets accepted American discourses by stressing China's democratizing and Christianizing tendencies in the twentieth century.[40]

Huang's preparations reflected both the promise and the risks he saw in the partnership between China and the United States. He understood that American attitudes toward China were at best paternalistic and at worst blatantly racist. Images of China in the United States had improved in the decade leading up to Pearl Harbor, but even the humanizing portrayals of ordinary Chinese in the writings of Pearl Buck or the ubiquitous United China Relief fundraising campaigns emphasized China's continued need for American help and guidance.[41] Huang was not exactly opposed to American guidance, but he had experienced the uglier side of American racial impulses during his time in the United States. Businesses had refused to serve him in California, and he had arrived in Cleveland just months after police arrested and fingerprinted every Chinese man in the city in response to a murder.[42]

Nearly two decades later, America's racist barriers to Chinese immigration remained in place, as did the extraterritorial system that exempted Americans from Chinese law, but Huang now saw himself in a position to improve relations between the two people. The attack on Pearl Harbor gave him the opportunity to showcase China's progress on a grand scale. He hoped that demonstrating that China could meet American standards would justify the Chinese laying claim to equal treatment. But by suffusing the hostel program with such ambitions, Huang's undertaking risked failure, even if it succeeded operationally by keeping the Americans housed and fed.

American Impressions

After the program got up and running, Huang took particular pride in hostel cuisine. When he traveled as part of the ROC's delegation to the November 1943 Cairo Conference, where Chiang and Roosevelt hashed out a strategy against Japan along with British prime minister Winston Churchill, he had the chance to talk to the president about his work. "I hear you are looking after my boys in China," Roosevelt said to Huang when they first met. "I understand you have been serving them water buffalo meat." Roosevelt expressed skepticism about the meat's taste and texture in comparison to the beef American soldiers were used to: "Isn't it too tough?" he asked. Huang assured him that "when buffalo meat is properly prepared and cooked, it can be quite tasty." The boys, Huang told the president, "have not noticed the difference."[43]

Huang was dead wrong. No matter whether writing during the war or looking back decades later, the army personnel who served in the China theater described the experience of dining on water buffalo meat as akin to eating a rancid rubber ball.[44] And taste was not the only sensory experience that failed to meet the standards WASC had set for itself.

But when soldiers first set foot in ROC-run hostels, the slow, dangerous, and stomach-churning journey to Yunnan left most of them simply relieved to be alive. The voyage from the continental United States to India could take nine weeks.[45] Enlisted men slept five high in canvas bunks and ate two monotonous meals each day. Officers could at least sit down to eat, but food and sleeping conditions were not much better. To avoid Japanese submarines, the ships had to change course every few minutes, turning and pitching the whole way.[46] Only the boozy shore leave in Perth offered a brief respite, while disembarking at Bombay threatened every human sense. "Whatever disease there is in this world it's over here, so take care of yourselves," officers warned.[47] In British India, GIs jostled uneasily against livestock, beggars, and lepers, encountering "unbelievable" poverty as they made their way across the country to the Assam airfields, the staging point for the flight to China. "It wasn't unusual to find dead bodies on the sidewalk or in doorways," a soldier named Angelo Ruvo recalled.[48] The journey's final leg was the most terrifying. More than five hundred aircraft crashed while flying over the Hump during the war.[49] According to Ruvo, as soldiers boarded the Kunming-bound Douglas C-47 Skytrains, a sergeant handed them parachutes and said, only half-jokingly, "I hope you guys don't have to use this, because if you do, and you're still alive when you get down over the Hump, it's too bad, you're better off dead."[50]

The soldiers found conditions in China far better than the shocking destitution they encountered in India, at least initially. "It seemed like the condition of the people was so much better than the condition of the people in India," anti-aircraft officer Jack Neal observed in Kunming.[51] It helped that WASC pulled out all the stops for new arrivals, making them guests of honor for banquets and various performances—Peking opera, acrobatics, folk music.[52] Most men also began their service in Kunming, which sat at 6,200 feet above sea level just north of the Tropic of Cancer, resulting in yearlong springlike weather. And the majority of hostels in the Kunming area were located outside city limits, within walking distance of nearby countryside that had plentiful wild game. Yunnan's stunning rural landscape evoked comparisons to the American Southwest. Anne Peeke, a graduate student at the University of Wisconsin, teased her husband, Jan, about becoming "too satisfied with China" after he spent two miserable months in India. Jan, a logistical sergeant with the Twenty-Third Fighter Group—the successor to the Flying Tigers—replied, "God, how could anyone in their right mind be satisfied with this place—though to be honest it's infinitely better than India."[53]

But it took only a few meals before disillusion set in, leaving many men pining for India's familiar creature comforts. Much on the menu tasted little better than water buffalo. Many soldiers considered eggs the single appetizing protein source, so Lieutenant Carl Kostol ate them at every meal.[54] Paul Hassett, a transport plane navigator, had the same idea, but confessed to his wife in July 1945, "My stomach turns at the sight of any egg now."[55] Another pilot recalled, "After I got home it was ten years before I'd eat another egg."[56] Huang's guests also chipped their teeth on pebbles mixed in with the rice, and even though he had assured U.S. commanders that food would meet War Department standards, frequent shortages left many hostels without fresh fruit or vegetables. When they were available, monotony was the rule—boiled cauliflower or cabbage for days or weeks on end.[57] Yet many GIs still preferred hostel food over local cuisine, much of which was fertilized with night soil (human excrement) and thus off-limits. "These Chinese eat this rot, but God damn it! We're not Chinese!" wrote cargo squadron officer Warren Arnett on the eve of Japan's surrender.[58] "When we think of those boys back there [in India] drinking ice-cold Coca Colas, a case and a half of beer a month, there is a bit of resentment among us," another soldier wrote in a 1945 letter home. Alcohol and soda never made it over the Hump.[59]

Even worse than the hostel food was the inescapable stench of human feces. "The first impression of China was the overpowering smell, recalled enlisted man James Brochon. "To be quite frank it stunk."[60] Hostel latrines did nothing to cover up the odor emanating from the night soil used as fertilizer across the country.[61] Urban areas also smelled like open latrines. Despite years of government campaigns against public urination and defecation, the practice persisted.[62] Cities and towns also lacked modern plumbing. Each morning, night soil collectors roamed the streets, depositing human waste into containers the Americans called "honey buckets" (see figure 1.3).[63]

FIGURE 1.3 Night soil collector in Chongqing.
(Paul LeRoy Jones Papers, Hoover Institution)

"There simply isn't any parallel," Jan Peeke wrote in 1943. "The smell of this country is like the smell of no other place."[64] China has "the ungodliest odor, and I do mean odor," he continued in another letter home.[65] According to P-38 pilot Harold Rosser, "You had to get in the air to get away from it."[66] Mary Krauss, an army nurse, agreed, describing Kunming to her mother as "very interesting but also very dirty. And odorous—Phew!"[67]

The hostels' surroundings and climate were considered little better. While Kunming had pleasant weather, Chongqing had "two seasons, both of them bad" (in the words of one war correspondent), and alternated between damp, sunless winters and sweltering summers with triple-digit heat indexes.[68] Mosquitoes filled the air, and men could feel mice running over mosquito nettings while they slept.[69] Lieutenant Samuel Etris wrote that beds in Kunming's Hostel No. 3 "were straw ticks only two inches thick stretched over ropes strung on a wooden frame. After a night on the ropes, one's back looked like a waffle."[70] Worse conditions awaited men at remote areas. Whitney Greenberg spent nearly three years with a combat cargo group and lived without showers or indoor housing at a hostel in Luliang, Yunnan. Captain Rafael Hirtz trained commandos at another isolated base in Yunnan, where "there were no showers . . . and I had just about every disease known to man."[71]

Even the visual environment evoked annoyance and disgust. Larger hostels were constructed in the classical Chinese style, so they looked imposing from afar. But closer inspection revealed infestations of cockroaches and rats.[72] "They are big," Jan Peeke told his wife. "If one could put a harness on them, as they do these Chinese midget interpretation of horses, I feel sure that the load pulled would be equally as big with rats."[73] Construction quality and furnishings left a lot to be desired as well. "Everything was crude," according to B-25 pilot Orlando Wood."[74] Soldiers also observed poor sanitary conditions when inspecting hostel kitchen facilities. During the summer of 1944, the fourteen hundred American soldiers stationed at Yunnanyi, a large airbase town approximately 180 miles west of Kunming, refused to eat at hostel mess halls for this reason.[75]

Sensory contact zones outside the hostels, where American personnel and Chinese from all walks of life engaged with one another in diverse ways, were even more revolting. Nearly everyone took liberty, or pass, in cities like Kunming, where—besides the mephitic smells, loud noises, and unsafe foods—they encountered visual indecency and came into physical proximity to dirty, diseased bodies. "I was shocked at first to see how desperately poor most people are," wrote staff sergeant Tom Hardwick in a letter to his mother. "The streets are very narrow, they are dirty, and they are crowded."[76] At least in India, the poor kept themselves clean, but according to lieutenant William Millner, "I don't think the Chinese ever bathed."[77] "They are a wonderfully clean race," Peeke joked in 1944, "bodies so caked with dirt and stuff that you have to scrape with a knife to find out if they have skin or not."[78] "What people wear can hardly be called clothes," another GI told his mother. "They are only rags, so torn and shredded I don't see how they manage to keep them on their bodies."[79] "Over here," staff sergeant Earl Revell wrote in 1944, "nothing is too dirty, filthy, or putrid for these people to wade into."[80] After three months in Kunming, Revell told his wife he wanted to write a book about "real life" in China to disabuse readers of all the "fantastic pieces of rubbish I have ever read—about the lure of the East. If you call a land that is overflowing with half starved, ragged, diseased, ignorant people a place that has 'lure' or 'charm,'" he continued, "then you refuse to let your mind believe what your nose and eyes are telling you."[81]

WASC's publications for U.S. forces represented Chinese people as aspiring Americans, but GIs found little evidence to support such claims. Public breastfeeding, as with urinating and defecating in the open, offended GIs' sensibilities, convincing them that the Chinese were shameless. "It is a common sight to see women with one on the breast, one on the back, and one in the fetal state," Peeke wrote. "It should be a trademark of China—no one else would bother copywriting."[82] While early on some men found it endearing to be surrounded by curious Chinese crowds, over time it became annoying. "Some misinformed individual stated that Chinese always mind their own business—he must have written that tome in a padded cell or flew over China at the altitude of eighty thousand feet," Peeke complained.[83] Chinese also appeared to lack the common sense Americans took for granted. They walked into busy streets without checking for oncoming traffic, performed poor-quality manual labor, and took far too long to finish routine administrative tasks. Rather than understanding these perceived deficiencies as the effects of war or poverty, Americans attributed them to innate stupidity or the hoary notion that Chinese were indifferent to human life. Comments such as "Life in China was pretty cheap" or "Death had no effect on the Chinese" were ubiquitous in wartime observations.[84] One colonel, for example, responded to witnessing a car wreck by writing in his diary, "The Chinese have no regard for life at all and no charity for suffering."[85]

Some officers, particularly during the alliance's early days, were impressed with hostel services, but Huang's hospitality failed to have the desired effect. The first guests, the forty or so men making up the army's

American Military Mission to China (AMMISCA), arrived in October 1941 to supervise lend-lease aid and advise Chiang's government. They spent several months at newly refurbished hostels while appraising the military situation. AMMISCA chief of staff Colonel Edward MacMorland, who had extensive experience working with ROC officials in Washington, described Huang as "one of the most capable Chinese I have ever met."[86] Of the hostel program, he wrote in his diary, "The WASC is, on the whole, doing a very good job."[87] But instead of recognizing WASC efforts as a contribution to the joint war effort in line with the principles underpinning mutual aid, MacMorland suspected ulterior motives. He thought WASC was feting American personnel because the ROC government wanted to blackmail the United States and get "someone else to win the war for them."[88] Brigadier General John Magruder, the Fifteenth Infantry veteran and former military attaché in China who commanded AMMISCA, agreed with MacMorland's assessment. He reported it back to the War Department, where army chief of staff George C. Marshall accepted it without comment.[89] Other early impressions echoed descriptions from the prewar treaty ports, where American soldiers and marines relied on "Chink coolies" to carry out all the routine tasks that could make ordinary military life a grind.[90] "My enlisted men never had to make a bed," said Seventy-Fifth Fighter Squadron commander John R. Allison. "The Chinese did everything; they cooked the food; they served the food; they cleaned your room."[91] None of these impressions elicited views of hostel staff or administrators as equals.

In contrast, these bodily encounters and impressions of Chinese dishonesty and servility fueled anti-Chinese resentment. The longer soldiers spent in the country, the lower their opinion of Chinese people fell. Graham Peck, a Chinese-speaking Office of War Information (OWI) employee and one of the most capable observers of wartime Sino-American relations, described "bitter personal hatred for the Chinese people" among military men in Chongqing. Most GIs in Kunming, he wrote, "seemed to have personally decided that all Chinese were despicable."[92] The largest army study of wartime morale revealed similar sentiments, with most enlisted men reporting that they had no idea why they were in China.[93] Earl Revell even tired of being waited on. "It may be "charming" for some people to have someone wait on you hand and foot," he wrote in reference to the hostels, "but to we Americans, that only makes us more anxious to go home." He was most explicit in a July 1945 letter to his wife: "This country is not fit for any white man. . . . I thought India was bad, but it never took out of me what it has in China."[94]

As Revell's letter reveals, these sensory engagements and frustrations contributed to a pernicious race-making process, similar to what U.S. military personnel went through while serving in the Philippines and Haiti.[95] Americans came to China with racist views about Asians, but they did not simply export domestic racism. Commanders warned newly arrived junior officers and enlisted men against using epithets like "Chink" or "Chinaman," reiterating the instructions from the *Pocket Guide to China*. This advice made a difference at first. Most diary entries and letters home that soldiers wrote during their first weeks in China referred to locals in nonracialized terms. But as GIs apprehended China through their senses and experienced other frustrations when interacting with Chinese people, the tutelary and assimilationist racial politics that underpinned Americans' understanding of their role in China gave way to more disparaging, bigoted views. The experience of living in China and grappling with its sensory offenses transformed and reinforced American racial constructs in specific ways. The term "Chink" returned to common usage, and a new epithet coined by American soldiers in China—"slope" or "slopey"—moved to the very center of popular culture in the China theater, becoming the preferred term used for referring to Chinese, whether in conversation with fellow soldiers or written in diaries and letters home.[96]

Tensions

These disparaging, racialized views of the Chinese also influenced how American personnel acted toward hostel staff and administrators. Seemingly minor incidents—at least from American perspectives—had major repercussions. On February 18, 1942, a fountain pen disappeared from the AVG Second Pursuit Squadron's ready room at Kunming's Hostel No. 2. Melvin Ceder, the squadron's acting police officer, and C. F. Bulger, its chief administrator, carried out a search of Chinese hostel staff that failed to reveal the missing pen. That same day, hostel manager Peter Shi (Shih) fired off a letter to Chennault, alleging that Bulger and Ceder had forcibly searched his staff while using "insulting language about China and the Chinese people." Chennault replied a few days later, disputing the hostel workers' account. "I am rather surprised that you would accept such a story since you know so well the record of this group for its faithful service and loyalty to China," he wrote. Chennault also told Shi that hostel workers needed to "obey" Ceder's "orders" and, "if required, to submit peaceably to a search of their persons if he so directs."[97]

In demanding that Chinese hostel staff demonstrate gratitude and submit to unlawful searches, Chennault gravely misjudged the depth of their anti-imperialist aspirations. Ending China's humiliation at the hands of foreigners and bringing about the country's rejuvenation had been the chief goal of Chinese reformers and revolutionaries for decades. It was instilled in textbooks and public discourse throughout the Republican era, providing Chinese with a clear framework for understanding and interpreting their engagements with all non-Chinese peoples, including Chennault and his men.[98] This nationalist project also underpinned the hostel program. For Shi and his staff, being subjected to racial abuse and an illegal search was an intolerable affront, with Chennault's response adding insult to injury. Making matters even worse, Chennault infantilized them. While using the conventional title "mister" in reference to Bulger and Ceder, he referred to adult hostel workers as "boys" in his letter to Shi. And instead of addressing Shi's complaints, he dismissed them with further paternalism by pointing to the AVG's combat record.[99] Another telling omission was Chennault's assumption of Chinese guilt. By early 1942, Chennault's pilots and ground crews had stolen huge stores of goods from the Rangoon docks and sold them on China's black markets.[100] Chennault ignored the possibility that one of his own men had snatched the pen.

The fraught combination of Chinese nationalism and racialized American resentment made such disputes both more likely to occur and harder to resolve. Whenever arguments broke out over subpar hostel facilities or services, U.S. military personnel and AVG volunteers attributed the problem to Chinese incapacity or dishonesty. Huang and his staff, on the other hand, reacted harshly whenever they felt like the Americans were not treating them with proper respect. The failure of American troops across the ranks to understand the depth of anti-imperialist nationalism in China would haunt the U.S. military throughout the war.

At the senior level, U.S. suspicions about WASC intentions sparked a confrontation between Huang and the U.S. Army's logistical branch, the Services of Supply (SOS). From mid-1941 until General Joseph Stilwell's arrival in Chongqing on March 4, 1942, the ROC had funded the hostel program, with Chennault's pilots contributing the nominal sum of $1 per day out of their $600 minimum monthly salaries paid by Chongqing. Actual costs were much higher, but Chiang's government was willing to foot the entire bill, as negotiations for a mutual aid agreement were already underway.[101] But because Stilwell accepted Magruder's conclusion that the hostel program was a scam, he went above Huang's head and pressured Minister of Military Administration He Yingqin into signing a provisional agreement for re-imbursement with the SOS, effective July 4—the day the AVG would be disbanded and replaced by the China Air Task Force's Twenty-Third Fighter Group. U.S. military personnel would continue to live in WASC hostels, but the U.S. Army would pay the Chinese government 85 fabi (equivalent to US$4.25 at the official exchange rate) per day for each man. Huang described the agreement as "another 'Unequal Treaty'" entered into by the Chinese government," requiring his agency to accept conditions that would be impossible to meet. When Minister He approved an extension of the pro-visional agreement in August without first notifying Huang, the WASC secretary-general was livid.[102]

Huang sent a long memorandum to Brigadier General Raymond Wheeler, the SOS commander, on September 9, outlining his grievances. He admit-ted to shortcomings in hostel work but stressed that the real issue was the U.S. Army's failure "to understand what extreme hardships China has gone through during these five years of war against a much stronger foe." He was doing his best, but his agency could not always adhere to the U.S. War De-partment's regulations. Nor could it afford to continue providing eighteen thousand gallons of gasoline per month or staff twenty-three *empty* hostels just in case of sudden changes in U.S. Army deployments, as the provisional agreement had stipulated. Inflation meant that WASC was already spend-ing an average of 120 fabi per day for each man, but Stilwell had refused to consider an adjustment, saying that "a man could stay comfortably in large hotels in America" for the equivalent of the original 85 fabi rate. "I won-der," Huang told Wheeler, "if that statement insinuated something or was it simply made by one ignorant of the present cost of living in China." Huang cited numerous other instances in which Americans accused the Chinese of cheating them. "These accusations have become so obnoxious that we hate to take on any more service than is prescribed as service proper" in the July 4 agreement, Huang wrote. But that was exactly what the Ameri-cans wanted, insisting on barbers, mechanics, and chauffeurs. The army made all these demands, Huang wrote, despite being three months behind and 3 million fabi in arrears in its repayments to Chongqing.[103]

More than anything else, Huang wrote, hostel work "has been handi-capped because so many Americans think they are crusaders in China and fail to treat their Chinese co-workers as comrades-in-arms."[104] Americans had difficulty conceiving of their role in any other way. Although the ar-my's instructions stressed the need to treat Chinese as equals, white Amer-icans were brought up to regard people from Asia as inferiors. Jim Crow racism was the norm at home. At the same time, ordinary Americans learned about China from missionaries and religious leaders who described the country as America's ward.[105] Depictions in popular culture reinforced this view, leading GIs to believe they had come to China in order to save the country. They also took it for granted that the Chinese would follow their lead. This understanding of China omitted crucial details, eliding the history of U.S. imperialism in the country and leaving the roots of Chinese sensitivity toward unequal treatment completely unexplored. And when soldiers arrived in China and found hostel workers waiting on them hand and foot, just like laborers employed by U.S. forces in the prewar treaty ports, they treated them like servants.

Disparaging views of Chinese hostel staff and the extraterritorial legal status U.S. military personnel enjoyed also meant that any argument could turn violent with little consequence for the Americans. Black market dealings between hostel staff and American personnel, though officially barred by authorities from both countries, were ubiquitous, especially in the cigarette rations every American soldier received. Soldiers did not take kindly to hostel workers who got too picky about the brand or price, or to those who tried to enforce the regulations, like Wang Haotang, a guard at Hostel No. 5 near Kunming, who suffered a broken leg in a beating at the hands of Private David Allan. While many GIs got away with such crimes, Allan was found guilty by court-martial. His punishment: a $35 fine.[106] The same court typically handed out six-month jail terms to GIs who hit other Americans, whereas causing serious injuries like broken bones could mean being locked up for several years.[107] Nor was Allan's case an exception. When Sergeant Paul Rock beat up three pantry workers at Hostel No. 11, he escaped with a reprimand.[108] After shooting hostel worker Kang Shihao to death for calling him a "son-of-a-bitch," Private Charles Phillips was sentenced to just five months of hard labor, despite telling criminal investigators he would happily do it again if given another chance.[109] Lax discipline for violent crimes against hostel workers illustrated that it was the Americans, in fact, who had a low regard for Chinese life.

Even senior hostel program administrators were subject to humiliating mistreatment. In early 1945, two young lieutenants arrived at Kunming's Hostel No. 1 to find the rooms they had been assigned occupied by Chinese officials. Hostel No. 1 was also the location of WASC's district headquarters for Yunnan, so the two lieutenants complained to Y. D. Wang, the provincial director. One of the rooms in question, Wang informed them, belonged to Ernest Moy, Huang's special deputy and WASC's chief liaison to the U.S.

Army. Before Wang could resolve the issue, one of the lieutenants, whose last name was McDonald, broke into Moy's room and dumped all his personal belongings and paperwork onto the floor of Wang's office. A few days later, McDonald barged into a memorial service being led by WASC's deputy director, a major general, and demanded that the room be vacated immediately so that the Americans could use it. He became aggressive and even threatened the general. Wang and Moy eventually calmed him down, with Moy reminding him that "in China today, such an intrusion, especially by a national of another country, upon an official and mandatory service[,] is a serious affront, intolerable to the national sense of the Chinese people."[110] That McDonald felt comfortable, as a lieutenant, ordering about Chinese generals and senior officials, insulting them, and trashing their rooms illustrated the failure of Huang's vision for the program.

Hostel staff, on the other hand, faced harsh discipline for crimes against American military personnel. Chongqing lacked the resources to address many of the Americans' complaints about the hostel program, but Chiang's government compensated by using severe measures to deal with theft—lashing out at the program's least powerful stakeholders. Violent crimes against American personnel were unheard of, but the combination of low salaries and easy access to U.S. military goods tempted some workers into stealing. A Kunming military court sentenced Hostel No. 1 orderly Zou Jiacai to seven years in prison for stealing a single coffee can and a screen used for projecting movies.[111] Lu Zhicheng and Zhang Guqing, workers at the same hostel, received lengthy sentences for taking whiskey and selling it to a restaurant.[112] Water carrier Zhou Zihuan got ten years for stealing blankets and cigarettes—two items Americans often pilfered and sold to Chinese.[113] For the crime of pocketing two cans of cocoa and some butter, Xie Chuwen, a hostel cook, earned three-and-a-half years behind bars.[114] American personnel also described seeing Chinese military police flog hostel workers for stealing.[115] Simple petty theft by these workers resulted in far harsher sentences than GIs received for violent crimes against workers, including murder.

At the senior level, Chiang tried to keep Huang and the Americans happy by deciding in late November 1942 to provide free board and lodging for all American troops in China. Huang had threatened to quit in his September 9 letter to Wheeler, but Chiang's decision convinced him to stay on the job. Chiang believed U.S. and Chinese authorities could reach a mutually satisfactory solution to the question of hostel program expenses. The June 2, 1942, mutual aid agreement between the two countries opened the door to a reverse lend-lease settlement.[116] China had little to offer the U.S. military after five years of war, and the Japanese blockade made it difficult for the U.S. government to supply its personnel in China, so Chiang's decision seemed like the most sensible way to contribute to the joint war effort in adherence to the spirit of the June agreement.

But Chiang's government and the U.S. military were not the hostel program's sole stakeholders. Chiang made his decision when just a thousand American personnel were stationed in China. As troop deployments increased sharply over the next year, the burden of accommodating the Americans fell mostly on Yunnan Province, governed by the ethnic Yi militarist Long Yun.[117] Long carefully guarded his autonomy from Chongqing. He kept close ties with neighboring warlords, refused to allow Nationalist secret police to operate in the province, and maintained control over local sales taxes.[118] Chiang and Long sparred over WASC's land use rights until early 1944. Chiang decreed that the central government would purchase any land the United States needed for hostels or other use in Yunnan, but Long saw this arrangement as an encroachment on his authority. Construction delays ensued, and hostel facilities remained inadequate. Commanders like Chennault and Stilwell seethed over the holdups, while GIs slept in tents.[119]

Keeping the Americans fed also became a source of tension. Meeting the War Department's fresh meat requirement fueled skyrocketing beef prices in Yunnan. Long Yun reported that agricultural output had also suffered because farmers had been trying to make a quick profit by selling off the water buffalo they normally used for plowing. In January 1944, Long refused to comply with a request from Stilwell to send fresh meat to feed Chinese and American soldiers stationed in India. American "consumption needs," Long wrote, "are massive. . . . They need thirty head of oxen each day, and recently news has spread that this could increase to eighty or ninety. There is no way Yunnan can meet this shocking number."[120] His province could not satisfy U.S. food demands in Yunnan, let alone in India, he informed He Yingqin in February.[121] Long banned food exports and ordered that all meat and vegetable requisitions go through local government agencies. Chennault's patience ran out in April. "The need is urgent," he warned Long, reminding him that the Fourteenth Air Force's ability to defend Yunnan "depended on adequate meat supplies."[122] Under pressure from Chennault, Stilwell, and Chiang, Long made up for shortfalls by importing water buffalo from Guizhou Province, but beef prices in Kunming still increased more than fivefold by June.[123] Shortages continued into the fall, when Chiang again ordered Long to raise purchase limits.[124] Whenever U.S.

needs clashed with those of the local population, the army usually won out, but only after lengthy delays that the Americans attributed to Chinese corruption and incompetence.

WASC's expenses added up rapidly. Opening a new hostel also meant building fuel and weapons depots, radio towers, garages, roads, warehouses, and fences, as well as clearing secure areas around the perimeter. Construction and land purchases for just nine Kunming area hostels in late 1943 cost 814 million fabi, which amounted to just over 1.75 percent of the Nationalist government's total 1943 expenditures.[125] For every two GIs at a hostel, WASC needed to hire one worker, and by June 1943 the agency had four thousand staff on the payroll—all of whom had to be housed and fed. Average daily cost per American guest also continued to creep up, reaching 180 fabi that same month. Foreign minister Song Ziwen first voiced concerns about the program's sustainability in early 1943, setting off alarm bells. "Stilwell is concerned, as is this Embassy," Ambassador Clarence Gauss told Secretary of State Cordell Hull, "regarding the spiraling of Chinese prices and the fantastic United States currency equivalents at which reverse Lend-Lease would be debited against United States at the present [20:1] official exchange rate."[126] Both Gauss and Song recommended that China and the United States negotiate a formal reverse lend-lease agreement, but the War Department demurred, doubting that an agreement would meet the army's needs.[127]

In January 1944, Chiang informed Roosevelt that China could no longer pay for the program, but reverse lend-lease negotiations stalled over the exchange rates question and American suspicions about Chinese intentions. According to Chiang, China's fiscal situation was now "incomparably worse than a year ago."[128] WASC now spent 300 fabi per day feeding each GI, enough for a Chinese soldier to eat for a month. Total monthly expenditures for the program had increased more than 2,000 percent over the past year. Unless the U.S. government provided financial assistance, Chiang warned, the army would have to start feeding its own men in China starting March 1.[129] Treasury secretary Hans Morgenthau pressured Chinese finance minister Kong Xiangxi to adjust the official exchange rate from 20:1 to 100:1. "We would be depreciating our currency by 500 percent, which would be fatal to our present situation," Kong replied. This adjustment, Kong insisted, would break "China's economic backbone."[130]

U.S. military and State Department officials believed that Kong's obstinance indicated that Chongqing "has not the slightest intention of cooperating with the United States."[131] Hostel service was poor, and U.S. commanders in the field suspected WASC of padding its returns. Negotiations continued as emergency cash infusions kept the program afloat, and on March 1, 1944, the SOS reached an agreement with Huang to take over control of hostel maintenance, construction, and non-foodstuff procurement.[132] U.S. commanders continued to believe that Kong was negotiating in bad faith, but they overestimated the extent of hostel program corruption. WASC's lists of personnel accommodated tracked closely to the army's personnel strength reports. And while Stilwell's headquarters claimed that Kong's 2 billion fabi estimate for total WASC expenses up to June 1944 was "a gross exaggeration," the army's estimate of 1.62 billion fabi was not that much lower.[133] And the exchange rate issue—the key sticking point in a reverse lend-lease agreement—stemmed not from Kong's obstinacy but from a genuine fear that the adjustment demanded by the U.S. Treasury would lead to the Nationalist government's collapse. But with the two parties still at odds in late August, the army's liaison officers to WASC recommended that they "should work toward taking over the supervision of hostel operations and operate them with civilian employees, thus eliminating WASC entirely."[134]

As Kong and Morgenthau tried to hash out a reverse lend-lease agreement, Huang made one last attempt to reshape perceptions of China, reaching all the way back to his OMEA playbook. On February 20, 1944, he launched the Friends of the Allied Forces movement.[135] WASC's dire financial straits meant that funding had to rely on membership fees. By summer, enough Chinese had joined to fund branches of the Friends of the Allied Forces Society in Chongqing, Chengdu, Lanzhou, Xian, Guilin, and Guiyang.[136] Any Chinese member or GI could visit for OMEA-style "wholesome" entertainment, such as opera performances or a meal. Huang promoted these facilities as venues for "proper social intercourse" between Americans and Chinese and places where GIs could "learn about cultural differences."[137] The Chinese press emphasized its role in promoting Sino-American equality. One feature in *Da gong bao*, wartime China's paper of record, read, "The two countries are complete equals. . . . All vestiges of the old days—arrogance and the sense of inferiority—should be swept away by the fire of war."[138] But few GIs bothered to visit. Less than a week after the Friends of the Allied Forces Society headquarters opened in Chongqing, the National Military Council's Foreign Affairs Bureau (FAB) recommended setting up a leisure club that would appeal to American soldiers' interest in alcohol and dancing girls. In addition, "To make life for allied troops more normal," FAB suggested, "we could open a brothel for a trial period."[139]

Chiang meanwhile tried to salvage the hostel program with the help of a liaison team recruited by his most trusted foreign advisor, an American missionary born in Zhejiang Province named Frank Price. Price recruited twenty Chinese-speaking Americans to help strengthen goodwill between U.S. and Chinese forces. The group arrived in Chongqing in late 1944, and Price placed Reuben Torrey, a Presbyterian missionary, in charge of WASC liaison work. Torrey set up a ten-day training program for hostel managers in Chongqing, which focused on ameliorating problems with food, hygiene, and living conditions. Other liaison team members took over management of individual hostels.[140] In January 1945, Torrey and his team began an inspection that took them to sixty hostels. They concluded that the program's difficulties stemmed from financial problems and a lack of cooperation from American personnel. "A large percent[age] of Army officers," Torrey wrote, did not know of or understand the agreement WASC had negotiated with the SOS the previous March. As a result, they failed to perform necessary upkeep or repairs and then blamed hostel staff for all their difficulties.[141] "Tak[ing] into consideration the many difficulties faced by [WASC], Torrey wrote to Chiang, "we feel that commendable work is being accomplished."[142]

Few American soldiers agreed with Torrey's assessment, but the army lacked the capacity to take over WASC operations, so Chongqing ran the program for the duration of the war, devoting a larger share of its national expenditure than the U.S. government spent on providing lend-lease aid to the ROC. Hostel program costs skyrocketed in 1945, reaching nearly 30 billion fabi, which accounted for 15.6 percent of ROC defense expenditures. Chongqing spent less than half of that on food administration for the entire *country*.[143] By comparison, U.S. expenditure on lend-lease aid to China in 1945, when nearly 80 percent of all wartime aid to the ROC was delivered, amounted to approximately 1.7 percent of U.S. defense spending.[144] Wartime hostel program costs totaled 34 billion fabi, which covered the construction, refurbishing, and upkeep of more than 190 hostels, staffed by a labor force of nearly thirteen thousand men. According to Huang's accounting, hostel kitchens served more than ninety-three million eggs and twenty-six million pounds of water buffalo meat over the course of the war.[145] But with continued disagreement over the exchange rate issue, the quality of hostel services, and American suspicions that WASC was padding its accounts, negotiations to settle these expenses went nowhere.[146]

· · · · · ·

By failing to insulate American soldiers from offensive sensory encounters, Huang Renlin's effort to showcase China's progress faltered along the very terms he had set for the hostel program back in 1941. He understood that

GIs would judge Chinese by their habits and manners. The sensory dimension, like other forms of Sino-American engagement, would be a site of negotiation between states—a struggle over the alliance's terms and bilateral relations more broadly. WASC hostels may have allowed GIs to distance themselves from civilians whose habits and hygiene made them recoil in disgust, but American troops still viewed hostels as another unpleasant environment, with horrible food, unsanitary kitchens, uncomfortable bedding, and rat and mosquito infestations. It was impossible for GIs to fully isolate themselves from China's offenses and affronts to the senses. WASC's efforts to convince American military personnel that China deserved a place among the civilized nations were met with scorn. The war ended with American troops circulating disparaging images and racist doggerel about China, focusing almost exclusively on offensive bodily encounters.[147]

The hostel program also fueled distrust at the alliance's highest levels, as U.S. officials and military commanders interpreted its sensory refinement failures and administrative shortcomings as evidence that the ROC was not committed to the joint war effort. By early 1942, Magruder and Stilwell had erroneously concluded that the hostel program was a Chinese scam to trick the Americans into winning the war for them. In contrast, Chiang and Huang actually believed that the hostel program aligned with the undergirding principles and letter of the law articulated in the 1942 mutual aid agreement. The logistical challenges of the China theater left the U.S. military dependent on the ROC for food and housing, and providing these services took advantage of China's limited potential. But like other wartime initiatives, the hostel program proved more difficult to administer than Chongqing had anticipated. Problems emerged with supply, land use, sanitation, and construction, among other issues, which frustrated U.S. commanders. But the army's chief complaint—that WASC inflated its expenses in order to cheat the U.S. government in a postwar reverse lend-lease deal—relied more on Stilwell's gut than hard evidence.[148] Chongqing continued funding the program long after its costs became unsustainable, still confident, even after V-J Day, that a reverse lend-lease agreement could be reached. But whereas the U.S. and UK governments settled their mutual aid account in December 1945, the fundamental American dissatisfaction with the hostel program led to the breakdown of U.S.-ROC negotiations, leaving Chongqing to foot the entire 34 billion fabi bill.[149]

In the end, the hostel program achieved the opposite of its declared aims, producing relations of hierarchy rather than equality. Huang had believed the program could reshape American perceptions and open up new possibilities in the GMD's larger anti-imperialist struggle. But living in China led American servicemen to exceptionalize differences between themselves and their Chinese hosts in primarily racial terms. GIs constantly referred to Chinese as "Chinks," "slopes," and "slopeys," encountering sensory violations each time they left their hostels that convinced them—for racial reasons—that no progress toward American-style civilization was possible in China. It was a nation, as Earl Revell wrote, "not fit for any white man."[150] The hostels themselves essentially reanimated the imperialist dynamics of the prewar treaty ports, with GIs infantilizing hostel staff as subordinate boys rather than partners. And there was a fine line, as physical assaults and illegal searches revealed, between seeing hostel workers as helpful, childlike coolies and seeing them as ungrateful thieves one had to control, sometimes violently. WASC administrators—representing the GMD elite—were dismissed as corrupt and incompetent, incapable of making a meaningful contribution to the joint war effort. The hostel program thus played a critical role in the unmaking of the U.S.-ROC alliance.

Communicating without Understanding

China's Interpreter Program

∙∙∙

On March 19, 1945, *Da gong bao*, wartime China's newspaper of record, published an op-ed by a man calling himself "Interpreting Officer Wang." Wang recounted his experiences as a Chinese-English interpreter serving with the U.S. and Chinese armies in India and Burma. Just weeks before, the ROC government had launched a drive—its largest of the war—to recruit several thousand young Chinese men to serve as interpreting officers alongside U.S. forces in China. But Wang warned prospective recruits on China's college campuses that they would find little, if any, satisfaction with interpreter duty. The ROC government's interpreter training program, he insisted, was "of no practical help to their designated work."

After graduation, matters would only get worse. Interpreting officers would spend long days and nights with arrogant, ungrateful, and poorly educated military officers—men whose jobs ought to be done by interpreters instead, he wrote. Wang described the work itself as "an inexplicable waste of manpower." Most interpreting officers, he explained, spent their days performing menial tasks, serving as "little more than office boys to the foreigners." Many others had nothing to do at all. "The entire system of 'interpreting officers,'" Wang concluded, "can be summed up in the phrase 'a waste of time.'"[1]

If hostels provided the alliance a backbone of physical structures that enabled GIs to eat and sleep in China, then interpreting officers like Wang were its lifeblood, facilitating communication between American military personnel and other Chinese. Both programs traced their origins to the summer of 1941, when Chiang Kai-shek ordered Huang Renlin to prepare for the American Volunteer Group's arrival in China. Less than a month after Huang began setting up the first AVG hostel, he wrote to university administrators in Sichuan and Yunnan, seeking suitable candidates for an interpreter training program scheduled to begin in July at the new War Area Service Corps headquarters in Kunming.[2]

The ROC's interpreter program, spearheaded by Huang, was built around a vision with ambitions similar to those of Huang's hostel program. Its consequent failure worsened the mutual distrust between Chinese and American allies but with greater implications for the legitimacy of Chiang's regime.

Wang's March 19 op-ed resonated widely, as allied authorities soon discovered, but the ROC's interpreter program still overcame many hurdles and achieved operational success. Over the course of the war, more than 3,300 male cadets—mostly upperclassmen from China's best universities—completed an ROC government-run training program and served as interpreting officers alongside U.S. forces.[3] The mobilization of these students and their service as military interpreters was a complicated issue. It required coordination and behind-the-scenes maneuvering by numerous networks of people who distrusted one another: military and civilian bureaucracies within the Chongqing regime; Chinese intellectuals and GMD secret police; missionary and Chinese state-sponsored colleges; the U.S. and Chinese armies; and a team of Chinese-speaking American missionaries reporting directly to Chiang. Even when these networks were able to cooperate, many layers of transition had to take place before translation on the ground could happen, as students who had learned English through Shakespeare and conversational primers had to master a technical vocabulary and prepare their bodies for the rigors of military interpreter duty. As interpreting officers, these young men mediated nearly every interaction between Chinese and American servicemen, wherever they took place. Seven of these interpreting officers actually died in combat.[4] Even the most mundane elements of alliance management, such as registering GIs at hostels, required their linguistic expertise. As Colonel John Middleton, commander of U.S. infantry training programs for Chinese forces in Yunnan, wrote in 1945, "Without interpreters the American mission in China will be most difficult to accomplish."[5]

But facilitating military cooperation between U.S. and ROC armed forces was not the Chinese interpreting officer's sole, or even most important, mission. Every Chinese authority figure associated with the program—its government administrators, the Western-educated professors who trained interpreter cadets, and senior Guomindang leaders—inculcated upon the minds of young recruits a vision that emphasized the interpreting officer's special role in sweeping away national humiliation. Yes, interpreters would enable Chinese and American soldiers to communicate. But more importantly they would aid China's search for wealth and power by introducing American values, technology, and habits to the Chinese Army. They would also help convince American soldiers that Chinese deserved to be treated as equals, making the interpreter program the second part of the answer to the question Huang Renlin had tried to solve with hostels and cultural outreach. As Chiang Kai-shek himself told a class of newly minted interpreting officers at an April 1945 graduation ceremony, "Henceforth we rely on you to raise the status of our country."[6]

But like the hostel program, China's interpreter project failed as both an alliance and a nation-building initiative. Once interpreting officers began their service, most found their government without the capacity to make good on the grandiose promises it had made to them, their duties beneath their dignity, their compatriots distrustful and unimpressed with their work, and their American allies unwilling to treat them as equals. Disagreements among the program's stakeholders also had a negative impact on interpreter recruitment, training, deployment, and retention. Wang's op-ed struck a nerve by highlighting these disappointments, which compelled Chongqing to draft government employees into interpreter service instead of continuing to enlist university students. Senior U.S. Army officers, for their part, viewed the program's administrative shortcomings as further evidence of the Guomindang's purported incapacities. These soldiers, like the Guomindang elite, viewed interpreting officers as agents of Americanization, but their paternalistic vision emphasized the interpreter's special role in strengthening U.S. influence in China at the *expense* of the Nationalist government.

Conflicting perspectives on interpreters' role in the alliance influenced how interpreting officers and GIs understood their encounters with one another, fueling a corrosive combination of American arrogance and Chinese hypersensitivity that harmed Sino-U.S. relations more broadly. Interpreting officers enabled communication but not mutual understanding. Their efforts to raise China's status vis-à-vis the United States and sweep away national humiliation proved unsuccessful.

The Chinese Interpreting Officer's Mission

The interpreting officer's mission was inextricably bound up with China's larger nation-building project. Huang recruited senior professors and administrators from Kunming's Southwest Associated University (Lianda) to run the training program before the first cadets arrived in July 1941. During World War II, Lianda was China's most prestigious higher educational institution, the wartime agglomeration of Peking, Tsinghua, and Nankai Universities.[7] Lianda eugenicist and evolutionary biologist Pan Guangdan oversaw the training center's day-to-day operations alongside Wu Zelin, a sociologist who had earned his PhD at Ohio State. Other key instructors and administrators from Lianda included the social activist and poet Wen Yiduo, head of foreign languages Chen Futian, Tsinghua president Mei Yiqi, and Peking University dean of academic affairs Fan Jichang.[8] Ma Yuehan, the training program's physical education director, had coached China's track-and-field team at the 1936 Berlin Olympics.[9] These men were among the leading scholars of China's Republican era. Like Huang, they had attended college or graduate school in the United States, and they were part of a generation of patriotic intellectuals driven by the desire to help the country stand up and free itself from foreign domination.[10] While the National Military Council's Foreign Affairs Bureau, which supervised the ROC's liaison with allied armed forces, took over administrative control of the interpreter program from Huang's War Area Service Corps in late 1943, these Lianda faculty continued to run the Kunming training center for the duration of the war.

The first cadets to enter the training program came from Lianda and the American missionary-run colleges in Chengdu. Their memoirs invariably cite patriotism when explaining their decision to enlist, but financial inducements were significant. New interpreting officers would earn between 140 and 180 fabi per month (between seven and nine U.S. dollars at official exchange rates) depending on their skill level, which exceeded what fresh graduates could earn as teachers or university instructors—if they were lucky enough to find work.[11] One member of the first training class, Li Shengting, signed up after seeing a poster on campus announcing that the American Volunteer Group was coming to China to support the war effort. He had just finished his junior year at Lianda. Kunming Episcopal bishop Zhu Youyu, who held a doctorate in social sciences from Columbia, conducted Li's oral entrance exam: translating a passage from *Reader's Digest* into Chinese and responding in English to a series of biographical questions. Li passed the test and joined the other successful candidates at the training center in Kunming, where they studied conversational English and American history, memorized aviation vocabulary, and practiced oral interpreting.[12]

Language work made up only 40 percent of the course, which also stressed physical conditioning. The emphasis on fitness drew from China's physical culture (*tiyu*) discourse, which attributed humiliation at the hands of foreigners to the physical weakness of the Chinese people. Ma Yuehan supervised intensive calisthenics drills while warning cadets "not to show weakness in front of the Americans." Interpreting officers, he said, "had to throw off the 'sick man of East Asia' hat by walking with their heads held high and their chests thrust forward."[13] "The sick man of East Asia," a term that originated with Western criticisms of the Qing government following the First Sino-Japanese War (1894–95), became a powerful symbol for Chinese who believed that physical education reforms could help transform the country into a modern nation-state.[14] Chiang Kai-shek himself channeled this discourse during a 1941 meeting of the Guomindang's Three Principles of the People Youth League. The Japanese despised China, Chiang said, "because they look down on the physical weakness of the Chinese people." If Chinese youth made physical education a priority over the next few decades, Chiang argued, "we will wipe away the shame of the 'sick man of East Asia'!"[15] Physical fitness thus came to have deeper meaning for recruits than simply possessing the strength and stamina necessary for work as military interpreters.

The training program's emphasis on hygiene and etiquette—much like the hostel program's—was built not only upon established nationalist discourses but also derived from the conviction that making a positive impression on American soldiers would generate respect for China. Hygiene was central to the Chinese school curriculum during the Republican era, with textbooks presenting it as both personal virtue and public necessity. It provided the basis for self-cultivation, which would enable students to develop strong bodies, become strong citizens, and thereby strengthen the ROC state.[16] It could also help improve American perceptions of China, for which, as Madeline Hsu has shown, many Chinese who attended college in the United States felt personally responsible.[17] With the hostel program, only the top administrators had gone to school in the United States, and this was more than sufficient to ensure a focus at WASC hostels on reproducing American hygiene and etiquette norms. Thanks to the Lianda connection, returning students played a more prominent role in the interpreter program, particularly while cadets underwent training. These instructors repeatedly urged new recruits to avoid appearing "uncivilized." Ma Yuehan, a Springfield College alum, pressed them to eat well, wash their hands, and brush their teeth. The Vanderbilt- and Columbia-educated Huang Renlin taught Western etiquette, stressing the importance of a firm handshake, punctuality, and proper table manners.[18]

The ROC government demanded loyal recruits. Huang's June 1941 request for suitable candidates noted the need for "obedience and pure mind" in addition to linguistic skills.[19] The Ministry of Education oversaw recruitment, and civilian intellectuals trained cadets to do their jobs, but the

GMD's National Military Council still ran the program and carried out political indoctrination. While in training in Kunming, cadets studied Sun Yat-sen's Three Principles of the People, Chiang's speeches, and party knowledge—the bedrock of Nationalist education in China since the late 1920s—under the supervision of staff from the National Military Council's Politics Bureau (*zhengzhi bu*).[20] While most college students were not aligned with the CCP or GMD, Chongqing did not trust civilian intellectuals, many of whom were Communists or at least liberal leaning.[21] From Chongqing's perspective, the interpreter's role in uplifting the nation was synonymous with shoring up Guomindang power.

After cadets completed training, they were subjected to military discipline and placed under the supervision of one of three central government military agencies: those assigned to work with the Flying Tigers or U.S. Army Air Forces reported to the Commission on Aeronautical Affairs (*hang kong weiyuan hui*), those who assisted with U.S. military training programs or logistics were assigned to the Foreign Affairs Bureau, while those stationed at hostels remained under WASC authority.[22] FAB was also responsible for providing interpreting officers to the Sino-American Cooperative Organization (SACO), the clandestine partnership between the U.S. Navy and China's Bureau of Investigation and Statistics (the Juntong)—the Nationalists' most formidable secret police agency—which, as of 1943, trained guerrilla fighters to operate behind Japanese lines.[23]

The Chinese government gave new graduates honorary officer rank and the title *fanyi guan*, meaning "interpreting officer," in another effort to convince Americans to view them as equals.[24] Huang Shang, an interpreting officer who published a book about his experiences in 1946, wrote that the title "interpreting officer" lacked the negative connotations associated with other terms used to describe interpreters in China. The words *fanyi*, meaning "interpreter," or *tongshi*, meaning "linguist," both implied subordination to foreigners.[25] Chiang Kai-shek made the same argument to more than 160 cadets graduating from the Kunming training center on April 2, 1945: "We don't want you to become the so-called '*fanyi*' or '*tongshi*' of thirty years ago, who simply translated language and became appendages (*fushupin*) dependent on foreigners."[26] By combining *fanyi*, the word for "interpreter," and *guan*, the character for "officer," this title placed interpreters on the level of Chinese and American military officers. To emphasize the point even further, the Chinese government assigned the rank of major, rather than lieutenant, as the minimum honorary officer rank of interpreting officers. According to interpreting officer Wang Yumao, an Education Ministry official, interpreters started off at the rank of major because "major is a relatively high rank, so it will prevent the Americans from looking down on you."[27]

Chinese authorities also stressed the interpreting officer's cultural broker role. Minister of military administration He Yingqin told a class of graduating cadets that they "would serve as a bridge to unite cultural relations between China and her allies."[28] Sichuan education commissioner Guo Yushou made a similar point during a recruiting trip to Chengdu, telling a group of college students that interpreting officers were responsible for helping Americans "see the best in Chinese life."[29] Chiang Kai-shek echoed Guo in his April 2, 1945, graduation speech describing "the mission of the military interpreter." In order to convince American troops to "respect our country and trust our military," Chiang said, interpreting officers had to explain to them "our military's strengths, our social customs, the beliefs and aspirations of our young soldiers, and the hardships we've endured during our revolution."[30] Chiang, He, and Guo—like Huang Renlin—recognized that American soldiers might fall back on racist stereotypes to explain China's poverty and military weaknesses. But while GIs could easily ignore WASC cultural outreach, they had no choice but to rely on interpreters. Through their daily engagement with U.S. military personnel, interpreting officers had a unique opportunity to influence American views.

Strengthening the Chinese military was another side to the cultural broker role. Without interpreters, Chinese troops had no way of mastering modern American weaponry and military tactics. But Chinese officials had a broader vision about how interpreters could improve the army's fighting efficiency. When Chiang told new interpreting officers that their main purpose was to serve China's soldiers, he barely mentioned linguistic expertise. Instead, he underscored the need to introduce American work habits to Chinese troops, particularly the average GI's "especially strong sense of responsibility," something Chiang believed his own officers lacked.[31] In February 1945, Chiang ordered his commanders to "study U.S. Army officers' efficiency, practicality, and willingness to accept new ideas, these three strengths, and learn from them with an open mind." If Chinese officers didn't want the Americans to look down on them, they had to emulate their strongpoints.[32] Chiang's views about interpreting officers' function vis-à-vis the Chinese Army found fuller expression in an instruction booklet titled *Ruhe zhidao guanbing yu mengjun xiangchu* (How to guide our troops to get along with allied soldiers), published by the National Military Council later that spring. This volume, which featured an introduction written by Chiang, lauded the positive traits and habits of the American people.[33] The inaugural issue of a government periodical for interpreting officers, *Yixun xunkan*, reprinted Chiang's introduction on its front page.[34] He Yingqin read aloud from the guide when delivering a speech in July at a training program graduation ceremony, reminding interpreting officers of their duty to "do as much as possible to introduce [these habits and traits] to our own officers and men so that they can understand the importance of self-respect and self-improvement and also eliminate their own bad habits."[35]

The positive habits and traits interpreting officers were supposed to introduce to the Chinese Army reflected what Chiang yearned for in China, rather than anything uniquely American. But by endowing GIs with traits and habits that Chinese troops supposedly lacked, such as "straightforwardness, valuing honor, being devoted to one's work . . . good hygiene, keeping one's promises, and assisting the old and weak," Chiang and other senior military commanders revealed their dim view of the average Chinese soldier.[36] In time, as we shall see, Chiang's projection of his own Confucian values onto American military personnel would prove to be a mismatch. But this framing of the interpreting officer's cultural broker responsibilities elevated their status above that of Chinese soldiers, playing to college students' self-image as an elite class. After all, the entire country of nearly 500 million people had fewer than 65,000 college students in 1942.[37]

The Kunming training program, a transnational endeavor involving American-educated intellectuals, central government officials, and students from elite universities, provided cadets with an ambitious nationalist framework for understanding their wartime mission. Ever since the 1830s, Chinese had tended to regard compatriots who interpreted for Westerners with suspicion, seeing them as stooges of foreigners, or even *hanjian* (traitors).[38] The interpreter program turned this logic on its head. Interpreting officers were trained to see themselves as a vanguard of national rejuvenation. Their healthy bodies and professional competence would demonstrate China's newfound vigor, earn America's respect, and strengthen the Chinese Army, thereby helping to ensure national revival.[39] Having lived under the shadow of humiliation their entire lives—observing national humiliation commemoration days, learning about foreign aggression in school, and surviving Japan's invasion—recruits found solace in this mission.[40] For example, more than sixty Lianda students volunteered for interpreter service after Tsinghua University president Mei Yiqi gave a speech on November 11, 1943, emphasizing the interpreting officer's role in ending national humiliation.[41] Interpreter service thus offered a sense of purpose that appealed to students' patriotism and intellectual ambitions, allowing them to serve the military by uplifting soldiers rather than joining them in the ranks. But it would prove much harder than anticipated.

Running the Interpreter Program

Problems emerged before the first interpreting officers began work in November. Recruitment numbers for the second cohort fell short of demand, compelling the Ministry of Education to impose a draft in late September calling on university foreign language departments to provide third- and fourth-year students.[42] All but four draftees from Sichuan University in Chengdu came from schools that had relocated to the interior to escape the Japanese. Lianda provided twenty-nine students. Another twenty-two came from Fudan and Central University in Chongqing, and nine each came from Zhejiang University in Guizhou and Wuhan University in Leshan.[43] The missionary colleges in Chengdu, however, refused to cooperate, since recruits from the first cohort did not receive the rice, clothing, or bedding they had been promised.[44] Because they were taught by Western missionaries, these students tended to speak better English than students at state-sponsored universities, so the largest reservoir of linguistically proficient students in the country was left untapped.[45] Meanwhile, the ROC government neglected to appropriate money for the Kunming training center, which forced Huang to use WASC funds "informally and without authorization" to keep it up and running, all while having to prepare hostels for the AVG.[46]

Recruitment shortfalls continued after Pearl Harbor, which frustrated U.S. Army plans for training Chinese forces and operating forward air bases. Between early 1942 and October 1944, the U.S. military presence in China climbed from just a few hundred men to more than twenty-eight thousand.[47] In India, where the U.S. Army operated its largest training center for Chinese armed forces at an old POW camp in Ramgarh, Bihar, deployments of American personnel also increased sharply. The Kunming training center kept up with demand in 1942 by graduating 206 interpreting officers—more than enough to translate for the 1,255 American soldiers stationed in China at year's end.[48] In 1943, however, U.S. troop deployments to the CBI theater climbed by over 600 percent, but only 104 new interpreters completed training.[49] "The effectiveness of assistance to Chinese Armies by American instructors has been severely limited by the lack of qualified interpreters," General Joseph Stilwell complained to FAB director Shang Zhen on July 16.[50] In the city of Guilin, a key eastern base for the U.S. Army Air Forces, American commanders dealt with the shortage by hiring ninety civilians as interpreters.[51] These civilian interpreters earned salaries "greatly in excess of those paid" by the Chinese government, which led many Kunming-trained interpreting officers to quit their jobs in protest after they discovered the pay discrepancy, further exacerbating the shortage.[52]

Financial and administrative difficulties grew acute. On January 8, 1943, Stilwell complained to He Yingqin that interpreting officers at Ramgarh had gone months without pay or proper uniforms.[53] Stilwell's deputy, Frank Dorn—the colonel who supervised training programs in Yunnan—had similar criticisms. While these interpreting officers got paid on time, Dorn argued that their salaries had failed to keep pace with inflation.[54] The more pressing problem, according to Dorn, was the ROC government's failure to provide most interpreting officers with the rice and clothing they had been promised to supplement their salaries and protect them from the elements.[55] "It is important," Dorn told Stilwell in September, "that the Chinese government fully realize that their interpreters cannot keep their backs warm or their stomachs full on promises; they must have something more tangible."[56] Dorn and Stilwell attributed these problems to corruption and incompetence.[57] Dorn singled out Kunming FAB branch officer Yao Kai, suspecting him of embezzlement and citing his "weakness in handling disciplinary cases" as the source of "unending trouble and the actual closing down on several occasions of the entire [Yunnan Chinese military] training program."[58] Missionary university administrators and local officials in Chengdu also cited graft and "broken promises" about food and clothing as the reason for their continued refusal to encourage students to enlist.[59]

Making matters even worse, many junior officers and NCOs found Kunming-trained interpreters from state-sponsored colleges poorly qualified. "Marvelous English these Chinese speak—the interpreters' favorite is 'about more than ten,' or 'I'll meet you at approximately about after three o'clock,'" Jan Peeke told his wife in October 1942. "Incidentally I'm still waiting," he joked.[60] Meanwhile, the challenge of dealing with local dialects made Charles Lakin's signal communication course difficult to teach. His interpreting officer, Li Huangtun, needed multiple interpreters of his own, "and by the time it got down to the end I'm not sure any of it was accurate," Lakin recalled.[61] A February 1943 report from the Heilinpu Infantry Training Center outside Kunming concluded that twelve of the fifteen interpreting officers serving there had "no prospects of satisfactory deployment" due to their poor English.[62]

By mid-1943, this alliance-building initiative had become a major source of tension between U.S. and ROC authorities. Chiang attributed administrative and financial problems to the program's divided authority structure. Depending on whether they worked for the Foreign Affairs Bureau, the War Area Service Corps, or the Commission on Aeronautical Affairs, interpreting officers earned different salaries, which led to resignations. Responsibility for pay, food, and uniforms was often unclear. Chiang and other Nationalist officials, including the powerful Juntong director Dai Li, believed that the U.S. Army's attempt to get around the problem by hiring civilian interpreters was both a security risk and an obstacle to recruitment. Japanese spies were found among the civilians hired by the U.S. Army for interpreter work in Guilin.[63] In the meantime, American commanders believed all fault lay with Chongqing. Both recruitment and retention had become serious problems, and Dorn's headquarters in Kunming anticipated needing 900 interpreting officers to staff its expanded training program for Chinese forces. But as of late June, only 160 interpreting officers were on duty and just 45 were undergoing training.[64]

On September 3, 1943, Major Loren B. Thompson, the army's newly designated officer in charge of interpreter affairs, met with Huang Renlin, FAB director Shang Zhen, Shang's deputy Wang Shimin, and vice minister of information Hollington Tong (Dong Xianguang, whose office carried out background investigations of interpreter recruits) to hash out a plan. They decided on a carrot-and-stick approach. "Compulsory service to a necessary extent" would be required from university students. But those who did serve would receive college credits for their work. The top 10 percent—according to semiannual interpreter performance reviews carried out by U.S. Army officers—would receive full funding from the Chinese government to earn graduate degrees in the United States after the war. To unify administration, FAB would take responsibility for all liaison work with U.S. forces as well as for pay, procurement, and work assignments.[65] Stilwell and Chiang approved the plan.[66] The generalissimo organized a committee on interpreter affairs and sent announcements to Lianda and other universities on September 29 outlining a proposed student draft. Two weeks later, he ordered Lianda to provide a hundred recruits for the next training class, which was scheduled for mid-November.[67] Chiang further unified administration by granting FAB supervision over interpreter training and, effective December 1, responsibility for all pay, subsidies, medical care, uniforms, and discipline.[68]

Support from Lianda proved crucial once again. Just days before training was scheduled to begin in Kunming, Mei Yiqi called together all Lianda students and urged them to "give up their studies and serve the country."[69]

In a rousing speech, Mei said that the lack of interpreting officers was preventing the Americans from training and equipping China's troops. It would be "a matter of humiliation for both China and China's colleges" if English-speaking students allowed this to continue.[70] British and American youth, he argued, had lined up to enlist when the war began, and now Chinese students had to follow their example.[71] Mei struck a nerve: over sixty students volunteered after hearing his speech.[72] Two weeks later, Mei presided over a meeting of Lianda's standing committee, which passed a resolution stipulating that all fourth-year male students would be drafted for interpreter duty after completing their end-of-semester exams.[73] In accordance with results of the September 3 meeting, Lianda's standing committee agreed to give draftees thirty-two academic credits in exchange for two years' interpreting officer service.[74] These draftees would make up the bulk of the 461 recruits comprising FAB's second interpreter training cohort, which started classes in Kunming on March 1, 1944. Under WASC authority, only 429 interpreting officers in seven cohorts had completed training in Kunming between July 1941 and October 1943.[75]

Lianda's example provided impetus for a nationwide draft carried out by the Ministry of Education in January 1944, just weeks after two Ramgarh-trained Chinese Army divisions had begun making contact with Japanese forces near the Burma-Assam border. All fourth-year male students except those attending medical, veterinary, or teacher training schools were eligible. Like students at Lianda, these draftees would receive academic credit and be eligible for government-supported graduate study in the United States after the war. But those who failed to complete their service would be expelled from school.[76] The draft applied to all private and public universities in China, but in practice only universities in Chongqing and Kunming followed Chiang's orders. The Chengdu missionary colleges did not participate.[77] In February, the National Military Council opened two new training centers in Chongqing to accommodate approximately 870 students drafted from Central University, Chongqing University, and Fudan University, which had relocated to the wartime capital in 1938. By early March, more than thirteen hundred recruits were undergoing training in Kunming and Chongqing, bringing Dorn's Chinese Army training plans within reach.[78] Stilwell thanked FAB director Shang Zhen in an effusive March 3 note, assuring him that the U.S. Army would refrain from hiring its own interpreters thanks to Shang's efforts to enlarge the program.[79]

Frank Dorn, now a brigadier general, sensed opportunity in the enlarged interpreter program, though not in terms of strengthening China's armed forces. On March 2, he sent a memo to all personnel in Y-Force, the Army command responsible for training programs in Yunnan, with orders to his subordinate commanders that the entire document be read aloud to all the officers and enlisted men of their commands. Dorn described interpreting officers—and college students more broadly—as "the future of China." Over the next thirty years, he wrote, they would supplant the "power cliques, incompetent, and selfish" men who ran the country and placed "obstacles in the way of further American influence." Dorn instructed soldiers to speak with interpreters about "American methods, living conditions," and other facets of life so that "these young men may judge for themselves as to how our type of modernized civilization may be adapted to the future needs of China."[80] His instructions—the most detailed to date on how American personnel should deal with interpreters—reinforced the "special relationship" myth.[81] But by defining interpreting officers as agents of Americanization who would help undermine the Chinese government, Dorn's vision ran counter to the Guomindang's goal of using interpreters to shore up its own power. It also made interpreting officers subordinate to American soldiers and reinforced the average GI's proclivity for judging interpreters by how well they conformed to American norms. Dorn's orders thus made conflict between American troops and interpreting officers both more likely to occur and harder to resolve.

The draft, however, proved to be a bust, leaving Dorn and Stilwell with fewer than half the qualified interpreters they had wanted. While the Lianda faculty-run Kunming training center had no trouble with the much larger March 1944 cohort, FAB's new training centers in Chongqing were not up to the task. Run by Hollington Tong, these centers screened draftees only for party loyalty, not English proficiency.[82] None of the 167 draftees from Chongqing University, for example, came from an academic division that emphasized English-language skills, such as foreign languages, social sciences, or humanities.[83] Nearly all recruits came from just three universities in Chongqing, where Minister of Education Chen Lifu's rigid political controls on higher education fell most heavily.[84] FAB sought just twenty draftees from the more politically freewheeling Guangxi Province, where many English-speaking refugees from Hong Kong resided, while the missionary colleges in Chengdu refused to participate due to lingering distrust of FAB.[85] Meanwhile, Tong's patchwork teaching staff included many men who could barely speak English, and they worked without textbooks or a curriculum. An inspection by U.S. Army colonel A. D. Fisken reported that no more than 150 of the 870 draftees in Chongqing had any chance of becoming competent interpreting officers. The others "offered very poor material," with most needing "a year or more of intensive English" before they could even begin learning military terms. Under pressure from the U.S. Army, Tong closed the Chongqing training centers and sent the best 130 draftees to Kunming to complete their course.[86] The War Area Service Corps concurred that most Chongqing program recruits "lacked the English proficiency needed for the job."[87]

The fiasco in Chongqing amplified existing tensions between U.S. forces and Chiang's government, but this was just one of the interpreter program's difficulties during the first half of 1944. Despite unifying all control over the program under FAB, the Chinese government continued to struggle in keeping interpreting officers paid, clothed, and fed. By June 1944, many had gone three months without receiving their salaries.[88] And while FAB was supposed to give interpreting officers four sets of uniforms upon graduation, many left Kunming without a single set.[89] Others went without food because FAB distributed monthly rice allowances in Kunming, leaving interpreting officers at remote posts with nothing to eat.[90] For those who fell ill—probably not an insignificant number given the lack of food and clothing—hospitals in Kunming charged exorbitant admission fees.[91]

Major Loren Thompson, the army's officer in charge of interpreter affairs, discovered further issues during a weeklong investigation in June. Chiang's December 1, 1943, directive placing FAB in charge of pay had not been fully implemented, and those men still drawing salaries from WASC or the Commission on Aeronautical Affairs earned two to three times as much as those who reported to FAB. This disparity encouraged recruits to slack while undergoing training, since the least qualified interpreting officers were assigned to hostels. At the same time, Thompson noted, English-speaking civilians hired directly by the U.S. Army in Guilin "performed as interpreters in a more qualified manner than student graduates of interpreter training schools." Thompson also found "many indications" that "a heavy 'squeeze' [was being] extracted" from interpreting officers' salaries in Kunming and Guilin. Prospects for attracting new recruits looked dim. "Due to the chain of broken promises made to the students by the Chinese government," he wrote, many college presidents, particularly in Chengdu, continued to oppose the program.[92] Only the backing of the Lianda professors at the Kunming training school—who, in addition to running the program, held press conferences to address critics and traveled to various universities to recruit new cadets—kept the program afloat.[93]

By late summer, however, support from Lianda was in doubt. According to reports from the U.S. consulate in Kunming, representatives from Lianda and other area schools traveled to Chongqing in July to press the central government to honor its obligations to interpreters.[94] Wu Zelin and Fan Jichang had previously warned U.S. Army liaison officers that "reports from interpreters concerning the subjects of pay, uniforms, rice, and hospitalization" had poisoned the atmosphere at the training center.[95] On August 31, consul general William Langdon told Ambassador Clarence Gauss that "dissatisfaction with the treatment of student interpreters may cause an outbreak of trouble if the Central government attempts to enlist additional students [from Lianda] as interpreters."[96]

As a result of these ongoing challenges, the Chinese government turned over many of its responsibilities to the Americans, and Chiang appointed a new FAB director with orders to make the interpreter program his top priority. In August, FAB phased out rice distribution and started paying the U.S. Army to feed interpreters at hostels. The bureau also started providing lump sum payments from which U.S. Army finance officers drew to pay interpreting officers' salaries.[97] The uniform problem dragged on until October, when the U.S. forces agreed to loan shoes, clothing, blankets, raincoats, and field gear to interpreters.[98] On October 15, Major General He Haoruo, who had a PhD in agronomy from the University of Wisconsin–Madison, became FAB director. General He's appointment coincided with the arrival in Chongqing of Frank Price's Chinese-speaking American liaison team, which assigned personnel to assist with both the hostel and the interpreter projects.

The new FAB director began working with Frank Price, Loren Thompson, and Chiang to tackle the program's many shortcomings. He convinced Chiang to set up a special revolving fund for interpreters in order to ensure that U.S. forces always had enough money on hand to pay salaries. He also acted on the generalissimo's orders to sack Kunming FAB chief Dai Zhaoran, a Virginia Military Institute graduate, for corruption.[99] In mid-November, General He and Price began preparing to open a new interpreter training institute in Chongqing. With Price serving as director, this training center employed eight members of Price's liaison team as instructors, who together compiled a curriculum titled Forty English Lessons for Interpreting Officers. To keep classes full, FAB began holding weekly entrance tests along with members of the American liaison team, and to keep standards high, Price's instructors conducted oral exams every Saturday. Cadets who failed were kicked out of the program. Meanwhile, He and Thompson—now a colonel—

worked out a system by which the U.S. Army would feed, clothe, and equip all interpreting officers beginning on January 1 in exchange for monthly gold and fabi reimbursements paid to the U.S. government. On January 23, He presided over the first meeting of Chiang's Special Committee on Interpreter Affairs, which assembled representatives from all organizations dealing with interpreters to coordinate progress toward He Haoruo's goal of training five thousand interpreting officers in 1945.[100]

He Haoruo and Thompson traveled to Chengdu in February to address long-standing opposition to the interpreter program at the city's missionary colleges. For years, U.S. military authorities in China had pressured Chiang's government to recruit students from Chengdu, but due to "broken promises, graft, embezzlement of funds, and drafting of students for interpreter duty," Thompson reported, Chengdu's university administrators had "consistently refused to encourage students to join."[101] He Haoruo assured reporters at a February 23 press conference that the days of conscription and broken promises were over. He and Thompson also met privately with the presidents of Chengdu's six universities, who agreed to back the program. Over the four-day trip, He spoke to around fifteen hundred students and one hundred professors. "Should there be no interpreters," He reminded them, "our allies would become deaf." Thompson and He then persuaded Sichuan governor Chang Chun and commissioner of education Guo Yushou to support them. As a result of the trip, Thompson wrote, FAB expected to entice around five hundred qualified recruits.[102] Eighty-two volunteers passed the first entrance exam on March 6 and left Chengdu to begin training.[103] Meanwhile, in Yunnan, Wu Zelin continued to advocate for the program, telling a group of college students, "Many students from allied countries have stepped onto the battlefield, [and] the same goes with students from Japan; what are you waiting for?"[104]

U.S. military authorities also stepped up their efforts to bolster the program. On January 14, 1945, the army opened an interpreters' pool in Kunming, where American officers ran a four-week orientation course for new interpreting officers covering tactics, map reading, military technology, and weapons. This course marked the first organized U.S. Army effort to help interpreters build up the language skills and technical expertise that their job demanded. The pool also gave veteran interpreting officers a place to live and train while awaiting redeployment or demobilization. In addition to opening the pool, Thompson began holding regular meetings with representatives from all army units using interpreting officers in order to help them keep up to date with regulations and address problems.[105] On March 1,

Colonel John Middleton, commander of the newly organized Chinese Training Center, which succeeded Dorn's Y-Force, reminded American personnel in Yunnan that "the Chinese interpreter is an officer and must be given the courtesy and respect due his position." Interpreting officers, he warned, should never be ordered to do anything but interpret and should never be placed under the authority of enlisted personnel.[106] Middleton recognized that all of the army's efforts in China depended on interpreting officers' expertise and goodwill.

Chinese and U.S. authorities had never cooperated so closely to manage the interpreter program, but on March 19, *Da gong bao* published Interpreting Officer Wang's op-ed, giving voice to simmering resentments just after FAB opened its largest recruitment drive of the entire war. The ROC government still believed that U.S. forces intended to carry out large-scale landings along the Chinese coast and joint ground offensives with the Chinese Army further inland. These operations would require thousands of new interpreting officers. Chinese authorities tried to contain the fallout by discrediting Wang and stressing the ongoing importance of interpreting work. Zhou Mingheng, the FAB branch director in India, where Wang served, dismissed him as a rabble-rouser. Some interpreters at Ramgarh might have little to do, Zhou admitted, "mainly because their English is not sufficient to do their work, or they are too lazy to learn or not reliable in carrying out promptly the various duties assigned to them."[107] He Haoruo lashed out at Wang in Chongqing during a March 30 press conference, while in Chengdu, education commissioner Guo Yushou warned that success or failure on the battlefield still depended on interpreters.[108] The Nationalist government, however, tacitly admitted failure in its damage control efforts on April 9, when Chiang ordered a draft of one thousand personnel employed by other party and military agencies for training as interpreting officers.[109]

Chongqing attempted to shore up morale by doubling salaries in May and launching a new periodical for interpreting officers.[110] Published every ten days beginning on May 10, FAB's *Yixun xunkan* (Interpreting dispatch) aimed to boost spirits, patriotism, and Sino-American cooperation.[111] *Yixun xunkan* portrayed interpreter service much like faculty at the Kunming training had promised it would be. Each issue included articles by interpreting officers describing their important, exciting work: clearing up misunderstandings between GIs and Chinese soldiers, translating for senior American commanders during the struggle to liberate western Yunnan, and teaching Chinese troops to use advanced weapons like flamethrowers.[112] Cover stories included speeches on interpreter duty by senior officials like

Chiang as well as paeans by American personnel on the indispensability of interpreting work. U.S. Army liaison officers with Chinese units, according to one piece plucked from the U.S. Office of War Information's Chinese-language newspaper *Xinwen ziliao*, "viewed interpreting officers almost as angels."[113] *Yixun xunkan* also highlighted improvements to interpreter welfare and urged those on duty to double their efforts in order to earn one of fifty spots reserved for "outstanding" interpreters in the United States, where one would earn $2,200 per year (around what U.S. Army captains were paid) interpreting for ROC Air Force pilots and then receive a graduate school education paid for by the Chinese government.[114]

But further trouble loomed. Disputes between GIs and interpreting officers, some of them violent, became a regular occurrence. Interpreters also began staging strikes at U.S. and Chinese military installations. On May 12, seventy-nine interpreting officers walked off the job at the U.S. Army's Kunming Field Artillery Training Center (FATC) in the largest strike of the war.[115] Meanwhile, despite Chongqing's crackdown on the press after Wang's op-ed appeared, another disgruntled interpreting officer published a damning account of the program in late June, this time on the pages of a Guiyang newspaper.[116] These incidents, along with the ongoing recruitment shortfall, convinced Chiang to send a joint Sino-American team into the field to investigate in July. Led by Perry Hanson, a Methodist minister working as one of Frank Price's liaison officers, the team included Lianda professor Dai Shiguang and U.S. Army captain William Yavelak, who had replaced Loren Thompson as the officer in charge of interpreter affairs. The team traveled to three provinces and spoke with hundreds of interpreting officers. "Almost without exception," Hanson wrote on August 8, "the men were disillusioned about their work and offered numerous complaints."[117] The gulf between the lofty expectations built up during the training program and the disappointing actuality of interpreter service had taken a heavy toll.

Realities of Interpreter Duty

More often than not, interpreting officers discovered that their duties were more pedestrian than they had been led to believe. "Any GI could do it," was the most common complaint Perry Hanson's team heard during their investigation.[118] Officials and training program instructors had described interpreter work as an almost sacred undertaking, but the actual job seemed anything but. Take Yang Xianjian, a Lianda student who volunteered in

July 1942 after seeing a recruiting poster on campus that described inter-preter service as "a glorious duty." After he completed training in Septem-ber, WASC assigned him to an air force hostel in Lanzhou. Yang made it to Lanzhou before any American personnel had arrived, and he spent another eight months there without seeing a single GI, passing the time by writing a pamphlet to teach hostel workers English, learning how to type, and study-ing palmistry. Bored and frustrated, he got permission to leave in July 1943. After hitching a ride on a charcoal-burning truck that broke down regularly, Yang spent more than a month on the road before arriving in Chengdu, where he contracted beriberi and spent another few weeks in bed. Now pen-niless, Yang "had to resort to selling my clothes and bedding in order to eat." He pleaded to Huang Renlin for a new assignment, and WASC sent him to the Chengdu Air Force hostel in October, where he finally met an Ameri-can serviceman, fifteen months after joining the program.[119]

While most interpreting officers had more contact with Americans than Yang did, the reality of their work still fell far short of expectations. Im-proving the fighting efficiency of the Chinese Army might have sounded ex-citing to recruits undergoing training, but in practice it routinely entailed long hours of translating vehicle repair manuals or safety instructions. Working at U.S. Army–run training facilities required translating sentence by sentence for American instructors, often enlisted men with no combat experience who simply read aloud from instruction booklets.[120] Those in the field also grew disillusioned. Hanson reported that the average interpret-ing officer had volunteered "often with high and real idealism to serve his country; he imagines himself as one who is about to do great things at great sacrifice to himself; but he finds himself checking trucks in and out of a small compound hundreds of miles from the front lines."[121]

Cultural intermediary work also seemed far removed from national re-juvenation. In the introduction to the National Military Council's *Ruhe zhi-dao guanbing yu mengjun xiangchu* (How to guide our troops to get along with allied soldiers), Chiang described Americans as "enterprising go-getters" who "valued honor . . . treated women with respect," and "served as a good model for our revolutionary soldiers."[122] But interpreting officers discovered otherwise, observing widespread shirking, drunkenness, sexual harassment, and other forms of misconduct among the GIs they worked with, including violence against Chinese civilians.[123] Even American com-manders in Chongqing admitted that their men were poorly disciplined and prone to alcohol-fueled malfeasance.[124] After waiting so long to work with American personnel, Yang Xianjian found most of them "simpleminded and uncultured."[125] Meanwhile, interpreting officers and U.S. military personnel rarely socialized while off duty, limiting the opportunity for informal discussions about Chinese culture. Elite Chinese aspirations that interpreters could somehow teach the indifferently educated and parochial mass of American troops to understand Chinese culture and look beyond the country's shortcomings rarely panned out.

To make matters worse, no one took their honorary officer rank seriously. During interpreting officer Huang Shang's training in Kunming, vice minister of education Gu Yuxiu told cadets about the meaning of "officer" in the title "interpreting officer." According to Huang, Gu said that interpreters "were now majors; in the future they could be lieutenant colonels, colonels, major generals, and could rise all the way up to commanders of group armies." Yet few interpreting officers earned promotions during the war, none beyond lieutenant colonel. At the same time, the Chinese Army refused to allow them to wear officers' insignia until July 1945, so the Chinese and American troops they translated for often had no idea about their honorary rank. "Yesterday we were majors, today we are mister," Huang wrote of his letdown after graduation.[126] "No one ever called me Captain Weng," recalled Weng Xinjun, another interpreting officer.[127]

The Chinese government's inability to meet its financial and administrative commitments also contributed to poor morale. After all, interpreting officers expected their work to help blot out national humiliation and persuade Americans to rethink their assumptions about China. But their own government embarrassed them in front of the well-equipped, healthy, and affluent GIs by leaving them cold, hungry, and poor. Despite at least six pay-scale revisions—bringing starting salaries from 140 fabi in 1941 to 26,000 fabi in 1945—and subsidies to account for differences in interpreting officers' ages, marital status, and location of service, inflation invariably eroded whatever gains were made.[128] The pay issue, along with Chongqing's failure to disburse salaries regularly or distribute other essentials like uniforms and equipment in a timely manner, led to resignations and strikes, which Chinese Army officers broke up by threatening to use force.[129] One interpreting officer even committed suicide following a dispute over his unpaid salary outside FAB branch headquarters in Kunming in February 1944, sparking protests by other disgruntled interpreters.[130]

Interactions with Chinese compatriots proved to be another source of disappointment. Once again, reality failed to meet the high expectations built up during the training program. Since few Americans spoke Chinese, interpreting officers became the U.S. military's public face. Their status thus depended, to a large degree, on how other Chinese viewed the Americans. When China's long-standing economic crisis became acute following Japan's Ichigo offensive, growing numbers of civilians looked to interpreting officers as middlemen who could connect them with American personnel. While some grasped the opportunity to make money from smuggling and black marketeering, others resented being treated like "brokers or wartime compradors." As one interpreting officer complained in June 1945, "Wherever we go we meet [civilian] friends who stretch out their hands and ask for chewing gum or Camel [cigarettes]." As the U.S. military's reputation declined in China during the final year of the war, civilians also lashed out at interpreting officers, calling them "false American soldiers" and accusing them of having "a relation with allied forces as masters and slaves."[131] Hanson's team confirmed large-scale animosity between the two groups, with some civilians employed by the U.S. Army even trying to undermine allied trust by telling GIs that interpreting officers "were in actuality government agents paid to spy on American activities."[132]

Hostel staff resented interpreting officers too, despite both programs' common purpose. They took umbrage at requests to house and feed them alongside American personnel, even though the Chinese government and the U.S. Army had reached an agreement in 1944 requiring hostels to do so.[133] Huang Shang described an incident in Guilin in which "the Americans all had hot showers, food, and went to bed, with each man receiving bedding and a pillow." But when Huang and his comrades asked for the same treatment, "the hostel worker gave us a strange look and refused. We spent the night on a shed floor."[134] Huang took the insult in stride, but other interpreting officers took a stand against what they perceived as unequal treatment. According to commander Colonel Norman McNeill, on May 4, 1944—the twenty-fifth anniversary of the seminal May 4 student protests in Beijing—nearly one hundred interpreting officers undergoing weapons training at the U.S. Army-run Kunming Infantry Training Center "formed into an unruly mob . . . with the apparent main intention of doing bodily harm" to the Chinese hostel manager in an "uprising against the food they had been receiving in their mess hall."[135] Dai Zhaoran, FAB's Kunming branch director, reported that "rioting" (*baodong*) broke out again two days later, leading to intervention by a Chinese infantry regiment and the arrest of two ringleaders whom Dai wanted shot to death.[136] Hostel staff saw interpreters as fellow Chinese and thus not qualified to enjoy the privileged treatment reserved, however grudgingly, for American personnel.

Relations between interpreting officers and Chinese soldiers were just as contentious. When Chinese forces launched the campaign to retake northern Burma in 1944, interpreting officer Shen Youkang and his comrades shared U.S. officers' mess and sleeping quarters, allowing them to live "far better" than the division's Chinese Army officers, which poisoned ties between the two groups.[137] Meanwhile, by framing the interpreter program as a means to uplift the army, the Chinese government encouraged interpreters to see soldiers as inferiors, an attitude that did them few favors. In his March 19 op-ed, Interpreting Officer Wang suggested making interpreters "munitions officers, technical officers, or even staff officers" because they were "far better than ordinary [Chinese Army] officers, whose knowledge of engineering, communications, and medicine is doubtful."[138] The soldiers the interpreters looked down on tended to side against them during their disputes with U.S. and Chinese authorities, such as during the first interpreter strike at Ramgarh, which was settled by threatening to execute the interpreters in accordance with Chinese military law.[139]

On the other hand, when Chinese soldiers clashed with GIs, interpreters found themselves in the middle of the conflict, distrusted by both groups. "The difference of these two tribes causes trouble for us interpreters," one man wrote in June 1945. "We are blamed by Chinese officers and Americans."[140] Huang Shang agreed, writing that whenever any trouble came up, "both sides dumped it on our shoulders."[141] By moving between languages and societies and thus being suspicious in situations where absolute loyalty is paramount, wartime interpreters, as historian Vicente L. Rafael argues, "are neither foreign nor native but both at the same time . . . [their task] thus mired in a series of intractable and irresolvable contradictions."[142] However, as Huang wryly noted, cases of Sino-American military success "were obviously the result of the Chinese and American officers' outstanding contributions."[143]

Communicating without Understanding

But according to Hanson's investigation, interpreting officers' most common grievances revolved around mistreatment at the hands of American soldiers. Many interpreting officers showed Hanson's team latrines and washrooms marked "For American Personnel Only." Others recounted being insulted by American enlisted men, denied timely medical treatment, or being forced to share segregated facilities with Black GIs. A few of the team's visits even coincided with interpreters' strikes against alleged American abuses. For some, mistreatment made the Americans eclipse the Japanese as immediate adversaries. Dai Shiguang tried to console one man by telling him, "Think of all the evil the Japanese have done to our country and by comparison how small your grievance is." The interpreter shot back, "The Japanese have never harmed me personally or mistreated me, yet the Americans have!" Hanson sympathized with these interpreting officers and blamed the U.S. Army for many of their difficulties, but he also thought that more than a few were too quick to see mistreatment in instances where none existed. When interpreters "did not have reason to complain about one thing," he wrote, "they discovered something else which did just as well."[144]

The emphasis on humiliation at the core of Republican-era nationalism made interpreters hypersensitive to the slights and insults they encountered when dealing with GIs.[145] They staged strikes and got into fights at numerous locations over perceived affronts regarding rations and latrine facilities.[146] Interpreting officer Wu Cunya went straight to General Zhang Shaoxun, commander of China's Eighty-Seventh Division, and was granted a transfer after an American captain asked him to do guard duty with a few enlisted men. "I am a captain in the Chinese Army and cannot be put on par with American enlisted men," Wu fumed.[147] Another interpreter, Cai Zukang, told Dai Zhaoran at the FAB office in Kunming that Major Fred Eggers and men under Eggers's command "had heaped insults on [him] and [his] country" before abandoning him in the mountains after he refused to help set up an antenna.[148] Eggers dismissed Cai's claims, telling Frank Dorn that Cai refused to help because he was unwilling to "do coolie work."[149] Dorn sided with Eggers, noting that Cai's attitude "was that he was on a higher intellectual plane than menials who might set up a radio or any other work in connection with training or the war effort in general. I consider him a traitor."[150]

By designating interpreters as agents of Americanization and holding them to American standards of soldierly conduct, U.S. troops aggravated these sensitivities about unequal treatment. Interpreters' vision of contributing to China's modernization did not include serving as junior partners under U.S. Army tutelage, which was how commanders like Dorn encouraged GIs to think. Dorn's influential March 1944 orders tapped into longstanding American assumptions about the paternalistic "special relationship" between China and the United States, fueling arrogance in a situation in which interpreters understood any whiff of inequality as the latest indignity in a long history of humiliation. Dorn's dismissal of Cai Zukang also drew on a culture of military masculinity specific to the China theater, in which Generals Stillwell and Chennault cultivated reputations as quintessential soldiers' soldiers. They bore hardships alongside the men in the ranks and loathed the petty "chickenshit" that made military life worse than it needed to be for American troops in other theaters.[151] Stilwell's 1942 walk-out during the retreat from Burma served as the cultural touchstone for all U.S. forces in China.[152] If the fifty-nine-year-old general could trudge out of the Burmese jungle on foot, then any soldier ought to be willing to get his hands dirty if the situation called for it. GIs applied the same standard to interpreters like Cai.

But interpreters were trained to see themselves as officers who existed outside the military and performed a specific high-level function. They embodied a traditional distinction between manual and intellectual labor that while not universal in Chinese culture, still dated back to the time of Mengzi.[153] To an interpreter, being asked to pull guard duty or set up an antenna was an insult; to an American officer, the interpreter's refusal was the insult.

American servicemen also took it for granted that they treated interpreters better than the Chinese government did, a belief heightened by the U.S. Army's takeover of much of Chongqing's responsibilities vis-à-vis interpreters over the winter of 1944–45. American personnel expected interpreting officers to be grateful for the equipment, food, and medical care Uncle Sam distributed. But to interpreting officers, these items became sources of stratification between themselves and American officers, with any difference seen as evidence of discrimination. Medical staff at the army's Twenty-Fifth Field Hospital in Burma, for example, bragged about reducing the death rate from wounds among Chinese soldiers to an admirable 3.5 percent, but Luo Daren, an interpreting officer at the hospital, took offense at seeing Chinese patients treated in a segregated ward "that was more like a prison."[154] In Ramgarh, American officers thought they were doing interpreters a favor by giving them secondhand Army khakis after the Chinese government sent them to India without proper clothing, but Zhang Zhiliang saw it as an insult. "Because Americans look down on the Chinese," he wrote, "they gave us their old uniforms."[155] Convinced that Chongqing bore responsibility for interpreters' morale problems, GIs were dismissive of their complaints. So while interpreter Liang Jiayou became outraged when an American lieutenant responded to his protest over damaged rations by shouting, "These rations are paid for by American taxpayers; you Chinese need to eat whatever we give you," most GIs would have emphatically agreed with the lieutenant.[156]

On May 12, 1945, American arrogance and Chinese sensitivity toward unequal treatment triggered the largest interpreter strike of the war. Mutual resentment had been building at the sprawling Kunming FATC complex—where one thousand GIs could train fourteen thousand Chinese soldiers at once. Interpreters complained about poor treatment, and U.S. staff grumbled over interpreting officers' worsening "attitude" problems.[157] On the evening of May 11, the interpreters nominated one of their own, named Ge Liang, to negotiate with FATC commander Colonel Garrison Coverdale after being told the U.S. Army could provide only one bus rather than the usual three to transport interpreting officers to Kunming on their normal Sunday off. According to Ge, Coverdale told him additional buses were not available and then went into a tirade about interpreters' ungratefulness. "If it weren't for American aid," Coverdale told Ge, "China would have collapsed long ago. You interpreters are a bigger threat to China than the Japanese are." Coverdale's comments, Ge said, "insulted my country and provoked the anger of interpreting officers," leading him and five colleagues to propose a strike. Seventy-three others joined them in walking off the job the next day.[158]

U.S. commanders had little sympathy for strikers who failed to meet American standards of military masculinity. FATC staff complained that despite providing interpreting officers with comfortable dorms, recreational facilities, and free transportation to Kunming, they "still felt they were not living in accordance with their just deserts."[159] Major Harry Smith, a liaison officer for interpreter affairs, agreed, writing, "It has been my experience that interpreters are a lot of greedy children and resent anything that does not benefit them directly."[160] Brigadier General Haydon Boatner, who replaced Dorn as commander of Yunnan training programs in January 1945, concurred, warning his men that interpreting officers were "immature in their thinking and actions."[161] This dismissal of interpreters as spoiled children echoed earlier criticisms of Filipinos working under American colonial tutelage. Interpreters, like hostel workers and Filipinos, failed the capacity test despite their linguistic contributions to the joint war effort.[162]

Chinese officials, on the other hand, sympathized with interpreting officers' complaints, especially when violence or racism threatened national dignity, but the ROC's dependence on U.S. Army goodwill limited Chongqing's options. FAB took a hard line on the May 12 strikers, charging Ge and the other five ringleaders with a "serious offense" (*daguo*) and issuing demerits to all other participants. Strikes of this size interfered with military plans, and FAB concluded that interpreters' May 12 actions were "selfish." But the agency also recommended that the Americans "be more respectful."[163] Throughout the spring and into the summer, He Haoruo and his deputy in Kunming, Yao Guanshun, pleaded with Wedemeyer and other American commanders to urge their men to treat interpreters with respect.[164] Just because they wore U.S. uniforms, He reminded Wedemeyer on April 29, did not mean they should be treated as U.S. soldiers—especially enlisted men.[165] On July 3, a Kunming military court dismissed charges against a senior interpreting officer accused of fomenting another large strike. The judge ruled that Li Songnian was not responsible when the thirty-nine interpreting officers he supervised failed to report for duty after an American private had shoved one of them for complaining about mess hall conditions. Although the judge's ruling hinged on whether or not Li had instigated the strike, the verdict implied that the assault by the American private had crossed a red line.[166]

Some American soldiers were blatantly racist, reacting to challenges with violence. Lieutenant John DiBaggis assaulted interpreting officer Hu Yimei in Yunnan for ignoring latrine notices reading "For American Use Only." DiBaggis's actions, Hu told Wu Zelin at the Kunming training center, "is not only an insult to me personally but to the country as a whole."[167] Enlisted men in Guizhou attacked interpreters who tried to enter a U.S. Army mess hall, leading to protests from He Yingqin.[168] He and other senior Chinese commanders reported additional assaults in China, Burma, and India, with most incidents occurring during the first half of 1945, including one in which an American enlisted man throttled an interpreting officer named Liu Maochun in front of dozens of other interpreters.[169] "Some American soldiers were deeply racist," Shen Youkang wrote in 1945 of his experience in Burma, noting that GIs were able to get away with pilfering by blaming it on Chinese soldiers—whom the Americans assumed to be crooked.[170] Even in disputes not ostensibly about race, such as when an American captain choked an interpreter into unconsciousness and threw him on the ground at Ramgarh for "being slack in his work," interpreting officers attributed the violence to racial animus.[171]

Nothing signaled a clearer repudiation of the interpreter's mission "to raise the status of the country" than being segregated alongside Black GIs. This happened mostly in Burma and India because of Chiang's reluctance to allow Black personnel into China.[172] After being pressed on the issue by Black war correspondent Frank Bolden and the left-wing writer Harold Isaacs in the spring of 1945, Wedemeyer allowed some Black army truck drivers to enter the country, but Chiang barred them from traveling east of Kunming.[173] Meanwhile, Chinese textbooks echoed the "racial science" of American white supremacists like Lothrop Stoddard by dividing the world into five major races, with Blacks portrayed as the least advanced group.[174] Influential thinkers including Kang Youwei went further, recommending that Blacks be eliminated through sterilization in order to improve the human race.[175] So when white GIs forced interpreters to sit beside Black cooks, engineers, and truck drivers at outdoor movie theaters in India or mess halls along the Burma Road, interpreting officers took it as an egregious affront: American whites viewed them not only as inferiors but as equal to a group Chinese regarded as primitive. Such incidents were among the only interpreter–U.S. personnel disputes that ended in gunfire.[176]

Other mistreatment allegations were less clear-cut. Many stemmed from unfamiliarity with evolving regulations regarding the status and treatment of interpreting officers. Hanson's team noted that this was a common problem even in early August, after numerous U.S. commands in China had issued orders stipulating that GIs treat interpreters as officers and refrain from assigning them any task beyond interpreting. Yet American personnel still mistook them for civilian laborers and ordered them to perform duties regarded as insulting: sweeping floors and serving enlisted men. Part of the fault lay with the Chinese Army for not allowing interpreters to wear officers' insignia until the final months of the war. Chinese and U.S. authorities also made frequent changes to the regulations that delineated evolving U.S. and Chinese government responsibilities vis-à-vis interpreters.[177] And because U.S. commanders rarely disciplined GIs for disputes involving interpreters, they had little incentive to keep abreast of the latest rules. American commanders circulated new regulations and procedures regarding the use of interpreting officers, but they appear to have attached a low priority to enforcing them.

American soldiers never understood the stakes interpreting officers attached to their interactions with GIs. They dismissed Chinese nationalism as a sham—a confidence trick used to fleece the U.S. government.[178] Both U.S. commanders and Chinese officials might have believed that interpreters had a special role to play in introducing worthy American values, habits, and technologies to the Chinese Army. But while interpreting officers and the Chinese stakeholders in the program expected their work to bring about more equal relations between Chinese and Americans, the U.S. Army's designs were shot through with paternalism, covert racial prejudices, and calculations of national interest inimical to the Nationalist government. The disparity between how Chinese and Americans saw the interpreter's role in the alliance constantly produced contradictions and tensions. Rather than "raising the status of our country," as Chiang had hoped, the interpreter program foreshadowed the U.S. imperialism of the postwar era, in which client states dotted with highly privileged U.S. military enclaves could move up the developmental ladder under, but only under, American tutelage.[179]

Hanson's team did find a few exceptions—instances in which Chinese and American expectations and experiences aligned. The dozen or so interpreting officers at the U.S. Army Signal Corps school in Anshun, Guizhou, lived together in clean, comfortable officers' housing. They encountered neither discrimination from GIs nor resentment from Chinese military personnel. At the veterinary school in the same town, senior American officers told Hanson, "We would have been lost without [our interpreters]; we depended on them for everything." Hanson also singled out the army's lieutenant in charge of interpreter affairs in Nanning, Guangxi, a veteran of the Burma campaign surnamed Gallagher. He had earned a stellar reputation for resolving disputes and treating interpreting officers with respect, with interpreters as far away as Zhanyi, Yunnan, praising his leadership abilities in their conversations with Hanson's team. "If only we had more Gallaghers," Hanson wrote.[180] Positive interactions recounted after the war in interpreters' memoirs highlighted similar experiences: being treated well at training centers; learning skills from older, patient specialists with the U.S. Army; and forming friendships that lasted until the Nationalist government's defeat in the Chinese Civil War.[181] In these cases, interpreting officers and Americans bonded during their shared experience of the war against Japan.

But Hanson's team recognized that such experiences were outliers. These were exceptions where everything came together: no trouble with pay, uniforms, food, or housing; mutually respectful relations with American personnel; living as equals with American officers without arousing the jealousy of their Chinese compatriots; and doing meaningful work. For this minority, interpreter duty resembled what men like Huang Renlin or Chiang Kai-shek had told them to expect. But for the vast majority of interpreting officers Hanson's team spoke with, the liaison group saw little hope. "I have come to the conclusion," Hanson wrote, "that basically the problems are insoluble arising as they do from the very situation in which interpreters are placed which in turn is immersed in cultural complexities of long standing, made more acute by tensions of war."[182]

· · · · · ·

The interpreter program ended in uproar. Nearly twenty-four hundred interpreting officers were on duty when the atomic bombings caught Chongqing by surprise and brought the Pacific War to an abrupt end. He Haoruo announced in late August that FAB would begin demobilizing interpreters in batches beginning September 15. Each man would receive bonus pay and transportation home. Around 150 interpreting officers gathered at the FAB office in Kunming that day. They expected severance pay, food, transportation, and news about who among them would be heading off to the United States for government-funded graduate study. The FAB office had nothing for them at all, which sparked a riot. Once again, the Chinese government had betrayed them, and the wealthy Americans—with all their aircraft, trucks, and Jeeps—failed to step in and help. Leslie Stewart, the army's deputy liaison officer for interpreter affairs, was on hand that day to assist FAB, but he fled the scene in his Jeep after interpreters shouted him down and called him a "god-damned son-of-a-bitch." For Stewart, it was a disappointing but fitting final act, with Chinese officials and interpreters once more demonstrating their incompetence and immaturity. "I have reached the end of my patience," he wrote.[183]

The program still succeeded operationally, helping to make the U.S.-ROC alliance a reality. The AVG and U.S. military took it for granted that the Nationalists would overcome the language barrier. Not until 1944 did the U.S. Army establish a Chinese-language training program, and this belated effort left graduates of the four-month course at Yale or Berkeley with nowhere near the proficiency required for interpreting work.[184] The U.S. Army also began deploying air service and signal units consisting of mostly Cantonese-speaking Chinese American military personnel in 1944, but the army viewed these groups as a supplement to assist aircraft maintenance work and further liaison relationships rather than as a substitute for, or key component of, the interpreter program.[185] It was the Chinese graduates of the Kunming and Chongqing interpreter training centers who facilitated every Sino-U.S. operational achievement in the China theater, as well as in Burma and India. From its origins in Huang Renlin's June 1941 letters to university administrators in Sichuan and Yunnan, the interpreter program gathered students, intellectuals, officials, soldiers, and missionaries into a transnational undertaking without precedent in Chinese history. By August 1945, morale problems aside, the program was operating at high efficiency, with Wedemeyer reporting, "Interpreting officers can be supplied for any mission on short notice. Special requirements in language, dialect, ability, etc., can be arranged in most cases within one week."[186]

But much like WASC's hostel and cultural outreach efforts, the interpreter program faltered along the very standards Chinese stakeholders had set for the initiative. The Nationalist government's inability to satisfy the U.S.

Army's demands frustrated senior American commanders throughout the war. Meanwhile, Chongqing's bungled efforts to meet its commitments to interpreters angered the Americans, potential recruits, university staff, and interpreting officers alike. Chinese officials and intellectuals expected interpreters to uplift the country, but the government lacked the capability to assist them in their task. Being clothed, fed, and paid were essential to being able to interpret, but ultimately only the U.S. Army could fulfill Chongqing's end of the bargain. The program thus became another source of tension in the alliance and further evidence of the Nationalist government's incapacity for managing its own affairs. U.S. commanders would have preferred to bypass the Chinese government and hire civilian interpreters directly, which is exactly what they would do after the war ended. For interpreters, mistreatment at the hands of American soldiers proved to be the hardest pill to swallow. Instead of uplifting the country alongside American majors and colonels, interpreting officers were ordered around by enlisted GIs and subjected to Jim Crow–style segregation. For most men, efforts to master English, adhere to American cultural norms, and show their allies that the Chinese deserved equal treatment came to naught.

Much of the misunderstanding and conflict between American soldiers, interpreting officers, and Chinese officials stemmed from the contradictory understandings Chinese and U.S. authorities held about the interpreter's role in spreading "American" habits and values. Throughout the first half of the twentieth century, Americans from all walks of life sought to remake China in their own image.[187] Senior U.S. officers like Stilwell and Dorn viewed interpreters as natural allies in this endeavor, identifying them as the key to strengthening U.S. influence in China at the Guomindang's expense. When making recommendations for promotion or commendation, American officers offered no higher praise than they did for interpreters like Colonel Sheng, chief interpreting officer for the Armored Force section at Ramgarh. Sheng "understands the American viewpoint," wrote Lieutenant Colonel Joseph Trent. "He is a friend to our country. His loyalty to our standards is unquestioned."[188] Chinese Nationalist government officials, on the other hand, considered party loyalty paramount. The "Americanization" they wanted interpreters to bring to the Chinese Army would strengthen GMD rule.

The program's alliance- and nation-building failures would have lasting consequences. Both the Nationalist government and the U.S. military wanted Chinese university students to support their visions for the country's future. Intellectuals at elite institutions like Lianda were already wary of the Nationalists before the AVG's arrival, and they identified with American culture, values, and ideas.[189] The Lianda scholars who ran the Kunming training center believed in, and helped develop, the interpreter program's transformative vision of Sino-American relations. But Chongqing's repeated betrayals intensified the demoralizing experience most students had as interpreting officers, which contributed to growing disillusionment with the Nationalists among the country's educated youth.

By turning educated youth against the ROC government, the interpreter program's failures were more significant than those of the hostel program. Hostels and cultural outreach aimed to uplift the country by improving American perceptions of China. Because the program's success depended entirely on how Americans viewed it, the ROC government could still present it as a triumph to domestic audiences; it could not make the same case for the interpreter program. Frank Dorn turned out to be right. American servicemen did in fact influence perceptions of the United States among interpreting officers and college students more broadly. But as we shall see, China's educated youth would play a central role during the postwar period in demanding that the United States leave China.

3 Unequal Partners

Military-to-Military Relations

On July 12, 1945, Brigadier General Haydon Boatner submitted a report on the ROC's best military unit: General Sun Liren's New First Army. Sun's men had spent more than a year at the U.S. Army's training center in Ramgarh, India, where Boatner's instructional staff of more than 750 American officers and senior enlisted men trained them to use modern American weaponry.[1] After completing the program at Ramgarh, they drove Japanese forces from northern Burma, which opened the Ledo Road connecting Assam to Yunnan. While in Burma, Sun's men took orders from an American headquarters and served alongside American service troops and liaison officers, who provided tactical advice and coordinated air support. The force epitomized the U.S. military's ambitions in China, and their combat record proved, according to Stilwell, that "the Chinese foot soldier, when properly led, trained and equipped, will give as good an account of himself in battle as any soldier in the world."[2] Though he loathed nearly every Chinese general he met, Stilwell gave high marks to Sun, China's first Virginia Military Institute graduate and a rare GMD field commander who earned his position through professional competence rather than personal connections. "You have laid the foundation for a new and efficient national force," he told Sun in October 1944, "and with this example, China can go on and build up an army that will make her free and strong."[3]

Yet according to Boatner, U.S. Army liaison officers encountered nothing but trouble with Sun and his Americanized New First Army. "There is no question," Boatner wrote, "that the attitude of the New First Army is anti-foreign." Ever since May 1942, he continued, "there has been repeated friction between the 38th Division, which is now the nucleus of the New First Army, with foreigners." He alleged that in recent weeks, Sun's troops had repeatedly assaulted American servicemen and threatened them at gunpoint. General Jia Yuhui, Sun's deputy chief of staff, had even ordered his men to shoot Colonel Lewis Leavell, the chief American liaison officer with the New First Army, following an argument.[4] According to Leavell, this particular dispute, and most others, stemmed from

Chinese commanders' refusal to follow American liaison officers' advice. "I know of no single instance," Leavell wrote in a report that Wedemeyer forwarded to Chiang Kai-shek, "where an American liaison officer has ever been consulted regarding training or combat functioning. Their suggestions are ignored."[5]

Sun and his divisional commanders denied the accusations leveled by Boatner, Leavell, and other American liaison officers. Disputes during the Burma campaign, Sun told Wedemeyer, arose from "absolute refusal" of American troops "to take into consideration the requests and suggestions, sometimes very appropriate, made by our men." He brushed aside allegations of theft, smuggling, assaults, and shootings as "malicious slander." "We welcome criticism," Sun continued, "but we cannot help wishing they [Boatner and senior liaison officers] had based their accusations on a little more adequate foundation of facts."[6] Meanwhile, General Li Hong, who replaced Sun as commander of the Thirty-Eighth Division when Sun was promoted to command the New First Army in August 1944, denied that his troops harbored anti-foreign inclinations. "The friendliness of the men and officers of the 38th Division is known to every American who has worked with this unit no matter for how long," he wrote on August 6, the day the *Enola Gay* bombed Hiroshima.[7]

The military-to-military relationship bound the United States and the Republic of China together during the war against Japan, and Sun's New First Army was its centerpiece. The ROC government established the hostel and interpreter programs discussed in chapters 1 and 2 in order to facilitate the very military cooperation that Sun's force exemplified. Built around two divisions that had retreated to India during the disastrous 1942 defense of Burma, the New First Army put its American training, equipment, and integrated Sino-American command structure to good use by becoming the first ROC military unit to defeat the Japanese in a large-scale offensive operation. From the American perspective, the New First Army provided the model for rebuilding the ROC's entire military along U.S. Army lines, while enduring colonial assumptions and the ROC's dependence on the United States meant that Sun's force became the Chinese army that the Americans wanted: although the reconquest of Burma boosted Chinese morale, the operation served America's strategic ambitions, not China's. But as this chapter shows, even when each side got what it wanted, Sino-U.S. military cooperation produced constant tensions and contradictions, adding to the distrust and resentment between the two allies.

Military-to-military cooperation between China and the United States went far beyond the New First Army, as the U.S. military undertook an unprecedented advisory and training role while carrying out equally trailblazing aerial operations. The United States did not deploy ground combat forces in China, but its army and navy carried out military aid and training programs for Chinese army, air force, intelligence, and guerrilla units that dwarfed anything the U.S. military had attempted in the Philippines or the Caribbean before Pearl Harbor.[8] Other U.S.-trained-and-equipped forces besides the New First Army carried out offensive operations with assistance from American liaison officers.[9] Both Chiang and Wedemeyer deemed these programs a success and pushed for a massive peacetime advisory mission just weeks after Japan's surrender.[10] Aerial operations, including the space-annihilating Hump air bridge and the Chinese-American Composite Wing—which integrated Chinese and American pilots into a single organization—also depended on U.S.-ROC military cooperation.[11] But while Chiang and Wedemeyer might have been satisfied with their mutual effort at the time of Japan's surrender, the men under their command did not always share their enthusiasm.

Although U.S. and ROC forces established a close relationship encompassing military advising, technical training, and army building, their military alliance was fragile and riven by core contradictions. As this chapter will show, the Americans treated American supremacy as an established fact and expected the Chinese to accept U.S. military prerogatives without question, while the Chinese were not always willing to go along, particularly when questions concerning national sovereignty were at stake. Stilwell, for his part, devoted nearly his entire tenure in China to taking unimpeded command over all Chinese armed forces, which led Chiang to request his recall in September 1944. Stilwell's successor, Albert Wedemeyer, respected Chiang's sensitivities about ROC sovereignty, which enabled him to make greater progress than his predecessor in building up China's armies. But violent confrontations between Chinese and American soldiers occurred far more frequently under Wedemeyer's tenure than Stilwell's. As Boatner's and Leavell's reports illustrated, Wedemeyer shared Stilwell's unwillingness to subordinate American power to Chinese authority. He reminded his liaison officers that they could not exercise command over ROC troops, but he also empowered them to halt air support and resupply if Chinese commanders refused to accept their advice. Stilwell's goals might have been nakedly imperial, but Wedemeyer and other senior American commanders were less interested in respecting ROC sovereignty than evoking it in order to legitimate American power.

The U.S. Military's Ambitions in China

Military cooperation, as it were, began with an exchange of military missions. On October 10, 1941, Brigadier General John Magruder, a Fifteenth Infantry veteran who had served in Tianjin during the 1920s, arrived in Chongqing as head of the American Military Mission to China (AMMISCA). He led a delegation of forty-three army officers and NCOs tasked with supervising American lend-lease aid distribution and advising the ROC government. Huang Renlin laid out the red carpet for Magruder, who quickly concluded that Chiang had little interest in carrying on with the war.[12] On January 5, 1942, less than a month after the two countries became allies against Japan, Magruder cabled Washington to report that Chiang intended to stop fighting the Japanese and stockpile American aid for future use against the Chinese Communists.[13] Magruder's dismissive views of the Nationalists dovetailed with Orientalist discourse about Chinese civilization and warfare. He denounced the ROC war effort as "deceptive symbolism" in a February 10 cable to the War Department, attributing the GMD's failures to the "age-long practice of Chinese commanding officers regarding their soldiers as static assets, to be conserved for assistance in fighting their fellow countrymen."[14] His chief of staff, Edward MacMorland, reiterated this view in his diary on March 2, writing, "They [the Chinese] are through and want someone else to win the war for them."[15] This assessment led Magruder to recommend to U.S. Army chief of staff George Marshall that the United States use lend-lease aid as leverage to force Chiang into compliance.[16]

The Magruder mission's appraisal became an article of faith for the U.S. Army in China, but it was dead wrong. The Nationalists were serious about fighting the Japanese. Magruder's team accused the GMD of abandoning the fight just as Chiang was pressing to send 100,000 of his best troops to assist in the defense of Burma, which came under Japanese attack on December 14.[17] Several factors contributed to AMMISCA's misreading of Nationalist intentions. Building on earlier patterns set by U.S. military attachés, Magruder reached his conclusions after meeting just a handful of ROC officials and without visiting any battlefronts.[18] (When the Sino-Japanese War broke out in 1937, Frank Dorn was assistant military attaché in China under Stilwell; both men based their reports largely on rumors and the English-language press.)[19] Many of Magruder's men, meanwhile, were inexperienced in China and poorly disciplined. Less than a third had been there before, and many had been forced into early retirement before World War II due to poor performance. White House envoy to China Laughlin Currie told Chiang that many AMMISCA members had no intention of helping the ROC government: they simply wanted to make a name for themselves and revive moribund careers.[20] Magruder fired a number of them for unsatisfactory conduct and other problems, including drunkenness. In December 1941, MacMorland admitted that he and Magruder "did a very poor job in picking them [AMMISCA staff] in the first place."[21]

While Huang Renlin did his utmost to ensure that Magruder and his staff were well taken care of in China, General Xiong Shihui had an entirely different experience leading the ROC's military mission to the United States. In early April 1942, Xiong and his staff left Chongqing aboard a U.S. Army aircraft. On several legs of the flight route to Miami, American officers forced Xiong and his comrades to give up their seats and move to the back of the plane so that all the whites could sit together. "The way Americans discriminate against the Chinese is despicable," Xiong wrote in his diary on April 3. Xiong encountered more of the same on the train from Miami to Washington, where his delegation had to sit in the railcar designated for Black Americans. "This discrimination was not random," he noted. "The way Americans look down on Chinese is deep seated and must be corrected."[22] On April 13, the delegation arrived in Washington, where the War Department rebuffed Xiong's request to join the highest allied military staffs—the U.S.-UK Combined Chiefs of Staff and the Combined Munitions Assignments Board—Xiong's main goal in coming to the United States. The Americans also refused to allow him to attend meetings of the Joint Chiefs of Staff.[23] "China is called an ally but in reality the country is treated as an inferior," he complained to Chiang in May.[24] Xiong's mistreatment led Chiang to protest to Roosevelt that the most difficult part of allied relations was the sense of superiority with which white Americans treated the Chinese.[25]

Magruder's assessment of Nationalist intentions and Xiong's frosty reception in Washington aligned with the broader American strategic consensus in favor of global dominance that had formed by 1941. As the historian Stephen Wertheim has shown, between the fall of France and the attack on Pearl Harbor, American foreign policy elites and senior war planners had decided that the United States needed to pursue military supremacy and take responsibility for leading the postwar world.[26] These postwar planners favored pursuing global dominance with Great Britain as junior partner, which provided justification for excluding the ROC from the Combined Chiefs of Staff.[27] Magruder, meanwhile, was the senior U.S. military figure in China, and the War Department never pushed back against his conclusion that the ROC would be an unreliable ally. Former U.S. military attaché in China Joseph Stilwell persuaded the reluctant secretary of war, Henry Stimson, to approve his appointment as Chiang Kai-shek's top American advisor after a January 14 meeting in which Stilwell said that gaining U.S. command over ROC armed forces would be the key to American success in China.[28]

Stilwell arrived in Chongqing on March 4, 1942, with orders to serve as Chiang's chief of staff and commander of U.S. forces in China, Burma, and India—including AMMISCA.[29] Chiang, for his part, wanted a chief of staff to give advice on military affairs, like the German and Soviet advisors had done in China before 1941. He grew alarmed after meeting Stilwell for the first time on March 6, when Stilwell outlined his duties in the CBI theater without mentioning his military advisory role, which Chiang saw as Stilwell's *chief* responsibility.[30] But Chiang did not have time to dwell on the meeting: Rangoon fell to the Japanese just two days later. Archibald Wavell, the British commander for the Far East, had rejected Chiang's offer to send Chinese troops to Burma until the fall of Rangoon was imminent, a decision stemming from imperial pride, logistical concerns, and long-standing anxieties about Chinese territorial ambitions.[31] As the British position deteriorated, however, Wavell agreed to accept the deployment of three Chinese armies (the Fifth, Sixth, and Sixty-Sixth), which made up the Chinese Expeditionary Force, in northern Burma.

Chiang reluctantly granted Stilwell command over the Chinese Expeditionary Force and instructed him to concentrate on the defense of Mandalay. Chiang believed that giving Stilwell command in Burma would protect his forces from British meddling and improve overall allied cooperation. Chiang could ill afford to lose his Fifth and Sixth armies, two of the ROC's best German-trained units, so he instructed that they only be used defensively, which would allow for an easier withdrawal to Yunnan if necessary.[32] The Japanese operated four hundred aircraft in Burma to the Allies' thirty-five and enjoyed similar advantages in artillery and naval support, so Chiang knew that a Chinese counteroffensive would be likely to end in defeat. Stilwell, however, without consulting Chiang, ordered two Chinese divisions to hurry south and launch a counteroffensive on March 21.[33]

The military situation quickly turned against the Chinese forces under Stilwell's command. On March 25, Japanese troops encircled the town of

Toungoo, which controlled the road from Rangoon to Mandalay, and sur-rounded the ROC's only mechanized division. Stilwell refused to order the Fifth Army's 200th Division to retreat while it still had time, which led di-visional commander Dai Anlan to go straight to Chiang, who allowed him to order a withdrawal. Dai's actions, however, provided fodder for Stilwell's accusations that Chinese commanders had refused to follow his orders. Meanwhile, partially as a result of information provided by documents cap-tured at Toungoo, which showed that ROC forces had moved too far south of Mandalay, the Japanese launched an attack against the Allies' logistical and command center at Lashio, to Mandalay's northeast, on April 3. Japa-nese forces took the city on April 29, and panic ensued.[34] Chiang ordered his armies to regroup farther north at Myitkyina, but Stilwell abandoned the men under his command on May 5 and retreated to India with a party of some eighty people. Sun Liren's Thirty-Eighth Division of the Sixty-Sixth Army also escaped to India, reaching the country with minimal losses while following a path slightly to the south of Stilwell's escape route.[35]

Other elements of the Chinese Expeditionary Force fared worse. The 200th Division made it back to Yunnan but lost nearly two thousand men during the retreat, including General Dai. The Fifth Army's other two divi-sions, the Ninety-Sixth and Twenty-Second, retreated northward to Myitky-ina, which fell to the Japanese on May 9. These divisions then split up, with the Twenty-Second Division under Liao Yaoxiang eventually reaching Assam, India, and the Ninety-Sixth Division returning to China. Japanese planes and hostile locals decimated their numbers as they made their escape, and disease and hunger ravaged both divisions. In order to survive, these troops resorted to looting and pillaging, laying the groundwork for lasting anti-Chinese resentment.[36] Meanwhile, the Fifty-Fifth Division of the Fifth Army was destroyed in battle, and the Sixth Army fell to pieces as it made its way back to Yunnan, looting heavily in Burma's Kengtung State.[37] Ca-sualties during the retreat were more than twice as high as those suffered in battle, and in all, the Chinese Expeditionary Force lost more than thirty thousand men.[38]

Chiang and Stilwell drew sharply conflicting conclusions about the cam-paign's failures. For Stilwell, whose walkout through the Burmese jungle earned him a hero's welcome in the American press—including a *Life* mag-azine cover—the ordeal reinforced his determination to seize unrestricted command over the ROC's armed forces.[39] He attributed the defeat to Chi-nese stupidity, unwillingness to take the offensive, and Chiang's meddling.[40] After his first meeting with Chiang on March 6, Stilwell had noted in his

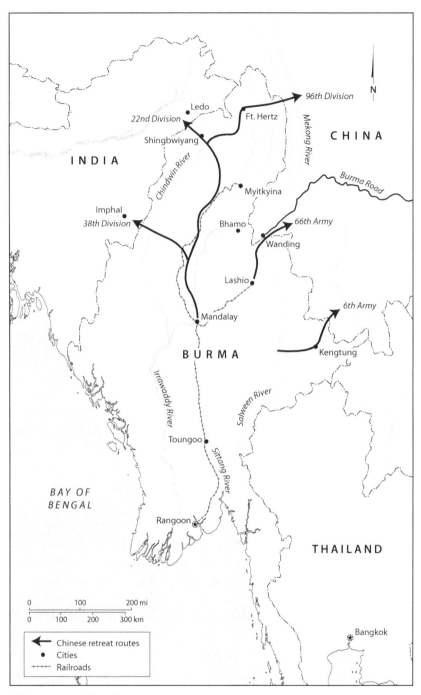

Chinese retreat from Burma, 1942

diary that Chiang "seems willing to fight."[41] But Stilwell interpreted Chiang's caution in Burma over the next two months as proof of Magruder's earlier appraisal. "Tomorrow or the next day I'll be going back to report to the G-mo [Generalissimo]," Stilwell wrote to his wife from New Delhi on May 26, "and I sure have an earful for him. He's going to hear stuff he never heard before and it's going to be interesting to see how he takes it."[42] Stilwell returned to China on May 29, bent on taking total control over Chinese forces without interference from the ROC government, "a structure," he wrote, "based on fear and favor in the hands of an ignorant, arbitrary, and stubborn man."[43] The power Stilwell now sought for himself, as the China scholar Ch'i Hsi-Sheng has shown, was one that no American general had even when it came to command over American troops.[44]

Chiang, on the other hand, lost trust in Stilwell as a result of his performance in Burma. He had given Stilwell command reluctantly on March 11, seeing it as a temporary measure that would help keep Chinese troops out of British hands and allow him to retain some degree of control after they entered British territory, since Stilwell was part of the ROC's chain of command.[45] But Stilwell had defied his instructions by launching a rash counteroffensive that risked the best forces Chiang had left. While in Burma, Stilwell also showed a lack of sensitivity to cultural and institutional differences. He and his men behaved arrogantly toward their Chinese counterparts. Stilwell also expected Chinese generals, who had never been trained to follow orders from a foreigner, to do everything he said, and he placed lower-level American officers in charge of higher-ranking Chinese officers. Much worse, from Chiang's perspective, Stilwell had abandoned the Chinese Expeditionary Force—some 100,000 men with inadequate supplies and medical care—without first organizing an orderly retreat. Chiang lost much of his best remaining forces, which weakened his ability to resist Japan and maintain power in Chongqing. Chiang was so outraged with Stilwell's actions and refusal to accept blame that he wrote in his diary on June 16 that Stilwell ought to be sent back to the United States and court-martialed.[46]

Chiang's assessment was closer to the mark than Stilwell's. While Stilwell told *Time* magazine's China correspondent Theodore White in 1942 that America's problems in China stemmed from "being allied to an ignorant, illiterate, superstitious, peasant son of a bitch," Chiang actually had the superior grasp of the military situation in Burma.[47] Stilwell had profound flaws as a military commander, and Chiang's reluctance to support his offensive strategy in Burma was well founded. Chiang understood that Japan's advantages in airpower, artillery, and naval support made any counter-offensive likely to fail. Meanwhile, whereas Chiang had decades of combat command experience and a proven track record of effective cooperation with foreign military advisors, Stilwell had neither. He had *never* commanded troops in combat, and his superiors had criticized him for having poor relations with colleagues while serving as military attaché in China before Pearl Harbor.[48] Stilwell also lacked any understanding of airpower and remained wedded to pre–World War I ideologies about the centrality of infantry offensives.[49] Whenever he encountered anything that challenged his assumptions, as the historian Rana Mitter has argued, Stilwell dismissed it as irrelevant or took it as a personal threat.[50] The contentious relationship Chiang and Stilwell established as a result of the disaster in Burma set the tone for the remainder of Stilwell's tenure in China, but as Xiong Shihui had learned during his frustrating journey to Washington, Stilwell's superiors in the U.S. War Department had little regard for Chinese perspectives. Marshall and Stilwell had been friends since the 1920s, and the army chief of staff trusted Stilwell's reporting on China without any reservations.

Stilwell rebuilt some of the trust he had lost in Burma by initiating a training program for the Chinese forces that had retreated to India. Even before Pearl Harbor, Chiang sought to modernize the ROC's armed forces along American lines. In March 1941, Chiang's brother-in-law Song Ziwen requested equipment to rearm thirty divisions when presenting the ROC's lend-lease requirements to the War Department.[51] The Burma crisis delayed the thirty-division program's launch, but on August 26, 1942, the U.S. Army opened the Ramgarh training center in Bihar, where nine thousand survivors of the Burma retreat—consisting of Sun Liren's Thirty-Eighth and Liao Yaoxiang's Twenty-Second divisions, redesignated as the Chinese Army in India (CAI)—began a hands-on instruction course.[52] The U.S. Army airlifted another three divisions to Ramgarh, bringing the CAI—also known as X-Force—up to five-division strength.[53] Stilwell had ample prewar experience with divisional-level training, and senior ROC commanders and officials, including Chiang, were pleased with Ramgarh's results (see figure 3.1).[54] Chiang's stopover in Ramgarh on November 30, 1943, on his way home from the Cairo Conference, reinforced his commitment to the program, as he remarked in his diary that Chinese officers still lagged behind the Americans when it came to "spirit, physique, and professional knowledge."[55] Chiang spent less than a day at Ramgarh, but a more in-depth early 1944 ROC Foreign Ministry investigation noted approvingly that "all of our officers were satisfied with instruction methods."[56]

FIGURE 3.1 Chinese cadets and American instructors at Ramgarh.
(Paul LeRoy Jones Papers, Hoover Institution)

The Ramgarh program also served Stilwell's ambitions. Stilwell's reputation as a selfless straight talker belied an image consciousness and egocentrism that rivaled that of General Douglas MacArthur.[57] Like MacArthur, Stilwell spun his escape from the Japanese into massive PR success despite leaving his men behind to suffer and die.[58] He also shared MacArthur's single-minded determination to avenge defeat in Southeast Asia by insisting that the reconquest of Burma begin immediately.[59] Ramgarh would train the force to carry this out while operating under Stilwell's terms: Chiang granted him command over the CAI on July 2, 1942—though Chiang implied that the Chinese would resume command after the CAI reentered Burma.[60] Meanwhile, White House backing and War Department materiel support meant that X-Force would be China's crack military unit, an American-commanded army far larger and better equipped than the colonial force MacArthur had controlled as field marshal of the Philippine Army before Pearl Harbor.[61] And because the military situation stabilized in late 1942, Ramgarh's accessibility allowed Stilwell to showcase his success. China "lacks an objective viewpoint common to cultures that have had long scientific education, [so] establishing any new project requires prolonged patient dealing with individuals," wrote *New York Times* correspondent Brooks Atkinson after a July 1943 visit. "But the instantaneous success of the program at Ramgarh," he continued, "where scientific diet, physical exercise and training with modern weapons has transformed willing Chinese soldiers into strong, skillful fighting men, has convinced high-ranking Chinese of the value of the experiment."[62] The State Department's China Hands also backed Stilwell's efforts. "If the Chinese Army is to be regenerated, it must be through General Stilwell," wrote John Paton Davies, Stilwell's political attaché, in 1943.[63]

Although Chiang and other ROC commanders approved of the Ramgarh program, Stilwell's control over the CAI remained a source of resentment. Stilwell commanded the CAI with a Chinese general as his vice commander and Haydon Boatner as his chief of staff. Another American directly under Stilwell oversaw Ramgarh.[64] In March 1943, Chiang combined three of the newly reorganized divisions at Ramgarh, including the Thirty-Eighth and the Twenty-Second, into the New First Army, under the command of General Zheng Dongguo. This made Zheng Stilwell's number two, but Stilwell ignored him and dealt directly with divisional commanders Sun Liren and Liao Yaoxiang instead.[65] Zheng complained to Chiang's son, Weiguo, about being ignored when Weiguo visited Ramgarh in September.[66] He also told Chiang about the problem during Chiang's November 30 visit, which led to Chiang noting in his diary that Stilwell "treated Zheng as a puppet and would not give him any command power. . . . There are many incidents like this, it is truly painful."[67] Stilwell was focused on eliminating perceived threats to his command, but he could also be petty. He refused, for example, to open a cooperative store for Chinese forces at Ramgarh even though the Americans stationed there had access to a PX.[68]

Military-to-military relations at Ramgarh were mixed, and most disputes involved struggles over authority. American officers viewed Ramgarh as a means to align the ROC military with U.S. strategic priorities, which Stilwell conflated with his own ambitions. He dismissed his first CAI vice commander, General Luo Zhuoying, because Luo insisted—in accordance with what Chiang had already implied to Stilwell—that Luo would assume command once the CAI began combat operations.[69] Stilwell's cold shoulder to Luo's replacement, Zheng Dongguo, no doubt reflected his perception of Zheng as a threat. In August 1943, Stilwell demoted the next Chinese general in the chain of command, CAI vice chief of staff Wen Mingjing, and replaced him with an American. Wen attributed his dismissal to bigotry: "American racial prejudices are deep-rooted; they don't respect Chinese people," he wrote.[70] According to Zheng, Wen's dismissal "outraged the entire CAI." The ROC military "had spent the entire Resistance War fighting for equality and freedom," Zheng protested to Chiang on August 18, and "we've already had to endure humiliation for the sake of preserving unity to an extreme degree, but Stilwell's measure has pushed me beyond my limits."[71] Sun Liren told Chiang that Wen's dismissal was not an isolated incident. "Ever since our army entered India, the Americans have consistently pursued a policy of breaking up high-level Chinese command structures," he wrote.[72]

The Americans understood Ramgarh in racialized terms. More than fifty thousand Chinese soldiers completed training there by October 1944, making Ramgarh the U.S. Army's largest-ever instructional program for a foreign military at that time.[73] Many Chinese servicemen arrived there sick, hungry, and bedraggled, including the personnel airlifted from China. American instructional staff referred to them using racial epithets like "Chink" in unit newsletters.[74] From the Americans' perspective, their success in training, equipping, and reorganizing these ragtag forces along U.S. Army lines affirmed the paternalistic vision that had underpinned U.S. imperialism in Asia since President William McKinley annexed the Philippines in the name of "benevolent assimilation."[75] Theodore White, for example, described Ramgarh as a "wonderland" for Chinese soldiers, who "were fed, for the first time, as much food and meat as they could stuff into their hungry bodies."[76] Colonel Arcadi Gluckman, an AMMISCA member who stayed on to serve in India, agreed that Stilwell's tutelary program had transformed the ROC's battle-depleted Twenty-Second and Thirty-Eighth divisions into China's most capable. But the tension between assimilationist and more disparaging, bigoted racial impulses was apparent in his assessment, as he described these troops as "loyal, hardy, docile, [and] fairly intelligent for a low class Asiatic."[77]

Ramgarh provided the model for the U.S. Army's less successful training program in Yunnan. Allied plans for the reconquest of Burma envisioned X-Force driving into Burma from India as fifteen Chinese divisions—designated as Y-Force—attacked from Yunnan. Colonel Frank Dorn, Stilwell's assistant attaché in China before Pearl Harbor, launched Y-Force training operations on April 1, 1943, opening a Field Artillery Training Center near Kunming. Compared to Ramgarh, where Chinese troops spent eighteen months retraining for combat, Y-Force instruction programs were brief. U.S. Army personnel ran six- to eight-week courses at the FATC, while American liaison officers worked with ROC units in the field, providing basic instructions. FATC programs, according to the center's final report, resulted in a level of attainment "below American standards."[78]

Neither the ROC government nor the U.S. Army supported Y-Force training with the same enthusiasm as they had for the Ramgarh program. The U.S. lend-lease contribution was minimal, while ROC Army commanders, who feared losing control of their troops, held back their best personnel. Training thus proceeded with limited supplies at a maddeningly slow pace. Chinese troops arrived in "appalling" physical condition, and the program operated well under capacity throughout 1943. Dorn and Stilwell attributed these problems to ROC corruption, factionalism, and the supposed ignorance of Chinese military commanders.[79] It was Dorn's experience with Y-Force that convinced him that Chinese interpreters might be able to help strengthen American influence in China at the expense of the Nationalists.[80] "With extremely rare exceptions," Dorn wrote to Stilwell from Kunming on January 4, 1944, "Chinese higher commanders and staff officers are stupid, self-seeking, irresponsible, and incompetent."[81] American liaison officers and instructional personnel judged Chinese units on their ability to accept and adhere to American methods, just as they did at Ramgarh. Those who failed to meet this standard were criticized as backward, unaggressive, childish, or anti-foreign.[82] At the same time, Chinese Y-Force personnel resented seeing American instructors living in WASC hostels while they slept in drafty tents. Unlike in Ramgarh, an ROC general, Chen Cheng, retained command over Y-Force, but he and other senior Chinese officers seethed at what they perceived as American scheming to wrest command out from under them by using lend-lease as leverage—a page from Magruder's playbook.[83]

The U.S. Navy took a different approach in China under Milton Miles, a Yangtze Patrol veteran who accepted a subordinate position in a partnership with the GMD's most powerful secret police agency, Dai Li's Bureau of Investigation and Statistics (Juntong). The Sino-American Cooperative Organization was established by a secret agreement on April 15, 1943, and from the start, Miles supported Dai as SACO's unquestioned chief.[84] U.S. Army officers criticized Miles for "accepting a secondary place and 'submitting' to a Chinese general," but Miles believed—unlike Stilwell—that Americans had to accept ROC leadership in order to work effectively in China.[85] Miles dismissed men from duty for using racial slurs against Chinese personnel and promoted those who facilitated close personal relations.[86] At Ramgarh, on the other hand, one American infantry training coordinator was christened "Chink Hawkins" in a unit newsletter simply because he showed "interest" in "the chinks."[87] Under Dai and Miles, SACO opened fourteen training camps scattered around China, where American sailors and marines taught Chinese recruits how to carry out sabotage and intelligence operations. SACO's largest camp, located eight kilometers west of Chongqing in a mountainous area called Happy Valley (Geleshan), trained Juntong secret police. According to GMD sources, Miles's men trained more than 49,000 recruits, though only 26,794 formally graduated from SACO camps.[88]

Miles might have rejected Jim Crow racism and respected Chinese sensitivities about national sovereignty, but American SACO personnel still upheld a set of racial assumptions. Miles and his men understood their work as uplift, and they offered racism as praise. Chinese SACO recruits did well, they believed, because of innate primordial qualities—feral adaptability, mule-like endurance, and boyish enthusiasm—rather than adult mastery.[89] In his best-selling 1920 book, *The Rising Tide of Color against White World-Supremacy*, Harvard-educated white supremacist Lothrop Stoddard identified the Chinese as a threat specifically because of their "untiring industry" and "self-denying thrift" under "conditions that would kill a man of a less hardy race."[90] These same racialized traits, according to SACO instructional staff, enabled the Chinese to become fine guerrillas under American tutelage. Taking it for granted that Chinese recruits "could work through long hours of unremitting toil with only a few bowls of rice" blinded American personnel to how SACO's extraordinary Sino-American disparities in food, pay, and living quarters generated resentment against them.[91] Training camp recruits ate just two meals of rice per day (one with a vegetable) and had meat once a week.[92] Their American instructors, on the other hand, had special chefs and individual food allowances equal to the allocation for several dozen Chinese. Salaries paid to American officers were ten times higher than those paid to their Chinese counterparts, and the Americans lived separately in Western-style housing.[93] Meanwhile, the U.S. Army and the State Department criticized Miles for training Dai's repressive secret police.[94]

Racial assumptions also fueled tensions in the U.S. Fourteenth Air Force's Chinese-American Composite Wing (CACW), Claire Chennault's attempt to train and equip the Chinese Air Force by integrating Chinese and American pilots and ground crews into a single organization. Disparities in treatment belied Chennault's claim that the CACW's Chinese and Americans served together as ostensible equals under his command. The ROC government was responsible for keeping Chinese personnel fed, clothed, and equipped, and Chongqing struggled to meet its obligations, just as it had with the interpreter program, which amplified resentment against the better-paid and better-equipped Americans while also reinforcing American assumptions about the GMD's incapacities. Chinese and American pilots carried out missions together, but they lived separately and ate at different canteens.[95] "Besides during pre-mission briefings or during the mission itself, I did not have many interactions with the Americans," recalled P-40 pilot Wang Songjin.[96] Even at the CACW's Liangshan, Sichuan, base, where Chinese and American officers shared a club, off-duty interaction was limited.[97] The failure to build camaraderie across national lines meant that minor disagreements could spark crises, such as in August 1944, when the unit's Chinese pilots refused to fly after an American officer kicked a Chinese officer during an argument.[98]

Burma, Ichigo, and the Stilwell Crisis

The U.S. Army's Ramgarh and Y-Force training programs were undertaken to prepare for the reconquest of Burma, where both Chiang and Stilwell sought to apply the lessons they had learned from the first Burma campaign. Chiang wanted to retain command over his forces, demanded joint U.S.-UK air and naval support, and urged the seizure of Rangoon, which would prevent the Japanese from reinforcing their troops.[99] Chiang instructed foreign minister Song Ziwen to convey his views at the May 1943 Trident Conference in Washington, where Churchill, Roosevelt, and their top advisors met to discuss Allied military strategy. "If this meeting can't provide guarantees on 500 airplanes for the China theater and guarantee American land, naval, and air involvement in taking Rangoon, then it will just be empty talk," Chiang told Song before the meeting began.[100] Roosevelt agreed to these conditions after Song addressed a Combined Chiefs of Staff meeting, and Chiang went forward with preparations. "Doing everything I can to help the U.S. and Britain recover Burma is the only strategy [for China] to follow," Chiang wrote in his diary on June 28.[101] Chiang's ties with Stilwell, however, worsened as a result of Stilwell's dismissal of Wen Mingjing and other measures he took to shore up his authority in the CAI. Their relationship grew so strained that Chiang made an official request for Stilwell's recall on October 15, only to change his mind a few days later on the advice of his wife, Song Meiling, and sister-in-law Song Ailing.[102]

When Chiang attended the Cairo Conference with Churchill and Roosevelt November 22–26, he threw his weight behind a proposal for the reinvasion of Burma code-named "Tarzan." According to this plan, Ramgarh-trained forces based in Ledo, close to the Burmese border, would invade the Hukawng

Valley and fight their way toward Myitkyina and Bhamo before linking up with Y-Force, which would enter Burma from the east after crossing the Salween River and dislodging the Japanese from western Yunnan. Meanwhile, seven divisions from British general William Slim's Fourteenth Army Group would attack Burma from Chittagong and Imphal, while U.S. and British long-range penetration forces under Frank Merrill and Orde Wingate would assist the Chinese troops making their way from Ledo. Roosevelt promised Chiang that Tarzan would be accompanied by another plan, codenamed "Buccaneer"—an amphibious operation in the Bay of Bengal that would sever Japanese communication lines and guarantee air superiority.[103] Chiang left Cairo feeling confident, having convinced the more powerful British and Americans to treat him as an equal. Not only had Roosevelt agreed to his conditions for ROC participation in the Burma campaign, but the December 1 Cairo Communiqué, jointly released by the three governments, gave Chiang his greatest diplomatic triumph by stipulating that Manchuria, Taiwan, and the Penghu Islands "shall be restored to the Republic of China" after Japan's surrender, ensuring the return of all Chinese territories lost to Japan since 1895.[104]

When it came to Burma, however, Chiang's triumph proved short-lived. Soviet premier Joseph Stalin had refused to come to Cairo because the Soviet Union remained neutral in the war against Japan, so Roosevelt and Churchill met with him at the Tehran Conference from November 28 to December 1. Stalin demanded that the Americans and British focus on the invasion of France. Roosevelt conceded and backed away from his commitments to Chiang. Operation Buccaneer was canceled on December 5, and the British sent all their landing craft to Europe for use in Operation Overlord. Chiang would get neither the air or naval support he had been promised, nor the attack on Rangoon. But the Americans and British still expected Chiang to carry out his share of the plan, with the Roosevelt administration hoping that increased lend-lease aid and support for the ROC's international standing vis-à-vis London and Moscow would soften the blow. The ROC protested against the Allies' about-face, to no avail. The Ramgarh-trained X-Force had already begun operations near Ledo in accordance with the plans laid out at Cairo.[105] According to Stilwell, on December 15 he "put it to" Chiang "as to the possible results of reneging on [the] Burma operation."[106] The march into Burma continued.

On December 18, Chiang unexpectedly gave Stilwell exactly what he wanted: unrestricted command over the Ramgarh-trained CAI divisions (the Thirty-Eighth and Twenty-Second) operating near Ledo. Chiang's decision floored Stilwell. "A month or so ago I was to be fired and now he gives me a blank check," he wrote in his diary.[107] Song Ziwen insisted that Chiang granted Stilwell command out of deference to Roosevelt. Chiang explicitly told Stilwell on December 18 that these troops would be the *only* Chinese forces Stilwell could expect to use until the Americans and British upheld their promise to China for a full-scale amphibious campaign in the Bay of Bengal. As Ch'i Hsi-sheng has argued, it is likely that Chiang granted Stilwell command of the U.S.-trained-and-equipped Ramgarh troops in order to prevent him "from asking for more, later." But Stilwell was already a step ahead of Chiang, determined to maximize his blank check. On December 19, he cabled Marshall and urged him to convince Roosevelt to press Chiang into attacking Burma immediately, including deploying Y-Force, which was still under ROC command, as soon as possible. Roosevelt relayed this message to Chiang the next day.[108]

Stilwell's X-Force fought its way through the Hukawng Valley and drove toward Myitkyina, but Chiang warned that committing Y-Force to the Burma campaign would leave China vulnerable. In January 1944, he told the Americans that concentrating Allied efforts in Europe in preparation for the invasion of France would invite an all-out Japanese offensive against central China. But Stilwell, whose forces had run into trouble in Burma, disregarded Chiang's concerns and attributed his caution, as was his wont, to Chiang's unwillingness to fight. Chiang held firm. He cabled Roosevelt on March 27 and told him that Y-Force had to remain in Yunnan because the ROC faced a Japanese offensive in China and Soviet meddling in China's northwestern Xinjiang Province. Under pressure from Stilwell and Marshall, Roosevelt replied on April 3, threatening to cut off all lend-lease aid unless Chiang sent Y-Force across the Salween River and into Japanese-occupied western Yunnan. Fearful of losing Allied support, Chiang acquiesced, sending forty thousand of his best remaining troops to the front under General Wei Lihuang and launching the Salween campaign.[109]

Just weeks after Marshall and Roosevelt coerced Chiang to deploy Y-Force, the generalissimo's warning came true when Japan launched Operation Ichigo, its largest ground campaign of the Second World War. Ichigo involved more than a half million troops, fifteen hundred artillery pieces, and two hundred bombers. Japanese forces had enough aviation fuel for an eight-month campaign and enough ammunition to last two years. Japanese commanders sought to neutralize U.S. air bases in China, establish an overland corridor to Southeast Asia, and annihilate the Nationalists' main remaining forces. Within a month, the Japanese took Henan and destroyed the Chinese units along the strategically crucial Peking-Hankou Railway. Despite Chiang's warning to the Americans, Nationalist troops were caught unprepared in Henan, where locals turned against them due to their ugly track record of corruption and heavy grain taxation. The Japanese attacked Hunan Province next. Stilwell, for his part, paid little attention to the war situation in China, and he refused a request from Chennault, whom he disagreed with about military strategy, to aid GMD forces at Hengyang, Hunan, where the Fourteenth Air Force operated a major airbase.[110] "Let them stew," Stilwell replied.[111] Nationalist forces, including a U.S.-trained regiment, hung on for forty-seven days at Hengyang, but the city fell on August 8, leaving the Japanese in control of the entire resource-rich province and the Nationalists utterly demoralized. Japanese forces then marched on to Guangxi Province practically unopposed.[112]

As Japanese forces advanced through central China, the troops under Stilwell's command suffered heavy casualties during the siege of Myitkyina, the main Japanese garrison in northern Burma. Myitkyina had transportation links with the rest of Burma, and control over its airstrip would allow Hump pilots to fly a less dangerous flight path to Yunnan.[113] Despite reservations from British military planners about the feasibility of seizing and holding Myitkyina ahead of the monsoon, Stilwell ordered an all-out drive against the city in early April, a month before the rains typically arrived. Stilwell commanded some thirty-six thousand Chinese X-Force personnel and around three thousand Americans in Brigadier General Frank Merrill's long-range penetration brigade, known as Merrill's Marauders. These forces took Myitkyina's airstrip on May 17 after a difficult march that left them sick and exhausted. But instead of flying in a fresh British division to take the city, Stilwell insisted—with an eye toward the American press corps at Myitkyina Airfield—that Merrill's battle-weary Marauders finish the job. Fighting dragged on for three months. At the same time, a Japanese counteroffensive trapped sixty thousand British Indian troops in the vicinity of Imphal, India, which threatened Stilwell's Assam supply base. British forces saved the day by breaking through and forcing the Japanese to retreat from Imphal on June 22, which turned the tide in Burma. Myitkyina's Japanese defenders abandoned the city on August 3, as the British advance had made their position untenable.[114] By this time, according to U.S. Army sources, more than twenty-five thousand Chinese soldiers had already died in Burma and western Yunnan, fighting a campaign without the Allied support Chiang had been promised at Cairo.[115]

While fighting raged on at Myitkyina, Stilwell convinced Marshall to back his bid for operational command over all Chinese forces, including the

Communists. In late June, the British asked Marshall to recall Stilwell from his position as Admiral Lord Louis Mountbatten's deputy commander in the South East Asia Command (SEAC) due to Stilwell's inability to get along with British commanders and his appalling treatment of his troops at Myitkyina. Marshall conveyed this request to Stilwell on July 1, seeking input from his old friend. Facing the prospect of losing the chance to avenge his 1942 defeat, Stilwell agreed to leave the SEAC so long as he be given full command power over the Chinese military. He told Marshall that this was the only way to prevent China's collapse.[116] Marshall endorsed Stilwell's proposal, which aligned with Orientalist assumptions—derived from military experience in China and the Philippines—about the need for white Americans to exercise command over Asians, as well as the consensus among U.S. military and State Department planners in favor of U.S. global leadership.[117] On Marshall's recommendation, Roosevelt wrote to Chiang on July 7, requesting that he place Stilwell in command of all Chinese armed forces. Angered and humiliated at what he perceived as an imperialist attempt to reduce the ROC to an American puppet, Chiang nonetheless felt compelled to go along, but he asked Roosevelt for time to make preparations and urged him to send a personal envoy to Chongqing to serve as a buffer between himself and Stilwell.[118]

Roosevelt's envoy, former secretary of war Patrick Hurley, arrived in Chongqing on September 6 determined to work out Stilwell's new position amid a series of military setbacks that had heightened tensions between Chiang and Stilwell. Hurley and Chiang reached an agreement on Stilwell's command over Chinese forces on September 14, but authority over lend-lease distribution remained unresolved. Chiang wanted Chinese control, but Stilwell refused to yield.[119] The next day, however, Stilwell returned to Chongqing from a visit to the front at Guilin. He barged into Chiang's office without an appointment and lashed out over the Nationalists' failure to hold the defensive line north of the city.[120] Chiang took offense because Stilwell had withheld much-needed fuel from the Fourteenth Air Force as Japanese troops advanced on Guilin, and he countered by demanding progress from Stilwell in Burma, where X-Force had remained stationed in Myitkyina for more than a month. On September 8, Chiang had requested that Stilwell use X-Force to attack the nearby city of Bhamo in order to relieve pressure on Y-Force, which had encountered tough resistance at Longling, the center of the Japanese line on the Salween front. Stilwell refused that request, so Chiang raised the stakes on September 15, warning that he would have to withdraw Y-Force units from Longling unless Stilwell attacked Bhamo within a week.[121] Stilwell left the meeting in a rage and sent a telegram to Marshall, reporting that Chiang intended to withdraw "behind the Salween and there wait in safety for the U.S. to finish the war."[122] He also fumed in his diary about lend-lease: "If the G-mo controls distribution, I am sunk."[123]

Tensions between Chiang and Stilwell boiled over into the alliance's worst diplomatic crisis on September 19, when Stilwell interrupted a luncheon to give the generalissimo a message from Roosevelt. The president's message, written the day after Marshall received Stilwell's September 15 cable, demanded that Chiang immediately place Stilwell "in unrestricted command of all your forces."[124] Hurley, who had been putting the final touches on Chiang's announcement of Stilwell's assumption of operational command, urged Stilwell not to show Chiang the message. Chiang had already agreed to the conditions Roosevelt had laid out, Hurley insisted, but no chief of state, he warned, "could tolerate such an insult as this letter," which was written in a blunt tone that surprised Hurley.[125] But Stilwell wanted to humiliate Chiang publicly, so as he wrote in his diary, "I handed this bundle of paprika to the Peanut [Chiang] and then sank back with a sigh. The harpoon hit the little bugger in the solar plexus, and went right through him."[126] Chiang simply replied, "I understand," and ended the meeting. Once alone in the room with his brother-in-law Song Ziwen, Chiang burst into tears, certain that Stilwell must have instigated the message.[127] "This is the worst humiliation in my life," Chiang remarked in his diary.[128] After mulling over his options for five days, Chiang asked for a meeting with Hurley on September 24 and officially requested Stilwell's recall.[129]

With the exception of Xiong Shihui, Chiang's advisors urged him to back down, but he held firm because the September 19 confrontation convinced him that Stilwell's continued presence would render him a mere figurehead in his own country. Chiang revealed his decision to his close military and political advisors on September 28, and only Xiong, who had been subjected to racist discrimination throughout his 1942 military mission to the United States, supported him.[130] Roosevelt replied with a compromise on October 5. He agreed to relieve Stilwell from duty as Chiang's chief of staff and end his control over lend-lease but wanted him to retain command over all Chinese forces in Burma and Yunnan.[131] Chiang rejected Roosevelt's offer on October 9, over the objections of minister of military administration He Yingqin, finance minister Kong Xiangxi, National Military Council Political Department director Zhang Zhizhong, and Wang Shijie, who would soon replace Song Ziwen as foreign minister. Chiang had actually made his mind up by September 23, writing that Stilwell's attitude when delivering the note made him realize that Stilwell would never accept an order from him again.[132] Chiang was waging a war for Chinese nationhood and sovereignty. He was unwilling to lead an American puppet government in Chongqing. Roosevelt accepted Chiang's request on October 18, bringing Stilwell's bid for proconsular authority in China to an end.

Military-to-Military Relations under Wedemeyer

Albert Wedemeyer, Stilwell's replacement, quickly established a cooperative relationship with Chiang and helped to stabilize the military situation. After arriving in Chongqing on October 31, 1944, and meeting with Chiang almost daily over the next few weeks, Wedemeyer realized Stilwell had been wrong about the ROC's commitment to the war effort. Chiang, for his part, found Wedemeyer respectful and constructive—a sharp contrast to Stilwell.[133] To prevent Japan's advancing forces from attacking Chongqing or Kunming, Wedemeyer airlifted the Twenty-Second and Fourteenth divisions from Burma to Guizhou and launched a B-29 firebombing raid against Wuhan, Japan's logistical and command center in China. Japan's Imperial General Staff decided to end the Ichigo campaign a few weeks later, overruling Ichigo's commander on the ground in China, who wanted to take Chongqing.[134] Chinese forces also made progress in Burma. On January 24, Y-Force and CAI units linked up at the Sino-Burmese border town of Wanding, bringing the Salween campaign to an end. Two weeks later, the first truck convoy from Ledo arrived in Kunming. Wedemeyer also set up an expanded training program, called the Alpha Plan, to equip thirty-nine Chinese divisions under the aegis of the U.S. Army's newly created Chinese Training Center (CTC). He integrated all liaison work into a new organization called the Chinese Combat Command (CCC). In addition, Wedemeyer established a Chinese Services of Supply (SOS) and launched a food program to improve nutrition in the ROC Army.[135] Chiang told Roosevelt on February 17 that the ROC military had benefited greatly since Wedemeyer's arrival.[136]

Training and liaison work continued to improve under Wedemeyer's watch. He sacked Stilwell's most trusted subordinate, Frank Dorn, after identifying him as an obstacle to the Alpha Plan. "Of all the general officers personally known to me," Wedemeyer wrote in Dorn's final efficiency report, "I would place him 499 of a group of 500."[137] Dorn had attributed Y-Force's difficulties to the poor qualities of its Chinese commanders, but with Dorn out of the picture, Wedemeyer took a more constructive approach by building up the ROC's officer corps along American staff lines.[138] He opened six new training schools under the CTC in 1945, including an Infantry Training Center that graduated more than four thousand officers.[139] Meanwhile, by August 1945, nearly two thousand American liaison personnel were serving with the Chinese Alpha divisions, all of which had begun at least the first half of a two-part, twenty-six-week training program as a unit.[140] Combat liaison work also made strides. On May 3, Chinese forces began a counterattack that repelled Japan's attempt to seize the large Sino-U.S. airbase in Zhijiang, in western Hunan. American air and ground teams operated with each frontline ROC regiment, while other liaison officers oversaw successful resupply efforts and evacuations of wounded personnel. Chinese troops, according to the CCC, "fought with great courage and not inconsiderable skill," which surprised both the Japanese and the Americans.[141]

While high-level military-to-military relations reached new heights during Wedemeyer's tenure, lower-level disputes became more frequent, as developments that had emerged during the Burma campaign increased tensions among the men in the ranks. On March 30, 1944, more than five months before Stilwell's showdown with Chiang, General Liao Yaoxiang reported that Merrill's Marauders had underwhelmed him during the first joint ROC-U.S. combat operations in northern Burma. "This unit of veteran American troops is a strong force but lacks backbone," he wrote. According to Liao, Merrill's men were undisciplined. When engaged in combat with General Shinichi Tanaka's Eighteenth Division near the Hukawng Valley town of Maingkwan, Merrill's men had retreated without orders as Chinese units continued to fight, abandoning bodies and equipment as they withdrew, and leaving the Chinese to deal with the mess they left behind. Chinese forces drove Tanaka's troops out of Walawbum, ten miles south of Maingkwan, but the operation was only a partial success because the Eighteenth Division escaped to fight another day. For Liao, the U.S. Army lost some of its luster, while Chinese forces proved their mettle. "In this battle, in comparison to Japanese and American forces, the results prove that our Revolutionary Army has recovered its self-confidence," he told Chiang.[142]

Confidence forged in Ramgarh and the Burmese jungle made Chinese forces more willing to challenge the Americans. Chinese military police in Assam, for example, refused to enforce a January 1945 U.S. Army order placing local bazaars off limits to Chinese troops in order to deter smuggling.[143] The opening of the Ledo Road gave Chinese soldiers the chance to participate in the lucrative smuggling rackets long dominated (as chapter 4 will show) by the American aircrews flying the Hump, and many of them took advantage of the opportunity.[144] With ROC authorities unwilling to enforce the off-limits order, American military police began patrolling the bazaars and searching Chinese military vehicles. On the evening of February 28, they confiscated hundreds of cigarette cartons and large quantities of batteries, soap, and cooking oil from two 6×6 trucks driven by Chinese personnel. A third vehicle made a run for it, resulting in a five-mile chase that ended after American military police opened fire, wounding the driver and a passenger, both privates in the Thirty-Eighth Division.[145] Divisional commander Li Hong supported his men. He reminded the Americans that they had confiscated the same daily necessities that any GI could freely purchase from a U.S. Army post exchange or an Indian bazaar—both of which remained off limits to Chinese troops but not Americans.[146]

Chinese resistance to anti-smuggling measures led some Americans to push for greater control over ROC military personnel, which triggered violence along the Ledo Road. ROC authorities sought to curb smuggling through joint inspections or Chinese military police supervision, and CCC commander Haydon Boatner agreed that cooperation with Chinese military police was essential when dealing with Chinese vehicle convoys.[147] But other U.S. commanders insisted that an April 1944 directive from Stilwell subjected CAI personnel on truck convoys to the control of U.S. Army military police.[148] Stilwell had issued this directive when all CAI personnel had been stationed in India or Burma, but with Chinese truck convoys now arriving in Yunnan, this arrangement violated ROC sovereignty. Efforts to enforce this directive in Baoshan, the first major military town that convoys passed through after entering China, led to confrontations, as Chinese officers and military police refused to cooperate with American personnel.[149] On May 19, Wedemeyer unilaterally halted all U.S. Army inspections of ROC New First Army–operated vehicles in Baoshan after Chinese soldiers pointed guns at a group of GIs attempting to seize contraband from one of their trucks. One Chinese officer had threatened "to kill all the Americans if they touched another vehicle" during the standoff, and an unknown assailant opened fire on the U.S. Army's operations headquarters at Baoshan with a machine gun less than an hour later.[150]

While in Burma, Chinese and American authorities usually backed their compatriots when investigating violent incidents involving Chinese or American troops, which added to tensions stemming from the alleged crimes under investigation. Sun Liren, for example, personally demanded murder charges against a sentry who had killed a decorated New First Army sergeant in early 1945, but U.S. Army investigators ruled that the killing was justified because the sergeant had entered a restricted area and threatened the sentry.[151] Another investigation carried out around the same time absolved an American MP of any guilt after shooting two Chinese kitchen staff at the Fourteenth Evacuation Hospital near Ledo, blaming the incident on the absence of Chinese military police.[152] Both American and British commanders reported that Chinese discipline deteriorated in Burma after the conclusion of combat operations, but misconduct targeted Burmese civilians rather than allied troops. Lieutenant General Daniel Sultan, who took over command of Chinese forces in Burma after Stilwell's recall, held Chinese commanders responsible for alleged CAI crimes against locals.[153] Crime along the Yunnan-Burma border reached epidemic levels in the summer of 1945, as Chinese soldiers—often deserters—robbed civilians and even took over entire towns, leading British colonial authorities to request U.S. Army assistance in rounding them up, a practice that had already generated anti-American backlash when carried out in India.[154]

Airlifts of New First Army personnel back to China also turned violent. On May 12, 1945, Lieutenant Colonel S. Y. Kao, commander of the Chinese military police corps at Ledo Air Base, saw two members of the American military police—both privates first class—drag two Chinese majors away from the crowded passenger terminal, kicking and punching them along the way. The two majors had been stranded at Ledo for three days, despite having valid travel tickets issued by CAI headquarters. Kao saw the MPs' actions as "an open insult of Chinese officers" and offered to help "settle the whole affair peacefully" through his interpreter, who told the Americans that Kao was the commanding officer of the Chinese military police. "I don't care who this damn colonel is," one of the Americans replied before forcing the two Chinese majors into a Jeep and driving them away. An armed standoff ensued, as around two dozen of Kao's men lined up outside with their weapons. An American officer who knew Kao personally talked him into leaving with his men, but Kao still insisted that the American MPs be "thrashed publicly for having mistreated the Chinese officers."[155] American investigators, however, recommended no criminal charges against the two enlisted MPs, "as they were fulfilling an order by a superior officer in the performance of duty."[156]

According to American liaison officers, New First Army discipline became even worse after the return to China. Chief liaison officer Lewis Leavell reported "continuous intimidations, threats, and delays" as he coordinated the loading of transport aircraft to bring troops from Yunnan to Guangxi, including having a bayonet thrust against his stomach by a Chinese enlisted man. On another occasion, he got into a fistfight with a Chinese colonel who had disagreed with him about the details of a particular flight. After he arrived in Kunming, Leavell discovered "disgraceful . . . misuse and abuse of New First Army vehicles."[157] Trouble continued at Baise, Guangxi Province, where the New First Army moved in to fill the vacuum left by retreating Japanese troops, who withdrew from positions in Guangxi after their failed western Hunan campaign. On July 5, Chinese personnel forced the American crew off a transport plane at gunpoint, convinced the Americans had intentionally made them airsick.[158] Just a week earlier, New First Army personnel crossing a river near Baise had opened fire on U.S. personnel after an argument over the loading of a Chinese truck convoy onto a ferry.[159]

By mid-August 1945, violent confrontations were a daily occurrence. On August 10, Wedemeyer addressed a message to all American personnel in China, writing, "There has been a marked increase in instances of Chinese-American friction in this theater which is in contrast to the growing spirit of cordiality and cooperation between the governmental and military leaders of the two allied nations."[160] In addition to fights and shootings at transportation bottlenecks like airfields and ferry crossings, Ramgarh-trained Chinese personnel began holding up GIs at gunpoint. Chinese bandits had robbed U.S. Army convoys in Yunnan a few times during 1943 and 1944, but not until the summer of 1945 did regular ROC military units start turning their weapons on American personnel, demanding rides, money, military equipment, and other goods.[161] Break-ins by Chinese military personnel also became more common at U.S. military warehouses and other facilities, reaching epidemic levels immediately after Japan's surrender. Chinese personnel also engaged in widespread looting in formerly Japanese-held territories and in cities like Kunming. As Chiang and Wedemeyer began hashing out an expanded postwar U.S. training and advisory mission, Nationalist China descended into a free-for-all, with Chinese troops snatching up whatever they could, and disgruntled GIs clamoring to go home.[162]

· · · · · ·

Two weeks after Japan's August 15 surrender announcement, Chiang, Wedemeyer, and Hurley, who now served as the U.S. ambassador to China, proposed the creation of an unprecedented peacetime U.S. advisory program—the American Military Mission in China—as a way for the Americans to build on their wartime efforts. Chiang envisioned a mission comprising four to five thousand American advisors, instructors, and technicians. They would spend at least five years in China, transforming the ROC's entire army, air force, and navy into highly mobile, well-supplied modern forces "capable of coping with any situation."[163] The generalissimo stated "categorically" to Ambassador Hurley that he sought "to adopt American equipment, tactics, and techniques as well as organization" throughout the Chinese military.[164] Chiang requested that Wedemeyer stay on in China to lead the mission. His services, Chiang told Hurley, "would be of great value in continuing the splendid relations that now exist between the United States and China."[165] Hurley supported the proposal enthusiastically. Wedemeyer did as well, though he told Marshall that he intended to decline Chiang's request to serve concurrently as his chief of staff, which "would inevitably draw me closer to political matters."[166] Marshall and the War Department threw their weight behind the proposal, which aligned with the long-standing tutelary vision for China, and by early October, planning for the mission had begun.[167]

High-level U.S. and ROC support for the advisory mission reflected the U.S. military's hard-won but uneven success in improving the fighting efficiency of ROC forces as well as each state's divergent postwar ambitions. Wedemeyer's thirty-nine division Alpha Plan, which dwarfed any previous U.S. Army training program undertaken in a colony or foreign country, was well underway when Japan surrendered. U.S.-trained and equipped Chinese forces, particularly the Ramgarh divisions, had also proven themselves in battle. But these triumphs were not unequivocal. American instructors and liaison officers complained endlessly about ignorant Chinese commanders and poorly educated, malnourished Chinese personnel. Wedemeyer himself conceded when trying to persuade Marshall to support the advisory mission that practically all Chiang's close advisors were "naïve and incompetent."[168] Only a small minority of Chinese troops earned the highest praise on offer from their American arbiters: "thoroughly sold on American methods."[169] Wedemeyer and Hurley nonetheless persuaded the War Department and Secretary of State James Byrnes that the advisory mission would help restore order to China and strengthen the U.S. position in East Asia.[170] Meanwhile, Chiang—as noted in a November 12 letter to the secretary of state by John Carter Vincent, director of the Office of Far Eastern Affairs— sought U.S. military backing in his struggle with Mao's Communists.[171]

The alliance with the United States, however, required the Nationalists to subordinate their military aims to U.S. strategic priorities, which often proved detrimental to ROC interests. Stilwell's ill-conceived, poorly executed 1942 campaign and retreat in Burma decimated the Chinese Expeditionary Force. His rash 1944 drive to Myitkyina, success in convincing

Marshall and Roosevelt to pressure Chiang into deploying Y-Force, and refusal to release lend-lease supplies for China's use during the Ichigo campaign all played out with predictably deleterious consequences to the ROC. As Chiang told Roosevelt on October 9, "We have taken Myitkyina but we have lost almost all of east China."[172] Stilwell, however, had no influence over other U.S. strategic decisions that undermined the Nationalist government. The War Department excluded China from the highest Allied strategic planning staffs, while Roosevelt canceled the amphibious operation in the Bay of Bengal during the reconquest of Burma. Roosevelt and the War Department were also behind the April 18, 1942, Doolittle Raid, in which sixteen B-25s took off from the aircraft carrier USS *Hornet* and bombed targets in Japan, triggering a brutal Japanese campaign against the local population in Zhejiang Province, where the American aircraft were supposed to land after completing their mission.[173]

Stilwell finally pushed too far by personally delivering Roosevelt's September 16, 1944, cable to Chiang. Two-and-a-half years in China as Chiang's chief of staff left Stilwell without any doubt that the Chinese Nationalists lacked the capacity to manage their own affairs. His push for unrestricted command over ROC forces was an extension of the racial logic that had always underpinned Western imperialism in Asia: the shared belief among American, British, French, Dutch, and Spanish colonizers that local populations were fundamentally incapable beings, in need of mentorship—and control—by civilized whites.[174] Chiang saw Stilwell's White House–backed bid as an attempt to turn the ROC into an American puppet regime, with him playing the role of Wang Jingwei, his onetime Nationalist Party rival who had defected to Japan and led the Japanese puppet regime in Nanjing until his death in 1944.[175] If Stilwell had any model in mind, it was probably Douglas MacArthur calling the shots as field marshal of the Philippine Army during the late 1930s, without interference from commonwealth president Manuel Quezon. But as Chiang understood, the era of Western colonialism in Asia had come to an end. Given the choice between turning military power over to Stilwell or facing Japan alone, Chiang stood firm.

Chiang won his showdown with Stilwell and got the American chief of staff he wanted in Albert Wedemeyer, but military-to-military relations at the lower level worsened during the war's final year. Battlefield success and being "thoroughly sold on American methods" were not enough, as American liaison officers' negative interactions with the ROC's crack Ramgarh-trained New First Army demonstrated. Meanwhile, Chinese personnel no longer believed that American servicemen deserved unquestioned deference. They began standing up for themselves against perceived violations of sovereignty, such as anti-smuggling measures. They also became more willing to use violence to get what they wanted in other situations, ranging from transportation disputes to armed robberies. Americans reacted by claiming or advocating for greater authority over Chinese personnel, which dovetailed with complaints from liaison officers in the field. According to a 1945 report, the chief difficulty faced by the Chinese Combat Command was "the fact that American personnel exercised no command function over the Chinese . . . [, which] further hampered the speed and efficiency with which operations could be carried forward."[176] American officers, Wedemeyer included, never questioned the assumption that they understood the Chinese Army's needs better than the Chinese did themselves.

The U.S. military achieved its aim of strengthening the fighting efficiency of ROC armed forces, but this effort, much like Huang Renlin's hostel program, still faltered along the very terms the Americans had set for themselves. The first section of the army's *Pocket Guide to China*, which carried the heading "Forget Your Old Notions," warned GIs that unless they treated Chinese as equals, "they would be playing right into the hands of the Japs." The Japanese, the *Pocket Guide* continued, "will harp on the color question first, last, and all the time. She will tell the Chinese what she has been telling them ever since Pearl Harbor—that Americans look down on nonwhite peoples and that the Chinese can never hope to be treated on equal terms of equality by America."[177]

Army war planners understood that anti-Chinese racism was toxic to the alliance. But Chinese military personnel, from Chiang Kai-shek, Xiong Shi-hui, and Sun Liren on down the ranks, needed no prodding from Japanese propagandists to grasp that their American comrades viewed them as junior partners—at best. Another Chinese group, as we shall see, fared even worse.

4 Living with the U.S. Military

Chinese Civilians

During his third mission with the Fourteenth Air Force's 373rd Bomb Squadron, Lieutenant John Gambardella's luck ran out. His B-24 got shot up over Guilin, and with his fuel tanks almost empty, the time came to "hit the silk."

Gambardella bailed out into the darkness somewhere over Guangxi Province. He hurt his ankle when he hit the ground and wrapped himself in his silk parachute to keep warm until daybreak. Recalling the *Pocket Guide to China*'s instructions on "how to spot a Jap," he examined footprints for signs of the wide space between the first and second toes that supposedly distinguished Japanese from Chinese feet—a result, according to the *Pocket Guide*, of the wooden sandals Japanese wore before army service. The five-foot-three, 106-pound bombardier found no suspicious imprints but still felt terrified when he limped into the nearest village, waving his .45 and yelling, "Ding hao! Meiguo feiji!" (Very good! American airplane!) Farmers gave this diminutive foreigner a wide berth while walking to their fields despite his passable Chinese pronunciation, but other villagers soon fed him and gave him a place to rest. A British missionary arrived a few hours later and told Gambardella that he "was in good hands." The next day, the locals began carrying him in a bamboo litter from village to village back to Yunnan, contacting missionaries or other English speakers along the way to reassure him at each stop. His civilian rescuers, Gambardella recalled, treated him like he was "something out of heaven."[1]

Engagements between American soldiers and Chinese civilians, such as the villagers who saved John Gambardella's life, were central to the making and unmaking of the U.S.-ROC alliance. Like hostel workers and interpreting officers, Chinese civilians facilitated many of the joint military operations discussed in chapter 3, particularly the aerial campaign. They built or expanded many military airfields and participated in most rescues of downed aircrews. They also contributed to the war effort by working for U.S. forces as drivers, mechanics, and unskilled laborers. Most contact between GIs and civilians actually occurred while American personnel were on the road or at liberty—engagements that took place without the mediation of trained hostel staff or interpreters. Each encounter reflected the power disparity between the Republic of China and the United States while also shaping soldiers' and civilians' mutual impressions. Some interactions, particularly the aircrew rescues, strengthened Sino-American ties. But for the most part, the more American servicemen and Chinese civilians interacted, the more they hated each other. This chapter tracks those interactions and how they sped the decay of mutual trust between Chinese and American allies.

Civilians and the War Effort

No American soldier left China with a greater appreciation for the country and its people than the downed airmen who owed their lives to Chinese rescuers. Claire Chennault described the rescues of U.S. airmen as "by far" the war's "most convincing demonstration of Chinese good will towards Americans."[2]

Many GIs agreed. "The Chinese would treat us like royalty," recalled Carl Kostol, a B-25 pilot who bailed out during a mission.[3] Captain Ralph Wilcox reported that the Chinese he encountered when lending Fourteenth Air Force assistance to rescue missions "were extremely friendly and could not do enough for us."[4] American officers rarely, if ever, had such kind words for Chinese soldiers or hostel workers. Many rescued airmen, including Gambardella, returned to China after the 1979 normalization of U.S.-China relations in order to pay their respects to the villagers who had saved their lives.[5] During the war, these rescues were crucial Fourteenth Air Force operations throughout the CBI theater. Chinese rescued more than nine hundred airmen between the AVG's arrival and Japan's surrender, a total, according to Chennault, of 95 percent of the American fliers who survived after bailing out or crash-landing.[6]

Civilians participated in most rescues, which were undertaken through an effective framework that predated the AVG's arrival and stretched from the ROC government in Chongqing down to the village level. The necessity of establishing a set of procedures and an infrastructure to facilitate rescues became obvious to ROC authorities on May 3, 1939, when the Japanese Navy launched the year's first large-scale bombing raid on Chongqing. While defending against the attack, Chinese Air Force vice squadron commander Zhang Mingsheng was shot down over Chongqing's south bank. He sustained major burns before he bailed out, and after he landed, local civilians mistook him for a Japanese airman and attacked him. Zhang's experience convinced

FIGURE 4.1
AVG blood chit: "This foreigner has come to help China fight. Soldiers and civilians, one and all, rescue him."

Chiang Kai-shek to issue orders stating that all airmen, whether Chinese or enemy, "must be captured alive or rescued" and brought to air force or civil authorities. Civilians who brought them in would receive large cash rewards.[7]

When the AVG arrived in China, Chongqing made sure civilians understood that these aviators were fighting on their side. To identify themselves as China's allies, all American airmen carried a silk blood chit, issued by the ROC's Aeronautical Affairs Commission and sewn onto their flight jackets, which featured China's flag and the characters that read, "This foreigner has come to help China fight. Soldiers and civilians, one and all, rescue him" (see figure 4.1). After Pearl Harbor and the creation of the CBI theater, the blood chit included an American flag and sometimes the CBI theater emblem. Local authorities in Yunnan also hung posters and distributed leaflets instructing people to look for the blood chit and demonstrating how to care for downed airmen. "Americans will never forget the people who helped them," read one poster. Many others displayed the slogan, "What we give, we get back."[8]

Not all rescues went smoothly, but early failures led to greater efforts from various Chinese authorities to educate rural populations and assist with returning airmen to their bases. In August 1942, an American pilot died after bailing out near Chongqing. U.S. Army Air Force investigators accused local civilians of murdering him, a charge ROC authorities rejected, pointing to a medical examination that concluded the man died from injuries sustained in his fall. This incident pressed the ROC government to double up on rural outreach and ensure that local authorities prioritized the rescue and protection of downed airmen.[9] The Chinese Communists also gave precedence to the rescue of American personnel who bailed out over areas under their control, earning high marks from Chennault.[10] Meanwhile, in Yunnan, U.S. commanders warned aircrews that bandits would hold them for ransom, but the archival record indicates that such admonishments were based on rumor rather than experience.[11] These rumors probably originated with cases of mistaken identity during the early days of the American presence. One AVG pilot who glided to a belly landing on a hill near Kunming a few weeks after Pearl Harbor, for example, spent an uncomfortable night with civilian rescuers who thought he was Japanese, but they took him to a Chinese Army post the next morning, where he cabled Chennault.[12]

In early 1943, the ROC government made civilian administrators responsible for the safety and well-being of all downed airmen. The GMD's Executive Yuan issued orders mandating that "when Allied [American] airmen are forced down, the local government must promptly rescue, host, and keep them protected."[13] Local authorities also had orders to protect their aircraft and belongings.[14] At the lowest level, rescue efforts relied on China's *baojia* system, the country's traditional arrangement of mutual responsibility and surveillance, which the Nationalists had revived in the late 1920s to restore control over local society. Every ten or so households were formed into a unit called a *jia*, and ten or so *jia* made up a *bao*.[15] Chiang ordered *baojia* chiefs to send rescue teams to locate wrecks and search for survivors whenever an aircraft went down.[16] *Baojia* chiefs also had orders to immediately inform county magistrates and nearby air force installations in the event of airplane crashes.[17] Over the course of the war, the rewards for rescuing airmen increased, and by the spring of 1945, the ROC's Commission on Aeronautical Affairs paid 100,000 fabi for every Chinese or American airman rescued from Japanese-held territory. Setting an equal rate for Chinese and American airmen demonstrated Chongqing's insistence that Chinese and American lives were of equal value.[18]

The U.S. Army reimbursed local officials and the Commission on Aeronautical Affairs for their expenses. Because some "local government and civilian organizations had spared no effort in hosting downed American airmen," daily expenditures for these operations ran as high as 10,000 fabi in 1944, leading Chongqing to crack down on lavish entertainment for American airmen and negotiate a daily reimbursement rate of 500 fabi per man with the U.S. Army. For medical expenses, however, Chiang and U.S. Army headquarters in Chongqing agreed that all airmen should receive whatever care they needed, regardless of cost, with the Americans footing the bill.[19] As in other areas of interaction with American soldiers, Chiang sought to base rescue efforts on the principle of equality: "Based on the cooperative spirit between allies," he ordered, "downed American airmen should be treated the same as Chinese soldiers." He also suggested that if costs could be kept low, "we do not necessarily need the Americans to reimburse us."[20] Chiang's instructions showed his cognizance of American anxieties about Chinese dishonesty when it came to finances. But rescue reimbursements, unlike compensations for hostel or interpreter program expenses, did not become a contentious issue.

While financial rewards incentivized civilians to save American lives, ordinary Chinese also participated in rescue efforts out of genuine gratitude. Despite all the problems associated with the U.S. military presence, the arrival of American airmen marked a turning point for civilians in Southwest China. From 1938 to 1941, Japanese aircraft waged an unprecedented bombing campaign that turned civilians in cities like Chongqing and Kunming into "front-line combatants." But after the United States entered the war, aerial operations against these cities largely ceased. In the summers of 1940 and 1941, when the foggy season had subsided, Japanese aircraft bombed Chongqing an average of once every two to four days, killing approximately six thousand civilians. Not a single raid occurred in 1942, and Japanese aircraft attacked the city just once in 1943.[21] Farther south, Japanese bombers had raided Kunming forty-five times before AVG P-40s first took to the skies above the city on December 20, 1941, shooting down three Kawasaki Ki-48 bombers and damaging seven others. Sixteen months passed before the Japanese attempted to bomb Kunming again.[22] American airpower boosted morale and gave respite to civilians who had grown accustomed to living under constant alert whenever the skies were clear. Rescues gave many civilians a chance to reciprocate when power relations were inverted, and American military personnel placed their lives in Chinese hands.

Civilians also kept U.S. aircraft in the skies by building and expanding military airfields, though most participation in these projects was compulsory. Airfield construction, like aircrew rescues, predated the arrival of American military personnel in China, but U.S. military requests led to dozens of new projects and the mobilization of more than a million civilian laborers.[23] The largest project began in late 1943, when the Sichuan provincial government conscripted more than 375,000 civilians from six counties around Chengdu to expand four bomber and nine fighter support airfields for Operation Matterhorn, the U.S. War Department's plan to crush domestic Japanese steel production with B-29 bomber raids.[24] Smaller projects, some still requiring over sixty thousand laborers, were carried out in 1944 and 1945. While conscript laborers performed most construction work, some projects relied on a combination of conscripts and contractors, and a few on contractor work alone.[25] Airfields were built or expanded based on U.S. Army request, and while the GMD National Military Council's Engineering Commission oversaw construction, U.S. Army resident engineers exercised ultimate authority at each jobsite.

Civilian laborers at airfields and other U.S. military facilities had less enthusiasm for the Americans than the compatriots who rescued them. While carrying out propaganda work for the Office of War Information, Graham Peck noted that pro-American sentiment among Chinese civilians "was especially shaky" near airfield construction projects, which he attributed to conscription and poor pay.[26] Workers were typically paid in rice and money based on the amount of work they accomplished, and large price fluctuations due to inflation caused tension at numerous jobsites. At Huangping County Airfield in Guizhou, for example, inflation far outpaced salary adjustments.

Working conditions made matters even worse (see figure 4.2). During the winter, most of the fifty-five thousand conscripts at Huangping had to work barefoot in the snow and carry all equipment to and from the jobsite by foot. Half of them ran away for the Chinese New Year.[27] Keeping workers fed was a huge logistical challenge, and food shortages occurred at construction sites in Yunnan.[28] Sanitary conditions were also poor. Despite the Sichuan Health Bureau's attempts to provide sanitary services at the B-29 airfield construction projects near Chengdu, 314 laborers died from dysentery, typhoid, and other infectious diseases during a five-month period in 1944.[29] Meanwhile, civilian laborers employed directly by the U.S. military staged strikes to protest physical abuse by American supervisors, and the U.S. Army

FIGURE 4.2 Airfield construction in Yunnan. (James B. Hinchliff Collection, Institute on World War II and the Human Experience, Florida State University)

paid 30,000 fabi to the family of one laborer who was shot to death by a GI during a motor repair shop strike in February 1945.[30]

At the more senior level, the GMD's Engineering Commission reported mostly cooperative relations with U.S. Army resident engineers, but several of these American jobsite supervisors got into trouble over their dealings with civilians. Captain James F. Byrne, the resident engineer at Luxian Airfield in southern Sichuan, beat up James H. S. Chang, manager of the guesthouse where Byrne resided, and threatened to slit Chang's wife's throat after an argument over the use of a kitchen. A court-martial imposed a one-time forfeiture on Byrne of half his monthly salary, a slap on the wrist compared to punishments for threatening and attacking a fellow GI.[31] The war ended before the provost marshal finished investigating Captain James Bohlkin, resident engineer at an airfield in Hu County, near Xi'an. Multiple sources told investigators that Bohlkin was throwing lavish parties for prostitutes, which he funded by defrauding the U.S. government and withholding wages from the thirty thousand Chinese laborers working at the airfield.[32]

In the most serious incident, First Lieutenant Gerald Clark, the resident engineer at Chuxiong Airfield in Yunnan, was sentenced to three years' hard labor for killing Yu Pinghui, a civilian contractor whom Clark had clashed with over price disputes and a labor strike. When agent Earl Miller of the provost marshal's Criminal Investigation Division (CID) investigated Yu's death, he discovered that Clark was also misusing funds and padding the payroll at Chuxiong. In his previous position as resident engineer at the Baoshan Airfield in Western Yunnan, Clark had also come under CID investigation for fraud.[33]

Airfield construction and aerial operations also made life difficult for civilians who lived nearby. Chennault admitted that construction projects contributed to food shortages and inflation not only at jobsites but also in surrounding communities. Once aircraft began flying, he wrote, aircraft noise, test firing, and emergency bomb jettisoning caused annoyance, property damage, and accidental deaths.[34] Disputes over payments for land requisitions also occurred because the government compensated people slowly and at unfavorable prices due to inflation.[35] This led farmers to attack the Chinese engineers carrying out preliminary surveys for airfields at Luxian and Xinjin, a B-29 staging base near Chengdu.[36] While airfield construction projects created jobs, the overall impact on nearby communities was mixed. Moreover, Operation Matterhorn achieved only marginal results despite the heavy burden it placed on Sichuanese civilians. Chengdu-based B-29s launched just nine raids against cities in Japan before the Joint Chiefs of Staff decided to move the aircraft to the Mariana Islands.[37]

American soldiers had never seen anything like China's airfield construction projects, but Chinese laborers did not earn the same respect from GIs as their compatriots who participated in aircrew rescues. On each jobsite, tens of thousands of laborers hauled gravel on their backs, crushed it with simple hammers, and then flattened the runways by pulling massive concrete rollers. The novelist Ernest Hemingway described one project for New York City's *PM* newspaper as what it must have been like to see men building the pyramids, with "every carrying stick . . . bent to its breaking point under a double load as the men worked twelve-hour shifts."[38] American servicemen also compared these construction projects to the pyramids while describing laborers as insect-like and indifferent to suffering.[39] "Some of the officers who have been here for a while say that a couple of times one of the workers has slipped under the roller," wrote one cargo pilot in 1945. "The others just plod along and would go back over him if they were not stopped. Death has no impression on them at all."[40] "It was amazing how they worked," said B-24 bomber pilot Melvin Lees, "steady like ants."[41] Another pilot agreed, recalling, "They looked like ants going after sugar—one line going one way, one line going another."[42] From the GIs' perspective, aircrew rescues humanized Chinese civilians, but airfield construction made manifest the striking differences between Americans and their primitive, ant-like hosts.

Smuggling and the Black Market

American airpower also gave U.S. personnel a tremendously advantageous position in China's black markets. Japan's coastal blockade and occupation of Burma led to critical shortages of practically every imported good in China, and many American air and ground crewmen eagerly filled the void. Smuggling and black-market dealing, like airfield construction and aircrew rescues, predated the arrival of U.S. forces. But almost immediately upon crossing into Chinese territory, American military personnel took advantage of their exemption from Chinese customs inspections to smuggle in a wide range of small, high-value items, which they usually sold to civilians. While many American servicemen and Chinese civilians profited from the underground economy and formed mutually beneficial illicit partnerships, they were not equals. American participation in the black market thus alienated local civilians—including many of those who participated in the trade—and stained the image of the AVG and the U.S. Army.

During the retreat from Burma, several AVG members and close associates began smuggling operations that would outlive their storied mercenary outfit. Although Long Yun had established a provincial anti-smuggling office shortly before Pearl Harbor, his border guards allowed AVG trucks to pass without inspection, which enabled transportation officer Raymond Hasty and several subordinates to enter China with booty looted from warehouses in Rangoon and Lashio.[43] A December 1943 provost marshal investigation into AVG smuggling concluded that Hasty and the other men stole large quantities of U.S. Army supplies and personal property belonging to U.S. diplomats. Hasty established a business in Yunnanyi, a key airbase town 270 kilometers west of Kunming, where he sold off his looted cargo supplies before leaving China and acquiring an interest in a Karachi cabaret that catered to U.S. military personnel. Army investigators believed that other ex-AVG men were still collaborating with Chinese civilians in Calcutta and Kunming in smuggling operations as of late 1943.[44] Rose Mok Carney, the Chinese civilian wife of ex-AVG member Boatner Carney, came up in numerous smuggling investigations, including, as we shall see in chapter 5, a scheme to bring Chinese prostitutes from Guilin to Kunming aboard a U.S. Army transport aircraft.[45]

Immunity from Chinese law and lax discipline made it easy for AVG members to participate in the black market. The Flying Tigers were practically untouchable. Japan's attack on Pearl Harbor and occupation of Shanghai's International Settlement effectively shut down the U.S. Court for China, which had exercised extraterritorial jurisdiction over American citizens in China ever since its establishment by Theodore Roosevelt's administration in 1906.[46] The only punishment AVG members were subject to was discipline by Chennault, a notoriously easygoing commander. Not until November 1942 did the U.S. Army's judge advocate general finish setting up a CBI theater branch, which meant that throughout the alliance's early days, American soldiers and AVG members could smuggle with impunity.[47] Based on rumors among American personnel, Chennault himself fell under suspicion for smuggling by the Office of Strategic Services, but an investigation into his activities failed to uncover conclusive proof.[48]

U.S. Army airmen continued to participate in the black market long after the AVG was disbanded, as inconsistent and uncoordinated anti-smuggling measures provided only minimal deterrence. Corruption at the GMD's Smuggling Prevention Office, which Juntong head Dai Li directed while simultaneously overseeing a massive nationwide smuggling operation, undermined American trust.[49] Stilwell rebuffed ROC foreign minister Song Ziwen's December 1942 request to establish a Sino-U.S. inspection office in Kunming with responsibility for joint searches of American aircraft.[50] U.S. Army authorities chose to deal with the problem on their own. Yet despite his recognition that smuggling was a serious problem, Stilwell did not begin implementing an anti-smuggling program for another year, and these efforts focused entirely on Assam, which meant U.S. Army aircraft were not searched for contraband after arriving in China.[51] Meanwhile, ROC authorities never received authorization to inspect U.S. aircraft.[52] U.S. authorities did end up disciplining some offenders. In late 1943, the Fourteenth Air Force charged twenty-two men for Hump flight smuggling, securing convictions or reprimands against thirteen. These men had smuggled medicine, cigarettes, cosmetics, piston rings, and large quantities of gold, but none received more than an eighteen-month sentence, while the others continued to fly.[53] As it took more than a year of training to prepare a pilot for duty, commanders believed that discharging or court-martialing every pilot caught for smuggling would have led to personnel shortages.[54]

Chinese civilians, on the other hand, faced potentially lethal consequences for smuggling. On November 25, 1942, an American pilot named William Kelling smuggled medicine worth 400,000 fabi over the Hump and gave it to Ge Zunxian, an employee at the Chuankang Civil and Commercial Bank. Chinese authorities arrested Ge for smuggling a few days later and discovered through his personal correspondence that he had previously colluded with other American pilots to smuggle. During interrogation, Ge admitted to working with a Calcutta-based partner named Chen Mengzhao, owner of the M.C. Chen Trading Company.[55] Foreign minister Song arranged Chen's extradition, and both Chen and Ge were convicted of smuggling and executed on October 16, 1943.[56] U.S. authorities questioned Kelling over his involvement, but because he was a civilian technical representative attached to the Fourteenth Air Force, the judge advocate general exercised no jurisdiction over his alleged crimes and recommended that no charges be brought against him.[57] The ROC's jurisdiction over ethnic Chinese civilians living in British India was murky at best, a subject of contentious negotiations between ROC and British colonial officials throughout the war, but this did not stop Chongqing from spiriting Chen out of Calcutta and bringing him to justice in China.[58] Disparities in punishment ensured resentment on the part of the Chinese.

American personnel had little trouble smuggling contraband into China. Fourteenth Air Force lieutenant William Milner's crew chief spoke Chinese and made a killing selling whiskey in Kunming. "He came back to the United States," said Milner, "and probably spent the rest of his time fishing.[59] Hu Guohua, a civilian airfield clerk, described the Yibin Airfield in southern Sichuan as "a wonderful place for smuggling." Flight crews brought in gold tolas (an Indian unit equivalent to 0.375 troy ounces) and rupees on practically every flight and sold them to the first civilian clerks and mechanics to offer them a good price.[60] Kunming-based pilot Whitney Greenberg explained how the system worked shortly after Japan's surrender: "I was an entrepreneur. Shanghai to Guilin to buy gold, take the gold and buy Chinese dollars in Kunming, take the Chinese dollars and exchange them into American dollars in Shanghai . . . tripled my money." Greenberg, like many other American smugglers and speculators, relied on privileged access to airpower and information. "The Chinese didn't know," he recalled, "how much the dollar was worth, how much the gold was worth . . . [and] because I was crew chief, I could take the flight any time I wanted to."[61] U.S. military aircraft, Greenberg knew, were rarely searched.[62] Cautious smugglers could always take precautions, like hiding gold in the plane's tail section, or medicine in its heater tubes, which posed a danger to the aircraft.[63]

Hump smuggling and theft by American personnel fueled a booming street-level black-market trade. In October 1943, Sergeant William Morris ran into Private Frank Berthaine and Sergeant Gene Yacavone, a couple of old acquaintances, at Billie's Café, a popular American hangout in Kunming. Morris, an India-based crew chief who flew the Hump regularly, bragged that he "had brought a great deal" of smuggled goods into China. The three hatched a scheme to steal canned milk from an SOS warehouse and sell it to a Kunming businessman who had purchased smuggled goods from Morris before. After the deal was done, a civilian mechanic who worked for Berthaine introduced the three GIs to other Kunming businessmen, who bought pilfered firearms. Over the next six months, Morris smuggled in cigarettes, medicine, cosmetics, and gold, and he and his partners in crime sold them to civilians they knew around town. Eager to capitalize on these connections, the three men spent much of their free time in Kunming stealing from U.S. Army warehouses, medical dispensaries, and WASC hostels. Morris evaded the theater provost marshal's anti-smuggling measures for more than six months before he was finally caught in June 1944.[64] He then laid out the details of his smuggling operation and testified in exchange for immunity against a female American civilian in Kunming who had brokered some of their deals.[65]

Contraband also made its way to Chinese black markets through the U.S. military's mail system. In September 1944, base censors in Kunming began intercepting packages containing contraband mailed from the United States. They also discovered letters written to friends and family members back home requesting Parker pen sets, cosmetics, clothing, sulfa drugs, jewelry, cigarettes, and other items. "All the stuff from home brings a good price," one corporal wrote. "A little ten cent lipstick brings $10 in our money."[66] The 407th Air Service Squadron of the Fourteenth Air Service Group, a unit composed almost entirely of Chinese American troops, "acquired a notorious reputation for widespread black-market activities" via the army's postal system. The base censor in Kunming confiscated twenty-five packages of contraband mailed to members of this unit during the summer of 1945.[67] Almost all of these goods made their way into civilian hands, with American soldiers reaping the biggest profits. At least one theater post officer—the soldier tasked with preventing smuggling through the mail system—was found by investigators "to have misused his official position to engage in black market transactions, such as the receipt through the mail of rupees [and the] sending and receipt of black market items." Criminal investigators also busted three members of the American military police outside

Chengdu for smuggling, reporting that the men had been "receiving an excessive number of packages from the United States every month" and dumping their goods on the black market during frequent trips into the city.[68]

American participation in the black market resulted in a large amount of U.S. military goods ending up for sale in Kunming and other towns, which heightened tensions between U.S. and Chinese authorities. GIs knew they could earn good money by selling rations, uniforms, firearms, and other U.S. government property to ordinary civilians, who would turn around and sell those items in public markets.[69] Many wealthier civilians who ran businesses that catered to American servicemen proposed larger deals for stolen goods, and these businesses themselves were sometimes established with capital accrued through black-market dealing with GIs.[70] The sight of so many goods intended for U.S. military use being sold by Chinese civilians frustrated American commanders, who blamed the problem on Chinese thieves. They pressured Chinese authorities in Yunnan and Chongqing to crack down. The Tobacco Monopoly Bureau barred foreign cigarette sales in May 1944.[71] In September, Long Yun's government announced a policy of "confiscation and severe punishment for anyone caught buying or selling U.S. military goods."[72] Local police carried out sporadic raids on areas known for selling American products, while U.S. Army investigators searched for suppliers.[73] These measures had little effect, as black-market trading increased throughout the first half of 1945. Even after Long imposed a ban on all trading in U.S. military goods in June 1945—backed up by joint patrols with the U.S. Army—markets broken up in one place reappeared elsewhere or quickly returned.[74]

Participation in the black market earned American military personnel a reputation as pilferers, and Chinese officials and civilians alike resented the way anti-smuggling measures let GIs off the hook. Despite going along with the U.S. Army's requests for a ban on trading U.S. military goods in 1945, Yunnan and ROC authorities laid much of the blame for China's black markets on the Americans. Long Yun and FAB director He Haoruo argued that the problem would persist as long as U.S. authorities failed to stop their own men from stealing U.S. military goods.[75] The writer Wang Pingshun criticized Long's June prohibition in the pages of the *Grand View Mansion Weekly*, arguing that "enforcement of the measure should begin with the party initiating the deal—the [American] seller." Wang wrote that it was "quite ridiculous" to ban the sale of articles with no military use, such as cigarettes and daily necessities. He sympathized with ordinary civilians, who often had few alternatives to black-market dealing thanks to unemployment and the worst inflation rates of the entire war. Besides, he insisted, "in view of the vast population in China—at least 300,000 strong in Kunming alone"—it would be far easier to make GIs the targets of discipline.[76] But American soldiers evaded suspicion and punishment for their participation in the black market by blaming Chinese thieves whenever U.S. government property went missing.

Theft and Profiteering

The widespread civilian theft of U.S. military goods gave pilfering GIs a ready alibi while also contributing to anti-Chinese resentment. Soldiers complained about theft no less than they did about hostel food. "There is really only one bad thing that we have found here in China, that wasn't so important a problem in India," Earl Revell wrote in 1944, "and that is stealing."[77] Warren Arnett agreed, telling his mother, "They [Chinese civilians] are dirty and born thieves."[78] "They used to steal us blind," recalled another GI.[79] Most American soldiers, as we have seen, already viewed the ROC government as an obstacle to the war effort, and civilian theft bolstered the conclusion that the rot went deeper. In April 1945, U.S. consular authorities in Kunming reported, "Growing criticism among our servicemen of the Chinese war effort and particularly of the profiteering and thievery of certain Chinese elements" had made it back to the United States. Profiteering and price gouging in everything from rickshaw fares to construction supplies had long angered GIs, but by spring 1945, theft had become the chief source of American resentment against local civilians.[80] On April 7, Chennault called a press conference in Kunming to request assistance in dealing with the surge in thefts that had followed Japan's Ichigo campaign, telling Chinese and American journalists that stealing had reached the point at which the average GI now believed "that every Chinese he sees about him is a potential thief."[81]

Civilian theft, like GI participation in the black market, ran the gamut from opportunistic pilfering to break-ins to sophisticated conspiracies that undermined military operations. Wealth gave American servicemen a leg up in the black market but also made them targets, though robberies were rare. When civilian employees stole from U.S. military facilities, it added to distrust and led to preventive measures that Chinese laborers found offensive, like full-body pat downs. Such petty theft was common, as was organized crime targeting fuel and vehicles. In December 1943, U.S. military police busted a civilian Chinese driver syphoning gas from a Jeep at Kunming's

U.S. Air Service Command. He admitted to being part of a scheme involving eighteen other civilian drivers employed at the same facility.[82] Car thieves in Kunming stole twenty-five U.S. Army Jeeps in two-and-a-half months over the winter of 1943 to 1944.[83] "So many vehicles have been stolen," an American major said to Chinese journalists a few months later, "that it has affected the capacity of Chinese and Americans to wage war."[84] The problem grew worse in 1945. In April, Chennault told Wedemeyer, "One of the principal problems confronting this command is the continuous loss of government equipment and personal property at all of our air bases by thievery."[85] Theft losses were staggering after the Yunnan-Burma oil pipeline opened in February 1945. During just two days in early June, thieves made away with 150,000 gallons—enough to fill the tanks of sixty-three B-24 Liberators.[86] By that time, civilians were stealing from the Yunnanyi Air Base daily, leading Wedemeyer to warn Chiang, "The many depredations constantly occurring at Yunnanyi are giving rise to violence and bloodshed."[87]

Wedemeyer's warning to Chiang revealed that U.S. military personnel were responding to the thefts by taking the law into their own hands. By late 1944, U.S. troops had begun undertaking sporadic searches for U.S. government property at homes and businesses in Yunnan—a blatant violation of ROC sovereignty and U.S. military regulations. In Zhanyi, northeast of Kunming, for example, the U.S. airbase commander twice sent armed GIs to search nearby Chinese-owned businesses and confiscate American cigarettes, uniforms, and other goods.[88] Long Yun reported that U.S. military police "sometimes exceeded their authority" in similar incidents elsewhere in the province.[89] Yang Chenren, a language professor in Kunming, complained directly to the ROC's Ministry of Foreign Affairs after an American MP stopped him on the street and stole his glasses. "Although the loss of a pair of spectacles is a trifle matter, yet such behavior on the part of a member of Allied [American] military police constituted a contempt for the Chinese people," Yang wrote.[90] American investigators, however, deemed the MP's actions "excusable" because Yang's glasses were "identical to the type issued by the United States military authorities."[91] In any of these incidents, Chinese may have very well purchased such goods from American personnel. These illegal and humiliating actions, which continued well into the summer of 1945, according to FAB director He Haoruo, added to accumulated grievances against the country's allied friends.[92] The American killing of civilian theft suspects made matters even worse.

In August 1944, the army theater's judge advocate in China made a ruling that allowed U.S. troops to shoot unarmed Chinese theft suspects in certain cases. The ruling stemmed from a case in which American sentries shot two Chinese civilians for stealing bricks. The judge advocate argued that U.S. military law allowed the killing of felons fleeing the scene of their crimes, and that any theft of U.S. military goods constituted a felony. His ruling contradicted a set of U.S. Army regulations promulgated in January 1944, which stipulated that firearms could be used only in self-defense or to prevent prisoners from escaping. ROC law, meanwhile, sanctioned lethal force only in cases of self-defense.[93] ROC authorities objected to this ruling, pointing out that Chinese sentries frequently saw GIs pilfering from military warehouses. "If Chinese guards would have also adopted the same method toward those U.S. soldiers of alleged burglary [sic] who used to creep into depots," China's Fifth Route Air Force headquarters reasoned, "it would be very hard for this headquarters to make good arrangements for any such result."[94] Meanwhile, at Yunnanyi, the base specified by Wedemeyer as a site of daily theft, GIs killed a number of suspected civilian thieves in May and June 1945, including one man named Liu Kaiqi, who was carrying water to sell at the airfield. "They [the Americans at Yunnanyi] don't only neglect human beings," stated Liu Kaiqi's father, "but also look down on our nation."[95]

U.S. and ROC investigations into civilian theft suspect shootings rarely reached the same conclusions. After GIs killed two suspected thieves at Yunnanyi on July 12, Chinese investigators lambasted American authorities for not capturing the men alive and voiced doubts that the suspects had attempted to steal at all.[96] American investigators displayed similar bias about Chinese eyewitness reports. "The undersigned has considerable experience dealing with the Chinese," wrote one investigator regarding a shooting that left one civilian dead and another injured, "from which he has learned that they frequently knowingly give false information." Thus, he concluded that the allegations that GIs had shot the men over an alleged theft of a 100 rupee note "were a complete fabrication."[97] Deep distrust made it difficult for ROC and U.S. authorities to see eye to eye. As with smuggling and the black market, Chinese officials believed that American soldiers were responsible for a far larger share of theft than U.S. commanders were willing to admit. One Commission on Aeronautical Affairs investigation found that American soldiers committed more than 46 percent of thefts involving U.S. Army Air Force property.[98]

But the power imbalance led ROC authorities to begin employing harsher anti-theft measures against their own people in 1945, moving in lockstep with anti-smuggling and black-market crackdowns. During a joint June 27 meeting about the Yunnan-Burma pipeline fuel theft, General Huang Qixiang, commander of the Chinese Combat Command, requested that GIs "shoot [Chinese] offenders who resist arrest, preferably wounding them so they could be interrogated as to accomplices." Huang's request stunned his U.S. Army counterparts, who asked him to put in writing.[99] For a Nationalist general to authorize foreign soldiers to shoot unarmed Chinese suspects on Chinese soil indicated the gravity of the theft problem and its impact on military operations. The relatives of theft suspects shot by American personnel typically appealed to Chinese authorities for help. But the GMD's dependence on the U.S. military pressed ROC military commanders to prioritize retaining American goodwill over protecting Chinese lives.

Accidents and Violent Crime

Traffic accidents caused by American military personnel and apparent GMD indifference also angered civilians. AVG pilots risked their lives every time they took to the skies in their beat-up P-40s, so it's no surprise that many also drove recklessly while on the ground. Chinese police were understanding at first. On May 22, 1942, an AVG member driving on the wrong side of the road in Chongqing seriously injured two civilians in a crash. "American AVG vehicles have been driving on the right when in the city, in accordance with the American custom," police wrote in their report. Chinese law, on the other hand, required traffic to keep to the left.[100] Police in Chongqing provided Chennault's outfit and U.S. forces with English translations of Chinese traffic regulations, but one week later an intoxicated AVG member hit a pedestrian a few blocks away. Chinese authorities had no recourse other than pleading to Chennault, warning him that "further drunk driving incidents will damage the AVG's reputation."[101]

Accidents became more frequent as U.S. troop deployments to China increased. In October 1944, Chiang urged U.S. Army headquarters in Chongqing to enforce traffic regulations in order to prevent collisions. "All allied vehicles must respect traffic rules and safety," he wrote.[102] In March 1945, municipal and central authorities in Chongqing held a traffic supervision conference to discuss traffic problems associated with the U.S. military presence, to no avail (see figure 4.3). "In recent days," the Chongqing Police Bureau reported on April 26, "accidents involving U.S. military vehicles have been happening one after another."[103] Deadly accidents also occurred in Yunnan. "Pedestrians have often been knocked down and killed by American military trucks" in Kunming, according to a December 1944 diplomatic

FIGURE 4.3 Three American soldiers and a Chinese traffic officer in Chongqing. (Paul LeRoy Jones Papers, Hoover Institution)

protest lodged by the ROC Foreign Ministry's special delegate in Yunnan.[104] Airbase construction led to deadly accidents even in the province's remote areas. "Ever since the highway in Luoping [near the American airfield approximately two hundred kilometers east of Kunming] was opened to traffic, reckless driving has caused a number of injuries and deaths," reported the village headman in Shawan Cun on May 4, after "a fast-running car belonging to the U.S. Army engineering section" killed a local woman.[105]

While GMD authorities repeatedly implored U.S. military commanders and officials to take measures to reduce accidents, government-affiliated newspapers downplayed the problem, leaving civilians with the impression that Chongqing was doing little, if anything, to protect them. The more accidents that occurred, the more outlandish the propaganda became. On April 28, 1945, the official GMD organ, *Central News Daily*, published a feature about an accident involving a U.S. Army convoy near Chengdu. According to the article, the American involved in the wreck gave first aid to the injured civilians. This was believable enough, but the author also wrote that the soldiers in question voluntarily handed over their driver's licenses pending legal settlement. "The town folk were deeply moved by their law-abiding spirit," the piece concluded.[106]

Despite pleas from Chinese authorities, U.S. military commanders did little until late spring 1945 to deter speeding, recklessness, or drunk driving. Fourteenth Air Force investigations in Kunming during August 1944 found U.S. base areas "characterized by reckless driving, speeding on narrow roads, and almost a total absence of military courtesy" while operating motor vehicles.[107] The army experimented by imposing a ten-mile-per-hour speed limit, but it hampered military operations and "was very commonly violated."[108] In May 1945, U.S. Army headquarters began referring soldiers to summary courts-martial for speeding and reckless driving.[109] By then, however, the army's reputation for dangerous behavior on China's roadways was well established. Meanwhile, in response to repeated complaints about drunk-driving accidents, Stilwell told Chongqing police chief Tang Yi in early 1943 that he had formulated new regulations to keep intoxicated soldiers from getting behind the wheel. But as late as June 1945, the U.S. Army's standard penalty for court-martial conviction on drunk-driving charges was just a $15 forfeiture—hardly a deterrent.[110]

U.S. commanders dismissed complaints from ROC officials because they believed Chinese civilians caused most collisions. GIs found China's roadways no less unpleasant than the country's sensory offenses and equally indicative of their host population's racialized inferiority. "The slope head driver," wrote Jan Peeke in 1942, "gets in his car, puts one hand on the horn button and takes off—right down the middle of the street—look[ing,] as a result, like a snowplow going up the sidewalks of 14th and F Streets during rush time."[111] It was also the custom, Peeke said, for pedestrians to walk in the street, "and if the walkers don't get out of the way, nothing to fear, just a few less mouths to feed in China."[112] The lack of orderliness frustrated GIs to no end—despite their own disregard for traffic laws. But instead of recognizing that most Chinese were unaccustomed to sharing the road with so many motor vehicles, GIs attributed differences in road etiquette to superstition and a disregard for human life. "The Chinese had a folk superstition that they picked up devils during the year," recalled a communications unit soldier, "and whenever possible they would rush across in front of a vehicle or airplane at a great risk to themselves in order to cut themselves free of the devils who shadowed them.[113] Major Norman Key of the Quartermaster Corps repeated the same story, remarking, "Life is so cheap, it was no big deal."[114] Warren Arnett put it in characteristic bluntness in 1945: "A Chink will cut across your path so his spirit will follow you and not him. . . . A lot of them get killed this way. Crazy people!"[115]

Civilians were also maimed and killed in accidental shootings by American personnel. Although U.S. military regulations in China stipulated that GIs could fire their weapons only in self-defense, indiscriminate shooting was common.[116] American soldiers enjoyed hunting and target shooting—while at liberty and sometimes from moving vehicles while on duty. Phone lines, porcelain insulators on telegraph poles, and road signs were favorite targets, but stray bullets sometimes hit civilians. In September 1943, for example, an American army engineer killed Li Fengshi and wounded Lei Zhilin, two civilians who had been shopping across the street from the grassy area where the American was taking target practice. FAB requested a court-martial for involuntary manslaughter, but U.S. authorities demurred, arguing that there had been no criminal intent.[117] Courts-martial for accidental shootings were rare. Unless an English speaker quickly alerted U.S. military authorities, Chinese police reports had to work their way up to the Ministry of Military Administration or FAB before reaching U.S. Army headquarters, a process that could take months.[118] In those cases, criminal investigators found it nearly impossible to identify the shooter or locate reliable witnesses. Other cases went uninvestigated because the Chinese reports were sent to the wrong U.S. military command.[119]

U.S. authorities did little to deter indiscriminate shootings, even though they damaged communication infrastructure, heightened tensions with

ROC authorities, and killed civilians. He Yingqin and He Haoruo pleaded with Stilwell and Wedemeyer numerous times to stop GIs from shooting at phone lines and telegraph insulators, to no purpose.[120] Between February and June 1945 alone, phone lines between Kunming and surrounding cities were severed by shooting ten times, delaying telephonic and telegraphic communications.[121] American commanders admitted that GIs were probably at fault each time.[122] In Chongqing, indiscriminate shooting by intoxicated American personnel became such a nuisance in late 1944 that the municipal police bureau imposed citywide limits on alcohol sales and ordered restaurants to stop serving GIs at 9:30 P.M. each night—two regulations that proved difficult to enforce.[123] Meanwhile, in cases in which U.S. military courts convicted American soldiers of wrongfully shooting civilians, the penalties were lighter than those imposed for pilfering, sleeping on post, or being absent from guard duty. Even near the war's end, after months of repeated pleas by Chinese authorities to halt indiscriminate shooting, GIs still got off easy for accidently shooting civilians, with minor fines or temporary confinement on base rather than jail time.[124]

Chinese civilians could request payment for damages due to shootings and vehicle accidents caused by U.S. military personnel under the 1942 Foreign Claims Act, but compensation decisions depended entirely on the American soldiers who handled claims, likely undercounting actual harm to civilians.[125] Payments varied widely, taking into account factors like earning potential and circumstances of wrongful death. The family of Li Fengshi, for example—the civilian killed by a stray bullet in September 1943—was paid around $320, a figure the ROC Foreign Ministry found scandalously low.[126] Another family received $483.33 after Li Benmao, their sole breadwinner, was killed by a U.S. Army vehicle in a hit-and-run accident near Zhanyi Airbase.[127] But the army paid just $15.50 for funeral expenses after an army truck crushed Liu Dongshi, a refugee woman without any relatives in Kunming.[128] When Sidney Rittenberg, a Chinese language specialist with the Judge Advocate General's office, paid the $26 compensation to the family of a twelve-year-old girl who died after a GI ran her over while trying to scare her, her father told him, "Our life is nothing."[129] American soldiers often remarked that Chinese had a low regard for human life, but disregard for Chinese lives by troops who claimed to be their allies disgusted and alienated many of the same civilians who had welcomed American troops to China after Pearl Harbor.

U.S. authorities also had jurisdiction over all criminal matters involving American military personnel in China. The extraterritorial system established in 1844, when U.S. envoy Caleb Cushing negotiated the Treaty of Wangxia with the Qing Empire, remained in effect when the Flying Tigers arrived in China in 1941. After the formation of the U.S.-ROC alliance, Stilwell convinced Chiang to allow U.S. military courts to fill in for the now-defunct U.S. Court for China. The GMD's National Military Council gave formal approval to Stilwell's request on August 8, 1942, granting the U.S. Army exclusive rights to apprehend and prosecute any GI that Chinese authorities suspected of committing a crime.[130] But the continued existence of U.S. extraterritorial jurisdiction in China provided fodder for Japanese propagandists while also fueling Chinese criticism against the United States, including speeches and op-eds by ROC first lady Song Meiling.[131] The Roosevelt administration finally relinquished U.S. extraterritorial rights in China on January 11, 1943, hoping to provide a morale boost to Chiang's government, but State Department officials insisted that the U.S. military retain exclusive jurisdiction over all American servicemen in China as a matter of wartime expediency.[132] On May 21, 1943, U.S. and ROC authorities signed an agreement granting the U.S. Army this right for the duration of the war and for a period of six months after hostilities ended, effectively continuing the extraterritorial system supposedly abolished in January.[133]

The ROC government approved the May 1943 Sino-U.S. jurisdiction agreement only after the State Department added a provision emphasizing reciprocal treatment for Chinese forces stationed in "any territory under United States jurisdiction," but some ROC officials still had concerns about the agreement's impact on civilians.[134] The jurist Wang Chonghui, a Yale Law School graduate and secretary-general of the ROC's Supreme National Defense Council, warned that further clarification was needed regarding Chinese powers to arrest GIs, hoping that the agreement would differentiate between U.S. forces' official and off-duty activities.[135] With Wang's warning in mind, the ROC's Legislative Yuan sought to amend the jurisdiction agreement during a September 9, 1943, session to finalize relevant regulations. But the U.S. Army rejected the legislative body's view that U.S. military jurisdiction "did not affect Chinese law regarding the powers to interrogate, apprehend, arrest, detain, search or question any American serviceman who has committed or has been suspected of committing a crime."[136] Uneasy ROC officials understood that the "specter of extraterritoriality" hung over the Sino-U.S. jurisdiction agreement, so they sold it to the Chinese public by comparing it to the agreements on which it was modeled: the 1942 United States of America (Visiting Forces) Act, which exempted American soldiers from criminal prosecution in British courts, and the 1942 National Security

(Allied Forces) Regulations (NSR), which gave the Americans full jurisdiction over their troops stationed in Australia.[137]

But the Sino-U.S. jurisdiction agreement differed in one crucial way from the British and Australia agreements, which permitted the shared policing duties that the ROC's Legislative Yuan tried but failed to obtain. When drafting its proposed September 9 amendment, ROC officials borrowed almost word for word from the Visiting Force Act, which stipulated that the agreement "shall not affect any powers of arrest, search, entry, or custody, exercisable under British law," so long as British authorities then delivered American personnel into U.S. custody.[138] Australia's NSR, meanwhile, gave Australian state police the right to arrest, detain, and investigate American personnel, even for misdemeanors and traffic violations. U.S. military commanders in Australia and Great Britain readily accepted shared policing duties because they recognized that they needed help keeping troops in line and agreed with host country authorities that chaos would ensue if local police had to ignore American crimes and wait for U.S. military police to show up.[139] U.S. military commanders had no such concerns in China, a country Americans had long associated with a racialized absence of law.[140] According to U.S. headquarters in Chongqing, the Sino-U.S. jurisdiction agreement gave Chinese authorities permission to detain GIs only "when an offense has been committed which would be repeated or aggravated if the offender is not taken into custody and then only when United States military authorities are remote from the locality."[141] Because American personnel took liberty in cities and towns near U.S. military installations, the jurisdiction agreement effectively barred Chinese authorities from detaining GIs under any circumstances.

American soldiers showed little respect for powerless Chinese law enforcement personnel. Chinese police or gendarmes who tried to intervene when they saw American soldiers beating up civilians or damaging property could end up getting assaulted themselves, and some GIs attacked police officers without any apparent cause.[142] Lenient discipline in such cases facilitated further misconduct. Three noncommissioned officers, for example, were released without charges after they paid for damages and medical costs following a drunken rampage at a Chongqing retail store, where they also attacked the Chinese police who attempted to stop them.[143] Police and gendarmes learned to avoid GIs altogether as a result of these beatings and other incidents in which American servicemen killed police without any consequences. On May 27, 1944, an American soldier shot a Chinese police officer to death in Kaiyuan, Yunnan, after the officer tried to break up a brawl between four GIs and a group of Chinese civilians. But because the U.S. military court ruled that the civilians had started the fight, the soldier who pulled the trigger was set free.[144]

The American refusal to share policing duties in China resulted in the very situation U.S. authorities had tried to prevent in Australia and Britain by sharing policing duties with local law enforcement: Chinese police had to ignore American crimes and wait for U.S. Army MPs to show up, often while large groups of civilians gathered to watch. In April 1944, Private First Class Norman Byrn spent a half hour destroying merchandise in Lin Sheng's Kunming music store during a drunken stupor before an American MP finally arrived to stop him. "This is only a small store and my whole family depends on this," Lin told investigators, who reported that Byrn broke 402 phonograph records and caused total damages of 530,000 fabi.[145] Just a week later, Sergeant James Gingell attacked a disabled cigarette vendor named Liang Nan in front of Kunming's Nanping Restaurant, located in the city's busiest pedestrian shopping area on Nanping Road, known as "GI Street." Gingell beat Liang in front of a large crowd and broke one of Liang's crutches over the head of the only witness who attempted to intervene: another disabled Chinese street vendor.[146] U.S. military commanders defended their men after such incidents by arguing that the majority of American servicemen were law abiding and respectful, but Chinese witnesses understood these crimes as part of a larger pattern of the U.S. military's disregard for Chinese sovereignty and well-being.

Accepting no help from Chinese police, U.S. military commanders in China failed to adequately supervise their men and punish malfeasance. Penalties for violent crimes against civilians were almost invariably more lenient than those for violent acts committed against fellow soldiers. In February 1945, the same military court that sentenced GIs to six months' hard labor for assaults on fellow American personnel imposed only a onetime $30 forfeiture on the one GI convicted of assaulting a civilian that month.[147] The previous month, technician James Humphries was sentenced to three years' hard labor for assaulting a fellow soldier with a weapon, but Charlie Goodrich, another technician, was given a six-month sentence for hitting a civilian in the face with a wine bottle.[148] In order to deter repeat offenses, Chennault recommended enacting a theater-wide policy to transfer any GI "who became involved in serious difficulties with Chinese civilians or military personnel" out of China, but his proposal never became official policy.[149] In Australia, on the other hand, offenders were often transferred to other areas.[150]

All the factors that facilitated violence against civilians is evidenced in a particularly brutal 1945 murder just outside Kunming. On February 23, Privates John Brennan and James Cooper got drunk at the Army's Ninety-Fifth Station Hospital and left to buy more liquor. Neither man had a pass to leave the hospital, and both had criminal histories. Brennan was a prisoner patient serving a six-month sentence. Cooper had two assault convictions for attacking Chinese, among other charges, and had been released days before after serving just one month of a six-month stint for hitting a Chinese soldier while drunk. After leaving the hospital around noon, they spent four hours drinking at a nearby out-of-bounds village. As the two stumbled back, they noticed an ox belonging to a farmer named Zhang Guoshui and decided to steal it and ride it to the hospital. Zhang, his sister, and his mother, Zhang Guoqing, gave chase. The two GIs attacked them, and a crowd, which included Chinese soldiers, gathered around. The terrified crowd, according to investigators, looked on, "afraid to intervene for fear of being shot or harmed," as Brennan and Cooper used bricks to beat the seventy-one-year-old Zhang Guoqing to death.[151] Although it is true that GIs murdered civilians in other allied countries, Zhang might have lived if Chinese police had the same powers their British and Australian counterparts were granted, or if U.S. authorities had undertaken measures they used elsewhere to prevent recidivism.

Zhang's killing drew nationwide attention and resulted in an uncharacteristically heavy punishment from the theater's judge advocate. Brennan and Cooper were arrested after witnesses followed them back to the hospital and alerted U.S. military police. Neither man denied the crime, but both attempted to "throw full responsibility on the other," according to investigators, who recommended murder charges. Both were sentenced to death, the only GIs in the China theater to receive death sentences for crimes against Chinese. In July, however, their sentences were commuted to life behind bars.[152] Unlike other violent crimes against civilians, Zhang's murder was publicized in Chinese newspapers, which highlighted the guilty verdicts handed down at Brennan's and Cooper's courts-martial as evidence that the U.S. Army took the protection of Chinese lives seriously. But Chinese civilians knew better by then.[153]

In contrast to the U.S. military, Chinese authorities dealt harshly with the handful of civilians who committed violent crimes targeting American troops. A ragtag bandit group comprising civilian militiamen, farmers fleeing conscription, and deserters from China's Eighth Army robbed three U.S. Army convoys in Yunnan between October 1943 and February 1944, injuring one GI.[154] The U.S. Army suspended training programs for Chinese forces after the third attack, which occurred near the town of Kaiyuan on February 19, and demanded swift retaliation. Long Yun had fired four county magistrates in response to the first two attacks and ordered their replacements to exterminate the bandits, but after the third attack, Chiang Kai-shek personally deployed an entire battalion from the Yunnan-Guizhou Pacification Headquarters with orders to eliminate the bandit threat once and for all.[155] These troops killed or captured more than sixty alleged participants in the Kaiyuan robbery. Never again did bandits attack another U.S. convoy.[156] Whereas Chinese officials rarely received anything more than empty assurances from U.S. commanders after deadly accidents and violent crimes against civilians, Y-Force commander Frank Dorn was thoroughly impressed with Chongqing's decisive crackdown, reporting that ROC forces had "taken most energetic steps to rectify this incident."[157]

· · · · · ·

The U.S.-ROC alliance's transformation into a military occupation placed an even heavier burden on civilians than it did on Chinese hostel workers, interpreters, or soldiers. American personnel mistreated hostel staff and interpreting officers, but because these two groups enabled the alliance to operate, U.S. and ROC authorities devoted resources and attention to shoring up their morale. Civilian morale was a lesser concern. No Chinese general ever suggested that U.S. forces shoot pilfering hostel staff—as General Huang Qixiang recommended in response to civilian fuel theft. Chinese soldiers meanwhile took heavy casualties during the Burma campaign and seethed at being treated like junior partners, but U.S. and Chinese military personnel also cooperated on programs that trained, equipped, and fed the ROC's best forces. Civilians benefited from the arrival of the American pilots who helped end Japan's terror bombing campaign, but they did so at the price of bearing the full social impact of the U.S. military presence over nearly four years of compromised sovereignty. Displacement, crime, and accidents caused by U.S. forces left civilians feeling angered and alienated, even if they recognized American contributions to the war effort.

In nearly every engagement between civilians and U.S. forces, GIs got their way, which spread anti-American resentment beyond the Chinese groups who worked alongside U.S. troops in an official capacity. GIs reaped the largest profits from smuggling while bearing few of the risks their civilian co-conspirators or buyers faced, while at the behest of the U.S. military, the ROC government met American land, food, and labor needs, regardless of the impact on the surrounding population. U.S. military commanders fretted over food and working conditions for Chinese interpreters and soldiers, but they treated ordinary civilians as a matter of negligible concern. They gave scant thought—compared to fellow American commanders stationed in Australia or Great Britain—to how GI crimes against civilians might affect the U.S. Army's image. Even as ROC authorities pleaded repeatedly to halt accidents and violent crimes, U.S. commanders did little, except in the most egregious cases, to punish or deter offenders. Thus, while ROC officials tried to protect civilians, the lack of results gave ordinary Chinese the impression that their government was indifferent to their complaints. Meanwhile, U.S. commanders' disdain filtered down the ranks, as GIs dismissed local civilians as indifferent to human life and often treated them accordingly, with few consequences. By spring 1945, memories of AVG P-40s downing Japanese Ki-48 bombers over Kunming had faded. From the perspective of civilians living in southwestern China, speeding U.S. Army jeeps, stray American bullets, and intoxicated GIs now ranked as greater threats to life and limb than the reeling Imperial Japanese Army and Navy.

Chinese civilians contributed to the U.S.-ROC alliance in numerous ways, but their interactions with U.S. forces convinced many American soldiers that *all* Chinese, not merely representatives of the ROC state, were obstacles, rather than partners, in the war effort. The missionary movement and the Luce publishing empire induced GIs to believe they had come to China to save the country. When they encountered difficulties with Chinese counterparts while carrying out their official duties, American servicemen could draw on Stilwell's categorical dismissal of the GMD to explain why Chinese military officers, interpreters, or hostel program staff were obstructing them. This allowed them to continue believing that other Chinese—be they Communists, ordinary soldiers, or the stoic civilians immortalized in United China Relief propaganda—were more amenable to American goals in China. Civilian theft and offensive sensory encounters undermined this assimilationist vision while bolstering the exclusionary racism that underpinned the U.S. Army's callous disregard for Chinese life and ROC sovereignty.

Still, as chapter 5 will detail, sex stood apart as the most contentious form of engagement between GIs and Chinese civilians. Only after this manifestation of the U.S. presence came to be perceived as an imminent threat to both Chinese sovereignty *and* manhood did civilians and other Chinese men finally find a voice with which to push back against their American allies.

5 GIs and Jeep Girls

Sexual Relations

· ·

At around 8:30 P.M. on April 14, 1945, three American soldiers left Chongqing's Sing Sing Café accompanied by three Chinese women. Several Chinese men confronted them as they walked toward Jifang Road, peppering the women with insults. The Americans took offense. A fistfight broke out. By the time police arrived, more than one hundred onlookers had surrounded the GIs and their female companions, pelting them with rocks and other debris.[1]

Over the next few weeks, the same scenario occurred, night after night. Hundreds of Chinese men and teenage boys congregated outside the U.S. Army's favorite Chongqing liberty spots: the Sing Sing, the Sino-Russian Café, and Victory House. Some cursed and spat at the women who fraternized with American personnel. Others pulled their hair, punched them, or hit them with rocks, leading to street brawls. "The general assumption," wrote *Time* correspondent Theodore White, "is that any girl with an American is a prostitute."[2] A Chinese police informant, on the other hand, told U.S. Army investigators that crowds had assembled because of rumors that GIs were molesting "decent girls" in the streets and forcing some women into Jeeps in order to rape them.[3] By early May, these disturbances had spread to Guiyang, Chengdu, and Kunming, while in Chongqing demonstrators were beginning to attack not just the women and soldiers but the American military police and counterintelligence agents who were trying to figure out what was happening.[4]

By spring 1945, the U.S. Army had worn out its welcome in China. The events of the previous years had taken a heavy toll on Sino-American relations. Unappreciative of WASC's costly efforts to keep them housed and fed, American personnel saw the hostel program as a scam. Chinese interpreters and soldiers, for their part, had grown sick of GIs treating them like second-class citizens in their own country. The Chinese civilians who in 1942 had gratefully welcomed U.S. forces as allies against the Japanese now associated the U.S. military presence with inflation, land appropriation, black marketeering, reckless driving, and drunken violence. But as this chapter shows, the backlash against Americans did not turn violent until the first half of 1945, triggered by outrage over sexual relations between American servicemen and Chinese women.

Two interrelated narratives about sexual relations emerged in China that spring. In March, government-backed newspapers began publishing articles, letters, and cartoons about "Jeep girls," an epithet coined to describe the Chinese women who fraternized with American servicemen. Jeep girls, this narrative alleged, rode alongside GIs in the U.S. Army's ubiquitous Jeep 4×4s while looking down on compatriots who bled and labored for the nation. Rather than serve their country, Jeep girls prostituted themselves to American personnel in exchange for luxury goods, comfort, or money. To be a Jeep girl, according to this narrative, was to betray China and relinquish one's womanhood: to become both a traitor and a whore. The second narrative alleged that American soldiers in Jeeps were snatching "respectable" women off the streets and raping them. It first appeared in police reports and street gossip during late 1944, before snowballing into a panic that swept through Southwest China over the months that followed. While one narrative focused on women's behavior and the other on the conduct of American personnel, both portrayed Chinese women's bodies as territory to be recovered, living embodiments of national sovereignty. By mid-April, Chinese men, convinced that women who associated with Americans were either prostitutes or rape victims, began violently confronting GIs and their female companions. The violence proliferated to such an extent that U.S. and ROC authorities were compelled to devise and deploy a Jeep girl counternarrative of their own.

Jeep girls became the channel through which all manifestations of resentment and resistance to the U.S. military presence intersected and converged. They represented the alliance's humiliating asymmetry by symbolizing American dominance over Chinese men. Gender had performed symbolic work in China throughout the late Qing and Republican periods, with male intellectuals and authorities repeatedly invoking the figure of woman in debates about Chinese culture and modernity.[5] The Jeep girl narratives resonated widely in 1945 because so many Chinese men had come to view the U.S. military presence as a threat to patriarchal gender roles and national sovereignty.

As other scholars have noted, sex workers and rape victims rarely speak or represent themselves directly in the historical record, so with few exceptions, such as police records, women appear in this chapter primarily when men wanted to condemn or rescue them.[6] Their silence, however, is crucial to the story. The wartime Jeep girl narratives reduced Chinese women to symbols in a propaganda battle among men seeking to control their sexuality and China's future. With Japan on the ropes, China's allied friends now stood in the way of irreversibly consigning foreign imperialism to the past. Sexual relations were not the alliance's seedy underside but the core site of its tensions during the final six months of the Second World War in Asia.

The Jeep Girl as Prostitute

The U.S. military contributed to the Jeep-girl-as-prostitute narrative by placing Chinese women into a single all-encompassing category: racially unsuited to marriage.[7] At the time of Pearl Harbor, thirty U.S. states enforced anti-miscegenation laws. As American personnel deployed to areas populated by peoples of non-European ancestry, War Department officials feared that a liberal marriage policy would upset this long-standing racial taboo. After all, even though the U.S. government strictly enforced anti-Asian immigration laws, including the Chinese Exclusion Act, American soldiers and military advisors living in China during the interwar years, such as Boatner Carney, still married Chinese women.[8] On June 8, 1942, in a move undertaken explicitly to prevent interracial unions, the War Department issued Circular 179, which stated that no military personnel on duty outside the United States could marry without his commanding officer's approval.[9] When soldiers in China began seeking permission to marry that fall, Raymond Ludden, the American consul in Kunming, informed U.S. Army Chaplain J. E. Tull that U.S. immigration law "specifically prohibited . . . the naturalization of Chinese."[10] Permission from commanding officers in China would not be forthcoming, even though many of them, including Chennault, slept with Chinese women.[11] Marriage policy in the CBI theater, like European colonial policy in Southeast Asia, thus relegated local women to the status of prostitutes or concubines, suited only for servicing sexual needs and preventing carnal relations between men.[12]

The War Department updated its policy after Congress repealed the Chinese Exclusion Act: American personnel contemplating marriage in China would now need to secure the *theater commander's* permission.[13] In contrast, the War Department *relaxed* marriage regulations in Europe, Australia, and New Zealand. Thus, while approximately forty thousand American servicemen married British women in the UK before Germany's surrender, not a single GI got married in China until June 3, 1945, when Wedemeyer allowed Wang Yabo, a Chinese American Fourteenth Air Force sergeant, to marry Zha Hailun, an American-educated clerical assistant employed at SOS headquarters.[14] The Guomindang-connected *Xinwen tiandi* magazine, which had stirred up resentment against Jeep girls during the spring, celebrated the marriage as a triumph of Sino-American friendship.[15] But this tokenistic union actually reinforced existing racial constructs. With her American bachelor's degree and service to the U.S. military in a traditionally female occupation, Zha embodied class and gender traits that buttressed the mid-century American rejection of scientific racism and its replacement with notions about the potential of "nonwhites" to mature into modern societies under American tutelage.[16] The marriage also failed to challenge the miscegenation taboo. More importantly, by deeming all but the smallest fraction of Chinese women as racially unsuited to marriage, U.S. policy made any Chinese woman who associated with American personnel vulnerable to being labeled a prostitute.

The army also tacitly encouraged prostitution among China-bound personnel. While its official guidebooks to Great Britain, Australia, and New Zealand mentioned little about women, its *Pocket Guide to China* enticed GIs with the prospect of exotic sexual adventure.[17] A section titled "Chinese Girls," accompanied by a drawing of a slender, busty, long-legged female dressed in a *qipao* gown, opened, "The modern Chinese girl, in her closely fitting gown, her bare arms and short hair, is often very pretty." The *Pocket Guide* warned against touching "the average Chinese girl" but assured readers they would find "Chinese girls in cabarets and amusements who may be used to free and easy ways."[18] Chinese language specialist Sidney Rittenberg recalled being shocked upon arrival in Kunming when a Chinese base commander "casually mention[ed] that he could get us all the women we wanted."[19] The officer's proposition, however, surely derived from experience with American personnel seeking "free and easy" women after the stifling transport ship journey from California and the perilous Hump flight.[20] The prewar U.S. military presence in China also left each service branch with rich and demeaning lore about Chinese concubines, taxi dancers, and prostitutes—whom American sailors, soldiers, and marines had all referred to as "pigs."[21]

Support for prostitution continued after arrival. The War Department arranged the mass distribution of condoms, while medical staff in China set up chemical prophylaxis stations. Unit commanders exercised indirect control over sex work by labeling certain brothels off limits and prohibiting officers and their men from partaking in sexual services at the same establishments.[22] In August 1942, U.S. forces set up seven military police posts at the "localities most frequented by American troops" in Kunming: four outside restaurants known for attracting sex workers, the other three inside the city's walled red-light district.[23] As more troops arrived, American commanders turned a blind eye when local authorities allowed the establishment of licensed brothels to serve GIs, or when Chinese-run social clubs for American troops—such as Long Yun's United Nations Club—became well-known gathering places for freelance prostitutes.[24] According to the American journalist John Hlavacek, the Fourteenth Air Force even carried out regular medical inspections at one brothel located near a forward airbase.[25] Both Stilwell and Wedemeyer denied that the army condoned prostitution in China in any way, but just one U.S. command—Naval Group China (SACO)—actively enforced an anti-prostitution policy.[26]

One U.S. Army captain actually ran a bordello. According to a provost marshal investigation, Gerald Reed, the base security officer for Kunming, operated an enlisted men's club that "was in fact a brothel." Investigators reported that Reed had collaborated with ex-AVG man and Chinese Air Force advisor Boatner Carney's wife, Rose Mok, to hire a dozen "dancing girls and prostitutes" in Guilin and fly them to Kunming aboard a U.S. Army transport plane. Stilwell placed Reed's club off limits on October 11, 1943, after medical staff confirmed that American personnel had contracted venereal diseases there but before the provost marshal had discovered the full extent of Reed's activities. Reed evaded disciplinary action and soon earned a promotion to major. He also continued to serve as base security officer until the arrival of Wedemeyer.[27] Stilwell did not care if GIs slept with prostitutes, only if they contracted a venereal disease. Chennault, for his part, might have had a hand in Reed's operation. According to rumors circulating around Kunming during the summer of 1943, he "gave personal vocal orders" to Reed to go to Guilin and "round up some girls for a whore house in Kunming."[28] If Chennault was involved, he left no paper trail, but Reed's scheme would have been difficult to pull off without the Fourteenth Air Force commander's tacit support, because aviation fuel shortages grounded Chennault's planes for long stretches during 1943.[29]

Both the War Department and the New Life Movement officially opposed prostitution, but American commanders and local officials in China had little interest in repressing it. This fit larger patterns. The Nationalists made only half-hearted and ineffectual efforts to stamp out prostitution during the Nanjing decade (1927–37).[30] U.S. policy, on the other hand, was of a piece with practices in occupied territories like Italy and France—where GIs ran brothels—and in nonwhite colonial territories including India, Africa, the

FIGURE 5.1 Chinese women and American enlisted men at a badminton exhibition organized for U.S. Army headquarters in Chongqing. (Paul LeRoy Jones Papers, Hoover Institution)

Middle East, and the Caribbean, where local businesses and governments operated brothels for the exclusive use of American troops.[31] In other allied nations, however, U.S. commanders suppressed prostitution while encouraging dating between white men and women, which created an environment more conducive to marriage.[32]

American servicemen in China came into contact with prostitutes more than any other single type of Chinese civilian, but not all interactions between GIs and Chinese women involved sex work, or even sex. More formal interactions connected American personnel with China's Westernized elite. For example, Lianda's Mei Yiqi allowed his daughter Zubin to date AVG pilot Peter Wright under the supervision of a chaperone in 1942.[33] Chinese Women's National Troop Comforting Society officer Tao Zigu (Lucy Chiang) was awarded the U.S. Medal of Freedom, Bronze Palm, for looking after the welfare of American personnel in the Kunming area and teaching them about China (see figure 5.1).[34] On a less formal basis, English-speaking Chinese women employed as clerks and typists for the U.S. Army socialized with American servicemen. Most of these women came from Hong Kong, Shanghai, or Tianjin.[35] According to one civilian employee who worked for the army in Kunming, she and her colleagues attended parties given by American personnel "just to be sociable and to make the party a success."[36] Growing numbers of young Chinese women also began patronizing the businesses catering to U.S. forces in Chongqing, Kunming, Guilin, and other cities. Some even took GIs as boyfriends.[37]

Chinese frowned upon intermarriage and mixing between Western men and Chinese women.[38] Conservative men associated with the New Life Movement, like Huang Jiade, believed that women who patronized dance halls or followed Western trends threatened the traditional social order.[39] Ordinary Sichuanese and Yunnanese also held conservative views about gender relations. To them, only prostitutes drank and socialized with men.[40] Guilin, on the other hand, was China's most open city. Young, well-to-do refugees from Hong Kong mingled with the Chinese artists, writers, and liberals who flocked there because of the city's autonomy from Chongqing.[41] According to Graham Peck, who ran Guilin's Office of War Information office, GIs enjoyed Guilin "mainly because of its swarms of pretty and often willing girls."[42]

Even in Guilin, however, patience with libidinous American personnel soon wore thin. Women from privileged backgrounds, according to Peck, were warned "to stop seeing so much of Americans," while local tabloids began printing "scandalous news about American aviators and their lady friends."[43] On March 15, 1944, an unattributed op-ed in the *Guangxi ribao*, Guilin's leading newspaper, channeled the "New Woman" discourse popular among prewar reformist intellectuals to attack women who patronized dance halls with American personnel: "These women . . . are not winning glory for China's New Women, they are humiliating them."[44] With conservatives, liberals, and ordinary folk all offended by the mixing between GIs and Chinese women, the Jeep-girl-as-prostitute narrative was beginning to take shape.

Guilin fell to the Japanese on November 11, but public interaction increased sharply over the winter in more conservative Sichuan and Yunnan, which caused resentment to boil over. The Ichigo offensive triggered a new refugee flow and the war's worst inflation, making more women dependent on GIs to earn a livelihood.[45] Kunming's food prices doubled in January alone, and by summer it took 3,250 fabi to purchase a single dollar on Chongqing's black markets, up from 470 in January.[46] Prostitution offered a harsh but available safety net, both symbolizing and shaping the ever more lopsided balance of power between China and the United States. Demand for sex work also increased because U.S. Army troop strength in China

FIGURE 5.2 The Nanping Theater on "GI Street," downtown Kunming. (James B. Hinchliff Collection, Institute on World War II and the Human Experience, Florida State University)

climbed from 27,739 at the beginning of December to over 58,000 in early June.[47] American buying power soared to new heights as well. By June, American privates earned $60 per month—ten times more than full Chinese generals.[48] As Huang Shang wrote, "They were naturally quite a catch" for sex workers.[49] Compared to soldiers from other countries during World War II, Americans were more powerful and attractive, invariably enjoying higher salaries, a better diet, more comfortable housing, and privileged access to black-market commodities. These disparities were more pronounced in China than in other U.S.-allied countries, even before inflation skyrocketed in early 1945.

Prostitutes flooded the streets wherever American personnel congregated during the war's final year, especially after Ichigo, heightening American arrogance and forcing Chinese men to recognize their relative weakness. Kunming's Nanping Theater area (see figure 5.2), downtown Chongqing around Minsheng and Minzhu Roads, and what remained of bombed-out Baoshan became unofficial red-light districts, bringing to Southwest China the riotous atmosphere of Shanghai's prewar French Concession—minus the glamour—and auguring the postwar camp towns outside U.S. bases in the Philippines and South Korea.[50] "The soliciting is more open here than in India," wrote intelligence officer Arthur Clark after he arrived in Kunming. "Many people who know little English have nonetheless mastered a few obscene expressions."[51] Pimps and streetwalkers accosted American troops anytime they entered these towns, even though the New Life Movement ostensibly barred prostitution in Chongqing.[52] Easy access to cheap sex reinforced American views of the Chinese as a subservient, pitiful people. Chinese men knew it, too. "It left a deep impression on me," wrote Huang Shang, upon seeing an American soldier with his arms around a girl "who couldn't have been more than sixteen or seventeen, too young to wear makeup but dressed in Western clothes, looking so pitiful and skinny next to her foreign boyfriend. . . . To think," he grieved, "that China had to rely on these women to 'promote harmonious diplomatic relations.'"[53]

The Chinese press began carrying stories attacking Jeep girls in early 1945. These articles implied that the Jeep girls' behavior served as a barometer for national decline. "Our Jeep girls," Zhu Junle wrote in the March 20 issue of *Xinwen tiandi*, walked around Chongqing with purses full of "French perfume, Three Flowers powder, and Tangee brand lipstick . . . foreign sentiment making them look down on everything: black-haired, black-eyed, yellow-skinned everything.[54] On May 2, the Chengdu edition of the Guomindang's *Central News Daily* published a letter that leveled similar charges: "You women, you are forfeiting everything! Soldiers bleed at the front lines as people in the rear areas sweat and toil." Chinese women, the author fumed, ought to attend to Chinese men: "Officers and men on the front lines are waiting for you . . . will you serve them?"[55] On May 3, Kunming's *Zhengyi bao*, a newspaper backed by Long Yun's provincial government, blasted Jeep girls for "snigger[ing] at her fellow country folks and flirt[ing] with foreigners."[56] The Kunming edition of the Guomindang's *Central Daily News* reported that "starved coolies" were lying in the streets as Jeep girls gushed over gifts from their "GI friends."[57] Less derisive pieces still portrayed the women in a negative light, though one editorial suggested that "they be given medals for helping bring in American gold dollars to balance the budget."[58] These articles echoed portrayals of the "modern girl" from the 1930s: the deceitful, greedy, and reckless young women who idolized the West and threatened China's national strength (see figure 5.3).[59]

Graham Peck interpreted the campaign against Jeep girls as a "much stronger indirect attack on the Americans," a conclusion endorsed by other scholars, but its core aim was to reappropriate women's bodies from American soldiers.[60] Female voices were conspicuously absent. An exposé in the April 20 edition of the *Xinwen tiandi*, supposedly written by "a real Jeep

FIGURE 5.3 *Lively Jeep Girls*: three images from a larger series titled *Allied Soldiers in Chongqing*. (*Xinwen tiandi*, 1945)

girl" named Shen Lusha, was more likely than not a male-authored satire intended to stir up further resentment: "Shen" spent two pages gushing over the luxury goods, cash, and extra rations that "Harry," her "international love," showered her with each month.[61] Like the interwar debates about China's "New Woman," the furor over Jeep girls was a male affair.[62]

So-called Jeep girls fraternized with American personnel for many reasons. Although power relations were unequal, these women still exercised agency. Refugees from Hong Kong shared their tastes in popular culture: they saw nothing wrong with going out to dance after work. For less privileged women, selling sex to GIs was perhaps the least unsavory choice among a handful of poor options—more lucrative than farming or labor at Chongqing's accident-ridden cotton mills.[63] Because of American wealth, even a civil servant's wife who occasionally dabbled in prostitution could earn more in ten minutes than her husband did in ten days.[64] Publications about Jeep girls elided these distinctions.

The Jeep-girl-as-prostitute narrative resonated because it soothed injured masculinity. During the war's final year, inflation decimated the incomes of public employees and men who held prestigious jobs. Professors, journalists, and civil servants became destitute as they watched pimps, smugglers, and black marketeers rise in the new social order.[65] They also witnessed their female compatriots become dependent on a foreign army with a long history of racist relationships with local civilians.[66] Jeep girls, from their perspectives, embodied a greater social disruption than the lower-class men whose standing rose during the war because they transgressed class, gender, and racial norms. These women, who had suffered no less from the war than men had, became scapegoats. Press censorship precluded direct criticism of the government and the U.S. military, but women were easier prey. The narrative's origin in government-backed papers, however, revealed both high-level frustration with the American presence and lower-level discontent at how the GMD had enabled Americans—and the women who fraternized with them—to behave. But this narrative had limited explanatory power when it came to addressing unwanted sexual advances by American personnel, a phenomenon that anyone who spent time near hostels or liberty spots became familiar with.

The Jeep Girl as Rape Victim

The second Jeep girl narrative relied on a more or less accurate rendering of American troops' propensity for sexism, racism, and sexual violence. Recent histories of World War II show that American servicemen committed widespread sexual misconduct around the globe, ranging from aggressive heckling to rape.[67] In China, excessive drinking mixed with racialized sexual entitlement, impunity, and contempt toward local men fueled harassment and violence against women. This fit the U.S. military's global pattern. According to the provost marshal at Kunming's Wujiaba Airfield, "Ninety-five percent of all violations were the result of the use of alcohol in some degree"—a statement that would have rung true nearly anywhere U.S. forces were deployed.[68] Sexualized masculinity, the belief that any woman on the street was fair game, and the encouragement of macho involvement in sexual activity epitomized by General George S. Patton's saying, "A man who won't fuck, won't fight," was another global phenomenon, common not only to U.S. forces but to military organizations regardless of nationality.[69] And of course U.S. forces stationed anywhere outside the United States, not just in China, were exempt from local laws, which facilitated misconduct. Finally, the scorn Chinese men experienced when interacting with GIs would have been familiar to men around the world, even within the United States, where American troops swaggered around New York City "just to show the slackers and café society toffs" that they "were real men on a real mission."[70]

While none of these ingredients were unique to China, the specific racial and power dynamics operating there made the mix uniquely explosive.

GIs at liberty in Australia did plenty of drinking, but they could also spend time at various social and sporting clubs. Welfare organizations set up popular activities for them on a far larger scale than anything WASC or the Chinese Women's National Troop Comforting Society could carry out, including kangaroo hunts and sailing trips. Civilians often invited them into their homes.[71] Britain had similar opportunities, plus effective joint institutional mechanisms for fostering cordial grassroots relations.[72] In China, on the other hand, despite Huang Renlin's best efforts, everything but eggs, alcohol, and sex workers was in short supply. With its lack of recreational options, China was more like Normandy under U.S. occupation than Britain or Australia. Sexualized masculinity among U.S. forces in China was also similar to that in France, where U.S. authorities promoted liberation as an opportunity for sexual conquest. But whereas sexual violence in France was exacerbated by the belief that battlefield victory entitled GIs to the sexual prerogatives of conquest, relatively few American personnel in China had experienced combat; in other words, they did not lash out at women due to post-traumatic stress.[73] Racial difference in China also influenced how American soldiers viewed women. Mary Krauss, a white army nurse serving near Kunming, told her parents that she had "fifty times as many chances to go out on dates and parties as a popular college sorority girl. . . . After all, there aren't many American gals in China."[74] White GIs might have considered French women easy and immoral, but they still saw them as fellow whites, not "pigs." The racial gap permitted American personnel to treat Chinese women as even more expendable.[75]

Legal impunity and the disregard for local men were also more pronounced in China. Lenient military courts, easygoing MPs, and Chinese police without arrest powers all played a role. American personnel in China also belonged to a dizzying array of commands, which left Chinese "bewildered" about where to take their complaints.[76] Unless American MPs caught suspects red-handed, Chinese allegations usually flowed up the chain of command to Chongqing, where FAB passed them to U.S. Army headquarters. This process could take two or three months. And because the Americans looked down on Chinese men, they did not take them seriously. When rapes occurred in Britain and Australia, U.S. commanders opened military courts to the press.[77] In France, U.S. authorities publicly hanged twenty-nine convicted rapists near the scene of their crimes to show locals that the army took sexual assault seriously.[78] Nothing similar happened in China, despite the central role of extraterritoriality in Chinese historical memory. And as other chapters have illustrated, the army's top-down disdain for the Chinese filtered through the ranks. Chinese men's poverty, smaller stature, and race all reinforced common perceptions that they were third-rate men. GIs might have hurled racist insults at Maori sailors and hit on Frenchwomen in front of their boyfriends, but they did so knowing that a fistfight might result.[79] The idea that Chinese men might fight back rarely entered their heads. Extraterritoriality, as Robert Bickers shows, left Americans in China confident that they could get away with just about anything.[80]

These troubling dynamics were apparent from the U.S. military's earliest days in Southwest China. The twenty-four sailors of the USS *Tutuila*, a Yangtze Patrol gunboat that became stranded in Chongqing before Pearl Harbor, made the police blotter frequently in 1940. On July 18, four of them beat passersby with glass bottles and harassed women outside Chongqing's centrally located Cathay Theater during an evening of heavy drinking.[81] Complaints about the sailors' continued misconduct led to another police investigation that fall. "Every night without exception," Detective Zong Yongyu concluded in his final October 18 report, "these sailors indulge in food, wine, women, and gambling." While intoxicated, Zong noted, they sometimes shoved sex workers into the Yangtze River.[82] Chongqing police could do nothing but protest to the U.S. embassy. After Pearl Harbor, soldiers on Stilwell's staff demonstrated similar proclivities. On October 7, 1942, two armed and intoxicated GIs trashed the *Shishi xinbao* newspaper office on Chongqing's Liziba Road, breaking windows, firing off rounds, and assaulting a *Central Daily News* deliveryman who happened upon them. Zhang Wanli, the paper's manager, told police that drunk American personnel "frequently stood at the intersection [outside the office] in groups of more than ten to harass women and disrupt traffic."[83]

Over the next few years, Chinese authorities reported occasional sexual assaults and attacks against Chinese men by GIs seeking prostitutes, but accusations increased sharply after the Ichigo campaign. By December 1944, "frequent late-night public drunkenness by American servicemen" looking for prostitutes had become a "threat to public safety," according to Chongqing police chief Tang Yi.[84] On January 26, He Haoruo forwarded Wedemeyer two police reports about sexual misconduct in nearby Baishiyi, including the first allegations about GIs using a Jeep when attempting to rape and kidnap a Chinese woman. According to the first report, Army Air Force personnel had "dragged a respectable lady" into their Jeep on October 20 "and made away with her" before Chinese guards forced them to release her. The second report alleged that American personnel were engaged in daily sexual misconduct, "roam[ing] about the streets of Baishiyi in the evening, try[ing] to get women by fair means or foul," sometimes going "so far as to knock at the doors of respectable citizens in their search for objects of desire, not hesitating to use firearms as a method of intimidation." If misconduct persisted, Chongqing gendarmerie headquarters warned, "this state of affairs may lead to untoward incidents in which the safety of American personnel may well be involved."[85] Wedemeyer promised to investigate, and Tang obtained U.S. military police assistance in carrying out joint patrols in Chongqing. But sexual misconduct continued.[86]

Officials like Tang and He had no alternative but to seek help from U.S. military authority figures, who were part of the problem. Of all the U.S. units stationed in China, only SACO enforced strict regulations to prevent sex crimes and misunderstandings. Milton Miles forbade "the public display of the sexual urge or any affection however slight toward any woman in China" and ordered severe disciplinary measures against violators.[87] Army units had no such policies. FAB deputy director Wang Shimin complained in March 1945 that instead of helping Tang rein in unruly GIs, U.S. Army military police actually flouted Chongqing's regulations against keeping prostitutes away from military facilities.[88] At around the same time in Kunming, Private Fred Mason, a member of the military police company that guarded Wujiaba, twice assaulted Chinese sentries who attempted to stop American troops from bringing prostitutes into the installation. After Wedemeyer replaced Gerald Reed as base security officer, a provost marshal investigation into Mason's conduct revealed that "military police had frequently and deliberately allowed prostitutes to enter the airfield."[89]

Commanders more senior than Reed also set poor examples, sending a clear message to the men in the ranks. Back in October, Lieutenant Colonel Raymond Wheeler, the commander of U.S. forces at Yunnanyi Airbase, drank heavily while standing at the back of the stage in full view of fifteen hundred American personnel attending a USO show. Wheeler twice interrupted the show, once bringing a donkey onstage, and a junior officer under his command tried to enter actress Jinx Falkenburg's dressing tent while completely naked.[90] Another lieutenant colonel, Harry McAleenan of the Chinese-American Composite Wing at Baishiyi, caused disturbances on consecutive nights in early May at Chongqing's Victory House, a hotel that catered to senior U.S. officers and served as the center of social life for the city's Chinese elite. On May 11, he drunkenly berated enlisted military police in front of Chinese guests, demanding they take him to a brothel. On the evening of May 12, Chinese attending a charity dance ball at Victory House were interrupted by a crying woman displaying bite marks on her skin. McAleenan, she asserted, had bitten her, beat her up, and refused to pay her for sex. Just thirty minutes later, another sex worker interrupted the ball after suffering a beating at the hands of a American army officer.[91]

Violence was a possibility whenever American personnel went looking for sex, especially if alcohol was involved. Intoxicated GIs searching for prostitutes barged into houses all around Yunnan. An American sergeant killed a man named Wang Anlin near Dali on December 19 after breaking into his home while searching for a brothel. The local police commander reported that Wang's wife agreed not to file charges after the sergeant paid her 50,000 fabi—seventeen dollars for her husband's life.[92] A few weeks later outside Baoshan, the next major town after Dali on the Burma Road, four American enlisted men rampaged through a village. Drunk on homemade liquor, they shot out locks and eaves on random houses, kicked down doors, killed farm animals, stole food, and struck a Chinese in the face with a rifle butt. The four had entered the village to find a comrade who had separated from the group earlier because "he wanted a girl."[93] American investigators discovered similar incidents near Yangkai Airbase in January.[94] Outside Yunnan, Baishiyi remained a hotbed of complaints through the winter and into the spring, with reports of GIs "molesting Chinese women" in their homes.[95] He Haoruo also forwarded to Wedemeyer rape allegations against American personnel in Sichuan and Hunan.[96]

GIs at times committed heinous acts of sexual violence. At around midnight on February 24, three intoxicated enlisted men—Harvey Miller, James Daffin, and Harold Hughes—entered a village near Yangkai Airbase to search for prostitutes. After forcing their way into two houses but leaving after the occupants "rais[ed] considerable hell," they kicked open the door to the home of a farmer named Yang Zhengcai. The three beat Yang with clubs and a bottle of rum. Daffin dragged Yang's wife to a nearby rice paddy, where he and Miller raped her. Hughes tried to rape the couple's nine-year-old daughter, but she resisted. Hughes then left her alone in the rice paddy and raped her mother. The three fled when they saw Jeep headlights approaching: a village magistrate had alerted the base. They evaded the MPs that night but confessed to the crime a week later after medics reported that Miller and Hughes were the only men to have taken prophylactics at the base dispensary on February 24. All three were sentenced to just six months' hard labor.[97] These short sentences belied the *Pocket Guide to China*'s claim that Americans treated "the Chinese as we treat any of our allies, and that we respect them as human beings on an equality with ourselves."[98] They were also far more lenient than the twenty-year sentences handed down by the same military court for a similar gang rape in India in June 1944, which also occurred during a home invasion and involved an aggravated assault on the victim's husband. In India, however, the perpetrators were Black.[99]

Other allegations were less clear-cut, some even fabricated, which reinforced American doubts about Chinese credibility. Proving rape in U.S. military court required evidence that sexual penetration had occurred and that the victim had resisted to the full extent that she was able.[100] Such evidence was difficult—if not impossible—to obtain weeks or months after an alleged crime had transpired. The provost marshal's criminal investigation division (CID) dismissed the reports from Baishiyi that He Haoruo had passed to Wedemeyer for this reason.[101] CID agents also concluded that prevalent rumors of Americans raping and murdering a girl near Baishiyi on April 25 stemmed from jealousy "over the fact that Americans have been seen with prostitutes and other Chinese women."[102]

Reporting delays and a lack of detailed evidence, such as license plate numbers, immediately raised red flags, but even timely, well-substantiated allegations could be dubious. On February 27, criminal investigators in Baoshan had both a license plate number and four suspects' names after Ma Weihan and his wife, Shagwan, reported that GIs in a Jeep had raped Shagwan the previous night. When pressed during questioning later that day, however, Shagwan admitted to sleeping with the Americans "of her own free will," while Ma, for his part, confessed to concocting the story in anger because one of the GIs had slapped him as they haggled over the price for sex with his wife.[103] From the provost marshal's perspective, some sexual violence, broadly in proportion with troop strength, was inevitable. But CID agents did not believe that the uptick in allegations indicated a worrisome increase in sex crimes. Chinese jealousy at GIs' success with local women, misunderstanding of loutish American behavior, or a desire for financial compensation were more plausible explanations.

While the vagueness of police reports and a few false rape accusations were sufficient to allow the army's criminal investigators to claim that nothing was amiss, rape hysteria was spreading. Economic desperation had compelled many Chinese, including Ma Weihan and Shagwan, to prostitute themselves or their partners to GIs—a harrowing, humiliating experience, particularly as the U.S. military's reputation deteriorated. The increase in fraternization alone generated deep indignation, tinged with Chinese racism and xenophobia, but as many of these experiences demonstrated, carousing could turn violent quickly. And while communication problems delayed the transmission of Chinese police reports, it could also take weeks or months for U.S. headquarters to reply, which gave the impression of American indifference.

Rumors thrive when a dearth of reliable information combines with fear.[104] By early May, these rumors had crept into both the Communist and the Nationalist Party–controlled press. "Many women are being dragged away to be 'Jeep girls' and deflowered," warned *Xiandai funv* (Modern woman), a progressive feminist biweekly edited by underground CCP members.[105] On May 13, the Guomindang's *Central News Daily* printed a letter to the editor threatening that "disturbances beyond imagination would arise" unless Chongqing stopped GIs from dragging women off the city's streets in their Jeeps, which the author claimed was happening "every night."[106]

Backlash

Chinese men began lashing out in mid-April, nearly a month before the *Central Daily News* printed a letter alleging nightly kidnappings, but these men targeted women, not Americans. The April 14 confrontation outside Chongqing's Sing Sing Café touched off weeks of similar incidents outside the city's liberty spots, where insults and physical violence against the women who fraternized with American personnel sometimes led to larger brawls. By ridiculing and assaulting so-called Jeep girls, men in Chongqing carried out their own version of France's *tonte* ritual, in which Frenchmen reasserted their masculinity and the virility of France itself by shaving the heads and ripping the clothes of women who had slept with German soldiers.[107]

As angry men humiliated Jeep girls in Chongqing, a U.S. Army counterintelligence investigation confirmed widespread anger about fraternization and panic over rape. Chinese-speaking counterintelligence agents Pardee Lowe and Andrew Lee spent two weeks on the case. On April 23, together with a high-ranking informant from the Chongqing Police Bureau, they sifted through a crowd of some five hundred people gathered outside the Sino-Russian Café on Minzhu Road, opposite the Sing Sing. The mob, according to the police informant, comprised "street urchins, shoe-shine boys, and street loiterers" who had assembled because of rumors that GIs were forcing women into Jeeps and molesting "decent girls" in the streets. But upon seeing women fraternizing with the Americans, the men began cursing them for "making money from foreigners in wicked ways."[108] Lowe and Lee also talked with ordinary civilians, police officers, and Chinese employed by the U.S. Army, none of whom had joined the liberty spot crowds, who reported witnessing American personnel abducting or attempting to abduct Chinese women. Two workers at the Li Xin Industrial shop, for example, claimed to have seen GIs trying to force women into Jeeps outside the Cathy and Wei Theaters each night, while a sweets dealer described a successful kidnapping involving three GIs in a Jeep on April 30. The agents could not confirm any of these allegations, but if left unchecked, Lowe and Lee warned, the panic could threaten the war effort.[109]

The army's counterintelligence section concluded that American misconduct lay at the root of the crisis. Poor behavior had been on their radar for some time. Lowe and Lee had actually started investigating tensions over sexual relations in late March, after a Chinese colonel stabbed a drunk American sergeant who had kicked down his door searching for a brothel.[110] Between just March 31 and April 9, Lowe and Lee confirmed incidents of intoxicated GIs molesting women in public, trashing shops and restaurants, crashing parties, starting a drunken brawl at Victory House, and harassing high-ranking Chinese officers.[111] On April 25, two days after mingling with the crowd outside the Sino-Russian Café, Lowe reported that American personnel in the Chongqing area "have recently committed every major offense that visitors to a foreign country are capable of performing," including rape.[112]

The counterintelligence section's final report, submitted to Wedemeyer on May 5, divided violations into four categories: inconsideration, offensive boisterousness, drunkenness, and law breaking. One-third of American personnel in the China theater, the agents estimated—approximately eighteen thousand men—were violators in one or more categories. "Boisterousness," as they defined it, included making lewd and vulgar remarks toward women, while "drunkenness" encompassed accosting women in public—an action that could involve physical assault. While counterintelligence agents insisted that such behaviors would be "entirely expected and strike no discord" in the United States—a dubious assumption—in China they intensified fears of sexual assault.[113] Most GIs who made vulgar remarks toward women or accosted them in the streets had no intention of committing rape, but that was not always clear to victims and bystanders, whether or not they understood English.

American misconduct and resentment against women triggered the Jeep girl crisis, but large crowds could not have congregated for weeks on end outside Chongqing's liberty spots without tacit approval from Dai Li's secret police. According to Dai's onetime protégé Shen Zui, some twenty thousand Juntong agents, informers, and runners worked in Chongqing. Juntong field officers, the most feared men in the city, operated inspection posts in every conceivable public facility. When antigovernment protests broke out in February, Dai's agents and other secret police suppressed them ruthlessly. They could have done the same with the liberty spot crowds if Dai had ordered them to. After all, the Juntong Social Investigations Group, a two-hundred-man force full of street thugs and petty criminals tasked with keeping social order in Chongqing, was run out of a hotel on Minsheng Road, just steps from Victory House, where many Juntong runners also worked as waiters. Most other restaurants and cafés had formal Juntong connections, so Dai's men would have known about any public incident involving American personnel in downtown Chongqing.[114]

The Juntong role in spreading rumors or inciting mob violence is less clear. The key archival files—the Chongqing Garrison Command's Investigations Department—are incomplete. But historical precedent and circumstantial evidence offer some clues. The Chinese had long associated Westerners with sexual lewdness, and local elites had used rape rumors to mobilize anti-British resistance during the First Opium War: the crowds that challenged British forces near Guangzhou were neither spontaneous nor peasant led, as later histories insisted.[115] The demographic profile Lowe and Lee's police informant identified on April 23 matched both the Juntong Social Investigations Group and Dai's preference for employing petty criminals and unemployed youth in street-level secret operations.[116] The Juntong also undertook an investigation of the liberty spot crowds at the counterintelligence section's request, which concluded that the demonstrators were all gainfully employed—perhaps an effort to throw investigators off the scent.[117] And while Dai gained power from his cordial partnership with the U.S. Navy, other Juntong members might have acted on their own initiative. Agents liked to throw their weight around, runners were poorly disciplined, and the Social Investigations Group operated without direct contact with Juntong headquarters.[118] At the very least, Juntong agents turned a blind eye, which facilitated and encouraged the demonstrations.

The situation outside Chongqing, however, where the Juntong wielded less authority, looked no better. Crowds blocked the paths of Jeeps and harassed women accompanying American servicemen in Chengdu, Guiyang, and Kunming, where GIs also clashed with local men over interactions with female students at Yunnan University.[119] On April 23, two intoxicated enlisted men with lengthy rap sheets and histories of violence against Chinese beat an elderly woman to death in front of a large crowd outside Kunming.[120] Friction over sexual relations also compelled U.S. authorities to place most of Baoshan off limits as of April 28.[121] On May 10, according to Chinese military sources, intoxicated GIs stationed at Laifeng Airfield near the Hunan-Sichuan border attempted to kidnap the wife of a local restaurant owner.[122] Two days later, U.S. Army censors obtained a letter from a Chinese stationed in Guizhou addressed to a comrade in India: "Two girls of my department were surrounded by a group of American soldiers who tried to drag them away. The girls got away when twenty or more boy students came to their rescue. . . . Any girl who is now seen riding in a Jeep with Americans should be ostracized."[123]

It did not take long before crowds began targeting U.S. troops directly, which forced Wedemeyer's hand. On May 8, several men assaulted an American major with the navy attaché office after he stopped to help rescue children from a house fire. A Chinese woman had been sitting in his Jeep, and she claimed that Chinese police and firemen participated in the assault.[124] Three days later, Chinese men armed with sticks and rocks attacked P. B. Smitty, an American MP on joint patrol with Chinese gendarmes. "The United States provides China with arms and equipment, and the Americans serving here get paid back with rocks and clubs," said Smitty after the attack.[125] A counterintelligence agent was hit with a rock while driving a Jeep the next evening, noting in this report that "it can be seen in the absence of girls, the resentment was transferred to any occupant of any Jeep."[126]

The Counternarrative

On May 16, Wedemeyer sent out a memo addressed to all American personnel in the China theater. "Public incidents which discredit America in the eyes of the Chinese," he warned, "have been increasing to an alarming degree in the last month or two." Little things, he wrote, such as yelling, public drinking, and slapping strangers on the back had lowered Americans "in Chinese public opinion to a noticeable degree." More serious were the behaviors Wedemeyer believed had caused Chinese men to lash out in Chongqing: "Accosting women in public places, often very offensively and in the presence of an escort. Public appearances with notorious prostitutes; fast and reckless driving—noisy joy-riding with cheap women sometimes in Army cars or Jeeps; drunkenness to the point of actually passing out in public; over-bearing and arrogant attitudes toward Chinese officers or police who are doing their duty." Present conditions, he warned, "cannot and will not be allowed to continue." Although Wedemeyer blamed a "small minority" of GIs rather than a full third of American personnel, his memo reflected the counterintelligence section's conclusions, admitting that sexual misconduct had caused Sino-American relations to deteriorate.[127]

In his May 18 memo to Chiang, however, Wedemeyer blamed the crisis on an anti-American newspaper campaign. Newspaper accounts alleging sex crimes, he told Chiang, were unduly vague and impossible to verify. "We cannot help but suspect that some undesirable elements are using this as a pretext for anti-American activity," he charged. In reality, he wrote, "Americans hold Chinese women in the highest regard. . . . The great majority of cases in which Chinese women have felt disrespected have stemmed from cultural differences." Wedemeyer conceded that some Americans had caused trouble, but he assured Chiang that he had taken measures to halt the misconduct. Now he wanted Chiang to use his Ministry of Information to make sure newspapers portrayed American soldiers "in the most positive rather than the most negative light." Failure to bring the press into line, Wedemeyer warned, would lead to serious consequences, and his men "would retaliate against embarrassment at the hands of crowds."[128]

Whatever the Guomindang's involvement in stirring up resentment and turning a blind eye toward anti-American demonstrators, Chiang immediately cracked down. From Chiang's perspective, U.S.-ROC military cooperation had reached unprecedented heights in mid-1945, so his dependence on the U.S. Army gave him little choice but to make Wedemeyer's demands his top priority.[129] But by investing his shrinking political resources in placating this American envoy rather than addressing the concerns of his own people, Chiang continued the downward spiral of repression that exacerbated opposition to Guomindang rule within China and among the U.S. State Department and the American press.[130]

Chiang's Ministry of Information promoted a new Jeep girl narrative, one diametrically opposed to the story that had defined the past two months. Rigid censorship was necessary, Chiang told Chongqing mayor He Yaozu, because "regardless of whether or not [allegations regarding Jeep girls] were the result of instigation by traitors, they had a negative influence on the feelings of American military personnel."[131] Rape rumors disappeared from Guomindang-backed newspapers, which now belittled the "unreasonable people" and "angry rumormongers" offended by fraternization.[132] The Office of Strategic Services (OSS) assisted Chiang by syndicating articles from *Damei wanbao* (*Shanghai Evening Post and Mercury*), an OSS-run black, or secret, propaganda outlet.[133] A column in the May 20 issue of *Liangzhou pinglun* (Fortnightly comment), for example, refuted the rape allegations published in the *Central Daily News* on May 13 and compared the behavior of the "howling mobs of hoodlums" in Chongqing to "Japs running amuck."[134] China's highest-selling magazine, *Xi feng* (West wind), echoed Wedemeyer's claim that "cultural differences," rather than American misconduct, led Chinese to assume the worst about GIs' intentions toward women.[135] And instead of seeing "Jeep girls" as symbols of national decline, authors now touted the benefits of fraternization. Intermarriage between GIs and Chinese women, the Cornell-educated agronomist Dong Shijin wrote in *Da gong bao* (L'impartial) on May 25, would aid the war effort and "the friendship between the two countries because no relationship is closer than marriage."[136]

Mayor He Yaozu and FAB director He Haoruo held a press conference at Chiang's behest on May 26 to reinforce this new narrative—at Victory House of all places. The FAB director told the incredulous Chinese journalists gathered at the U.S. Army's favorite liberty spot that "the Allied [American] troops that have come to China are noted for their strict observance of discipline, and their friendly feeling and polite behavior toward the Chinese people are especially well-known."[137] The mayor repeated similar absurdities in a *Da gong bao* editorial the next day, stressing that Sino-American cooperation was "especially" gratifying in Chongqing. Most GIs, he wrote, "by giving our girls a lift in their Jeeps, are simply helping the girls—a chivalrous act that merits emulation."[138] The two men expressed more nuanced views outside the public eye. He Haoruo passed sexual misconduct and other crime allegations to Wedemeyer almost daily, while the mayor told the director of Chongqing's Social Affairs Bureau on May 29 that GIs caused "almost constant trouble," especially at places like Victory House, because they "lacked proper entertainment facilities."[139]

Chiang also turned his security forces, including the Juntong, against anyone who made liberty inconvenient for American personnel. Citing P. B. Smitty, the American MP attacked in Chongqing on May 11 while on a joint patrol with Chinese gendarmes, Chiang vowed to stamp out both anti-American demonstrations and price gouging.[140] To prevent anti-American mobs from forming, English-speaking foreign affairs police would accompany U.S. military police on crowd-control duty.[141] Police also posted English speakers at each substation.[142] On May 27, theaters began showing slideshows warning people to keep clear of American soldiers or face severe punishment. Paramilitaries from the Peace Preservation Corps began reinforcing the police who protected American liberty spots, and posters went up around the city advising parents that they would be held responsible if minor children bothered American personnel.[143] To prevent price gouging, gendarmes and Juntong agents from the garrison command headquarters began joint patrols on June 15. Any business that charged American customers more than Chinese customers, or did not mark prices using Arabic numerals, would be shut down.[144]

To reverse declining support for the U.S. military among his own armed forces, Chiang drew on the same playbook he had used to address interpreter morale problems. On May 27, he ordered the Chinese Army to "spare no effort in giving cooperation to our allied friends." The Americans, he said, should be emulated for their discipline and "respect for women."[145] These orders were quoted from the National Military Council's lengthy publication *Ruhe zhidao guanbing yu mengjun xiangchu* (How to guide our troops to get along with allied soldiers), which also assured Chinese servicemen that "Americans held up women at an unimaginable level."[146] Meanwhile, Mayor He discussed a plan with security forces and city government representatives for educating police, gendarmes, and civil servants about cultural differences in gender relations between China and the United States.[147]

Wedemeyer lent a hand in propagating this new narrative during his final weekly press conference for the month of May. He told Chinese journalists that men in France and England had also attacked local women for fraternizing with GIs. American personnel "were the best paid soldiers in the world," said Wedemeyer. They liked spending money, and women around the globe found them attractive. Wedemeyer implied that Chinese men might have similar luck in the United States because people were naturally attracted to foreigners. Many fights had broken out between American and British soldiers undergoing training together in Alabama because of local women's preference for the latter.[148] Wedemeyer avoided mentioning another related global phenomenon: widespread sexual misconduct by American personnel.

Chiang's and Wedemeyer's counternarrative revealed the conspicuous inequality between the two allies while providing fodder for the generalissimo's domestic critics. Wedemeyer declined to take Chiang into his confidence and instead pushed him into taking measures that undermined his own position in China. By branding all Chinese who took offense at American misconduct as ignorant or treacherous, Chiang alienated large swaths of the Chinese populace, including his own soldiers, police, and secret agents. Tightening control over the press may have halted publication of unsubstantiated sex crime rumors, but it also weakened trust in the government.

Printing outright lies about the harmonious state of Chinese-American relations in Chongqing did not alter reality: the image of well-disciplined GIs placing women on a pedestal was so at odds with what ordinary Chinese had observed around the country that few people could have taken such articles, or the National Military Council's *Ruhe zhidao guanbing yu mengjun xiangchu*, seriously. In doing everything Wedemeyer wanted and trusting the American general to weed out misconduct, Chiang wagered on the American general's ability to produce quick and decisive results.

Chiang's throw of the dice failed to pay off. U.S. commanders implemented only minor changes aimed at reducing misconduct, but even these measures met with numerous setbacks. In Kunming, Brigadier General Haydon Boatner's plan to expand recreational opportunities and understanding about Chinese culture quickly fizzled out. Non-military goods remained in short supply, and his special service library managed to locate just one book about China.[149] A theater-wide 11:00 P.M. curfew from Monday through Friday (allowing an extra hour on Saturdays and holidays) and a ban on pleasure driving reduced venereal disease rates in the city. But military police shortages, slowness in reporting derelictions, and frequent troop movements hampered investigations of earlier sex crimes while allowing new violators to slip through the cracks. Meanwhile, the army's disciplinary crackdown elicited complaints from enlisted personnel and pushback from Washington. GIs in Yunnan accused military police of abusing their power, while the War Department warned that lengthy prison terms reflected poorly on the military. "Resorts to courts-martial to enforce discipline evidence a lack of leadership in the unit commander," wrote Major General Gilbert Cheves, the SOS commander in China.[150]

American personnel continued to commit sex crimes and assault Chinese women. Neither the new curfew nor warnings of harsh consequences stopped Private Omar White from assaulting a Chinese couple in Kunming with a wine bottle on May 17, for which he earned just one night in the stockade.[151] But a court-martial did sentence two enlisted men to life behind bars for a June 15 rape they committed in Luoping, near the Yunnan-Guangxi border. Down the road in Baise, a strategic Guangxi military town, more than four hundred Chinese saw an intoxicated sergeant named Raymond Belitz try to stab a Chinese professor and knock his seriously ill wife, Madame Liang, out of a Jeep after Belitz caused a drunk-driving accident. Two CID agents who happened to be in Baise to investigate other allegations against American personnel subdued Belitz before he stabbed anyone. The Chinese professor, ironically, had come to Baise as part of an ROC government-sponsored lecture tour undertaken to help rebuild trust between American personnel and Chinese civilians.[152] The town had been on edge after two nights of violence that began when GIs pushed a sex worker into a river and ended when several American soldiers carried out a drive-by shooting in Baise's red-light district that left a civilian with two bullets in his neck.[153] These incidents were part of an overall increase in violent crime committed by American personnel against Chinese civilians in June and July.[154]

False rape accusations also continued, provoking confrontations between American personnel and ROC authorities. Gendarmes forced three GIs to flee at gunpoint after an alleged rape in Shiqiaopu, a village outside Chongqing, on May 15. On May 24, two days before he lauded GIs' "strict observance of discipline" at the Victory House press conference, He Haoruo demanded that Wedemeyer arrest the three men for kidnapping and rape. One of the alleged victims was married to a detective at the Chongqing Police Bureau. He Haoruo provided a license plate number, which enabled military police to arrest three men from the 1066th Quartermaster Truck Company. The GIs claimed that the women were prostitutes, procured from a pimp at Victory House for 3,000 fabi apiece. Army MPs and Chinese police questioned the pimp, who verified the GIs' account. When questioned a second time, alleged victim Luo Guangru admitted to making up the rape allegations. The Chongqing city government had threatened to arrest any woman riding in a U.S. Army vehicle for prostitution, and Luo feared that a solicitation charge would embarrass her husband on the police force.[155]

The clearest indication that Chiang's campaign had failed to produce the desired results came from the Chinese Army. During the spring, when crowds began forming outside liberty spots in Chongqing, U.S. forces did not report a single attack on American military personnel by Chinese armed forces. But by summer, U.S. commanders warned that Americans now faced "an ever-increasing number of incidents involving intimidation of U.S. personnel at the point of a gun by Chinese soldiers and officers."[156] Chiang's forces had begun taking matters into their own hands.

Many confrontations involved women. On May 16, four unidentified Chinese soldiers killed Sergeant Joseph Diltz near Luliang Airbase in Yunnan. Diltz had long flaunted his associations with Chinese women. He went a step too far when he put his favorite sex workers up in rooms that were supposed to be reserved for housing Chinese Air Force officers.[157] Farther west in Baoshan, Chinese soldiers opened fire on American personnel in two separate incidents. They shot at an officer driving a Jeep on June 13 because two

Chinese women were aboard, resulting in a standoff involving an entire Chinese Army platoon.[158] On July 4, soldiers from the same platoon abducted two Black GIs at gunpoint after hearing rumors that Black American personnel were raping women in Baoshan, culminating in a shoot-out.[159] Four days later, Chinese soldiers drew their weapons on a group of American enlisted men sitting with two Chinese women at a café in Chongqing. The GIs pleaded for help from three Chinese officers seated at a nearby table, who ignored them. Finally, an English-speaking Chinese major got up from his chair and shouted, "I don't want American soldiers to go with Chinese girls!"[160]

· · · · · ·

The Jeep girl narratives enabled Chinese men to speak up for the nation by speaking on behalf of Chinese women. Each narrative aligned with prominent Republican-era discourses that elevated female virtue as a means of dealing with the loss of masculinity. As the impact of capitalism and urbanization threatened traditional gender roles during the 1920s and 1930s, patriarchal writers portrayed chaste widows and virtuous wives as the embodiment of the nation. Wartime literature continued to represent women as the essence of virtue, with rape victims symbolizing the defiled purity of the invaded nation.[161] This trend did not end with Japan's surrender.

Popular films released between 1945 and 1949 depicted the war as bringing out the worst in Chinese men, who had been unable to prevent the Japanese invasion, while portraying women as strong and patriotic.[162] In spring 1945, precisely at the juncture when Chinese men found themselves unable to stand up against the U.S. military in any other way, they turned around and demanded all the more from their female compatriots.

By linking anxieties over race, gender, and nation, Jeep girls became the most conspicuous and humiliating symbol of China's subordinate position in the U.S.-ROC alliance. While Stilwell's contentious tenure as senior U.S. commander in the CBI theater culminated in a diplomatic crisis that weakened Chiang's stature in the United States, it did not provoke a wider backlash targeting American servicemen in China. The average Chinese civilian or soldier knew nothing of Chiang and Stilwell's uneasy relationship. Their perceptions of the U.S. military derived, in large part, from the actual conduct of American troops in China. While on duty or at liberty, GIs alienated the Chinese they interacted with as a result of crime, deadly accidents, and the mistreatment of interpreters and hostel workers, among other problems. But only sexual relations and sexual misconduct triggered a violent response by adding this co-dimension of gender to accumulated grievances over racial discrimination and compromised sovereignty.

This violent backlash against Jeep girls and American servicemen made Chiang Kai-shek's contradictory political requirements untenable. His alliance with the United States entailed managing a delicate balance between responsiveness to U.S. demands and remaining popular enough at home to maintain legitimacy. Chiang found himself on the rocks with both constituencies in early 1945. Many U.S. diplomats and military commanders had soured on him years before, but the Stilwell crisis shattered his formerly untarnished image in the American press, raising the possibility that the White House could abandon him. Meanwhile, his domestic standing had reached a low-water mark in the wake of Ichigo. Doing anything to jeopardize his relationship with Wedemeyer was not an option, but neither was appearing indifferent as GIs harassed and assaulted women in the wartime capital. By allowing the press to stir up resentment and demonstrators in Chongqing to become unruly, Chiang took a gamble. Time and again, his Foreign Affairs Bureau had implored U.S. commanders to curb sexual misconduct, but to no avail. Perhaps Chiang believed that anti-American demonstrations would pressure Wedemeyer into halting liberty in Chongqing or confining sexual relations to special government-run brothels, as Tang Yi had suggested. Instead, Chiang found himself backed into a corner, and his dependence on U.S. goodwill left him little choice but to placate his American chief of staff.

Chiang's response satisfied Wedemeyer at the expense of local needs at a time when the sovereignty issue had become more significant, which damaged his government's legitimacy. Sex work serving American personnel had become a hated public spectacle, and it seemed that everyone in Chongqing—from homeless street kids to the mayor's office—was convinced that sexual assault had reached epidemic levels. Chiang's sudden reversal, after weeks of inflammatory newspaper reporting and demonstrations that occurred with tacit government support, made him appear more concerned with protecting foreign sexual predators than their female Chinese victims. The GMD alienated soldiers, bureaucrats, and civilians with official pronouncements that belittled demonstrators while lauding American soldiers for their exemplary conduct and respect for Chinese women. Back in 1943, the ROC government's decision to grant the U.S. military exclusive criminal jurisdiction over its troops in China had not generated any public controversy, but by spring 1945, Chinese from all walks of life—including senior government officials—had grown wary of the impunity and violations of sovereignty that this agreement had facilitated. The counternarrative Chiang fell back on was unpersuasive in these new circumstances, a fact made clear by the wave of attacks against American soldiers by Chinese military personnel. For a leader like Chiang, who viewed himself as Chinese nationalism personified, giving into pressure from Wedemeyer was a costly decision.

The ROC government would come to regret this response, as well as allowing the Jeep girl narratives to be deployed in the first place. Jeep girls would also return to haunt the Americans. In her pioneering analysis of the U.S. military's global base network during the Cold War, the feminist scholar Cynthia Enloe argues that without delicate adjustment of relations between local women and foreign men, any military presence can spark off enough nationalist resentment to subvert the very structure of a military alliance.[163] The furor over Jeep girls that erupted in the spring of 1945 did not topple the U.S.-ROC alliance, but it did damage the U.S. military's image in wartime China more than any other factor to date. The Chinese Communists refrained from exploiting what could have been a major propaganda coup against the GMD, as neither U.S. Army investigators nor Chiang's government found evidence of Communist agitation among the anti-American demonstrators in Chongqing. But the CCP was watching.

After Japan's surrender, these troubling patterns of American sexual misconduct and perceived GMD indifference would continue, but in an entirely new geopolitical context. Soon enough, the Communists would prove Enloe correct by deploying the Jeep-girl-as-rape-victim narrative as a crucial propaganda tool in their efforts to seize and consolidate power.

6 **Everything Comes Undone**

The Postwar Occupation

On the eve of Japan's surrender, soldiers in Sergeant Earl Revell's 653rd Engineer Topographic Battalion passed around a poem called "Panorama of China." Modeled on a rhyming account of American soldiers' impressions of Italy, "Panorama of China" summed up the failures of Huang Renlin's hostel program and the overwhelming desire of American personnel to go home.

While the poem's author wrote a few lines about China's impressive landscapes and temples, he devoted far more space to enumerating everything he loathed about the country and its people. None of the poem's criticisms reflected domestic racism or prewar anti-Chinese animosities. Rather, they revealed the contingent and dynamic nature of American racial formations in China, illustrating how the country's sensory offenses and affronts congealed into racialized resentment against "Chinks" and "slopies":

If I were an artist with nothing to do,
I'd paint a picture, a composite view,
Of historic old China, in which I'd show,
Visions of contrast, the high and the low,
There'd be towering mountains, a deep green lea,
Filthy brats yelling "Ding how" at me.
High plumed horses, and colorful carts,
Two-toned dresses on hustling tarts.
I'd show Chinese coolies, seemingly merry,
Dejected old women, with too much to carry.
A dignified old gout with a Fu-Man-Chu beard.
Bare bottomed children with both ends smeared.
Temples and tombs and mud houses too,
Hostels and mountains and marvelous views,
Houses made of wood, bricks and of mud,
People covered with scabs, scurvy and crud,
Poverty and want, men craving for food,

Picking through garbage, practically nude.
Stately temples, with horrible smells.
Stone fronted tombs, a place for the dead,
Noisy civilians clamoring for bread.
Grass fringed paddies, swept by the breeze,
Peasants wading in mud up to their knees.

Ancient idols with legends replete,
A sensual lass with scars on her f[ee]t
Creeping roadways, with a spangled theme,
Alleys that wind like a dope fiends' dream.
Rice fields set on the side of a hill,
A single latrine with privacy nil.
Two by four shops with shelving bare,
Gesturing merchants filling the air.
Narrow gauge sidewalks, more like a shelf,
Butt-puffing youngster, scratching himself,
Lumbering carts, hugging the road,
Non-descript trucks frequently towed,
Diminutive donkeys loaded for bear,
Coolie drawn taxis, soaking a fare.
Determined pedestrians, courting disaster,
Walking in gutters where movements are faster,
Chinese drivers all accident bound,
Weaving and twisting to cover the ground.
Home made brooms, reed tied to sticks,
Used on the streets to clean off the bricks.
Rickshaws and pushcarts, blocking your path,
Street corner "SLOPIES" needing a bath.
Soldiers galore with manners quite mild,
Profile woman, all heavy with child.

Arrogant wretches, picking up snipes,
Miniature apartments of various types.
An ugly maiden, a smile on her face,
Breath smelling of onion, fouling the place,
A listless housewife, with bound up feet,
Washing and cooking right out in the street.
The family wash, a tattle-tale gray,
Hangs from a cord, blocking the way.

Families dining from one common bowl,
Next to a fish store, a horrible hole.
Chinese Zoot-suiters, flashingly dressed,
Barefooted beggars looking depressed.

Mud smeared children, clustering about,
Filling their jugs from a community spout.
A dutiful mother, with a look of despair,
Picking the lice from her small child's hair,
Capable craftsmen, skilled in their art,
Decrepit old shacks, falling apart.
Intricate needlework, out on display,
Surrounded by rot, filth and decay,
Elegant baskets, weaved out by hand,
Odorous shops where leather is tanned.
An alley-way shop—a black market store,
Crawling with vermin, no screen on the door.

I've neglected the war scars, visible yet,
But those are the things we want to forget,
I'm glad I came, but darned anxious to go,
Give it back to the "Chinks," I'M READY TO BLOW![1]

To soldiers like Revell and his comrades, the Chinese had proved themselves unworthy of further U.S. assistance and tutelage, but because of the
shifting geopolitical situation, the Truman administration was not yet willing
to "give China back." The U.S. government immediately turned its attention to perceived Soviet expansion in North China and Manchuria. At the
same time, because both parties believed civil war was imminent, the CCP
and GMD set out to solve their differences through force of arms.[2] Meanwhile, both Chiang and Wedemeyer feared that Mao's Communists and the
Soviet Red Army would exploit the void left by Japan's surrender, so less than
forty-eight hours after the war ended, the Marine III Amphibious Corps—
veterans of the horrific battles for Peleliu and Okinawa—received a warning
order to prepare for deployment to China. Most of these men, who had been
training for the invasion of Japan in Guam, were thrilled to receive word that
they were headed to the Marine Corps' favorite prewar stomping grounds
on a new mission: Operation Beleaguer.[3] By late October, the entire occupation force—approximately fifty-three thousand marines—had landed
in North China and taken up positions in the vicinity of Tianjin, Beijing,

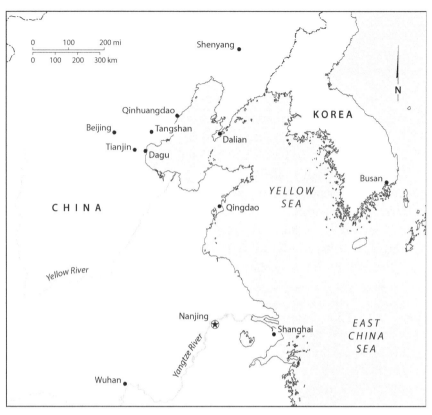

North China, 1945

Dagu, Qinhuangdao, and Qingdao, with orders to assist Chiang's forces, receive the enemy's surrender, and repatriate Japanese troops.[4]

Finding themselves in Earl Revell's "Panorama of China," rather than the Orientalist playground they had expected, the marines lashed out, fulfilling the inexorable transformation of an uneasy wartime alliance into a military occupation characterized by mutual loathing. The sensory affronts, price gouging, and rampant theft the marines encountered enraged them no less than it had the soldiers of Frank Dorn's Y-Force. Making matters even worse, U.S. support for GMD forces resulted in sniping and occasional attacks by Communist troops. Even Chiang's soldiers and police officers sometimes harassed the Americans, who continued to behave recklessly. The Nationalists, for their part, dropped all pretenses about influencing American perceptions or cooperating with U.S. forces in order to realize ROC nation-building aims. The hostel, interpreter, and military training programs ceased operations, leaving U.S. forces to do little but occupy and dominate.[5] Compared to the U.S. Army's deployment in Southwest China from 1941 to 1945, the marines in North China caused more vehicle accidents, committed more violent crimes, and were quicker to resort to deadly force when dealing with suspected thieves—who were often children. The Chinese had welcomed the marines in early October, but this enthusiasm quickly gave way to outrage.

While ground-level Sino-American relations deteriorated largely along the patterns described in previous chapters, the entirely new political context enabled the CCP to harness anti-American resentment and turn it against Chiang's Nationalists. The emergence of a robust press and superpower competition played crucial roles. From Japan's surrender to early 1947, Chiang's government tolerated the publication of Communist, liberal, and independent newspapers in areas under its authority, including the cities occupied by marines. Communist papers and underground party activists made hay of American misconduct and disregard for Chinese sovereignty while pinning the blame on Chiang.[6] Liberal and independent papers also condemned American misconduct and urged the U.S. government to withdraw its troops. Meanwhile, continued U.S. military support for the GMD, particularly the air and sea lifts of hundreds of thousands of Nationalist troops, allowed the CCP to make a persuasive case that the marines were helping Chiang wage civil war. The ROC could have leveled similar charges against Moscow. The Soviet forces that occupied Manchuria between August 1945 and April 1946 terrorized the local population and systematically deindustrialized the entire region.[7] But because Chiang still believed there was potential for cooperative relations with Soviet premier Joseph Stalin, the ROC protested quietly through diplomatic channels rather than ginning up public resentment through official news organs.[8] The Soviets also concealed their massive arms transfers to the Chinese Communists, so only U.S. forces were tarnished with fomenting civil war.[9] After Soviet troops completed their withdrawal, U.S. forces bore the full brunt of the anti-imperialist anger that had become central to civil war politics and only intensified after the CCP launched a major propaganda campaign against the U.S. military presence in late June.[10]

Operation Beleaguer was supposed to shore up Nationalists, but it actually helped bring about their downfall. U.S. logistical support enabled Chiang's forces to enter Manchuria using a flawed strategy. As the historian Harold Tanner shows, the Nationalists focused on controlling Manchuria's cities and railways, which Communist forces did not depend on. The region's terrain negated the advantages of the GMD's American weaponry while making it impossible to encircle CCP base areas adjacent to the Soviet Union.[11] The Truman administration also imposed an arms embargo on the ROC for ten crucial months after Nationalist forces began their offensive in Manchuria, based on misjudgments about the state of GMD military supplies. But the U.S. military presence provided the greatest windfall to the Communists in the political realm. Outrage over rape once again became the catalyst though which all variables causing resentment against U.S. forces intersected and converged, but this time the CCP was ready. When two drunk marines raped a nineteen-year-old Peking University student named Shen Chong on Christmas Eve 1946, underground Communist Party members in Beijing spearheaded what became the largest protest movement of the Nationalist period. Hundreds of thousands of demonstrators took to the streets across the country to demand that U.S. forces leave China. On January 6, Truman ordered his envoy General George C. Marshall to end his efforts to mediate between the GMD and the CCP. Marine Corps troop strength in China dwindled rapidly, as the State Department concluded that further military assistance would only heighten anti-GMD and anti-American resentment.[12]

Scholars have rightly rejected the decades-long debate in the United States over who "lost" China, but the fact remains that the U.S. military presence did indeed play a significant role in Chiang's defeat. Both Chiang's defenders and his detractors in these Cold War debates were mistaken. Chiang did not lose the civil war—as members of the China lobby insisted—because of State Department perfidy. Nor did his defeat in 1949 stem from his refusal to follow Stilwell's advice and his unwillingness to fight the Japanese, as "Stilwell myth" supporters argued. After the Cold War ended, newly available Soviet and Chinese archival sources affirmed that the CCP had always been oriented toward Moscow and indigenous revolution. This revelation buried the "lost chance" thesis, first articulated by leftist American scholars during the U.S. war in Vietnam, which posited that the Truman administration had missed an opportunity to reach an accommodation with the CCP before 1950.[13]

In fact, as this chapter will show, the U.S. military did indeed lose a chance in China, though it had nothing to do with reaching out to the CCP. The real missed opportunity was the failure of American military personnel to get along with their allies. Despite the centrality of racism in American society at the time of Pearl Harbor, the army's *Pocket Guide to China* opened with a passage admonishing GIs to treat Chinese as equals. This demonstrated that American military planners recognized the crucial importance of showing respect and consideration for Chinese dignity and nationalist sensitivities about unequal treatment. They understood that the prewar treaty-port world had come to an end. But from theater commanders on down to fresh draftees, the U.S. forces that deployed to China failed to heed this warning. After Japan's surrender, the U.S. military offered limited but undeniable support to the GMD while individual servicemen behaved with the brutal, everyday racism of imperialism—driving recklessly, beating rickshaw pullers, shooting theft suspects, assaulting women. As a result, they undermined the legitimacy of Chiang's regime while giving the Nationalists just enough rope to hang themselves in Manchuria.

The Mission

The marine occupation began auspiciously in October 1945, with thousands of Chinese civilians lining the streets to embrace their victorious allies. ROC officials worked behind the scenes to make sure the arrival went smoothly. Du Jianshi managed the operation in Tianjin. His résumé included artillery training at Fort Leavenworth; a PhD in international relations from the University of California, Berkeley; coordination of the Magruder Mission; and serving on China's delegation to the June 1945 San Francisco Conference, which resulted in the creation of the United Nations Charter.[14] In Beijing, the GMD's North China Military and Propaganda Committee (*Huabei junzheng xuanfu weiyuan hui*) ordered that foreigners be treated with respect, while the city's police bureau greeted newly arrived U.S. forces by organizing representatives from schools and commercial organizations to join armed police in welcoming them.[15] But even though the ROC government stage-managed these receptions, enthusiasm for U.S. forces was genuine. As Democratic League politician Luo Longji wrote in *Xi feng*, the U.S. military had made the largest contribution to victory in the Pacific War.[16] The Americans, for their part, felt sincerely welcomed.[17]

But the marines entered what Wedemeyer described on the day of Japan's surrender as "an enormous pot, seething and boiling."[18] A Soviet force of more than 1.5 million men had smashed through Japanese lines and penetrated far into central Manchuria after just a week of fighting. Astonished U.S. military commanders had expected that it would take the Russians a month to begin gaining ground.[19] On August 9, the same day the Soviets had launched their offensive, Mao ordered his forces to seize Shanghai, Nanjing, Tianjin, Tangshan, and Baoding. Over the past year, the CCP had exploited the opportunities created by the Ichigo offensive to double the size of its armies and fan them out across North China in preparation for the showdown with the GMD. While the CCP called off its plans to seize large cities in the face of Soviet and U.S. opposition, Communist forces had still taken control of more than 150 towns at the county level and higher in North China by the time the marines landed near Tianjin.[20] They also controlled the outskirts of all the cities the marines planned to occupy, along with the surrounding rail networks. Thus, while Luo Longji recognized the need for postwar cooperation with the United States, he also wrote that the marine landings "have made the complicated situation in China even more complicated, and the dangerous situation even more dangerous." For this reason, he concluded, "Our welcome for the U.S. marine landings is filled with anxiety."[21]

U.S. forces had strict orders not to interfere in domestic strife, but their very presence in formerly occupied areas, as observers like Luo Longji noted, represented a clear intervention in support of Chiang's government. Truman's General Order No. 1 excluded CCP forces from participating in Japan's surrender.[22] Japanese forces actually cooperated with puppet government soldiers—under Chiang's orders—to keep CCP troops from entering major cities immediately after the war ended.[23] After the official surrender ceremonies, which took place in Nanjing on September 9 and occurred slightly later elsewhere, the U.S. military prioritized the massive air and sea lifts of approximately 500,000 Nationalist troops into areas that had been under Japanese occupation.[24] The repatriation of Japanese military personnel began only after the transfers of GMD forces were complete. From October 1945 until January 1946, the marines oversaw the entire repatriation process, concentrating disarmed Japanese troops in major port cities like Tianjin and then sending them to Japan aboard U.S. Navy landing ships.[25] GMD forces took charge of the process in late January but continued to rely on U.S. personnel for security and shipping.[26]

The U.S. military's air and sea lifts of GMD forces helped convince Chiang that he could crush the Communists in a matter of months. On July 28, he had written in his diary that a military struggle in Manchuria would be extremely difficult and possibly futile. But the Truman administration and the Joint Chiefs of Staff wanted him to unite the region, with China proper under his control. In late October, the U.S. Navy's Seventh Fleet transported two of his crack, largely American-trained-and-equipped armies to Qinhuangdao, a city recently secured by marines that was located just south of the Great Wall. With these sixty thousand well-armed troops at his disposal, Chiang decided to fight his way into southern Manchuria, and on November 13 they crossed the Great Wall at Shanhaiguan under the command of Du Yuming, a veteran of the first Burma campaign.[27]

The Truman administration, however, sought to avert civil war. Its overriding aim was to limit Soviet influence in China by forcing the GMD and CCP into a coalition government under Chiang's leadership. The Red Army's speedy conquest of Manchuria, refusal to allow the U.S. Navy to land Nationalist troops there, and systematic looting of the entire region alarmed U.S. military commanders and government officials. They feared Stalin was going back on his agreements at the February 1945 Yalta Conference, where Roosevelt and Churchill had conceded to granting the Soviets a sphere of influence in Manchuria but with the ROC government retaining full sovereignty.[28]

In mid-November, the situation took a turn for the worse, at least from the American perspective. Stalin was failing to comply with the August 14, 1945, Sino-Soviet Treaty of Friendship, which stipulated that the Soviet Union would withdraw its forces from Manchuria three months after Japan's surrender.[29] Soon afterward, on November 26, Patrick Hurley—the U.S. ambassador to China—resigned in a shocking public display, insisting that his difficulties in China stemmed from communist sympathizers in the U.S. Foreign Service. It was the last straw for Truman, and within hours the president had appointed former army chief of staff George C. Marshall as his special envoy to China. Marshall arrived in China on December 20 with a public directive to encourage democratic reform and avert a civil war. He also had private instructions from Truman—leaked to Chiang's ambassador to the United States from an unknown source—to back the generalissimo even if he resisted Marshall's efforts.[30]

While Marshall managed to persuade both sides to accept a cease-fire agreement on January 10, putting the paper agreement into practice proved impossible.[31] Neither the Nationalists nor the Communists put much faith in Marshall.[32] Meanwhile, the United States continued to support Chiang's ambitions in Manchuria, putting transport planes at his disposal to ferry 200,000 troops there and providing him with $500 million worth of military supplies.[33] GMD forces pushed farther into Manchuria following the Soviet withdrawal, entering a region with terrain and infrastructure ill-suited to their American weaponry and the mobile, logistics-dependent style of fighting they had learned from U.S. Army advisors in Ramgarh and Yunnan.[34] As Chiang's forces attempted to exert control over Manchuria, the marines continued to guard airfields, railways, and ports in North China.

U.S. military and GMD forces finished repatriating Japanese personnel in July 1946—three months after Soviet forces had departed Chinese territory—but the marine occupation continued.[35]

"The Hell-Hole of Creation"

The marines arrived in China with high hopes for their mission. "China duty was considered the cream of duty assignments," wrote James Fackler, an infantryman with the First Marine Division at Okinawa. Fackler heard salacious anecdotes from the few old "China Marines" still serving in his outfit, "as well as the common, almost legendary, stories that had been handed down over the years."[36] Survivors of horrific combat in the Pacific, Fackler and his comrades looked forward to celebrating their victory. They still had a mission to complete, but the war was over and there would be plenty of time for the easy living that had earned China duty its celebrated place in Marine Corps lore: sex, booze, servants, exotic surroundings, and the green light to run wild. Like the American soldiers still stationed in Southwest China, every marine was eager to return home, but a stint in the Marine Corps' favorite prewar stomping grounds beat doing occupation duty in Japan.[37] "When the word passed that North China was our destination, most of us were delighted," recalled E. B. Sledge, the Peleliu and Okinawa veteran whose memoir, *With the Old Breed*, remains the most famous account of the U.S. Marines in World War II. Sledge wrote that after dropping anchor off Dagu Bar and boarding the train for Tianjin, "all the men were in high spirits and very excited about the prospects of pleasant duty in China."[38]

But disillusionment set in almost immediately, beginning with the same sensory offenses and affronts that made soldiers like Earl Revell loathe serving in China. On the train to Tianjin, an odor emanating from a toilet that "indicated it had not had the attentions of a plumber for a considerable time" and a coach that "lurched, yawed, and leaned one way and then the other" gave E. B. Sledge and James Fackler a premonition of the olfactory and haptic transgressions to come.[39] Abject poverty and public defecation made an immediate, deep impression, coming up frequently in diaries and letters home as well as in memoirs and veterans' newsletters. The cries of begging children also left a deep impression.[40] Even the fabled city of Shanghai caused the Americans to recoil in disgust. Lieutenant Carl Johnson described the city to his wife after his first day there as "the hell-hole of creation."[41]

Sanitation and hygiene deficiencies were especially revolting. Transporting Nationalist troops, according to American personnel, was a bodily encounter like no other. Chinese soldiers urinated, defecated, and expectorated all over the deck; threw up in aircraft cabins; bathed in urinals; and rinsed their toothbrushes in the head. American servicemen had to disinfect ships and aircraft to rid them of germs and odors.[42] GMD forces showed a profound failure, in American eyes, to act with the bodily discipline required of "civilized" men.[43] Civilians were no better, they discovered. "Nothing was clean," recalled one marine, as others described "stinking" inhabitants living like "pigs" in putrid surroundings, desperate for the privilege of picking through Marine Corps garbage.[44] "When we first got to China, you wanted to vomit," said Walter Grzeskiewicz of the Second Marine Division.[45] The chief distinction marines made between themselves and Chinese, like their colonial predecessors had in the Philippines, was between clean and dirty bodies.[46] The Chinese, they believed, were inhumanly filthy. With filth came disease: cholera, typhoid, dysentery, trachoma, malaria, schistosomiasis, leprosy, syphilis, and gonorrhea.[47] "Colds are about as common as chinks up here," Carl Johnson told his wife, Marion, during his third week in China. "You can't be too careful with these people, they're pretty dog gone filthy."[48]

Price gouging, scams, and robberies also contributed to disillusionment. The goodwill these marines encountered upon their arrival seemed to evaporate as soon as the victory parades ended. Rickshaw and tricycle fares skyrocketed "almost overnight," according to E. B. Sledge.[49] The Tianjin Committee for Hosting Allied Forces warned police on December 15 that rickshaw pullers were colluding with prostitutes "to cheat American servicemen," often the new arrivals who had just stepped off the train.[50] At markets in Tianjin and Beijing, opportunists acting as interpreters jacked up prices and split their profits with crooked police officers.[51] "Had fun watching the gooks," Johnson wrote after his first trip to one of Shanghai's markets. "I think their greatest pleasure in life is to argue about prices." Hawkers followed him so persistently, according to Johnson, that "it takes quite a few 'no's' and a last disgusted shove to make some of them shove off."[52] The China edition of the military's *Stars and Stripes* newspaper published many letters to the editor complaining of rip-offs.[53] ROC authorities tried to help. On November 24, the Beijing Police Bureau ordered all merchants in the city to halt profiteering, and three weeks later they publicized a bilingual rickshaw and pedicab fare table.[54] Police in Tianjin followed their lead in early 1946 by setting rickshaw fares and deploying plainclothes police to the city's popular Quanye Bazaar.[55] But inflation made price standardization difficult, and disputes continued to occur. Marines also fell victim to armed robberies while taking rickshaws at night.[56]

Morale sunk further with the realization that commanders had not been entirely forthcoming about their mission. It happened quickly to E. B. Sledge and the marines of K Company. They stopped in Tianjin only so another heavily armed locomotive could be switched onto their track in case the Communists attacked them on their way into Beijing. "Our holiday mood was dampened . . . the war was over, and we had had our fill of fighting," he wrote. The ride into Beijing proved uneventful, but Sledge and his comrades soon found themselves engaged in gunfights with CCP troops in isolated outposts and along the railroads: "We had survived fierce combat in the Pacific, and now none of us wanted to push his luck any further and get killed in a Chinese civil war."[57] These sentiments were widely shared, as many marines were shot at while on duty despite the Communists being constrained by orders from Yan'an not to engage the Americans.[58] Even the train carrying Major General DeWitt Peck, the First Division's commander, was attacked.[59] At least thirteen marines died from hostile fire during operations in North China, including four killed in a July 29, 1946, CCP ambush at a village called Anping along the Tianjin-Beijing Highway that left another twelve wounded.[60] Army personnel also came under fire and took casualties in skirmishes between Chinese forces during the weeks following the atomic bombings.[61]

Chinese Communist forces had orders to avoid open hostilities with the marines, but the combination of U.S. support for the Nationalists and anti-American CCP propaganda led some local commanders to act more aggressively. During the months immediately following Japan's surrender, CCP forces tried to sabotage rolling stock and track along the railroad lines patrolled by marines. Communist troops also occasionally shot at trains and the Marine Corps detachments guarding rail bridges.[62] The July 1946 ambush at Anping, on the other hand, occurred a month after the CCP's Central Committee launched a major propaganda campaign against the United States, demanding the withdrawal of Marine Corps personnel.[63] The CCP forces that attacked the marines at Anping—the Eighth Route Army's Fifty-Third Regiment—had been subjected to four days of mass meetings denouncing U.S. China policy, which resulted in a local decision to block the Beijing-Tianjin Highway with two oxcarts and open fire on a Beijing-bound marine truck convoy. Although the CCP Central Committee soon discovered that its troops had launched the ambush, the Communists blamed the incident on U.S. forces and demanded an apology.[64]

U.S. military personnel also clashed with Nationalist soldiers and police. A Shanghai police officer shot three enlisted men on November 4, 1945, after a brawl at the Shanghai racecourse, while GMD soldiers in Shanghai carjacked unarmed U.S. forces at gunpoint.[65] Marines, soldiers, and sailors in other locations complained of unprovoked aggressive behavior against them by Nationalist cops and military personnel, including shootings and armed robberies.[66] Chiang himself admitted that poorly disciplined Nationalist and provincial forces had attacked U.S. Army installations around Southwest China throughout October 1945.[67] Witnessing the ROC government's harsh measures against suspected Communist agents, such as the shooting of a female schoolgirl in Qingdao for passing out CCP propaganda, contributed to the growing ill will toward the Nationalists.[68]

But just as with the war against Japan, theft was the main complaint. The problem reached new heights after V-J Day owing to the presence of better-supplied U.S. forces, the relaxation of wartime security measures, and the collapse of civil order following Japan's surrender. Poorly paid Chinese day laborers employed at Marine Corps facilities stole to supplement their meager incomes.[69] Unlike wartime hostel workers, they were not subject to military law, so convictions resulted in fines or short jail sentences, rather than lengthy prison terms. For example, Li Wenling got fifty days for pocketing six flashlight bulbs at Beijing's Nanyuan Airport, while Xu Decheng was fined 60,000 fabi for sewing six pairs of gloves into his jacket at a Marine Corps slaughterhouse, equivalent to a month's pay.[70] Larger items also disappeared. Thirty-eight marine Jeeps and trucks were stolen off Beijing's streets during the second half of 1946, and another thirty-seven vehicles vanished over the same period while being shipped to the city from Shanghai, which had a far higher crime rate.[71] Wedemeyer reported the "astounding" theft of 170 Jeeps in the city during March 1946 alone.[72] Warehouse and storage depot break-ins also occurred daily. "Hungry Chinese would go over the wall to steal anything that wasn't tied down," James Fackler recalled.[73] In December 1946, the Seventh Service Regiment's Engineer Supply Lot—one of eight warehouses the marines operated in just a single Tianjin police district—reported an average of five burglaries per week.[74]

The marines wanted out. They were repelled by their bodily encounters with Chinese people and resented having to risk their lives in an escalating domestic struggle after the war they fought had ended. A theft epidemic fueled violent racist anger at a people whose lives many marines came to view with callous disregard. "Practically every leatherneck now stationed in China," read the January 9, 1946, cover story in the *North China Marine* newspaper, was asking "when are we going home?"[75] Marines in China did not take part in the demobilization demonstrations that occurred in Asia during early 1946, but at least three hundred army personnel staged a protest march in Shanghai on January 11, demanding to leave the country.[76] One piece of doggerel that made the rounds in late 1945 put it more bluntly, describing China as "the place that god forgot, where the food will turn your stomach and you'll catch the Chinese rot. When I climb the golden stairway, old St. Pete will know me well, and he'll say, 'Come on to Heaven for you've served your hitch in Hell.'"[77] At the same time, for many Chinese, simply being around American servicemen was itself a kind of hell.

American Brutality

Just a few weeks after the marines landed in October 1945, Tianjin's regional military commander Sun Lianzhong warned Chiang that American personnel "were engaged in frequent lawlessness."[78] In November, marines in Tianjin robbed Chinese bus and trolley ticket sellers, soldiers, suit makers, jewelry and camera stores, factories, and homes.[79] During an evening crime spree on December 23, three marines attacked a pedicab driver, robbed a pedicab factory, broke into a nearby fresh goods store, and then mugged a pedestrian. Marines had already robbed the store twice in December.[80] As of early 1946, Tianjin police were still investigating twenty-six robberies involving American personnel.[81] Commanders elsewhere, including in Taiwan, reported robberies and muggings.[82] Violence against civilians and police was also common. Soldiers billeted in Shanghai's luxury hotels while awaiting transportation home entertained themselves by throwing firecrackers and garbage at Chinese walking the streets below.[83] They also beat up civilians "for no good reason," according to army investigators.[84] Over a twelve-day period in early 1946, marines assaulted police officers from a single Beijing precinct in four separate unprovoked attacks.[85] In Tianjin, attacks were so common that Chiang personally ordered the mayor to investigate after a marine grabbed an eighteen-year-old woman off the streets and tried to rape her in his barracks.[86] U.S. military police in Qingdao also documented assaults, robberies, and murder, while hunting accidents and indiscriminate firing from vehicles led to injuries elsewhere.[87]

Rickshaw pullers and pedicab drivers, viewed by many Americans as petty crooks, took frequent beatings.[88] Most attacks followed price disputes or attempts by intoxicated American personnel to ride off with pedicabs: a joke to the Americans but a threat to one's livelihood for impoverished Chinese drivers. Physical assaults were the norm, but on November 1, an unidentified marine shot rickshaw puller Liu Enhua in Beijing. Liu nearly died and had to spend two months in a hospital that lacked the funds to keep him fed.[89] That same evening in Tianjin, Kong Qingnian was taking two marines home from a bar when they "suddenly jumped down and knocked [him] unconscious." Kong awoke and gave chase, but the marines got away with his pedicab.[90] Two attacks in December escalated into confrontations with Tianjin police. In one case, a marine suspected of assaulting another driver and throwing his pedicab into a river punched a police officer in front of the precinct's foreign affairs section commander while being questioned. U.S. military police let him go with a warning.[91] In the other case, police at the Hai dadao substation watched two marines take a pedicab from a driver and ride away. As soon as officer Sun Rutian exited the door to give chase, the marines went after him. They charged into the substation with their fists swinging, threatened the commander, and broke the windows before running away. U.S. military police paid compensation to the driver but failed to track down the suspects.[92]

While most assault victims were poor or middle class, elites were not entirely immune. On January 23, Zhang Shaosong, director of the Shanghai Municipal Government's Civil Affairs Department, was riding in his chauffeured sedan along Avenue Joffre when a U.S. Army Jeep overtook him and forced his vehicle to stop. A soldier, who appeared intoxicated to Zhang, exited the Jeep and assaulted Zhang's driver, Chen Jinzhang, knocking a tooth out and leaving Chen dazed and bloody in the street. Seconds later, Zhang told investigators, two drunk American sailors climbed into his sedan. One pinned Zhang to his seat as the other took the wheel and sped down Avenue Joffre. The two fled on foot after crashing into a pedicab near Route Père Robert. Despite having a license plate number and testimony from several Chinese and Russian eyewitnesses confirming Zhang's and Chen's account, the provost marshal declined to press charges. The Jeep in question had supposedly been checked in a few hours before the collision, and besides, wrote the investigator, "the victim [Chen] was quite capable of defending himself. He admitted having had police training."[93]

Misconduct continued throughout 1946, with some crimes rivaling the callousness of violence committed during Japan's occupation. On August 18, 1946, three marines raped two Chinese girls ages eleven and thirteen in Tianjin.[94] On September 22, a sailor beat rickshaw puller Zang Da Erzi (also known as Zang Yaocheng) to death in Shanghai over a fare dispute.[95] The next evening in Tianjin, an eleven-year-old girl named Hu Xiaomei drowned during an incident involving three intoxicated marines. Chinese witnesses—the pedicab driver who alerted police and the two fourteen-year-old girlfriends accompanying Hu—told police the marines had accosted the three girls and pushed Xiaomei into the river. The other two struggled free, but "Xiaomei was too small," her friends said, "so she couldn't get away and the American soldier threw her into the water."[96] American investigators accepted the marines' version of events: that the three girls were beggars, and Hu Xiaomei had fallen into the water while pestering them for money. They released them and dismissed the girls' statements as "useless, misleading information used to gain claims from the U.S. government."[97] Hu's distraught mother challenged this account in letters to the mayor and police commissioner. Hu's older brother supported the family with a successful business, so her daughter had no reason to beg, her mother wrote. Marines "constantly caused trouble" in Tianjin, she continued, and warned presciently that "unless the government finds a way to stop this, there will be backlash from the Chinese people."[98]

CCP-affiliated periodicals published a constant stream of allegations against U.S. forces, while government-connected newspapers downplayed the violence. The Communist Party's Xinhua News Agency, for example, described the Zang and Hu killings as part of a pattern of "escalating" American violence against civilians in Shanghai, Beijing, and Tianjin.[99] And while Shanghai's *Shen bao*, edited by a member of the Guomindang's right-wing CC Clique, blamed Zang's death on an "intoxicated American sailor," it buried the story in a short back-page summary on September 24.[100] An October 4 *Shen bao* editorial walked back this account, questioning whether an American had in fact killed Zang and assuring readers that the case, "which had no political meaning whatsoever," would be dealt with according to U.S. military law.[101] *Shen bao*'s reversal echoed reporting in Nationalist-affiliated newspapers during the Jeep girl crisis. On the other hand, Shanghai's second paper, the leftist *Wenhui bao*, which employed several underground CCP members, published more than forty pieces about Zang's case. Authors linked it to frequent assaults on civilians by American personnel and called on U.S. forces to hold an open trial.[102] The *Wenhui bao* also took the lead in promoting the U.S. Forces Out of China Week campaign, a series of press conferences and meetings focused on problems stemming from the U.S. military presence. The campaign, run by nonpartisan organizations in Shanghai, opened just hours before Zang's death.[103] On September 29, after Zang's younger brother had spoken at a campaign meeting, the CCP's Central Committee issued a directive making "U.S. Forces Out of China" its propaganda slogan.[104]

Newspapers, including CCP, liberal, and independent publications, also devoted substantial space to reporting on vehicle accidents—the leading cause of death and injury at the hands of American servicemen. Japan's surrender ended transportation bottlenecks and freed up supplies, allowing U.S. forces to bring many motor vehicles to China. The sharp increase in traffic, which occurred alongside rapid population growth as war refugees returned home, had an immediate impact.[105] According to ROC statistics, Shanghai had the country's deadliest roads. During the 120-day period beginning on September 12, 1945, U.S. military vehicles were involved in 495 accidents there, killing or injuring 244 Chinese.[106] In a November 10 letter to the *Stars and Stripes*, an American sergeant wrote that army truck drivers in Shanghai "speed on narrow streets—in heavy traffic, disregard traffic rules, tip vehicles, smash ricshas [*sic*] . . . look upon the Chinese people as skum [*sic*]."[107] In Beijing, police found American personnel fully or partially at fault for eighty-three accidents between October 1946 and January 1947, the majority of which caused injuries or death.[108] Tianjin police reported 248 vehicle accidents in the year following Japan's surrender, resulting in 330 deaths.[109] They found American personnel responsible for more than 90 percent of these collisions.[110] Based on these figures, a summer 1946 investigation by the Democratic League–affiliated *Minzhu bao* newspaper concluding that U.S. military vehicles had killed over one thousand Chinese in the ten months after V-J Day was probably not far off—though U.S. authorities would have disputed responsibility for many of those accidents.[111]

The physical danger U.S. forces brought to the streets and alleyways of the cities they occupied further galvanized anti-American sentiment. "Not a day went by without seeing the misdeeds of American servicemen in Shanghai written up in the city's newspapers and magazines," wrote Ling Hong in *Minzhu zhoukan* (Democracy weekly), a magazine that claimed no party affiliation but was in fact co-founded after Japan's surrender by the publisher Xu Boxin, who had joined the CCP in 1944.[112] The high frequency of vehicle wrecks, the impression that Americans were almost always at fault, and the often-belligerent behavior of the servicemen involved made easy work for Communist Party propagandists, such as the cartoonist Zhang Ding. Zhang's 1946 depictions of drunk-driving "Americans run amok in Shanghai" on the pages of the *Northeast Pictorial* (*Dongbei manhua*) simply illustrated the scenes reported each month in the Nationalist Party's police blotter.[113] GMD-affiliated publications might have downplayed American misconduct, but there was little difference between depictions of American behavior in CCP publications and what appeared in internal ROC correspondence and police records.

Anti-American sentiment crossed party lines and spread to those who had initially welcomed the U.S. military presence. Nationalist police attributed most collisions to careless driving and speeding on the part of American personnel.[114] Police themselves sometimes suffered injuries, including in drunk-driving and hit-and-run cases. In March 1946, the U.S. Army's public relations officer in Nanjing "created a particularly embarrassing situation" by crashing head-on into a Chevrolet sedan owned by the Nanjing Police Bureau after getting drunk at an embassy dinner. Marines and American soldiers also assaulted Chinese accident scene investigators.[115] GMD organizations, such as Beijing's People's Committee for the Protection of Freedom (*Beiping renmin ziyou baozhang weiyuan hui*), described accidents caused by American servicemen as a leading "threat to citizens' lives."[116] On January 19, 1946, former interpreting officer Huang Shang, now working as a journalist, published an article castigating U.S. personnel for "practically turning Shanghai into their own world, with Jeeps plowing through and leaving a trail of injuries and destruction in their wake. Feeling toward Americans," he wrote, had changed. "You no longer see anyone giving them the thumbs up sign or shouting 'ting hao.'"[117] Jin Chongji, a high school senior in Shanghai, who later became a leading historian, wrote that vehicle accidents and violence against civilians "made every self-respecting Chinese realize that even though China had won the war, the era of foreigners throwing their weight around in China had not ended."[118]

Although ROC and U.S. authorities had anticipated trouble with traffic accidents, they failed to devise mutually satisfactory prevention and investigation measures. Following the Japanese practice, Chinese traffic moved on the left, which had contributed to wartime collisions, since U.S. military vehicles were in effect being driven on the wrong side of the road. In June 1945, Wedemeyer persuaded Chiang to transfer all traffic to the right-hand side beginning January 1, but many accidents still occurred due to vehicles traveling in the wrong direction.[119] In September, Wedemeyer's headquarters drafted a joint investigation procedure calling for a "courteous, tolerant spirit of cooperation" among Chinese police and U.S. MPs.[120] But according to Beijing police commissioner Chen Chao, this plan failed to materialize. His men found the Americans difficult to work with. Slow response times, shortages of English-speaking Chinese foreign affairs police, and the continued tendency among Chinese and American investigators to exonerate their compatriots made matters worse.[121] U.S. authorities blamed most accidents on the carelessness of Chinese pedestrians and cyclists, while Chinese civilians and police officers expected motor vehicles to yield to cyclists and pedestrians under most circumstances.[122] Joint prevention efforts were too late and half-hearted to make much of a difference. In Beijing, U.S. marines and local police set up the Joint Office of Sino-American Police (JOSAP) on October 4, 1946, which carried out a "traffic safety week" starting on October 27 but devoted more energy to dealing with Chinese thieves.[123] U.S. and Chinese authorities in Tianjin followed suit on December 14, deploying joint traffic safety patrols along the city's three busiest thoroughfares, but only for a week.[124]

The extension of the 1943 jurisdiction agreement left the question of compensation entirely in American hands. Wedemeyer forbade troops to settle traffic disputes privately, so as with criminal cases, requests for damages were passed from Chinese municipal governments to the U.S. Foreign Claims Commission.[125] Marine commanders relaxed Wedemeyer's policy in the event of minor accidents, which could be settled by cash payment and the signing of a civilian release form, but disputed cases and collisions resulting in injury or death still went to the Foreign Claims Commission throughout the occupation period.[126] While the commission often paid out, the procedure could take more than a month, compelling those with urgent expenses to look elsewhere for money. Sometimes hospitals lacked the funds to pay for ongoing care.[127] And in many cases where Chinese police investigators found the Americans at fault, the commission refused to pay damages. In August 1946, the left-wing *Xinmin bao* newspaper wrote to Tang Yongxian, who succeeded Chen Chao as Beijing police commissioner, to express concerns over accident victims not being properly compensated.[128] Rejected damage claims led victims and their families to argue that the Americans—and by implication the ROC government—held Chinese lives in low regard.[129] Tang admitted that the police bureau needed more English speakers and foreign affairs officers to handle negotiations with the Americans but assured the paper that his men "were working nonstop" to secure damages for accident victims.[130]

Two early 1947 accidents involving children scavenging at the dumping grounds behind the USMC's First Medical Battalion on Tianjin's Xinkai Road illustrate the damage such collisions did to families. On January 14, a trailer attached to a Marine Corps truck driving along Xinkai Road struck and killed fifteen-year-old Guo Darong. Guo had been scavenging coal with her older sister Erfu. According to Erfu, Darong tried to get out of the way, but the trailer's front wheel passed over her head, crushing her skull. The driver, Corporal Roland Gatheval, insisted that Guo had been killed because she tried to grab the truck's skid chain. But Erfu insisted that Gatheval had thrown down the chain after the collision, a version of events backed up by Chinese investigators.[131] Nevertheless, the Marine Corps investigator insisted that Erfu was too young to be a reliable witness, and the Foreign Claims Commission refused to pay damages, leaving an impoverished family with one daughter dead, another traumatized, and funeral expenses beyond their means.[132] The Marine Corps also refused to accept responsibility after a dump truck driven by Private First Class Robert Stone ran over fourteen-year-old Yin Erwu, breaking his pelvis. This accident, wrote investigator Joseph Brill, "was due to the anxiety of the beggar boys to pilfer the contents of the rubbish."[133] To the families of these victims and other impoverished Chinese who heard similar stories about vehicle accidents, the CCP's straightforward narrative of American imperialist recklessness abetted by Chiang's Nationalists made sense, just as it did to the families of hit-and-run victims, who had no recourse whatsoever unless a witness wrote down a license plate number.

The often deadly measures U.S. forces adopted in response to theft aroused even greater indignation. Policy varied from unit to unit, but the August 1944 ruling of the CBI theater's judge advocate allowed American personnel to use deadly force to protect government property.[134] Admiral Charles M. Cooke Jr., commander of the U.S. Naval Force, Western Pacific, ordered that firearms be used against civilians only as a last resort—after calls to halt and warning shots had failed to stop suspected thieves. Even then, Cooke insisted that men shoot to disable rather than kill.[135] But by early 1946, before break-ins reached epidemic levels, sentries at some Marine Corps facilities in Tianjin had strict orders to shoot to kill after firing warning shots.[136] Marines killed numerous suspected thieves there in 1946, including several unidentified boys whom police believed to be only thirteen years old. Police precinct commanders and Mayor Du Jianshi criticized such killings as "excessive force," well beyond the scope of protecting U.S. government property.[137]

American military police also targeted Chinese civilians suspected of possessing stolen U.S. military goods, repeating actions that had caused outrage over violations of Chinese sovereignty in Kunming during 1945. On September 5, 1946, an American MP fired five shots at a middle school student named Cao Guiming in Beijing, wounding him in the left leg. The MP opened fire because Cao was wearing a pair of U.S. military-issue trousers and had refused orders to halt. Police inspector Du Jun described the shooting as an outrage, writing that U.S. military police had "no right to exercise jurisdiction over Chinese people and especially should not be wantonly shooting at them." Chinese police, he noted, could only use firearms for self-defense. The shooting took place near the hotel hosting the Communist Party's representatives to Marshall's Executive Headquarters in Beijing, and correspondents from all the major newspapers came to investigate.[138] The incident received national coverage in the weeks before the Zang Da Erzi killing. *Da gong bao* reported that Cao had been watching a chess game when the MP spotted him, jumped out of a Jeep, and then kicked him in the back—causing the terrified teenager to run away. Communist Party organs, including *Jiefang ribao* and the Xinhua News Agency, highlighted the case as one of numerous atrocities committed over the past two months. In Chiang's Republic of China, one article noted, Chinese had "no freedom of wearing trousers."[139]

As had been the case during the war, American personnel were rarely disciplined for such shootings. Authorities refused to bring charges in nearly all cases where theft had occurred, however minor. A week before Cao Guiming was shot in Beijing, a marine sentry killed eighteen-year-old Wu Liuxiao for stealing a few boxes of pencils in Tianjin. Other guards had actually caught Wu and started beating him, but he struggled free and managed to run almost forty yards down Consular Road before he was shot in the back.[140] A few weeks later, Gu Hanling bled to death with a bullet in his back on another Tianjin street after snatching a case of beer from a Marine Corps truck. The driver shot him dead as Gu fled. In both cases, the provost marshal recommended that the Americans not be held responsible.[141]

U.S. authorities also refused to accept responsibility in cases of attempted theft, such as when Guo Zenglin, a civilian employee at Seventh Service Regiment's Engineer Supply Lot in Tianjin, entered the warehouse area through a fence after work hours. A sentry shot Guo dead after ordering him to halt and firing two warning shots. Investigators found no evidence Guo intended to steal but still concluded that sentries had discovered him "before he had a chance to get into any of the warehouses."[142] Guo's tragic death marked the end of a spiral into penury that countless Chinese experienced in the horrible wave of official corruption and inflation that marred the Nationalists' postwar takeover. Guo took the poorly paid job at the supply lot after the once-successful small business he owned failed due to price increases. He left behind a wife, a son, and three daughters—the youngest born just four days before he died.[143] If families of shooting victims succeeded in clearing the names of the dead—which proved difficult—they had a chance of receiving compensation, but in these cases U.S. authorities ruled the deaths accidental and declined to bring charges.[144] In such cases, including the death of eighteen-year-old Zhou Erbao, killed while gathering firewood outside a marine base, and sixteen-year-old Hua Sanhuan, shot in the back of the head while waiting for her father to return from work on a U.S. naval vessel, it could still take months for the Foreign Claims Commission to pay damages.[145]

Prosecutions only happened in the most egregious cases. The day after Cao Guiming was shot, Private First Class William V. Sears chased down a civilian cutting millet near the boundary of a Marine Corps base at Tianjin's French arsenal and shot him twice in the head. A court-martial sentenced him to fifteen years for murder, finding that Sears knew full well the victim had simply been cutting millet and had vacated the area after Sears ordered him to leave.[146] Chinese investigators noted that the millet field was approximately fifty meters from the French arsenal's boundaries and that Sears shot the victim, a farmer named He Wanshun, while He was eating lunch.[147] The provost marshal also court-martialed two marines for the death of Sun Yugui, who was shot six times after grabbing on overcoat through an open window. Sun stole the jacket after he had entered the courtyard of the headquarters of the First Marine Division's battalion motor pool through a narrow alley, so investigators ruled that the two sentries had ample time to simply corner Sun in the courtyard and arrest him.[148]

Most of the measures the ROC government implemented to deal with theft and violence targeted its own people, particularly the poor and vulnerable, reviving yet another widely loathed wartime pattern. Chiang banned rickshaws in Shanghai after Zang Da Erzi was killed, sparking anti-American backlash in a city where an estimated half-million people relied on income from rickshaw pullers, who numbered more than 100,000. The municipal government also tried to wipe out street peddling, kicking off three days of rioting beginning on December 1, when police imposed martial law and began raids. ROC police targeted street peddling because American personnel complained of price gouging and because hawkers often sold U.S. military goods, which led to incidents like the Cao Guiming shooting. A street peddling ban in Tianjin also resulted in violence and anti-American backlash.[149] Meanwhile, local police in Tianjin, convinced that Americans would do little to halt the shooting of the poor Chinese children who gathered near bases to beg or collect garbage and were sometimes mistaken for thieves, recommended deploying its own sentries to chase them away.[150]

Ordinary Chinese also resented the hypocrisy behind draconian U.S. military and ROC government anti-theft measures. Official corruption during the Guomindang reconversion period was notorious and widely publicized by late September 1945.[151] The Chinese also knew that American personnel got away with a tremendous amount of stealing, smuggling, and black marketeering. In addition to looting and robberies, American personnel frequently sold U.S. military goods to street peddlers, which was illegal under U.S. military law. They pilfered much of what they sold to peddlers from the same warehouses where American sentries shot Chinese dead for stealing. Meanwhile, savvy army aircrewmen, their craft honed through wartime Hump smuggling, made a killing trafficking in opium, weapons, gold, and various currencies immediately after the war ended.[152] Even senior commanders got into the act. Lieutenant Colonel William Evans, the army's chief civil affairs officer for Taiwan, stole half the Japanese Army's gold bullion supply in Taipei—sixty kilograms—and sold it off in Shanghai. Evans left the service and returned to California a wealthy man, having made $108,000, equivalent to approximately $1.5 million in 2020 dollars. Despite the U.S. Army finding overwhelming evidence of Evans's guilt, a federal judge dismissed all charges against him, causing outrage in China, where Chinese officers who smuggled gold aboard U.S. military aircraft were executed.[153]

Sexual relations, however, remained the most explosive source of resentment. A massive sex industry catering to newly arrived marines and departing army personnel sprung up practically overnight. Government officials and businessmen returning from Chongqing competed with locals to set up ventures that could quickly bring in U.S. dollars. In Qingdao, some fifty nightclubs and over four hundred cafés and restaurants primarily serving marines had opened by early 1946 (see figure 6.1).[154] Establishments like Dave's Nightingale, the Tumble Inn, and the Little Café advertised their beautiful hostesses, while higher-end prostitutes distributed business cards with their addresses listed in English and Chinese.[155] A parallel boom occurred in Tianjin. Carl Johnson was responsible for enforcing curfew near the city's French arsenal in January 1946, a village, he described to his wife, consisting of "thirty bars, or cafes or whatever you want to call them. Each one is a house of prostitution to put it mildly." The going price, he wrote, "is about fifty cents."[156] Hospital corpsman ran prophylaxis stations inside Tianjin's larger brothels, as marines played a more direct role in venereal disease control than the army had in Southwest China during the war, including examining prostitutes for disease.[157] Venereal disease rates nevertheless dwarfed wartime levels, climbing as high as 382 per 1,000 men for the entire First Marine Division in June 1946.[158] Public interaction between

FIGURE 6.1 American marines and their dates in Qingdao.
(China Marines Association Collection, Marine Corps History Division)

American servicemen and local women in the cosmopolitan former treaty ports was also more common than it had been in Chongqing and Kunming.

The Chinese press continued attacking Jeep girls, particularly the better-educated women whose fraternization with American personnel posed the greatest threat, in authors' minds, to national sovereignty, Chinese identity, and gender, class, and race norms. Commentators chastised Jeep girls for their vanity and slavishness.[159] One author praised Beijing's "very conservative young women" for ignoring American advances, unlike the easy, English-speaking "girls" of Shanghai, who happily sold their bodies for U.S. dollars.[160] Shanghai's female students, another author warned, had embarked on "a devilish path" by pursuing their "golden dreams of an easy life with American husbands who offered comforts that pure Chinese could not enjoy." Not only had these women forsaken "China's tradition of valuing spiritual over material pursuits" but, like the British girls who had fallen for GIs, they would inevitably be spurned by their American lovers, resulting in such shame that "suicide by hanging would be of no use."[161] Numerous tabloids published lighter-hearted but nevertheless cautionary tales about former starlets who had fallen on hard times: the Shanghai actress Chen Lu, who contracted an "unmentionable disease" and fled to Qingdao to be a Jeep girl; Bai Guang, a movie star now "thick with several marines" and supporting nine relatives through "shameless acts"; and the dancer Yao Baobao, spotted looking "poorly dressed" and walking "hand-in-hand with an Allied friend."[162]

American personnel also continued their wartime pattern of sexual misconduct. Police reported sexual assaults by American personnel in Tianjin, Beijing, and Qingdao, including cases in which marines tried to force women into Jeeps.[163] Three marines stationed in Qinhuangdao admitted to "drinking about forty cans of beer" and then breaking into a home in a nearby village and assaulting four people, including a pregnant woman, while looking for prostitutes.[164] Meanwhile, the "public incidents" Wedemeyer had warned about during the Jeep girl crisis—excessive drunkenness, accosting women, and arrogant attitudes toward Chinese police officers trying to do their jobs—occurred wherever marines took liberty. On February 2, 1946, a large crowd witnessed two intoxicated marines assault a pedicab driver just blocks from Beijing's forbidden city. The two marines let the pedicab driver go when they spotted a young woman walking nearby and grabbed her. They then beat a traffic officer who tried to intervene to a bloody pulp, requiring hospitalization.[165] Combined with reckless driving and frequent violence against civilians, such scenes fueled apprehension that rape was occurring more frequently than the press was letting on. So while the sexual assault rate never approached the levels in U.S.-occupied Germany and Japan or Soviet-occupied Manchuria, Chinese civilians still lived in fear.[166] After all, they had expected better behavior from their wartime allies than civilians in Axis countries and Manchukuo had expected from their conquerors.

On June 24, 1946, the Communists began a centralized campaign to exploit American misconduct for propaganda purposes, while some Chinese men, including police, took matters into their own hands. On July 1, 1946, the CCP's Beijing Urban Work Committee issued a directive instructing party members to inform the public about "atrocities" committed by American personnel, including sexual misconduct.[167] But it was Nationalist police who first gave indication that the sort of backlash that erupted in Chongqing in spring 1945 was once again on the horizon. On September 18, an MP named Francis Janzen was standing on Nanjing Road in Shanghai with his Chinese girlfriend when a police officer approached and began berating the woman in Chinese. He also told Janzen that "it was forbidden for an American to speak with a Chinese girl." Another police officer arrived and said the same thing, and a shoving match broke out. More police officers arrived, their guns drawn, and began beating Janzen, who ran away, pursued by civilian men who threw stones at him.[168]

As winter approached, American personnel reported a marked increase in hostility toward the U.S. military presence. Brigadier General Omar Pfieffer, a commander in Qingdao who made frequent trips to Shanghai, noted that anti-Americanism "was a little worse" with each visit. Demonstrators heckled him during his Thanksgiving holiday in the city, and he stayed in a private home in order to avoid demonstrators.[169] Weeks before, a public opinion survey published in Shanghai's *Wenhui bao* claimed that 98.9 percent of 18,907 respondents favored the withdrawal of U.S. forces from China.[170] Writing in the highly regarded *Guancha* semi-monthly on November 9, the leading liberal journalist Chu Anping slammed American personnel for "running around violently, beating up students, taking liberties with women, crushing pedestrians to death with their vehicles, and showing utter contempt for China."[171] Meanwhile, the signing of a new Sino-American Commercial Treaty on November 4 triggered a nationwide uproar. Newspapers across the political spectrum—even those affiliated with the Guomindang's right wing—unanimously criticized it as a "new unequal treaty" that ceded China's economic autonomy. The CCP compared it to the notorious "Twenty-One Demands" Japan had presented to the Yuan Shikai government in 1915 and proclaimed November 4 as "National Humiliation Day."[172] Two weeks later, the Marshall Mission entered its death spiral when Zhou Enlai informed Marshall that he was leaving Nanjing for good.[173] And on December 18, President Truman issued a statement on U.S. China policy, reiterating America's supposed commitment to noninterference in Chinese affairs, which was roundly condemned for its emptiness and hypocrisy.[174]

Quit China!

Resentment against the U.S. military presence exploded into a nationwide protest movement after the alleged rape of a nineteen-year-old Peking University (Beida) student named Shen Chong by two intoxicated marines on Christmas Eve in 1946. Shen told investigators two marines seized her as she walked home from a movie at around 8:30 P.M. They pushed her across the street to the Dandong Polo Grounds, where one marine, later revealed to be Private Warren Pritchard, kept guard, while the other—Corporal William Pierson—raped her twice and then dragged her to a nearby shack. Pritchard left for the Beijing Hotel, a block to the east, and Pierson tried to rape Shen again, but a group of Chinese police and soldiers who heard what was going on pulled Pierson off and called JOSAP. Military police took Pierson into custody and brought Shen to the hospital, where a Chinese doctor found evidence of sexual intercourse, including minor vaginal lacerations, but could not determine if rape had occurred. Pierson insisted that Shen had consented, but investigators found inconsistencies in his statements and recommended disciplinary action.[175] The municipal police bureau tried to keep news from getting out, but several newspapers reported the incident on December 26. College students from the city's leading universities held emergency meetings, and on December 30, at least four thousand students took to the streets to demand that U.S. forces quit China (*gun chuqu*). Demonstrations spread to Tianjin and Shanghai two days later, while students in other cities planned their own marches. The Anti-Brutality Movement had begun.[176]

While uncertainty about the exact details of what transpired on December 24 still remain, few, if any, Chinese doubted Pierson's and Pritchard's guilt.[177] The Nationalists' immediate response—claiming on December 28 that Yan'an had dispatched Shen to instigate an anti-American movement by seducing a marine and then sending club-wielding members of the Three Principles of the People Youth League to interrupt student meetings in Beijing—backfired. Shen's father, a department chief in the Ministry of Communication, came out publicly, and student anger at the ROC government intensified.[178] And despite the government's public-facing reaction, internal correspondence revealed that ROC officials also believed that Shen had been raped.[179] After all, Chiang's government had been dealing with widespread American misconduct for five years. Anyone, for that matter, who had spent time around U.S. forces since the AVG's arrival in 1941 had most likely seen intoxicated American personnel behaving aggressively toward woman. Public incidents, as Wedemeyer admitted in spring 1945, had facilitated the spread of rape hysteria across Nationalist-controlled China without any Communist agitation. Now, however, similar feelings existed in areas that had welcomed marines as liberators on V-J Day but had experienced a year in which the Americans had behaved like occupiers. But this time around, liberal newspaper reporting, CCP propaganda, and anger over U.S. China policy had further amplified the resentment American personnel generated through their own poor conduct.

More than a year of urban political work put the Communists in a strong position to harness and take control of the movement. Underground party members now held leading positions in student organizations at the three Beijing universities that formed the core of the burgeoning protest campaign. The CCP controlled two student groups at Beida, where Shen was enrolled. The Beixi (northern group) answered to Yu Diqing, a native of Hebei

Province who had joined the party in 1936, while four former Lianda students led the Nanxi (southern group).[180] On December 26, Yu met with Nanxi leaders and discussed the "tremendous opportunity" they had "to strike a blow against Chiang and the United States" by using the Shen Chong case "to start a protest movement."[181] Liu Junying, a female underground party member at Beida, chaired a meeting of all student groups that same evening, during which participants voted to contact student groups at Beijing's other schools in order to stage strikes and prepare for protest marches. The CCP also had a strong underground presence in student government and departmental committees at Tsinghua, where party members put up big posters in the dining hall to spread word of the incident and helped persuade more than one thousand students to sign up for a protest march. At the smaller Yanjing University (Yanda), which had only around seven hundred students, all student government leaders had participated in the CCP underground.[182]

Thanks to the actions of CCP activists and the students Frank Dorn described as the future of China, the Anti-Brutality Movement swept across the country with tremendous momentum, quickly becoming the largest protest movement of the Nationalist era. The ironic failure of both U.S. and Nationalist visions for the wartime alliance revealed itself most clearly in the crucial role played by students from Beida, Tsinghua, and Nankai universities—the three schools that had formed the backbone of the wartime interpreter program while joined together as Southwest Associated University (Lianda) in Kunming. While Beida and Tsinghua students initiated the protests in Beijing, Nankai students co-organized the student march in Tianjin on January 1, one of the first demonstrations outside Beijing.[183] Another key source of wartime interpreting officers—Nanjing's government-supported Central University—led a three-thousand-strong march to the U.S. embassy on January 2, plastering Ambassador J. Leighton Stuart's residence with signs reading "God Damned United States Army Leave China." Deep indignation existed even at schools without a Communist presence.[184] By the end of January, an estimated 500,000 people joined protest marches and strikes spearheaded by students in over twenty-five cities. In addition to the rape case, demonstrators shouted slogans referring to Zang Da Erzi's death, shootings, vehicle accidents, and other crimes. University professors; the Democratic League; and leading business, cultural, labor, and women's movement figures also expressed support for the movement and the students' main demand: that U.S. forces leave China.[185]

As students took to the streets, the Communists elevated the Anti-Brutality Movement to the level of a "second front" in the Civil War. On

December 31, the CCP's Central Committee instructed party cadres in major cities and overseas Chinese communities to "launch and resolutely continue protest marches." In places where demonstrations were not feasible, petitions should be circulated demanding that Shen's rapists and other American personnel who committed crimes "be tried in Chinese courts, just as overseas Chinese who commit crimes in the United States are." The instructions closed with a call to "isolate Chiang and the United States and oppose America's colonization of China."[186] Beginning on New Year's Day, the Communist Party's two mouthpieces—the *Xinhua ribao* and the *Jiefang ribao*—abandoned all moderation in attacking the United States and used the movement to frame the Nationalists as enablers of American imperialism.[187] Four days later, the Central Committee hailed "the remarkable success and influence" of demonstrations in Beijing, Tianjin, and Shanghai: "We can see the basis for this patriotic movement grows stronger by the day, and it is already inextricably connected to victory in our war of self-defense in liberated areas."[188] Zhou Enlai expanded on this theme during a February 1 Political Bureau meeting, explicitly referring to the movement as a "second front" that had united people across the social spectrum, including capitalists, against the U.S. military presence.[189]

The ROC government only succeeded in further alienating the public with its response to the Anti-Brutality Movement. Protest bans and club-wielding thugs made students more supportive of the campaign. Once the depth of public anger became clear, the Nationalists actually backtracked, providing police protection to protest rallies in Shanghai for the first and only time.[190] And while the official press demanded punishment for Pierson and Pritchard, editorials in Nationalist Party organs strained credibility by continuing to stress Sino-American friendship and faith in U.S. military justice.[191] The Communists, on the other hand, through their December 31 instructions calling for Chinese jurisdiction, co-opted public outrage even though they failed to offer a sustained legal critique of the extraterritorial rights U.S. forces enjoyed in China.[192] Public outrage intensified after the Nationalists launched another crackdown on February 17, arresting and beating up thousands of student activists in five cities.[193] By February, the movement had undermined Nationalist legitimacy across the country and given the CCP its greatest victory to date in the urban battle for hearts and minds.

Making matters even worse for the ROC government, the Anti-Brutality Movement exploded just as the tide began to turn on the battlefield and economic stabilization efforts failed. Between mid-December and early April,

Communist forces turned back four Nationalist offensives in southern Manchuria, leading to a strategic transformation in the civil war's most important theater. For the first time, key CCP commander Lin Biao's Northeast Democratic United Army held the initiative. Marshall ended his mediation mission and left China on January 8, allowing both sides to concentrate their attention on military issues.[194] Nationalist armies, however, were running out of ammunition as the U.S. arms embargo imposed in August 1946 began to bite. But Soviet arms shipments to the Communists continued apace, and Lin's Soviet-trained chief of staff Liu Yalou arranged the transfer of numerous military industrial factories to CCP control.[195] Meanwhile, as Lin's forces captured weapons and inflicted thousands of casualties on Du Yuming's Nationalist troops, the government's February 16 emergency economic reform program collapsed. The wage freezes and price ceilings on essential commodities implemented in order to slow inflation fell apart after only a month in the face of rice riots, hoarding, and black marketeering.[196] The Nationalists were in terrible shape.

Many Chinese welcomed Pierson's January 22 conviction on rape charges, but the Communists called on students to continue the Anti-Brutality Movement. A panel of seven military judges found Pierson guilty after a five-day court-martial and sentenced him to fifteen years.[197] But as the Communists warned, the verdict, imposed by "a so-called 'military court'" that made a mockery of Chinese sovereignty, was still subject to final approval in Washington. "The movement may have started with the Shen case," wrote the author of a January 29 *Xinhua ribao* editorial, but "incidents of U.S. military brutality in China are too numerous to count, so the movement cannot be limited to the rape of Ms. Shen."[198] On March 8, activists formed the Nationwide Anti-Brutality Student Federation (*Quanguo xuesheng kangbao lianhe hui*), a move supported by the CCP.[199] By summer, radical activists completely dominated the student movement across the country.[200]

Highly publicized deadly incidents continued even as troop deployments dwindled, affirming the CCP's warnings that American brutality would continue until all U.S. forces left China. Marine Corps sentries in Tianjin killed three unarmed theft suspects and wounded a fourth over a four-day period in early February. Three of them were shot while running away.[201] According to five Chinese eyewitnesses working at a Marine Corps warehouse, the other suspect, a fellow laborer named Li Fuyou, was strip-searched, beaten, and shot in cold blood for allegedly stealing a monkey wrench.[202] Li, investigators pointed out, had testified three months earlier in a court-martial against a marine accused of assaulting a Chinese worker with a hammer.[203]

On March 17, an MP named Lloyd West killed a thirteen-year-old boy in Beijing. West claimed the boy, a middle school student named Wang Fengxi, had tried to scale a perimeter fence, but several Chinese witnesses insisted that Wang was shot while playing with marbles.[204] Marine Corps investigators refused to bring charges or consider compensation claims in the Tianjin cases, while a court-martial acquitted West.[205] Less than two weeks later, an intoxicated sailor stabbed a rickshaw puller to death in Qingdao hours after a sentry killed an alleged thief at a nearby storage compound, leading to student protests at Shandong University. While the sentry escaped without charges, the sailor in question was convicted of voluntary manslaughter.[206] The verdict, however, failed to bring any closure to student activists, who considered a U.S. military court-martial on Chinese soil an intolerable vestige of foreign imperialism.

Another blow came on August 11, when the secretary of the navy, John Sullivan, overturned Pierson's conviction, giving further credence to CCP attacks on Chiang and the Americans. Although the Naval Sentence Review and Clemency Board concluded that evidence presented in the case was sufficient beyond a reasonable doubt to support the guilty verdict, the navy's judge advocate, General O. S. Colclough, issued a report in June advocating Pierson's exoneration. Colclough misrepresented evidence introduced during the court-marital and discounted Chinese witness testimony in favor of Pierson's drinking companions' accounts, yet his recommendation prevailed.[207] The Chinese Foreign Ministry protested to the U.S. embassy—to no avail.

Communists described Sullivan's decision as "the result of Chiang's government selling out the country and the American imperialists trying to destroy China." The "U.S.-Chiang humiliation of the Chinese people has reached its apex," according to the CCP-controlled *Qunzhong* (The masses), "but Chiang's government had nothing to say about it—not even a fart."[208] Some government-controlled papers did in fact criticize the reversal, but with hyperinflation ravaging the cities and Du Yuming's forces now confined to a few key urban areas in Manchuria as a result of Lin Biao's summer offensive, the Nationalists had more pressing concerns.[209] After all, another violent incident—the Nanjing drowning deaths of two Nationalist soldiers thrown off a bridge by a drunk American corporal celebrating his last night of bachelorhood—had already taken the story's place in the headlines.[210]

· · · · · ·

The last marines departed Qingdao on May 25, 1949, bringing the U.S. military presence in wartime China to an end. On June 2, the People's Liberation

Army (PLA) marched into Qingdao unopposed.[211] Though fighting still raged, the main military confrontations of the civil war were over. The Nationalists' political and military collapse followed quickly after Lin Biao's forces completed the Liao-Shen campaign on November 11, 1948, in which they captured China's largest industrial base and eliminated 472,000 of Chiang's best troops—including the Ramgarh-trained New First and New Sixth Armies. Lin's forces came through the Great Wall passes and seized Beijing and Tianjin in January, while other Communist armies destroyed a force of more than a half-million Nationalist soldiers during the Huai-Hai campaign in the area around Xuzhou, Jiangsu Province. Tens of thousands of PLA troops crossed the Yangzi River on April 21 and occupied the Nationalists' capital at Nanjing two days later. Wuhan, central China's main industrial and transportation center, fell on May 15, and the Communists completed their takeover of Shanghai by the end of the month. As the PLA continued to advance in the West and in the South, Chiang accelerated his efforts to prepare for a last stand in Taiwan. He left Chengdu aboard a DC-4 on December 10, never to return to the mainland.[212]

The Truman administration's policy of providing limited military support to the Nationalists facilitated Chiang's pursuit of a fundamentally flawed strategy in Manchuria, helping to pave the way for his defeat. Without encouragement from senior U.S. military commanders, the marine occupation, and the U.S. Army and Navy's air and sea lifts of Nationalist troops, Chiang might have reconsidered his campaign in the Northeast. Instead, U.S. backing added to Chiang's unwarranted self-assurance about the prospects of defeating the Communists on the battlefield. Under Du Yuming's command, the Nationalists fought a three-year struggle against Lin Biao's forces in a region ill-suited to their American weaponry, way of fighting, and strategy of capturing major cities and transportation lines—which the Communists did not depend on for manpower or material resources. At the same time, Lin's forces had the additional advantage of being adjacent to the Soviet Union, North Korea, and the Soviet-controlled areas of the Liaodong Peninsula, ensuring that Nationalist forces could never outflank or encircle them.[213] Defeat in Manchuria was a blow from which the Nationalists never recovered. In the last two weeks of October 1948 alone, Chiang lost the equivalent of thirty-two divisions there—almost as many troops as the Americans had trained in Ramgarh and Yunnan over the entire Second World War.[214]

The U.S. military presence did incalculable harm to the Nationalists in the political realm. Having learned little from their wartime experience in Southwest China, American personnel behaved like an imperial occupying force, showing none of the deference to local sensitivities and sovereignty characteristic of an ally. The lack of empathy among American personnel serving in China was matched only by the cluelessness of the American press, which, with a smattering of exceptions, dismissed the Anti-Brutality Movement as an outburst of irrational, ungrateful anti-Americanism. Few newspapers bothered to mention the rape case that had sparked the protests.[215] The last thing any Chinese wanted to deal with after Japan's surrender, recalled Jin Chongqi, "was another foreign power acting like a conqueror, running roughshod over Chinese sovereignty, and disregarding Chinese dignity and interests by throwing their weight around on Chinese soil and even wantonly killing and raping our compatriots."[216] But that was exactly what the Chinese got, making easy work for Communist activists, newspapers, and front organizations.

Assigning blame for Chiang's defeat began even before the civil war ended, and Chiang and his American China lobby defenders argued that the conflict might have turned out differently if the Truman administration had placed fewer limits on U.S. involvement. The U.S. military pushed for more vigorous military and political support for Chiang's government in mid-1947, but by late 1948, Americans were convinced that Chiang and the Nationalists were not worth saving. Further military support, as the Truman administration recognized, also risked Soviet intervention in China.[217] In addition to discounting the very real possibility of war with the Soviet Union, Chiang and the armchair generals of the China lobby ignored the lessons of the marine occupation. Deploying more American military personnel in China would have meant more soldiers, sailors, and marines like Earl Revell—men who would have arrived in China feeling like they had come there to save the country, only to grow disillusioned, embittered, and hateful toward the Chinese. They would have been responsible for more vehicle accidents, shootings, assaults, and sexual violence. George Marshall and American diplomats in China believed that further military aid would increase anti-Americanism because the Chinese public had grown weary with Chiang's regime. But they failed to see how deeply the misconduct of U.S. military personnel had contributed to disillusionment with the Nationalists.

Epilogue

The Occupation of China's Long Shadow

. . . .

On August 5, 1949, the U.S. State Department released to the public a report titled *United States Relations with China, with Special Reference to the Period 1944–1949*. Known upon publication simply as the China White Paper, the report placed sole blame on the Chinese Nationalists for their impending defeat in the Chinese Civil War. The China White Paper was a bombshell, making immediate headlines across the United States.[1] In issuing the report, which comprised historical narrative and State Department files dating back to 1844, the Truman administration sought to counter Republican Party attacks on the president's China policy and to humiliate Chiang Kai-shek and the Nationalists, whom Truman and Secretary of State Dean Acheson now viewed as a lost cause. They hoped the White Paper's documentary record would speak for itself and persuade the American public that the time had come to dump their erstwhile wartime ally.[2] In the letter of transmittal that prefaced the White Paper, Acheson wrote that "the ominous result of the civil war in China was beyond the control of the government of the United States. Nothing that his country did or could have done within the reasonable limits of its capabilities," he continued, "could have changed that result."[3]

The White Paper clocked in at 1,054 pages, but it contained not a single document or piece of analysis that reckoned with the conduct of American military personnel in China. This lapse derived in part from expediency. Acheson and Truman wanted to publish quickly, so the report's State Department compilers did not examine records from the military or other government bureaucracies. But U.S. diplomats in China had reported extensively on friction between American soldiers and locals, so the omission stemmed first and foremost from a deeper cause. The military commanders, diplomats, and policy makers charged with thinking about America's relationship with China clung to a series of illusions rooted in a conveniently selective historical memory. Acheson opened his letter of transmittal by citing the long-standing "ties of closest friendship" between China and the United States.[4] Racist violence, deadly accidents, and black marketeering by American servicemen had no place in this "special relationship" myth, nor did the longer history of prewar American imperialism in China. The report's compilers also took it for granted that American observers understood China's needs and realities better than the Chinese did themselves. They never questioned the actions or observations of men like Magruder, Stilwell, or Wedemeyer. While the United States might not have been responsible for the fall of the Chinese republic, it was not the benevolent innocent bystander portrayed by the China White Paper either. U.S. forces indeed contributed to the GMD's defeat.

The Truman administration succeeded in breaking with the Chinese Nationalists by January 1950, but the White Paper placated neither the president's critics nor Chiang's enemies. Under pressure from the Department of Defense and the CIA, Truman authorized covert aid to the Nationalists until the Communists took Guilin in late November 1949. On January 5, however, nearly a month after Chiang left mainland China, the president announced that Washington would not provide military assistance to protect Taiwan. Acheson reiterated Truman's message a week later, declaring Taiwan (and Korea) outside the U.S. defense perimeter in the Asia-Pacific region during a speech at the National Press Club.[5] Meanwhile, Republican attacks intensified. On February 9, Senator Joseph McCarthy launched his namesake political campaign with a speech in Wheeling, West Virginia, in which he claimed, among other accusations, that Communist Party agents working at the State Department had torpedoed Chiang Kai-shek.[6] Mao Zedong, for his part, interpreted the White Paper as irrefutable evidence of America's imperialist designs in China. He responded with a series of scathing essays that took particular umbrage with Acheson's claims of long-standing Sino-American friendship. Mao's narration of Sino-American relations since the 1840s, unlike Acheson's, addressed the conduct of U.S. forces in China, noting sarcastically that Shen Chong's rape and the U.S. Navy's decision to free her attackers "counts as another expression of 'friendship.'"[7]

Enduring resentment of the U.S. occupation would soon be used to justify a new war. The United States revived military support for the Nationalists and deployed forces to Korea after the North Korean People's Army launched attacks across the length of the thirty-eighth parallel in June 1950, attempting to reunify the Korean peninsula under Communist control. As U.S. troops reversed North Korean gains and pushed toward the Chinese border, Mao ordered Chinese forces into Korea and launched a massive domestic political campaign that turned painful memories of the U.S. military presence during the 1940s into a historical touchstone of the New

FIGURE E.1 The U.S. military presence in 1940s China as portrayed during the Resist America and Aid Korea campaign, 1950. (*Meidi qin Hua shi*, Chinese Pamphlet Digitization Project, Center for Research Libraries)

China.[8] The Resist America and Aid Korea campaign of the People's Republic of China (PRC) spurred the country's war-weary population into supporting a potentially catastrophic war against the United States through an unprecedented propaganda drive. Propagandists expanded the Communist Party's reach into daily life by fanning out across China to spread "hatred" (*choushi*), "spite" (*bishi*), and "scorn" (*mieshi*) for American imperialism to every school, factory, neighborhood, and village in the country.[9]

The Resist America and Aid Korea campaign employed a sophisticated array of tools, each reinforcing the others. Literate, urban audiences read about violent crimes and deadly accidents involving American military personnel in dozens of books, pamphlets, and pulp magazines. Despite overblown titles like *Inveterate Hatred* and *America: A Murderous, Blood-Drinking Country*, these accounts focused on the actual sources of wartime anti-American sentiment and often highlighted real legal cases, like Shen Chong's rape and the shooting death of thirteen-year-old Wang Fengxi in Beijing.[10] Comics and pictorials like *The History of America Imperialist Aggression in China* (see figure E.1) and *The U.S. Military's Violence in China* (see figure E.2) introduced the same stories to less sophisticated audiences, as did photograph, cartoon, and art exhibitions.[11] The killing of Shanghai rickshaw puller Zang

FIGURE E.2 Image of Chiang Kai-shek and an American serviceman as portrayed during the Resist America and Aid Korea campaign, 1950. (*Meidi qin Hua shi*, Chinese Pamphlet Digitization Project, Center for Research Libraries)

Da Erzi was turned into a play.[12] Perhaps most ubiquitous were the thousands of newspaper articles devoted to the campaign, which provided the basis for group study sessions that propagandists found "very effective." Workers at Beijing's Electric Power Bureau, for example, "were able to make connections to violent American behavior in Beijing [during the 1940s]" by reading accounts about the conduct of U.S. forces in Korea.[13] The campaign also saturated the airwaves, accounting for two-thirds of daily programming on the People's Radio, including a lecture series on crimes committed by U.S. forces in China and songs like "Paper Tigers Aren't Scary." Meanwhile, in schools and universities, all politics classes became Resist America and Aid Korea classes.[14]

The campaign reached its zenith at denunciation meetings (*kongsu hui*)— carefully choreographed mass rallies where local residents often shared personal stories of mistreatment at the hands of U.S. military personnel. Propagandists laid the groundwork in advance by researching past American, Japanese, and GMD "crimes against the masses" in each area, while spreading propaganda and carrying out patriotic education. "In many coastal cities, as well as Wuhan, Chongqing, Chengdu, Kunming, Guiyang and Xian, all the places where American troops were stationed and slaughtered Chinese, you can criticize violence by American soldiers," instructed Liao Gailong, the National Resist America and Aid Korea Association's Propaganda Bureau vice director. Liao wrote that it was fine to "criticize" Japanese and GMD crimes, "but everything must be put on the shoulders of the American imperialists, our mortal enemy." Liao also emphasized the importance of "finding and cultivating" local "activists" (*jiji fenzi*) who could speak about their negative interactions with American troops during the meetings.[15] "Ordinary people like hearing about real people and events," reported the Communist Youth League's Beijing office. "They aren't willing to listen to long-winded sermons."[16]

Party officials believed that the emotionally charged atmosphere and collective sharing of crimes and accidents involving U.S. military personnel made denunciation meetings the campaign's best tool for cultivating hatred of American imperialism. "In Shanghai, as in all other places around the country, denunciation meetings are the most effective propaganda method," concluded the city's propaganda committee some nine months into the campaign.[17] Earlier reports described "hearing about a young woman from the district named Zhen Lin who was killed by an American military vehicle" as the "most powerful moment" during a ten-thousand-person-strong meeting in the city's Gaoqiao district. Everyone in attendance "was outraged" after another man announced that "his son's wooden leg was bestowed by an American Jeep."[18] Sixteen people supposedly fainted while hearing about "the cruelty and violence of American imperialism" at a meeting that occurred around the same time in Beijing.[19] These rallies had the feverish energy of evangelical Christian revival meetings in the United States and aimed to inspire similar conversion experiences.[20] The Communist Youth League's Propaganda Bureau in Beijing noted that previously apathetic middle school students understood the limits of their knowledge—or at least became afraid to express "incorrect" ideas—after "hearing from people who've been harmed by American imperialism."[21]

In Southwest China, denunciation meetings called attention to every source of civilian resentment against the U.S. military that had materialized during the Second World War. In Chengdu, Li Ceji recounted the deaths that occurred during the B-29 airfield construction projects.[22] Another former airfield worker described going three months without pay and watching drunk American personnel charge into homes when looking for prostitutes.[23] Farmers belonging to the Yi minority in Yunnan explained how they were unfairly compensated for land appropriated to build hostels and airfields.[24] According to participants at a meeting near the former U.S. airfield at Liangshan, "Jeeps killing people was a dime-a-dozen occurrence."[25] Residents in

Kunming discussed how American soldiers harassed women near the Nanping Theater, while Zhang Guoshui described the day (discussed in chapter 4) that two intoxicated GIs beat his mother to death outside the U.S. Army's Ninety-Fifth Station Hospital.[26] Others shared stories about the beating and killing of suspected thieves, while discussion of American involvement in the black market echoed the Chinese Nationalists' wartime complaints, arguing that American military goods for sale in Kunming were smuggled in or stolen by the Americans themselves.[27] Speakers also stressed GMD complicity in the U.S. military's violations of Chinese sovereignty, such as searching Chinese-owned shops in Zhanyi and confiscating American goods.

The Jeep-girl-as-rape-victim narrative reemerged powerfully during these meetings. Participants almost invariably raised rape allegations, with many people claiming to have seen Americans dragging women off in Jeeps. "The people of Kunming can also clearly remember how the [GMD] reactionaries would do everything they could to cover up American violence," recalled Xia Yu, alluding to the Jeep girl counternarrative the Nationalists tried to popularize under pressure from Wedemeyer. "The U.S. military now wants to come back and humiliate our wives and sisters once again," Xia warned.[28] Li Longhui echoed Xia's claims during a meeting in Chongqing, describing how Nationalist police blew him off when he tried to report a sexual assault. "If we don't resist now," he told the audience, "American Jeeps will carry back those savage, inhuman soldiers to humiliate us again."[29] Accounts like Xia's and Li's reconfigured gender in a specific way that aided CCP state building, framing support for the war as a means to reclaim Chinese masculinity. This narrative also reasserted patriarchy, depicting Chinese women solely as victims—or potential victims—to be defended.

Harnessing memories of the U.S. military occupation through the Resist America and Aid Korea campaign helped the Communists consolidate power, building on lessons learned during the Chinese Civil War. Communist Party rule was still fragile when the Chinese People's Volunteer Army crossed the Yalu River and entered Korea just one year after Mao proclaimed the founding of the People's Republic. Many civilians opposed the new regime, which also had to contend with food shortages, roving bandit gangs, social turmoil, and escalating GMD morale operations along the Chinese coast.[30] Fear of U.S. military power and admiration for American culture remained prevalent, too.[31] The party's anti-American campaign bolstered Mao's regime by marginalizing dissent, pumping new life into the Communist revolution, and redefining Chinese citizenship, making hatred of the United States a key pillar of national identity.[32] While Resist America and Aid Korea propaganda included huge exaggerations and many outright lies, including allegations that American missionaries engaged in the mass murder of Chinese orphans, the campaign's grounding in the widely shared anti–U.S. military sentiment that emerged during the 1940s enabled it to resonate widely.[33]

The Korean War also enabled the Chinese Nationalists to consolidate their rule on Taiwan, underpinned by a revived U.S.-ROC alliance that quickly fell into troubling wartime patterns. U.S. and ROC officials learned some lessons from the 1940s. Neither Chiang nor the Pentagon wanted U.S. ground forces in Taiwan. Admiral Arthur Radford, chairman of the Joint Chiefs of Staff, actually pushed back against State Department pressure in 1955 to station a U.S. Marine division on the island by arguing that their high salaries relative to those of Chinese troops and their sexual relations with Chinese women would alienate locals. The U.S. government deployed a fighter-bomber squadron, and a Military Assistance and Advisory Group (MAAG) instead, the latter unit a direct outgrowth of the wartime Y-Force and Ramgarh training programs, the first major U.S. military initiative to train and equip the armed forces of an allied state. Like their predecessors who deployed to Southwest China, MAAG and Air Force personnel enjoyed all the trappings of colonial overlords: wealth, Western-style housing, privileged access to valuable commodities, and full diplomatic immunity. These power disparities fueled misconduct and a sense of racial superiority on the part of American personnel and resentment on the part of the Chinese—just as they had during the 1940s.[34]

Sino-American tensions would erupt into anti-American riots in Taiwan after a U.S. military court-martial in Taipei acquitted an American soldier of killing a Chinese man. MAAG sergeant Robert G. Reynolds shot Liu Ziran to death on March 20, 1957, telling investigators he had acted in self-defense after his wife spotted Liu leering at her from outside a window while she bathed. Reynolds claimed that Liu charged at him with a metal pipe, but neither American nor Chinese police found such a weapon at the crime scene. In the weeks leading up to the trial, the island simmered with anti-American resentment. Newspaper coverage raged against the continued humiliation of diplomatic immunity. For years, ROC authorities had demanded—to no avail—a status of forces agreement (SOFA) like the NATO and Japan SOFAs, which allowed host governments to exercise jurisdiction when American troops committed crimes against locals while off duty. Reynolds's May 23 acquittal sparked outrage. In another echo of wartime Chongqing, ROC authorities turned a blind eye the next day as hundreds of demonstrators surrounded the U.S. embassy. The crowed quickly swelled into the thousands and grew violent, with rioters storming the embassy compound and attacking MAAG facilities elsewhere in Taipei, injuring eleven Americans. U.S. authorities believed elements of the ROC government were behind the riots, but Chiang cracked down quickly, just as he had done in response to earlier anti-American demonstrations on the mainland. U.S. policy toward Taiwan remained unchanged.[35]

American servicemen's interactions with Chinese civilians during the 1940s and 1950s also established patterns that followed the U.S. military elsewhere in Asia. U.S. forces displaced civilians in South Korea and Japan in order to build sprawling bases with American-style suburban neighborhoods and recreational facilities.[36] English served as the lingua franca in every partnership. Particularly during the Cold War, American buying power distorted local economies no less than it had in China, and sex work became central to the economic and social landscape around practically every base. The political scientist Katharine Moon estimates that more than one million South Korean women have worked as sex providers for the U.S. military since 1950.[37] Meanwhile, extraterritorial provisions shielded American personnel from local jurisdiction, fueling high violent crime and accident rates. Both power disparities and race influenced the U.S. government's refusal, until the mid-1960s, to grant the ROC, South Korea, or the Philippines jurisdiction rights on par with those granted to Japan and NATO allies beginning in the early 1950s.[38] This disparity recalled the wartime decision to deny Chinese authorities the powers of arrest granted to British and Australian police. As it was, each SOFA included a "courtesy clause" that enabled U.S. authorities to pressure host countries into transferring their jurisdiction rights back to the Americans. Between 1967 and 1991, for example, U.S. authorities in South Korea retained jurisdiction in more than 99 percent of the cases that Seoul was legally entitled to handle.[39] These patterns have persisted up to the present.

American servicemen in Asia continued to commit brutal sex crimes against women and girls, which galvanized opposition to U.S. military bases across the region. In Japan, as the historian Jennifer Miller shows, public opposition to the U.S.-Japanese alliance during the 1950s linked sex and nationhood, as it had in China. Japanese who opposed the alliance with the United States used discussions and images of prostitution, rape, and sexual violence as metaphors for national trauma.[40] A nationwide grassroots anti-base movement would emerge in South Korea for the first time in 1992, after the shockingly grotesque rape and murder of sex worker Yun Geum-i by U.S. Army private Kenneth Markle.[41] Korean feminists argued that government officials had violated the Korean nation by allowing American troops to abuse Korean women, the same narrative that had animated China's 1947 anti-brutality protests.[42] In 1996, President Bill Clinton and Prime Minister Ryutaro Hashimoto held an emergency summit in California to defuse tension on Okinawa after three American servicemen dragged a twelve-year-old girl into a rental car at knifepoint and gang-raped her at an isolated beach, sparking mass protests and moves toward a referendum on the bases.[43] Sexual relations and violent sex crimes committed by American servicemen also energized the anti-base movement in the Philippines, which succeeded in evicting U.S. forces in 1991.[44] U.S. military sexual violence remains endemic in Asia: sixty-five U.S. Marines were imprisoned for sexual offenses on Okinawa between January 2015 and December 2017.[45]

The experience of the U.S. military in wartime China provided a clear example of how a history of foreign imperialism and lasting sensitivities connected to race, gender, and nation provided a framework through which local populations understood their interactions with Americans, but it was not a lesson applied elsewhere in Asia. U.S. allies in Korea and Southeast Asia fell under foreign domination before the twentieth century, while Okinawans lived under direct U.S. military rule from 1945 until 1972. But only on Japan's main islands have U.S. forces in Asia made a sustained—albeit reactive— effort to insulate society from the U.S. military presence, largely by concentrating bases in Okinawa.[46]

U.S. military authorities showed considerably more care as they managed interactions with local populations in Western Europe. In Great Britain, U.S. forces proactively reduced their visibility by operating out of existing bases and integrating into British housing patterns, schools, and social life.[47] The U.S. military also invested tremendous effort and resources into building a more egalitarian relationship with West Germany, beginning in the early 1950s. European civilians have remained more supportive of the U.S. presence, and prior to the Iraq War, protests focused mostly on issues like nuclear weapons, not the conduct of American troops.[48] Resistance in Asia, however, illustrated the degree to which the U.S. military presence in the region revived old colonial dynamics.[49]

The experience in China also cast a long shadow over U.S. imperial statecraft in Asia. Both the so-called loss of China and the specter of PRC expansionism propelled the Kennedy administration to escalate the military advisory presence in South Vietnam.[50] The military partnership with Saigon, like Taiwan's MAAG program, had roots in the U.S. military's army-building program in China. Dependence on U.S. military and economic aid left South Vietnamese president Ngo Dinh Diem facing the same dilemma Chiang Kai-shek had confronted, compelling him to forfeit domestic support by binding his nation-building aims with U.S. foreign policy objectives, despite pursuing goals that often diverged from Washington's ambitions in the region.[51] American officials in South Vietnam, for their part, mirrored predecessors in China with their unquestioned faith in their capacity to mentor Diem's troops and impart effectiveness. But as battlefield setbacks mounted for Diem's security forces, his alliance with the United States unraveled. Instead of questioning the premises informing America's role in Vietnam, U.S. officials lashed out over Diem's corruption, authoritarianism, and failure to follow American ideas for political and military reform.[52] Joseph Stilwell and Frank Dorn had discussed engineering Chiang's elimination over similar frustrations, but the Kennedy administration took action by pledging nonintervention against the South Vietnamese generals plotting to remove Diem, which paved the way for the November 1, 1963, coup that toppled his government.[53] Kennedy's successor, President Lyndon Johnson, committed the United States to war in Vietnam in order to avoid—as he said on more than one occasion—being "the President who saw Southeast Asia go the way China went."[54]

The U.S. war in Afghanistan revealed the enduring influence of patterns that emerged in China more than fifty years before the 9/11 terrorist attacks. Over nearly two decades, the United States spent more than $2 trillion attempting to remake Afghanistan along American lines, above all through army building. U.S. forces relied on thousands of locally hired Afghan interpreters to train and equip some 300,000 Afghan security personnel, providing them with mountains of modern American weaponry.[55] Throughout the conflict, American officials and media outlets upbraided Afghan prime minister Hamid Karzai's administration for its corruption, rarely pausing to consider how U.S. military and economic aid contributed to the problem. At the same time, ordinary American troops racialized the host country population with the same speed and consistency their predecessors had in China, Korea, and Vietnam, with pejoratives like "Haji" and "goat fucker" standing in for "Chink," "slope," and "gook." Many Afghans sided with the United States after U.S. forces toppled the Taliban in 2001, but the conduct of American military personnel, particularly the killing of civilians, energized anti-American sentiment as the occupation dragged on.[56] The Taliban, like the Chinese and Vietnamese Communists before them, exploited grassroots resentment against the U.S. military presence, drew sustenance from across the border, and built up armies that proved more capable than their American-trained-and-equipped compatriots, prevailing with remarkable ease against Afghan government forces after U.S. troops departed in 2021.

In the wake of the failure in Afghanistan, we would do well to heed the lessons of the tormented U.S.-ROC alliance. Had Dean Acheson and his staff undertaken a more thorough accounting of the U.S. military's role in China before publishing the White Paper in 1949, they might have drawn some of the following conclusions. First, building up foreign armies that will advance U.S. policy objectives is a daunting task. American arms, equipment, and know-how cannot imbue a foreign army with fighting spirit, particularly without the air support and logistical networks that U.S. forces take for granted.[57] Second, army building is inherently paternalistic and neo-colonial. The hierarchical relationship it creates predisposes American commanders to blaming junior partners—rather than reexamining their own assumptions—whenever difficulties emerge. Third, history matters. Americans might overlook the past and profess good intentions, but victims of racism and foreign imperialism do not forget so easily, especially when Americans have been complicit in their suffering. Fourth, maintaining extraterritorial legal jurisdiction over American military personnel facilitates misconduct and promotes prejudice against the host country population. Placing U.S. troops outside local law turns them into an occupying force. In a divided society, each of these factors can be turned into weapons against a U.S.-allied government. U.S. officials failed to learn any of these lessons in 1949. Whether they do so today remains to be seen.

Notes

Introduction

1. Regulations respecting the Laws and Customs of War on Land, annex, the Hague, October 18, 1907, article 42.

2. B. Zhang, "China's Quest for Foreign Military Aid," 303.

3. Immerwahr, *How to Hide an Empire*, 283–87, 295–97.

4. Tunner, *Over the Hump*, 59.

5. Tow, "Great Bombing of Chongqing," 256–82.

6. Van de Ven, *China at War*, 172–78.

7. This figure includes more than 65,000 army and 3,100 navy personnel stationed in China in August 1945 and more than 53,000 marines and sailors who arrived in October 1945. The total figure is probably slightly higher because of the need to account for replacement troops, whose arrival relieved others but did not increase the total count. Personnel Strength—China Theater, Jan. 1945 to Jan. 1946, RG 493, UD-UP 590, box 11, Charts on Strength, NARA; SACO Troop Strength charts, August 31, 1945, RG 38, NHC-75, box 6, Personnel S-1 folder 17, NARA; "III Amphibious Corps War Diary, 1 October to 31 October 1945," *China Marine Scuttlebutt*, December 2003, 26. According to China's 2010 census, 71,493 Americans were residing in Mainland China. See "Major Figures on Residents from Hong Kong, Macao, and Taiwan and Foreigners Covered by 2010 Population Census," National Bureau of Statistics of the People's Republic of China, April 29, 2011. On the prewar population, see Pomfret, *Beautiful Country and the Middle Kingdom*, 4.

8. Both China studies scholars and historians of U.S. foreign relations and military history followed this approach, which originated with the publication of journalists Theodore White and Annalee Jacoby's *Thunder out of China* in 1946 and *The Stilwell Papers*, edited by White, in 1948. For examples, see Romanus and Sunderland, *Stilwell's Mission to China*; Romanus and Sunderland, *Stilwell's Command Problems*; Romanus and Sunderland, *Time Runs Out in CBI*; Tuchman, *Stilwell and the American Experience in China*; Schaller, *U.S. Crusade in China*; Alexander, *Strange Connection*, 1–72; Eastman, *Seeds of Destruction*; Dreyer, *China at War*, 256–311.

9. Van de Ven, *War and Nationalism in China*; van de Ven, "Stilwell in the Stocks," 243–59.

10. Mitter, *Forgotten Ally*, 239–364; Ch'i, *Jianbanuzhang de mengyou*; Chang, "Nationalist Army on the Eve of the War," 83–104; Jay Taylor, *Generalissimo*, 194–381. T. Yang, *Xunzhao zhenshi de Jiang Jieshi*.

11. For World War II–focused scholarship, see Schaller, *U.S. Crusade in China*; X. Liu, *Partnership for Disorder*; Mitter, *Forgotten Ally*, 239–364; Ch'i, *Jianbanuzhang*

de mengyou; Babb, "Harmony of Yin and Yank"; K. Xu, *ZhongMianYin zhanchang kangri zhanzheng shi*. For Chinese Civil War–focused scholarship, see Gallicchio, *Scramble for Asia*; Spector, *In the Ruins of Empire*, 3–72, 215–25, 242–56; H. Zhang, *America Perceived*, 9–145; Kurtz-Phelan, *China Mission*; Westad, *Cold War and Revolution*.

12. Morden, *Women's Army Corps*, 21–23, 31, 47; Mary Krauss to A. P. Krauss, March 11, 1943, folder 14, Mary Theresa Krauss Collection, FSU.

13. Romanus and Sunderland, *Stilwell's Command Problems*, 104, 263; Converse et al., *Exclusion of Black Soldiers*, 139.

14. Wedemeyer to MacArthur, August 21, 1945, Albert C. Wedemeyer Papers, box 87, folder 1, HIA.

15. Kraus, *China Offensive*, 3.

16. This figure includes housing, revolving funds, construction, and operation and maintenance at overseas bases but excludes the salaries paid to personnel stationed there. See *Operation and Maintenance Overview*, 179; Vine, *Base Nation*, 115–33, 195–213, 217–31; Gillem, *America Town*, 88–89.

17. Juvinall, "Heaven or Hell," 205–9; Ryan, "Left Behind."

18. Karlin, "Why Military Assistance Programs Disappoint," 111–20; Whitlock, "Unguarded Nation"; Bacevich, *America's War for the Greater Middle East*, 275, 317, 348–52.

19. Vine, *Base Nation*, 135–48, 163–91, 262–87; Höhn and Moon, *Over There*, 1–30, 337–58; Donoghue, *Borderland on the Isthmus*, 128–85, 204–29; C. Johnson, *Sorrows of Empire*, 151–86; A. Johnson, *Night in the American Village*; Enloe, *Bananas, Beaches, and Bases*, 1–87.

20. Kovner, "Soundproofed Superpower," 87–109.

21. Hobsbawm, *The Age of Extremes*, 216–22; Von Eschen, *Race against Empire*, 25–28; Bayly and Harper, *Forgotten Armies*, 106–286, 423–64.

22. Immerwahr, *How to Hide an Empire*, 230–31.

23. Duara, "Cold War as a Historical Period," 457–59.

24. Duara, "Chinese World Order in Historical Perspective," 1–12; Duara, "Cold War as a Historical Period," 460–64. The Soviet Union, as Duara argues, also fits into this framework. See also Arrighi et al., "Historical Capitalism, East and West." On developmentalism and U.S. imperialism, see E. G. Miller, *Misalliance*; Ekbladh, *Great American Mission*; Immerwahr, *Thinking Small*.

25. For comprehensive studies of the global U.S. military base network and post-1945 U.S. empire, see Vine, *Base Nation*; Vine, *United States of War*, 225–359; Immerwahr, *How to Hide an Empire*; Gillem, *America Town*; Sandars, *America's Overseas Garrisons*; Cooley, *Base Politics*; A. P. Baker, *American Soldiers Overseas*; Man, *Soldiering through Empire*; C. Johnson, *Sorrows of Empire*, 23–37. On anti-base resistance and blowback, see Lutz, *Bases of Empire*; Yeo, *Activists, Alliances, and Anti-U.S. Base Protests*; C. Johnson, *Blowback*. For analyses of race and gender, see Höhn and Moon, *Over There*; K. H. S. Moon, *Sex among Allies*; Enloe, *Maneuvers*; Enloe, *Bananas, Beaches, and Bases*; Höhn, *GIs and Fräuleins*; S. Cheng, *On the Move for Love*; Yuh, *Beyond the Shadow of Camptown*; Sturdevant and Stoltzfus, *Let the Good Times Roll*; Alvah, "U.S. Military Personnel and Families Abroad," 247–68; Briggs,

Reproducing Empire; Angst, "Sacrifice of a Schoolgirl." On U.S. military bases and cultural exchange, see Kim, "*My Car* Modernity," 63–85; Kim and Shin, "Birth of 'Rok'"; Roberson, "'Doin' Our Thing.'" For a review essay on bases and military occupations, see Fredman, "Military Occupations and Overseas Bases in Twentieth-Century U.S. Foreign Relations," 596–612.

26. McCoy, *In the Shadows of the American Century*; Kramer, "Power and Connection"; Kramer, *Blood of Government*; Neptune, *Caliban and the Yankees*; Rotter, "Saidism without Said."

27. Kramer, "Power and Connection," 1378–83.

28. Exceptions include Cathcart, "Atrocities, Insults, and 'Jeep Girls,'" and Masuda, *Cold War Crucible*, which deals primarily with the Korean War. Hong Zhang examines culture during the Chinese Civil War but does not draw on Chinese archives. See Zhang, *America Perceived*.

29. Misconduct was still common among U.S. forces in other allied countries and in the United States itself, but U.S. commanders in Britain, Australia, and New Zealand made greater efforts to cooperate with host country authorities and foster mutual understanding between U.S. troops and local civilians. See especially Reynolds, *Rich Relations*, 42–43, 95–105, 143–49, 161–98, 210–14, 260, 383–91, 403; Barker and Jackson, *Fleeting Attraction*, 110–36; Bioletti, *Yanks Are Coming*, 75. On the U.S. home front, see Blower, "V-J Day, 1945, Times Square," 70–87; Hiltner, *Taking Leave, Taking Liberties*. On occupied Europe, see Goedde, *GIs and Germans*; Roberts, *What Soldiers Do*; Willoughby, *Remaking the Conquering Heroes*; Lilly, *Taken by Force*. On Japan, see Kovner, *Occupying Power*; Kramm, *Sanitized Sex*; Shibusawa, *America's Geisha Ally*; Dower, *Embracing Defeat*; McLelland, *Love, Sex, and Democracy*; J. M. Miller, *Cold War Democracy,* 26–70. For comprehensive studies of the postwar occupations, see Carruthers, *The Good Occupation*; Madsen, *Sovereign Soldiers*.

30. On prewar American empire, see Kramer, *Blood of Government*; Kramer, "Power and Connection," 1348–91; Go and Foster, eds., *American Colonial State in the Philippines*; Tillman, *Dollar Diplomacy by Force*; McPherson, *Invaded*; McPherson, "Irony of Legal Pluralism in U.S. Occupations"; Renda, *Taking Haiti*; Foster, *Projections of Power*; Gobat, *Confronting the American Dream*; McCoy and Scarano, *Colonial Crucible*; Utset, *Cultural History of Cuba*. For studies that show continuities in American empire across the twentieth and twenty-first centuries, see Bender and Lipman, *Making the Empire Work*; Blower, "Nation of Outposts," 439–59; Bacevich, *American Empire*; Donoghue, *Borderland on the Isthmus*; Lipman, *Guantanamo*.

31. On imperial race-making, see Kramer, *Blood of Government*, especially 124–30, 196–205; Kramer, "Race-Making and Colonial Violence in the U.S. Empire," 169–210. The literature on gender and imperialism is vast and widely cited throughout this book. Key monographs I have depended on include Hoganson, *Fighting for American Manhood*; Goedde, *GIs and Germans*; Bederman, *Manliness and Civilization*; Enloe, *Maneuvers*, Enloe, *Bananas, Beaches, and Bases*; Renda, *Taking Haiti*; Roberts, *What Soldiers Do*; Shibusawa, *America's Geisha Ally*.

32. On bodily encounters in colonial India and the Philippines, see Rotter, *Empires of the Senses*.

33. On extraterritorial power and status of forces agreements, see Scully, *Bargaining with the State from Afar*; C. Johnson, "Three Rapes," 1–19; Ruskola, *Legal Orientalism*; Zheng, "Specter of Extraterritoriality," 17–44; Bickers, *Out of China*, 124; Vine, *Base Nation*, 40, 138, 264–66.

34. Kramer, *Blood of Government*, 196–205, 305–13; Rotter, *Empires of the Senses*, 14–46; Capozzola, *Bound by War*, chaps. 2–3.

35. Kramer, "Power and Connection," 1380–82.

36. On sovereignty and legitimacy, see Sheehan, "Problem of Sovereignty in European History," 1–15; Reilly, "Sovereign States of Vietnam."

37. Plating, *Hump*, 160; Immerwahr, *How to Hide an Empire*, 284–85.

38. On the Xi'an Incident, see van de Ven, *China at War*, 57–72; Jay Taylor, *Generalissimo*, 121–37.

39. On the American impulse to reform China and the belief in a paternalistic "special" relationship between the United States and China, see Hunt, *Making of a Special Relationship*, especially 299–304; Jespersen, *American Images of China*, 3–9; Jacobson, *Barbarian Virtues*, 25–38; Pomfret, *Beautiful Country and the Middle Kingdom*, 40–68, 137–49, 178–89. On the interplay between assimilationist and exclusionary (or segregationist) forms of racism, see Kendi, *How to Be an Antiracist*; Kendi, *Stamped from the Beginning*, especially 13–14; Immerwahr, "Ugly American," 7–20. On Buck and Luce, see Jespersen, *American Images of China*; J. Bradley, *China Mirage*, 130–67; Herzstein, *Henry R. Luce, Time, and the American Crusade in Asia*, 9–78; Leong, *China Mystique*, 27–33, 101.

40. On American and American-educated contributions to China during the late Qing and Republican era, see Pomfret, *Beautiful Country and the Middle Kingdom*, 123–41, 150–54; Guoqi Xu, *Chinese and Americans*, 74–104, 139–203; Brooks, *American Exodus*, 41–74.

41. In 1928, 5,692 marines deployed to Nicaragua during the Sandino Rebellion. For the rest of the 1920s and 1930s, however, no more than 2,500 U.S. troops were stationed in Nicaragua, the Dominican Republic, or Haiti at any given time. See McPherson, *Invaded*, 14, 27, 35, 59, 68, 80, 200, 231–32. The last American occupation forces left the German Rhineland in February 1923. See A. P. Baker, *American Soldiers Overseas*, 21–22.

42. On the Boxer Uprising and the 1900–1901 China Relief Expedition, see Pomfret, *Beautiful Country and the Middle Kingdom*, 109–17; P. A. Cohen, *History in Three Keys*; Hunt, "Forgotten Occupation."

43. During Chiang's Northern Expedition (1926–28), the U.S. Navy sent seventeen destroyers, eleven submarines, and three cruisers to China, along with numerous support vessels. See *River Patrol and Other U.S. Navy Asiatic Fleet Activities in China*, Annual Reports of the Department of the Navy, Gale Archives Unbound. On the Yangtze Patrol, see Kemp, *Yangtze Patrol*; Braisted, *Diplomats in Blue*.

44. Cornebise, *United States 15th Infantry Regiment in China*; G. B. Clark, *Treading Softly*, 56–77; Coffman, "American 15th Infantry Regiment in China," 58–59.

45. On the Philippines, see Capozzola, *Bound by War*, 14–150; Kramer, *Blood of Government*, 218–23, 248. On the Caribbean, see Renda, *Taking Haiti*, 13–18, 89–130; McPherson, *Invaded*, 53–110.

46. Joseph Castner to Charles Summerall, June 21, 1927, Gale Archives Unbound: Political, Economic, and Military Conditions in China. On treaty port racism, see Cornebise, *United States Army in China*, 87–93; Bickers, *Out of China*, 17, 57.

47. Van de Ven, *War and Nationalism in China*, 9–13; Dorn, *Sino-Japanese War, 1937–1941*, 9, 201.

48. On how interwar service in China shaped attitudes toward the Chinese, see Ch'i, *Jianbanuzhang de mengyou*, 640–42. On prewar China service of senior U.S. officers in China during the 1940s, see Grieve, "Belated Endeavor," 15–17; Cornebise, *United States Army in China*, 121–75, 220–21.

49. Letcher, *Goodbye to Old Peking*, 10.

50. On the Fifteenth Infantry, see Coffman, "The American 15th Infantry Regiment in China," 57–74. On the navy and the marines, see "Subject File of Communicable Disease," RG 52, Controls Section 1942–1952, box 44, Venereal Disease 1938 to 1946, folder 2, NARA; "10 Year Syphilis Study," undated, RG 52, box 45, Subject Files 1943–1951, NARA.

51. Romanus and Sunderland, *Stilwell's Mission to China*, 27.

52. Mao, "Report to the 2nd National Congress of Worker's and Peasant's Representatives," January 23, 1934, www.marxists.org/reference/archive/mao/selected-works/volume-6/mswv6_18.htm#s3.

53. Chiang and Jaffe, *China's Destiny and Economic Theory*, 80–81.

54. The following is a short list of works that have been key to my own thinking about Chinese nationalism during the 1930s and 1940s: Oyen, *The Diplomacy of Migration*, especially 13–68; Ch'i, *Jianbanuzhang de mengyou*; van de Ven, *War and Nationalism in China*; Hershatter, *Women and China's Revolutions*; Duara, "De-Constructing the Chinese Nation"; Duara, *Rescuing History from the Nation*; Callahan, "National Insecurities"; Callahan, *China*; S. Zhao, "Chinese Nationalism and Its International Orientations," 1–33; S. Zhao, *Nation-State by Construction*; P. A. Cohen, "Remembering and Forgetting National Humiliation in Twentieth-Century China," 1–39; Dikötter, "Culture, 'Race,' and Nation," 590–605; Sun, "Minguo shiqi de guochi jinianri," 16–19; Harrison, *China*; Lu, "Sport, Nationalism, and the Building of the Modern Chinese Nation-State," 1030–54; Morris, *Marrow of the Nation*; J. Yang, "Xiangxiang minzu chiru," 1–42; J. Yang, *Bingfu, huanghuo yu shuishi*; M. Johnson, "Anti-Imperialism as Strategy," 123–45.

55. On the German advisory role in China, see Ch'i, *Jianbanuzhang de mengyou*, 65–67, 87, 181–82; B. Zhang, "China's Quest for Foreign Military Aid," 283–88; Chang, "Nationalist Army on the Eve of War," 86–87, 95–97, 102–4; Harmsen, *Shanghai 1937*. On the Soviet role, see B. Zhang, "China's Quest for Foreign Military Aid," 288–93.

56. Pomfret, *Beautiful Country and the Middle Kingdom*, 234–43.

57. Harmsen, *Shanghai 1937*, 75–78; Ch'i, *Jianbanuzhang de mengyou*, 633–37.

58. Quoted in Tuchman, *Stilwell and the American Experience in China*, 239.

59. Manela, "Fourth Policeman," 214–30.

60. U.S. Army Service Forces, *Pocket Guide to China*, 2–3.

61. On War Department backing for Stilwell's plan to take command of China's armies, see Ch'i, *Jianbanuzhang de mengou*, 76–92; Yu, *Dragon's War*, 164–66.

62. "Attached Report on Theft of Building Materials and Incidental Shooting," August 21, 1944, RG 493, UD-UP 419, box 244, Correspondence 1944, NARA.

63. On anti-Americanism in the press, see M. Johnson, "Anti-Imperialism as Strategy," 123–31. For GMD files on Soviet misconduct, see "Sulian jundui zai dongbei," file no. 020-021803-0022 to 020-021803-0024, wajiao bu dang'an, AHA.

64. On this pattern repeating in U.S.-occupied Korea less than one year later, see Man, *Soldiering through Empire*, 24–28.

Chapter 1

1. "Kunming mengjun zhi shenghuo," *Da gong bao*, February 15, 1945.

2. "Major-General Huang Talks on the Rations of the U.S. Armed Forces in China," *Guomin gong bao*, February 15, 1945, China Press Review 41, RG 208, OWI Overseas Branch, Information File on Asia, box 380, unmarked folder, NARA.

3. Van de Ven, *China at War*, 179–202; Lary, *Chinese People at War*, 157–61.

4. Young, *China's Wartime Finance and Inflation*, 265–68; van de Ven, *War and Nationalism in China*, 269.

5. Wakeman, *Spymaster*, 344; "Political Reports for January and February 1945, February 20 and March 17, 1945," RG 84, China, Kunming Consulate, Classified General Records, 1944–1949, box 3, Classified Files, 1945, NARA.

6. Van de Ven, *War and Nationalism in China*, 272–74.

7. Allen, "Mutual Aid between the U.S. and the British Empire," 247, 254–55.

8. "Principles Applying to Mutual Aid in the Prosecution of War against Aggression," Executive Agreement Series 251 (Washington, DC: Government Printing Office, 1942), 2.

9. On the Guomindang, nationalism, and nation-building in the Republican era, see Tsui, "Clock Time, National Space, and the Limits of Guomindang Anti-imperialism," 921–45; Duara, "De-Constructing the Chinese Nation," 15; Callahan, "National Insecurities," 200–210; Cohen, "Remembering and Forgetting National Humiliation in Twentieth-Century China," 6, 11–15; Dikötter, "Culture, 'Race,' and Nation," 590–91; Callahan, *China*, 69–76; Harrison, *China: Inventing the Nation*, 2–6, 169–84, 190–223.

10. Lou Stoumen, "What It's Like for GIs in China," *Yank*, October 20, 1944.

11. This chapter's sensory approach draws from the work of Andrew Rotter. See Rotter, *Empires of the Senses*.

12. This is the WASC figure. See "WASC Graphic Report of Four Years' Service," Huang Renlin Papers, box 1, folder 2, HIA.

13. A few scholars discuss hostels or hostel services briefly, but most have ignored the program entirely. See Mitter, *Forgotten Ally*, 339–41; Zhang, "Cong Minguo dang'an kan 1944 nian zhu Dian Meijun roulei gongying fengbo," 20–22; Romanus and Sunderland, *Stilwell's Command Problems*, 291.

14. U.S. Army Service Forces, *Pocket Guide to China*, 2.

15. "Huang Renlin renshi diaocha biao," undated, file no. 129000100325A, AHA, Xindian Branch. On Chiang's Office of Personal Attendants, see Chor, "Making of the Guomindang's Japan Policy," 218–19.

16. "A Graphic Report of Four Years' Service," Huang Renlin Papers, box 1, folder 2, HIA.

17. Chennault, *Way of a Fighter*, 31, 50.

18. On Soochow University, see X. Xu, "Southern Methodist Mission to China." On other American missionary-run schools in China, see Bays and Widmer, *China's Christian Colleges.*

19. "The Memoirs of J.L. Huang," chap. 2, Huang Renlin Papers, box 1, folder 1, HIA.

20. "Regarding the Future WASC Service for the Caring of US Army Personnel in China," September 9, 1942, RG 493, UD-UP 419, box 246, Subsistence Total Costs, NARA.

21. "Memoirs of J.L. Huang," chap. 2, p. 20, Huang Renlin Papers, box 1, folder 1, HIA.

22. "Memoirs of J.L. Huang," chaps. 2 and 3, Huang Renlin Papers, box 1, folder 1, HIA. On the Northern Expedition and Chiang's military reforms, see Jay Taylor, *Generalissimo*, 107–9; van de Ven, *War and Nationalism in China*, 131–37. On Kong, see Coble, *Shanghai Capitalists and the Nationalist Government*, 161–207.

23. On CTCA-YMCA efforts, see Bristow, *Making Men Moral.*

24. Jeremy Taylor, "Production of the Chiang Kai-shek Personality Cult," 99–100.

25. "Memoirs of J.L. Huang," chap. 4, Huang Renlin Papers, box 1, folder 2, HIA. On the New Life Movement, see Oldstone-Moore, "New Life Movement of Nationalist China," Thomson, *When China Faced West*, 155, 165–69.

26. "Memoirs of J.L. Huang," chap. 4, p. 10, Huang Renlin Papers, box 1, folder 2, HIA.

27. "Memoirs of J.L. Huang," chap. 4, Huang Renlin Papers, box 1, folder 2, HIA.

28. The total number of Soviet military advisors, technicians, experts, and aviation volunteers in China totaled about five thousand. See Zhang, "China's Quest for Foreign Military Aid," 291.

29. On official hospitality, see Brady, *Making the Foreign Serve China.*

30. Zhang, "China's Quest for Foreign Military Aid," 294–95.

31. Romanus and Sunderland, *Stilwell's Mission to China*, 15–16.

32. Moser, *China-Burma-India*, 8–9. On Japan's strategic bombing campaign, see van de Ven, *China at War*, 123–29; Tow, "Great Bombing of Chongqing and the Anti-Japanese War," 256–82.

33. Chennault, *Way of a Fighter*, 107–9.

34. "Regarding the Future WASC Service for the Caring of Army Personnel in China," September 9, 1942, NARA.

35. Chennault, *Way of a Fighter*, 73–74; Zhang, "China's Quest for Foreign Military Aid," 292.

36. "Memoirs of J.L. Huang," chap. 9, Huang Renlin Papers, box 1, folder 2, HIA. On tensions between Long and Chiang, see Eastman, *Seeds of Destruction*, 10–14; Xie, *Long Yun zhuan*, 149–62; T. W. Wu, "Contending Political Forces during the War of Resistance," 60–61.

37. Huang Renlin zhi Zhong-Mian yunshu zongju, February 25, 1942; Zhong-Mian yunshu zongju ge zhan Meiji fuwu renyuan zhaodai banfa, February 16, 1942, file no. 54-24-413, pp. 1–3, 39–41, YPA.

38. Huang, *Memoirs of J.L. Huang*, 117–18.

39. "Memoirs of J.L. Huang," chaps. 4, 5, and 9, Huang Renlin Papers, box 1, folders 1 and 2, HIA.

40. See Fei Xiaotong, "Rural Economy of a Typical Chinese Village in Yunnan," *Information Pamphlets on China*, Series B, no. 1, 12; Wang Zuoliang, "Trends in Chinese Literature Today," *Information Pamphlets on China*, Series A, no. 4; Lei Haizong, "China: A Century of Decline and Revival (1839–1937)," *Information Pamphlets on China*, Series A, no. 5, 3–4; Lei Haizong, "The Chinese Empire (221 B.C.–1839 A.D.)," *Information Pamphlets on China*, Series A, nos. 3, 4. On the Philippines, see Kramer, *Blood of Government*, 370–72.

41. J. Bradley, *China Mirage*, 130–31; Jespersen, *American Images of China*, xv–58; Leong, *China Mystique*, 12, 18–20, 23–56.

42. "Memoirs of J.L. Huang," chap. 3, Huang Renlin Papers, box 1, folder 1, HIA; Bieler, *"Patriots" or "Traitors,"* 122.

43. "Memoirs of J.L. Huang," chap. 10, Huang Renlin Papers, box 1, folder 3, HIA.

44. See, for example, Milton McGee Collection, AFC/2001/001/37418; Carl Kostol Collection, AFC/2001/001/56123, VHP.

45. Richard Goon Collection, AFC/2001/001/50828, VHP.

46. On the Pacific passage, see Bailey and Farber, *First Strange Place*, 40–41.

47. Angelo Ruvo Collection, AFC/2001/001/74195, VHP.

48. Angelo Ruvo Collection, AFC/2001/001/74195, VHP.

49. Plating, *Hump*, 248.

50. Angelo Ruvo Collection, AFC/2001/001/74195, VHP.

51. Jack M. Neal Collection, AFC/2001/001/11316, VHP.

52. Diary entry, May 31, 1942, Robert Tharpe Smith Collection, AFC/2001/001/199658, VHP.

53. Jan Peeke to Anne Peeke, September 11, 1942, Jan Alonzo Peeke Collection, MSS box 129, folder 3, AFC/2001/001/1530, VHP.

54. Carl Kostol Collection, AFC/2001/001/56123, VHP.

55. Paul Hassett to Charlotte Hassett, July 28, 1945, Paul E. Hassett Papers, box 1, folder 5, WVM.

56. John Forrest Green Collection, AFC/2001/001/15799, VHP.

57. Wyndham Manning Collection, AFC/2001/001/72846, VHP.

58. Warren Arnett to Martha Arnett, August 7, 1945, Warren Jefferson Arnett Collection, AFC/2001/001/11032, VHP.

59. Earl Revell to Leona Revell, July 22, 1945, Earl M. Revell Collection, box 2, folder 3, USACMH.

60. Unpublished memoir, p. 51, James Brochon Collection, AFC/2001/001/09874, VHP.

61. Yin, "Treatment of Night Soil and Waste in Modern China," 51–70.

62. See Chongqing shi weisheng ju zhi Chongqing shi jingcha ju dian, February 24, 1940, file no. 61-15-05085, p. 120; Chongqing shi weisheng ju zhi Chongjing shi jingcha ju, April 4, 1944, file no. 61-15-04342, p. 239; and Chongqing shi disi qu fenqu suo baogao, November 20, 1946, file no. 57-7-00196, p. 66, CMA.

63. "A Sailor's Chinese Duty," p. 29, MSS box 137, Kenneth Miller Collection, AFC/2001/001/01623, VHP.

64. Jan Peeke to Anne Peeke, May 17, 1943, Jan Alonzo Peeke Collection, AFC/2001/001/01530, VHP.

65. Jan Peeke to Anne Peeke, October 31, 1943, Jan Alonzo Peeke Collection, AFC/2001/001/01530, VHP.

66. Harold Rosser Collection, AFC/2001/001/69876, VHP.

67. Mary Krauss to A. P. Krauss, April 21, 1944, Mary Theresa Krauss Collection, folder 15, Center for the Study of World War II and the Human Experience, FSU.

68. Eskelund, *My Chinese Wife*, 181.

69. Daniel Baer Collection, AFC/2001/001/81024, VHP.

70. Unpublished memoir, p. 25, Samuel Etris Collection, AFC/2001/001/76860, VHP.

71. Rafael D. Hirtz Collection, AFC/2001/001/00094, VHP.

72. Daniel Baer Collection AFC/2001/001/81024, VHP; Gigi McGuire, unpublished memoir, p. 54, Gigi McGuire Collection, AFC/2001/001/12158, VHP.

73. Jan Peeke to Anne Peeke, October 27, 1942, Jan Alonzo Peeke Collection, MSS box 129, folder 3, AFC/2001/001/1530, VHP.

74. Orlando Wood Collection, AFC/2001/001/51477, VHP.

75. "Report of WASC Liaison Office on Mess Conditions at Yunnanyi," August 1, 1944, RG 493, UD-UP 349, box 14, WASC Correspondence, 1943–1945, NARA.

76. Tom Hardwick letter, June 25, 1945, Tom Hardwick Collection, AFC/2001/001/297, VHP.

77. William Millner Collection, AFC/2001/001/57101, VHP.

78. Jan Peeke to Anne Peeke, February 15, 1944, Jan Alonzo Peeke Collection, AFC/2001/001/01530, VHP.

79. Warren Arnett to Martha Arnett, June 14, 1945, Warren Jefferson Arnett Collection, AFC/2001/001/11032, VHP.

80. Earl Revell to Leona Revell, May 20, 1945, Earl M. Revell Collection, box 2, folder 3, USACMH.

81. Earl Revell to Leona Revell, February 24, 1945, Earl M. Revell Collection, box 1, USACMH.

82. Jan Peeke to Anne Peeke, February 15, 1944, Jan Alonzo Peeke Collection, AFC/2001/001/01530, VHP.

83. Jane Peeke to Anne Peeke, January 16, 1944, Jan Alonzo Peeke Collection, AFC/2001/001/01530, VHP.

84. Diary, 1941–1942, May 13, 1942, MacMorland Papers, box 1, USACMH. See also Daniel Baer Collection, AFC/2001/001/81024; Warren Arnett to Martha Arnett, May 30, 1945, Warren Jefferson Arnett Collection, AFC/2001/001/11032; Arthur Perry Hauge, "With the Flying Tigers in China," unpublished memoir, p. 20, Arthur Perry Hauge Collection, AFC/2001/001/02877.

85. Norman Victor Key Collection, AFC/2001/001/01162, VHP.

86. Diary, 1941–1942, January 17 and August 13, 1942, Edward E. MacMorland Papers, box 1, USACMH.

87. Diary, 1941–1942, August 14, 1942, Edward E. MacMorland Papers, box 1, USACMH.

88. Diary, 1941–1942, February 18 and March 2, 1942, Edward E. MacMorland Papers, box 1, USACMH.

89. Ch'i, *Jianbanuzhang de mengyou*, 47–53, 635–36.

90. Letcher, *Goodbye to Old Peking*, 10.

91. John R. Alison Collection, AFC/2001/001/7422, VHP.

92. Peck, *Two Kinds of Time*, 492, 634.

93. "Morale in the CBI Theater," October 9, 1944, RG 493, UD-UP 36, box 205, Morals and Conduct, July 1 to October 30, 1944, NARA.

94. Earl Revell to Leona Revell, July 22, July 25, and February 24, 1945, Earl M. Revell Collection, box 2, folder 3, USACMH.

95. Kramer, *Blood of Government*, 124–30, 196–205; Renda, *Taking Haiti*, 101–4.

96. Jan Peeke to Anne Peeke, December 3, 1942, Jan Alonzo Peeke Collection, AFC/2001/001/01530, VHP.

97. Chennault to Peter Shih, February 23, 1942, Claire Chennault Papers, box 2, folder 3, HIA.

98. On national humiliation and rejuvenation, see Harrison, *China: Inventing the Nation*, 2–6; Callahan, *China*, 69–76; Dikötter, "Culture, 'Race,' and the Nation," 590–91; M. Song, *Young China*; S. Zhao, "Chinese Nationalism and Its International Orientations," 4–5.

99. Chennault to Peter Shih, February 23, 1942, Claire Chennault Papers, box 2, folder 3, HIA.

100. Ford, *Flying Tigers*, 199–200.

101. "Memoirs of J.L. Huang," chap. 9, Huang Renlin Papers, box 1, folder 2, HIA.

102. "Regarding the Future WASC Service for the Caring of US Army Personnel in China," September 9, 1942, RG 493, UD-UP 419, box 246, Subsistence Total Costs, NARA.

103. "Regarding the Future WASC Service for the Caring of US Army Personnel in China," NARA.

104. "Regarding the Future WASC Service for the Caring of US Army Personnel in China," NARA.

105. Jespersen, *American Images of China*, 3–9; Pomfret, *Beautiful Country and the Middle Kingdom*, 43–45, 178–89, 237–39, 278–79.

106. "Special Court Martial 13," December 30, 1943, RG 493, UD-UP 7, box 29, Charges, Proceedings, and Trials, NARA; and Case No. 44K, October 16, 1943, RG 493, UD-UP 365, box 64, Morals and Conduct, 1943–1944, NARA.

107. See JAG Monthly Reports, RG 493, UD-UP 419, box 246, Monthly JAG Report folder, NARA.

108. "Misconduct of Technical Sergeant Paul Rock," June 20, 1945, RG 493, UD-UP 541, box 85, 250 Discipline, NARA.

109. "Case #627-186," July 27, 1945, RG 493, UD-UP 309, box 670, Fatal Shooting of Chinese Civilian by Pvt. Charles Phillips, NARA.

110. Ernest K. Moy to Major Joseph De Pietro, January 18, 1945, RG 493, UD-UP 349, box 13, WASC Correspondence, 1945, NARA.

111. "Kunshi pan di 76 hao," June 19, 1945, file no. 54-18-53, YPA.

112. "Wei nipan Lu Zhicheng deng daomai gongyong caiwu yi an," August 22, 1945, file no. 54-18-56, YPA.

113. "Wei nipan Li Gui deng daofei xianyi yi an," May 16, 1945, file no. 54-18-56, YPA.

114. "Wei nipan Xie Chuwen qiequ gongyong caiwu yi an," April 29, 1945, file no. 54-18-56, YPA.

115. "With the Flying Tigers in China," p. 30, Arthur Perry Hague Collection, AFC/2001/001/2877, VHP.

116. "Principles Applying to Mutual Aid in the Prosecution of the War against Aggression."

117. By June 1944, twenty-two thousand GIs were stationed in China. "Cost of Subsistence at WASC Hostels," August 27, 1944, RG 493, UD-UP 419, box 246, Subsistence Total Costs, NARA.

118. Israel, *Lianda*, 83–95; Wu, "Contending Political Forces during the War of Resistance," 60–61.

119. Chennade zhi Long Yun dian, June 13, 1943, file no. 1106-3-1449, p. 3, YPA; Long Yun to Stilwell, November 13, 1943, and Stilwell to Shang Zhen, January 5, 1944, RG 493, UD-UP 419, box 245, Correspondence, NARA.

120. Long Yun ling Luo Peirong dian, February 7, 1944, and Long Yun ling minzheng ting dian, February 8, 1944, file no. 1106-4-2753, pp. 1–3, YPA.

121. Zhang, "Cong minguo dang'an kan 1944 nian zhu Dian Meijun roulei gongying fengbo," 21.

122. Chennade zhi Long Yun dian, April 8, 1944, file no. 1106-4-2752, p. 26, YPA.

123. *Kunming shi wenshi ziliao (Kangri zhanzheng—wujia)*, 324. A half kilo of beef sold for 250 fabi on June 25, 1944.

124. Zhang, "Cong minguo dang'an kan 1944 nian zhu Dian Meijun roulei gongying fengbo," 20; Mitter, *Forgotten Ally*, 339–41; SOS Liaison Office to WASC, August 9, 1944, RG 493, UD-UP 419, box 245, Correspondence, NARA.

125. Zhou, *Jiang Zhongzheng zongtong de dang'an: Shilue gaoben*, 56:586–90; U.S. ambassador Clarence Gauss reported total Chinese government expenditures of 48 billion fabi for 1943. See "The Ambassador in China to the Secretary of State," March 3, 1944, U.S. Department of State, *Foreign Relations of the United States: Diplomatic Papers, 1944, China*, 904–7 (hereafter cited as *FRUS*).

126. Ambassador in China to the Secretary of State, January 23, 1943, *FRUS: 1943, China*, 525.

127. Ambassador in China to the Secretary of State, *FRUS: 1943, China*, 524–27; "Draft Note from the Chinese Minister of Foreign Affairs (Soong) to the Secretary of State," May 15, 1943, and Memorandum of Conversation by the Chief of the Division of Far Eastern Affairs (Ballantine), July 2, 1943 *FRUS: 1943, China*, 524–27, 538–40, 552–54.

128. Ambassador in China (Gauss) to the Secretary of State, January 16, 1944, *FRUS: 1944, China*, 837.

129. Ambassador in China (Gauss) to the Secretary of State, January 16, 1944, *FRUS: 1944, China*, 837–39.

130. Ambassador in China (Gauss) to the Secretary of State, January 28, 1944, *FRUS: 1944, China*, 868–70.

131. Memorandum by the Deputy Director of the Office of Far Eastern Affairs (Joseph Ballantine) to the Under Secretary of State (Stettinius), February 29, 1944, *FRUS: 1944, China*, 877–79.

132. "WASC Proposals Presented to the USAF," March 18, 1944, RG 493, UD-UP 365, box 74, WASC Activities in the China Theater, NARA.

133. "Cost of Subsistence at WASC Hostels," August 27, 1944, RG 493, UD-UP 419, box 246, Subsistence Total Costs, NARA; "WASC Graphic Report of Four Years' Service," Huang Renlin Papers, box 1, folder 2, HIA; "Personnel Strength, China Theater," RG 493, Black Book China #1, box 15, Records Related to Histories, Charts on Strength, NARA.

134. "WASC Operations," August 28, 1944, RG 493, UD-UP 419, box 244, Correspondence, 1943–1944, NARA.

135. "Xin yun zonghui Mengjun zhiyou she jianze," March 31, 1944, file no. 290-1-1079, pp. 153–63, CMA. The movement was carried out under the authority of the New Life Movement General Association, which Huang Still directed.

136. Sun, "Zhankai 'Mengjun zhiyou' yundong," *Xinyun dao bao*, 39–41; Mengjun zhiyou she tonggao, July 13, 1944, file no. 290-1-50, p. 52, CMA.

137. "Mengjun zhiyou she zongshe kaimu," *Da gong bao*, 1944.

138. "Jing ai mengjun," *Da gong bao*, April 19, 1944.

139. Junshi weiyuan hui waishi ju zhi Chongqing shi zhengfu dian, April 27, 1944, file no. 53-10-52, pp. 6–7.4, CMA.

140. Erksine, "Frank W. Price," 420–35; C. T. Johnson, *Ambassador to Three Cultures*, 218–22.

141. "Operations of War Area Service Corps," April 19, 1945, RG 493, UD-UP 349, box 13, WASC Correspondence, NARA; Reuben Torrey to Carl Dutton, April 14, 1945, RG 493, UD-UP 365, box 75, WASC Activities in the China Theater, NARA.

142. "Report of Liaison Officers to His Excellency Generalissimo Chiang Kai-shek on the War Area Service Corps," undated, RG 493, UD-UP 365, box 75, WASC Activities in the China Theater, NARA.

143. Young, *China's Wartime Finance and Inflation*, 332–33; "WASC Graphic Report of Four Years' Service," Huang Renlin Papers, box 1, folder 2, HIA.

144. Zhang, "China's Quest for Foreign Military Aid," 303; Daggett, "Costs of Major U.S. Wars," 2–5.

145. "WASC Graphic Report of Four Years' Service," Huang Renlin Papers, box 1, folder 2, HIA.

146. "Staff Study of Reverse Lend Lease," July 16, 1945, RG 493, UD-UP 590, box 20, G-5 USFCT Procurement Branch History, NARA: APO 879 Memorandum, July 11, 1945, and "WASC," June 26, 1945, RG 493, UD-UP 349, box 13, WASC Correspondence, 1945, NARA.

147. See, for example, "Panorama of China," Earl M. Revell Collection, box 2, folder 15, USACMH; "The Village Queen," *Hedron Daily News*, August 28, 1946, Jerry Cassidy Personal Papers, box 1, McHD.

148. Romanus and Sunderland, *Stilwell's Command Problems*, 291.

149. On the U.S.-UK settlement, see Allen, "Mutual Aid between the U.S. and the British Empire," 243–47.

150. Earl Revell to Leona Revell, July 22, July 25, and February 24, 1945, Earl M. Revell Collection, box 2, folder 3, USACMH.

Chapter 2

1. Wang fanyi guan, "Lun fanyi guan," *Da gong bao*, March 19, 1945.

2. "Junshi weiyuan hui zhandi fuwu tuan zhaopin yingwen yiyuan jianze," June 25, 1941, file no. 120-1-181, pp. 141–42, CMA.

3. Other scholars estimate that the Chinese government trained as many as five thousand interpreters. See Luo, "Dian-Mian zhanyi zhong de junshi fanyi," 232; Zuo, "Kangzhan shiqi mengjun zhong de Zhongguo yiyuan," 168; Wu, "Kangzhan shiqi Jiang Jieshi de 'yiyuan' renzhi ji peiyu," 302; Y. Yang, *Erzhan Zhong-Yin-Mian zhanchang Zhongguo yiyuan*, 4–5. These estimates fail to take into account two factors: the U.S. Army refused to work with nearly six hundred interpreters trained in Chongqing in early 1944 because of their poor English skills, and some interpreters began work before they finished training or without any training at all. See "Interpreting Officers with United States Force in China Theater," April 1, 1945, RG 493, UD-UP 300, box 615, Interpreting Officers, 1945, NARA; "Junshi weiyuan hui yiyuan xunlian weiyuan hui diwu ci changhui jilu," June 29, 1945, RG 493, UP-UP 297, box 646, Minutes of Meetings, NARA; "Disan qi yiyuan biye dianli," undated, file no. 1032-1-30, YPA.

4. Guo, *Surviving in Violent Conflicts*, 45.

5. "Interpreters," March 1, 1945, RG 493, UD-UP 297, box 645, Interpreters Pool CTC, NARA.

6. Chiang Kai-shek, "Jundui yiyuan de shiming," in *Xian zongtong Jiang gong sixiang yanlun ji*, 56–60.

7. Israel, *Lianda*, 169–72.

8. For more on these figures, see Israel, *Lianda*; Dikötter, *Discourse of Race in Modern China*, 157–58; Fang, *Wen Yiduo zai Meiguo*; Guldin, *Saga of Anthropology in China*, 63, 143; Ye, *Seeking Modernity in China's Name*, 107–13; Y. Zhang, "Returned Chinese Students from American and the Chinese Leadership," 64–65; Chung, "Better Science and Better Race?," 783–802.

9. Morris, *Marrow of the Nation*, 172.

10. K. Yang, "Pan Guangdan yu ta de shidai," 1–7.

11. "Junshi weiyuan hui zhandi fuwu tuan zhaopin yingwen fanyi jianze," June 25, 1941, file no. 120-1-181, pp. 141–42, CMA; Chang, *Kangzhan shiqi de guojun renshi*, 89–95; Zhang and Guo, eds., *Guoli xinan lianhe daxue shiliao (er) huiyi jilu juan*, 247–48.

12. Li, "KangRi shengzhan wo zuo fanyi san nian yu," 54–55; A. Y. Y. Tsu, *Friend of Fishermen*.

13. Guo Guanqiu, "Liangci zhengdiao zai Meijun zhaodai suo," in *Guoli xinan lianhe daxue babai xuezi congjun huiyi*, ed. Xinan Lianda, 19.

14. Morris, *Marrow of the Nation*, 3; J. Yang, "Xiangxiang minzu chiru," 1–42.

15. Chengdu tiyu xueyuan tiyushi yanjiusuo, *Zhongguo jindai tiyushi ziliao*, 420–31.

16. Zarrow, *Educating China*, 98–100, 113–15.

17. Hsu, *Good Immigrants*, 58.

18. Guo Guanqiu, "Liangxi zhengdiao zai Meijun zhaodai suo," 19.

19. "Junshi weiyuan hui zhandi fuwu tuan zhaopin yingwen yiyuan jianze," June 25, 1941, file no. 120-1-181, pp. 141–42, CMA.

20. T. Guo, *Surviving in Violent Conflicts*, 49–54; Zarrow, *Educating China*, 35–36, 39, 115–30.

21. Israel, *Student Nationalism in China*, 178.

22. Shang Zhen cheng Jiang Jieshi dian, September 30, 1943, file no. 763-46, pp. 1–6, SHAC.

23. "Junshi weiyuan hui waishi ju fenpei ZhongMei hezuo suo fanyi mingce," undated, file no. 763-1329, pp. 175–79, SHAC. On SACO, see Wakeman, *Spymaster*, 282–305; Shen, "SACO."

24. "Jinhou kangzhan zhong yiyuan zeren zhongda," *Saodang bao*, April 21, 1944.

25. Huang, *Guanyu Meiguo bing*, 131–32. Chiang, "Jundui yiyuan de shiming," 60.

26. "Fanyi xunban diyi qi biye, disan qi kaixue," *Yiyuan xunkan*, May 20, 1945, file no. 763-423, p. 57, SHAC.

27. Wang, "Wo zuo Meijun fanyi guan de rizi," 77.

28. "First Batch of Interpreters Ready for Work," *Yenching News* (Chengdu edition), April 22, 1944, RG 493, UD-UP 300, box 653, Chungking-Chengtu Trip, NARA.

29. Kuo Yu-shou, "The Twofold Mission of the Interpreting Officer," undated, RG 493, UD-UP 300, box 653, Chungking-Chengtu Trip, NARA.

30. Chiang, "Jundui yiyuan de shiming," 59.

31. Chiang, "Jundui yiyuan de shiming," 59. On Chiang's low opinion of Chinese officers compared to U.S. Army officers, see Ch'i, *Jianbanuzhang de mengyou*, 424–25.

32. Ch'i, *Jianbanuzhang de mengyou*, 694.

33. *Ruhe zhidao guanbing yu mengbing xiangchu*, June 18, 1945, file no. 53-10-142, pp. 312–15.108, CMA.

34. "Weizuo xunling," *Yixun xunkan*, May 10, 1945, file no. 763-423, p. 57, SHAC.

35. "Yixun ban xueyuan jieye li, He zongzhang qinlin xunhua," *Saodang bao*, July 9, 1945. On He Yingqin's military service during the war, see Worthing, *General He Yingqin*, 177–239.

36. "Ruhe zhidao guanbing yu mengbing xiangchu," June 18, 1945, file no. 53-10-142, pp. 312–15.108, CMA.

37. T. Guo, *Surviving in Violent Conflicts*, 63–64.

38. Wong, "Translators and Interpreters during the Opium War between Britain and China (1839–1842)," 51–53; Chiang, "Junshi yiyuan de shiming," 60; Huang, *Guanyu Meiguo bing*, 133, 138–39.

39. On strengthening the state by improving the quality of the people, see Duara, *Rescuing History from the Nation*, 139; Sigley, "*Suzhi*, the Body, and the Fortunes of Technoscientific Reasoning in Contemporary China," 539–43.

40. Most interpreters fled their home provinces to escape the Japanese invasion. See "Guoli Chongqing daxue 33 nian di er xueqi yingzheng yiyuan mingce," June 26, 1944, file no. 1010-4-204, pp. 49–55, CMA; "Interpreting Officers with United States Forces in China Theater," April 1, 1945, RG 493, UD-UP 300, box 651, Interpreting Officers 1945, NARA. On humiliation commemoration days and the emphasis on victimization in the school curriculum, see Callahan, *China*, 69–76; P. A. Cohen, "Remembering and Forgetting National Humiliation in Twentieth-Century China," 11–15; Dikötter, "Culture 'Race,' and Nation," 590–91; Harrison, *China: Inventing the Nation*, 190–91, 198–99; Sun, "Minguo shiqi de guochi jinian ri," 16–19.

41. Weng, "Nan wang de junshi yiyuan shenghuo," 1–3; Y. Yang, *Erzhan Zhong-Yin-Mian zhanchang Zhongguo yiyuan*, 3.

42. "Zhandi fuwu tuan gong han zidi 3107," September 22, 1941, file no. 5-6731, pp. 71–72, SHAC.

43. "Ganbu xunlian ban di'er qi xueyuan xiaobie ji xingming ce," undated, file no. 5-6731, pp. 21–26, SHAC.

44. Missionary-run schools in Chengdu included West China Union University, Nanjing (Jinling) University, Yenching University, and Cheeloo University. Loren Thompson to Executive Officer, February 28, 1945, RG 493, UD-UP 300, box 653, Chungking-Chengtu Trip, NARA.

45. "Chinese Interpreters' School," March 14, 1944, RG 493, UD-UP 299, box 648, January-February-March 1944, NARA.

46. "Inspection Trip Report," June 16, 1944, RG 493, UD-UP 299, box 649, June-July 1944, NARA.

47. This number includes approximately 27,000 GIs plus 1,200 sailors. See Grieve, "Belated Endeavor," 17; Zhou, *Jiang Zhongzheng zongtong de dang'an: Shilue gaoben*, 59:142–44; Troop Strength Graph, undated, RG 38, box 6, chap. 6, Personnel S-1, folder 15, NARA.

48. "Interpreting Officers with United States Forces in China Theater," April 1, 1945, RG 493, UD-UP 300, box 651, Interpreting Officers 1945, NARA.

49. On December 31, 1943, 8,174 soldiers were stationed in China and 86,120 in Burma and India. See Romanus and Sunderland, *Stilwell's Mission to China*, 267; Romanus and Sunderland, *Stilwell's Command Problems*, 258, "Administrative and Staff Narratives," December 31, 1943, box 17-1, Stilwell Papers, HIA.

50. Stilwell to Shang Zheng, July 16, 1943, RG 493, UD-UP 299, box 648, July-August-September 1943, NARA.

51. "Interpreters," February 19, 1943, RG 493, UD-UP 299, box 648, February-March-April 1943, NARA.

52. "Employment of English-Speaking Chinese Interpreters," March 3, 1943, RG 493, UD-UP 299, box 648, February-March-April 1943, NARA.

53. FAB no. 251, January 8, 1843, RG 493, UD-UP 299, box 648, February-March-April 1943, NARA.

54. "Interpreters," September 17, 1943, RG 493, UD-UP 299, box 648, July-August-September 1943, NARA.

55. "Interpreters," October 25, 1943, RG 493, UD-UP 299, box 648, October-November-December 1943, NARA.

56. "Interpreters," September 29, 1943, RG 493, UD-UP 299, box 648, July-August-September 1943, NARA.

57. On Dorn's and Stilwell's Orientalist views, see van de Ven, *War and Nationalism in China, 1925–1945*, 6–12.

58. "Interpreters," October 25, 1943, and "Misunderstanding between Interpreter and Capt. Eckes," December 4, 1943, RG 493, UD-UP 299, box 648, October-November-December 1943, NARA.

59. Loren Thompson to Executive Officer, February 28, 1945, RG 493, UD-UP 300, box 653, Chungking-Chengtu Trip, NARA.

60. Jan Peeke to Anne Peeke, October 10, 1942, Jan Alonzo Peeke Collection, MSS box 129, AFC/2001/001/1530, VHP.

61. Charles Lakin Collection, AFC/2001/001/82918, VHP.

62. "Interpreters," February 19, 1943, RG 493, UD-UP 299, box 648, February-March-April 1943, NARA.

63. Wu, "Kangzhan shiqi Jiang Jieshi de 'yiyuan' renzhi ji peiyu," 296–300.

64. T. G. Hearn to Shang Zhen, June 26, 1945, RG 493, UD-UP 299, box 648, February-March-April 1943, NARA.

65. Loren Thompson to Forward Ecehlon HQ, Kunming, September 4, 1943, RG 493, UD-UP 299, box 648, July-August-September 1943, NARA.

66. Stilwell to Shang Zhen, September 7, 1943, RG 493, UD-UP 299, box 648, July-August-September 1943, NARA.

67. Zhang and Guo, *Guoli xinan lianhe daxue shiliao (er) huiyi jilu juan*, 308–10; Memorandum to the Chief of Staff, October 12, 1943, RG 493, UD-UP 299, box 649, October 1944 Orders and Memos, NARA; FAB no. 834, November 3, 1943, RG 493, UD-UP 299, box 648, October-November-December 1943, NARA.

68. "Interpreting Officers with United States Forces in China Theater," April 1, 1945, RG 493, UD-UP 300, box 651, Interpreting Officers 1945, NARA; "Interpreter Procurement and Accounting," December 3, 1943, RG 493, UD-UP 299, box 648, October-November-December 1943, NARA.

69. "Lianda Mei weiyuan mian tongxue congjun," *Yunnan ribao*, November 10, 1943.

70. Weng, "Nan wang de junshi yiyuan shenghuo," 1–3.

71. Fu, "Mianbei zhangchang wubai tian—yige suijun yiyuan de huiyi," 69.

72. Yang, *Erzhan Zhong-Yin-Mian zhanchang Zhongguo yiyuan*, 3.

73. Zhang and Guo, *Guoli xinan lianhe daxue shiliao (er) huiyi jilu juan*, 315–17; Israel, *Lianda*, 368.

74. "Lianda si nianji nan sheng yilv canjia fuyi," *Sao dang bao,* December 12, 1943; Li, "Wo zhe yi jiu si si de [yuan]," *Qinghua xiaoyou tongxun*, 44–45.

75. "Interpreting Officers with United States Forces in China Theater," April 1, 1945, RG 493, UD-UP 300, box 651, Interpreting Officers 1945, NARA.

76. Jiaoyu bu zhi Sichuan shengli jiaoyu xueyuan dian, March 1944, file no. 122-5-49, pp. 8–11, CMA; "Guoli Zhongyang daxue fengling zhengdiao si nianji xuesheng chongren yiyuan banfa," *Guoli zhongyang daxue xiaokan*, 1944:3.

77. Jiang Wenbin, "Danren fanyi canyu kangRi zhanzheng de jingli," in *Erzhan Zhong-Yin-Mian zhanchang Zhongguo yiyuan*, ed. Yang, 129–31.

78. "Guo nei daxue sheng san qian ming jiang diaochong junzhong tongyi guan," *Yunnan ribao*, February 2, 1944; Wu, "Kangzhan shiqi Jiang Jieshi de 'yiyuan' renzhi ji peiyu," 300–302.

79. Stilwell to Shang Zhen, March 3, 1944, RG 493, UD-UP 299, box 648, January-February-March 1944, NARA.

80. Dorn to all personnel of Yoke Force, March 2, 1944, RG 493, UD-UP 300, box 650, INT-Directives-SOP, NARA.

81. See Wang, "Zai long de yingchen xia: Dui Zhongguo de xiangxiang yu Meiguo guojia shenfen de jiangou," 156–73; Hunt, *Making of a Special Relationship*, 299–304; Jespersen, *American Images of China*, 3–9.

82. Wu, "Kangzhan shiqi Jiang Jieshi de 'yiyuan' renzhi ji peiyu," 300–302.

83. "Guoli Chongqing da xue 32 niandu di er xueqi yingzheng yiyuan xuesheng jiao baogao jianbiao," undated, file no. 120-4-18, pp. 28–30. Sixteen draftees came from the sciences, ninety-six from engineering, and fifty-seven from business and management.

84. Eastman, "Nationalist China during the Sino-Japanese War," 172–93.

85. "Zheng zhao daxue sheng fuwu yuanzheng jun," *Guangxi ribao*, February 4, 1944.

86. Fisken to Chief of Staff, March 14, 1944, and Stilwell to Shang Zhen, March 17, 1944, RG 493, UD-UP 299, box 648, January-February-March 1944, NARA; "Interpreters' School," April 10, 1944, RG 493, UD-UP 299, box 648, April-May 1944, NARA.

87. Junshi weiyuan hui zhandi fuwu tuan dai dian, September 11, 1944, file no. 763-46, p. 60, SHAC.

88. Stilwell to Yang Hsuan-cheng, July 16, 1944, RG 493, UD-UP 299, box 649, June-July 1944, NARA.

89. Memo to the Chief of Staff, October 12, 1944, RG 493, UD-UP 299, box 649, October 1944, Orders and Memos, NARA.

90. Headquarters USF CBI Theater to FAB, May 14, 1944, RG 493, UD-UP 296, box 644, Correspondence File 8/44-5/45, NARA.

91. "Interpreters," October 9, 1943, RG 493, UD-UP 299, box 648, October-November-December 1943, NARA.

92. "Inspection Trip Report," June 16, 1944, and "Interpreter Problems," June 23, 1944, RG 493, UD-UP 299, box 649, June-July 1944, NARA.

93. "Jin hou kangzhan zhong yiyuan zeren zhongda," *Saodang bao*, April 21, 1944; "Yi xun ban sanqi liuyue chu kaixue," *Guangxi ribao*, May 25, 1944.

94. "Chinese Interpreter Corps," July 13, 1944, RG 84, Kunming Consulate General Records 1938–1949, box 60, Kunming, vol. 12, NARA.

95. "Interpreters," March 18, 1944, RG 493, UD-UP 296, box 643, Correspondence (February to August 1945), NARA.

96. "Activity among Chinese University Students at Kunming," August 31, 1944, RG 84, China Kunming Consulate, Classified General Records, 1944–1949, box 1, Kunming 1944, vol. 2, NARA.

97. "Interpreters' Food Costs," May 29, 1944, RG 493, UD-UP 299, box 648, April-May 1944, NARA; "Stilwell to Yang Xuancheng, June 30, 1944, RG 493, UD-UP 299, box 649, June–July 1944, NARA.

98. "Interpreting Officer Procurement and Accounting," October 31, 1944, RG 493, UD-UP 299, box 649, October 1944, Orders and Memos, NARA.

99. Zhou, *Jiang Zhongzheng zongtong de dang'an: Shilue gaoben*, 59:116–17. "Inspection Trip Report," June 16, 1944, RG 493, UD-UP 299, box 649, June-July 1944, NARA.

100. "Meijun xuyao yiyuan wuqian," *Da gong bao*, March 7, 1945.

101. Office of Interpreter Affairs Report, February 28, 1945, RG 493, UD-UP 300, box 653, Chungking-Chengtu Trip, NARA.

102. "FAB Director General He Haoruo's Speech," February 23, 1945, and Office of Interpreter Affairs Report, February 28, 1945, RG 493, UD-UP 300, box 653, Chungking-Chengtu Trip, NARA.

103. "Fanyi kaoshi jiexiao," *Zhongyang ribao* (Chengdu edition), March 11, 1945.

104. Wang, "Baogao fanyi guan," *Xi feng*, February 1, 1945.

105. "Report of Progress," February 28, 1945, and "Minutes of American Representatives of Units Utilizing Interpreters," January 29, 1945, RG 493, UD-UP 297, box 646, Chinese Training Center, 1945, NARA.

106. "Interpreters," March 1, 1945, RG 493, UD-UP 297, box 645, Interpreters Pool, CTC, NARA.

107. "Comment on the Article 'On Interpreter-Officers,'" April 26, 1945, RG 493, UD-UP 215, box 5, Interpreters, NARA.

108. "He Haoruo juzhang tan: Jun zhong yiyuan jiwei deli," *Da gong bao*, March 31, 1945; "The Two-fold Mission of the Interpreting Officer," undated, RG 493, UD-UP 300, box 653, Chungking-Chengtu Trip, NARA.

109. "Junshi weiyuan hui yiyuan xunlian weiyuan hui disi ci chahui baogao ji taolun shixiang," undated, RG 493, UD-UP 299, box 650, Memorandums for Record, NARA; Chongqing shi jiaoyu ju ling shi shu geji zhong deng xuexiao dian, April 17, 1945, file no. 107-4-413, p. 35, CMA.

110. Chongqing shi jiaoyu ju ling shi shu geji zhong deng xuexiao dian, April 17, 1945, file no. 107-4-413, p. 35, CMA.

111. "Yixun xunkan zhenggao jianyue," undated, file no. 763-423, p. 70, SHAC.

112. "Wo zenyang zuo fanyi gongzuo," June 30, 1945; Shao Hui, "Zhandi shenghuo: Junzhong riji pianduan," May 10, 1945; Fan Hongyuan, "Nankan jixing," May 30, 1945, all published in *Yixun xunkan*, file no. 763-423, pp. 74, 82, 85, 93.

113. "Meiguo junguan yanzhong de wo guo fanyi guan," June 20, 1945, *Yixun xunkan*, file no. 763-423, p. 87, SHAC. For the original, see "Meiguo junguan yanzhong de wo guo fanyi guan," *Xinwen ziliao*, June 2, 1945, file no. 61-1-10, pp. 79–97.1, CMA.

114. "Faling yu xiaoxi," "Youxiu fanyi guan xuanpai fu Meiguo," May 20, 1945; "Yindu yiyuan shenghuo sumiao," May 31, 1945, all published in *Yixun xunkan*, file no. 763-423, pp. 76, 78, 87, SHAC.

115. Huang Deji cheng Yao Guanshun dian, May 14, 1945, file no. 763–58, SHAC.

116. Interpreting officer complaint, June 28, 1945, RG 493, UD-UP 296, box 643, Correspondence (August to September 1945), NARA.

117. Perry Hanson to Frank Price, August 8, 1945, RG 493, UD-UP 299, box 651, TIAO Section, 1945–1946, NARA.

118. Hanson to Price, August 8, 1945, NARA.

119. Yang Xianjian, "Liang nian fanyi shengya luxing guomin waijiao," in *Erzhan Zhong-Yin-Mian zhanchang Zhongguo yiyuan*, ed. Yang, 132–38.

120. Hua Renjiao, "Qianxian nan shangqu, junzhong duo jianwen," in *Xinan, Guoli xinan lianhe daxue babai xuezi congjun huiyi*, 120.

121. Perry Hanson to Frank Price, August 8, 1945, RG 493, UD-UP 299, box 651, TIAO Section, 1945–1946, NARA.

122. *Ruhe zhidao guanbing yu mengbing xiangchu*, June 18, 1945, file no. 53-10-142, pp. 312–315.108, CMA.

123. See, for example, Mei Zuyan, "Meijun Y-Force zongbu he Dianxi qianxian zhihuisuo de yiyuan shenghuo," in *Xinan, Guoli xinan lianhe daxue babai xuezi congjun huiyi*, 139–41; Guo, "Liang ci yingzheng," in *Xinan, Guoli xinan lianhe daxue babai xuezi congjun huiyi*, 19; Yang Baohuang, "Wo wei Meijun dang fanyi," in *Xinan, Guoli xinan lianhe daxue babai xuezi congjun huiyi*, 56.

124. Headquarters Memorandum, December 19, 1944, and "Discipline," July 7, 1945, RG 493, Morals and Conduct, NND 813515, box 95, Morals and Conduct, December 1944 to May 1945 and July to September 1945, NARA.

125. Yang, "Liang nian fanyi shengya luxing guomin waijiao," 136.

126. Huang, *Guanyu Meiguo bing*, 139–40.

127. Weng Xinjun, "Zhong-Yin gonglu tongche hou de paixiao," in *Xinan, Guoli xinan lianhe daxue babai xuezi congjun huiyi*, 147.

128. On pay, see "Junshi weiyuan hui fanyi xunlian weiyuan hui di wuci changhui jilu," June 29, 1945, RG 493, UD-UP 296, box 646, Minutes of meetings, NARA; He Haoruo zhi Weidemai dian, July 22, 1945, file no. 763-417, pp. 36–37, SHAC; "Yuanzhengjun yiyuan deji daiyu heding," *Saodang bao*, April 10, 1944; "Yiyuan daiyu jijiang tigao," *Saodang bao*, May 19, 1944; "Yiyuan daiyu biaozhun waishi ju xin liding," *Xinxin xinwen*, March 19, 1944. On subsidies, see Zhang and Guo, *Guoli xinan lianhe daxue shiliao (er) huiyi jilu juan*, 318–19; Special Committee for Interpreter Affairs Meeting Minutes," June 23, 1944, RG 493, UD-UP 299, box 649, June-July 1944, NARA.

129. "Employment of English-Speaking Chinese Interpreters," March 3, 1943, RG 493, UD-UP 299, box 648, February-March-April 1943, NARA; Kwan, *Dragon and the Crown*, 54; Dai Zhaoran cheng Yang Xuancheng dian, June 13, 1944, file no. 763-58, p. 31, SHAC.

130. FAB records state that the interpreting officer in question, He Zongyi, killed himself as a result of mistreatment from both FAB and U.S. forces, while fellow interpreting officer Weng Xinjun claimed that He committed suicide over the pay issue. See Weng, "Nan wang de junshi yiyuan shenghuo," 11–12; "Junshi weiyuan hui waishi ju yiyuan He Zongyi yin Meijun ji Kunming banshi chu qianhou paichi beipo zisha qingxing," file no. 763-59, SHAC.

131. "Interpreting Officer Complaint," June 28, 1945, RG 493, UD-UP 296, box 643, Correspondence (August to September 1945), NARA.

132. Perry Hanson to Frank Price, August 8, 1945, RG 493, UD-UP 299, box 651, TIAO Section, 1945–1946, NARA.

133. Norman McNeill to Huang Renlin, January 30, 1945, RG 493, UD-UP 300, box 652, Mess, 1945, NARA.

134. Huang, *Guanyu Meiguo bing*, 135–36.

135. "Interpreters Report," May 19, 1944, RG 493, UD-UP 299, box 648, April–May 1944, NARA. On the May 4 movement, see Manela, *Wilsonian Moment*, 176–96; Wasserstrom, "Chinese Students and Anti-Japanese Protests, Past and Present," 59–65.

136. Dai Zhaoran cheng Yuan Xuancheng dian, May 10, 1944, file no. 763–58, SHAC.

137. Shen Youkang, "Wo zenyang zai Meijun zhong dang fanyi guan," *Xuesheng shidai* 1, no. 4/5: 13–14.

138. Wang fanyi guan, "Lun fanyi guan," *Da gong bao*, March 19, 1945.

139. Haydon Boatner to Hoover Institution, December 12, 1975, Haydon Boatner Papers, box 2, Biographical File, HIA.

140. "Interpreting Officer Complaint," June 28, 1945, RG 493 UD-UP 296, box 643, Correspondence, August to September 1945, NARA.

141. Huang, *Guanyu Meiguo bing*, 138.

142. Rafael, "Translation in Wartime," 242, 245. See also M. Baker, "Interpreters and Translators in the War Zone," 197–222.

143. Huang, *Guanyu Meiguo bing*, 138.

144. Perry Hanson to Frank Price, August 8, 1945, RG 493, UD-UP 299, box 651, TIAO Section, 1945–1946, NARA.

145. Scholars have documented how humiliation can foster outrage and militant reactions in China in response to perceived foreign slights. See S. Zhao, *Nation-State by Construction*, 35; Tsu, *Failure, Nationalism, and Literature*, 10; Dikötter, "Culture, 'Race,' and Nation," 590–91.

146. Gu Shurong, "Meijun de 'Zhongguo' jiyang zhan," and He Yizhong, "Dang Meijun yiyuan de jingli: Yi fu Zhongguo shoukao he yi fu Meiguo shoukao," in Xinan, *Guoli xinan lianhe daxue babai xuezi congjun huiyi*, 98–99, 134–35; "Report of Incident," February 2, 1945, RG 493, UD-UP 296, box 644, Correspondence File 8/44-5/45, and "FAB Kunming Branch Office No. 3076," May 1, 1945, RG 493, UP-UP 296, box 643, Correspondence File 8/44 to 5/45, NARA.

147. Wu Cunya, "Yaowang Longling san ge yue," in Xinan, *Guoli xinan lianhe daxue babai xuezi congjun huiyi*, 133.

148. "Summary of Report Submitted by Interpreter Cai Zukang to Brigadier General Yao Kai," October 24, 1943, RG 493, UD-UP 299, box 648, October-November-December 1943, NARA.

149. "Report on Interpreter Tsai," undated, RG 493, UD-UP 299, box 648, October-November-December 1943, NARA.

150. "Misunderstanding between Interpreter and Capt. Eggers," December 4, 1943, RG 493, UD-UP 299, box 648, October, November, December 1943, NARA.

151. On "chickenshit" during World War II, such as sadism disguised as discipline, frequent unnecessary inspections, and obsession with personal appearance, see Fussell, *Wartime*, 79–95.

152. Dorn later immortalized the experience in a book. See Dorn, *Walkout*.

153. Mengzi wrote, "Those who work with their minds rule people; those who work with their hands are ruled by people." See X. Song, *Teachers' Schools and the Making of the Modern Chinese Nation-State*, 114–15.

154. Tuchman, *Stilwell and the American Experience in China*, 422; Luo Daren, "Jieye manyou sheshi dan," in Xinan, *Guoli xinan lianhe daxue babai xuezi congjun huiyi*, 90.

155. Zhang Zhiliang, "Dianxi de jiyang zhan," in Xinan, *Guoli xinan lianhe daxue babai xuezi congjun huiyi*, 158.

156. Liang Jaiyou, "Yu paobing lian gongfu qianxian," in Xinan, *Guoli xinan lianhe daxue babai xuezi congjun huiyi*, 70.

157. "History, Chinese Training Center," October 1, 1945, RG 493, UD-UP 590, box 14, CTC HQ's Final Report; "Interpreting Officer," April 10, 1945, RG 493, UD-UP 296, box 642, Correspondence (February to September 1945), NARA.

158. Huang Deji cheng Yao Guanshun dian, May 14, 1945, file no. 763–58, SHAC; "34 nian 5 yue fen yiguan chengfa biao," undated, RG 493, UD-UP 296, box 644, Correspondence File, 1945, NARA.

159. "Final Report of FATC, 1943–1945," undated, RG 493, UD-UP 590, box 15, CTC Field Artillery Training Center Final Report, NARA.

160. H. R. Smith to Joe Keeton, May 15, 1945, RG 493, UD-UP 296, box 646, Chinese Training Center, 1945, NARA.

161. "Interpreters," June 20, 1945, RG 493, UD-UP 541, box 82, 231.3 Interpreters, 1945, NARA.

162. Kramer, *Blood of Government*, 310–13.

163. Huang Deji cheng Yao Guanshun dian, May 14, 1945, file no. 763–58, SHAC.

164. Waishi ju Kunming banshi chu gong han 3067, May 3, 1945; Waishi ju Kunming banshi chu gong han 3927, July 7, 1945, RG 493, UD-UP 296, box 644, Correspondence File 8/44-5/45, NARA.

165. FAB no. 2625, April 29, 1945, RG 493, UD-UP 297, box 646, Chinese Training Center, 1945, NARA.

166. Kun shi pan zidi 75 hao, July 3, 1945, RG 493, UD-UP 296, box 644, Correspondence File, 1945, NARA.

167. Hu Yimei to Wu Zelin, June 21, 1944, RG 493, UD-UP 365, box 64, 250.1 Discipline, NARA.

168. Headquarters, 57th Army, Guizhou, February 20, 1945, RG 493, UD-UP 541, box 67, 000.5, February 7 to July 21, 1945, NARA.

169. Shang Zhen to Stilwell, June 18, 1943, RG 493, UD-UP 299, box 648, February, March, April 1943; FAB Kunming Branch Office to FAB Liaison Officer, Undated, and Case #75, Kunming Office, Southwest Military Transport Military Law Supervision Branch, Provost Marshal Department of the National Military Council], July 3, 1945, RG 493, UD-UP 296, box 644, Correspondence File 1945; Kunming Branch Office, FAB, Subject: Temporary Assignment of Duty of IO Liu Shichuan, July 27, 1945, RG 493, UD-UP 296, box 643, Correspondence (February to September 1945), NARA.

170. Shen Youkang, "Wo zenyang zai Meijun zhong dang fanyi guan," *Xuesheng shidai* 1, no. 4/5 (1945).

171. Dai Li zhi Shang Zhen dian, June 15, 1945, file no. 763-63, p. 13, SHAC.

172. Black engineering battalions played a leading role in the construction of the Ledo Road connecting Assam to Yunnan. See Daugherty, *Allied Resupply Effort in the China-Burma-India Theater*, 181–97.

173. Bolden and Isaacs investigated the issue in China after Chinese drivers replaced Black GIs on the first convoys from India to Kunming in early 1945. U.S. commanders denied that Chiang had prohibited Black personnel from entering the country, but SOS commander Gilbert Cheves admitted "off the record" that he didn't want Black soldiers in Kunming because the city was "a rotten town" with just a few liberty spots, where fights between Black and white troops were likely to break out. "In these dark streets if fights were to start a colored man would start to cut; records show that he is a good cutting man," Cheves said on February 6. Chiang officially prohibited Blacks from traveling east of Kunming on August 20—affirming a tacit practice already in place. See "Conference: Newspaper Correspondents—Brooks and Bolden," February 6, 1945; Wedemeyer to Hurley, May 15, 1945; and Wedemeyer to MacArthur, August 21, 1945, Albert Wedemeyer Papers, box 87, folder 1, HIA.

174. Zarrow, *Educating China*, 226, 234.

175. Sihn, "Eugenics Discourse and Racial Improvement in Republican China," 463–64; Dikötter, "Racial Identities in China," 405.

176. Liang Jiayou, "Da guizi qu," in Xinan, *Guoli xinan lianhe daxue babai xuezi congjun huiyi*, 32.

177. Hanson to Price, August 8, 1945, RG 493, UD-UP 299, box 651, TIAO Section, 1945–1946, NARA.

178. Ch'i, *Jianbanuzhang de mengyou*, 291–93, 639–43.

179. See Duara, "Cold War as a Historical Period," 463–68.

180. Hanson to Price, August 8, 1945, RG 493, UD-UP 299, box 651, TIAO Section, 1945–1946, NARA.

181. Cheng Yaode, "Fanyi shenghuo huiyi," 168–69, and Zhou Mingdao, "Zai paobing xunlian zhongxin de rizi," 145–46, in Xinan, *Guoli xinan lianhe daxue babai xuezi congjun huiyi*.

182. Hanson to Price, August 8, 1945, RG 493, UD-UP 299, box 651, TIAO Section, 1945–1946, NARA.

183. Leslie Stewart to H. R. Smith, September 1945, RG 493, UD-UP 300, box 652, Officer in Charge of Interpreter Affairs-Kunming Area, NARA.

184. Radio WARX-49489, October 20, 1944, RG 493, UD-UP 590, box 11, China Theater History, October 20, 1944, to December 31, 1944, NARA.

185. K. S. Wong, *Americans First*, 163–92.

186. Headquarters Memo, August 21, 1945, RG 493, UD-UP 300, box 650, INT Directives-SOP, NARA.

187. Pomfret, *Beautiful Country and the Middle Kingdom*, 178–79.

188. Assignment of Interpreter, June 23, 1945, RG 493, UD-UP 297, box 645, Assignments of Interpreting Officers, NARA.

189. Israel, *Lianda*, 367–70.

Chapter 3

1. Setzekorn, *Rise and Fall of an Officer Corps*, 61–63, 73–74.

2. "Article Five on the Chinese Training Center," undated, RG 493, UD-UP 590, box 14, Chinese Training Command Press Releases, NARA.

3. K. Shen, *Sun Liren zhuan*, 305.

4. "Misconduct of New First Army," July 12, 1945, RG 493, UD-UP 541, box 67, 000.5, New 1st Army Incidents, NARA.

5. Albert Wedemeyer to Chiang Kai-shek, August 5, 1945, RG 493, UD-UP 590, box 15, Contact Liaison with New First Army, NARA.

6. Sun Liren to Albert Wedemeyer, December 31, 1945, RG 493, UD-UP 265, box 62, 000.5, Crimes, from Jan. 1, 1946, NARA.

7. "Discipline of the 38th Division," August 6, 1945, RG 493, UD-UP 541, box 67, 000.5, Crimes folder, from July 22, 1945, NARA.

8. On the Philippines, see Capozzola, *Bound by War*, 34–45, 96–102, 132–45, 178, 180. On the Caribbean, see Renda, *Taking Haiti*, 15, 20, 101–16, 123–25.

9. On U.S. Army advisory and training programs, see Gallicchio, "Other China Hands," 46–58; Romanus and Sunderland, *Stilwell's Mission to China*, 151–52, 212–20, 292–96; Romanus and Sunderland, *Stilwell's Command Problems*, 27–32, 139, 320–21, 338, 352, 367, 375; Romanus and Sunderland, *Time Runs Out in CBI*, 24–49, 56–65, 94–96, 233–46, 262–69, 272–73, 295, 314–16, 359, 368–78, 380; Spence, *To Change China*, 257–58; Setzekorn, *Rise and Fall of an Officer Corps*, 55, 60–67; Babb, "Harmony of Yin and Yank," 76–83, 119, 125–42, 147–50; Westad, *Restless Empire*, 268; Ch'i, *Jianbanuzhang de mengyou*, 300–302, 311–13, 665, 670–77, 692–97; Cao, "Establishing the Ramgarh Training Center," 1–10; Ch'i, *Nationalist China at War*, 110–11; van de Ven, "Stilwell in the Stocks," 248–50. On U.S. Army liaison work and combat cooperation, see Gallicchio, "Other China Hands," 59–64; Romanus and Sunderland, *Stilwell's Command Problems*, 45–48, 119–59, 204–56, 312–16, 331–60; Romanus and Sunderland, *Time Runs Out in CBI*, 77–141, 276–90; Setzekorn, *Rise and Fall of an Officer Corps*, 64, 67–69, 72–75; Babb, "Harmony of Yin and Yank," 160–12; Yu, *Dragon's War*, 88–103, 177–93; Ch'i, *Jianbanuzhang de mengyou*, 434–44, 459–518; van de Ven, *War and Nationalism in China*, 47–51, 54; Mitter, *Forgotten Ally*, 315–18, 332–33. On the U.S. Navy's training program for the Chinese Juntong, see Wakeman, *Spymaster*, 285–307; Kush, *Rice Paddy Navy*; Yu, *Dragon's War*, 104–42. On intelligence cooperation, see Yu, *OSS in China*.

10. Setzekorn, *Rise and Fall of an Officer Corps*, 11, 55, 84–86.

11. On air force training and Chinese-American Composite Wing operations, see Romanus and Sunderland, *Time Runs Out in CBI*, 26, 172–73; Romanus and Sunderland, *Stilwell's Command Problems*, 323; Warnock, "Chinese American Composite Wing," 21–30; Xu, "Chinese Air Force with American Wings," 77–78; Guo, *Feihu xinzhuan*. On the Hump, see Plating, *Hump*; Liu, *Tuofeng hangxian*; Immerwahr, *How to Hide an Empire*, 283–87, 295–97.

12. "Dian-Mian gong lu gongwu ju zi di 13022 hao," October 15, 1941, file no. 54-22-246, YPA.

13. Ch'i, *Jianbanuzhang de mengyou*, 47–48.

14. "The Military Mission in China to the War Department," February 10, 1942, *FRUS: 1942, China*, 13–16.

15. March 2, 1942, diary entry, Edward Elliot MacMorland Papers, box 1, Diary 1941–1942, USACMH.

16. U.S. Ambassador to China Clarence Gauss supported Magruder's recommendation. See Grieve, "Belated Endeavor," 193–94.

17. Ch'i, *Jianbanuzhang de mengyou*, 108–11.

18. Ch'i, *Jianbanuzhang de mengyou*, 47.

19. Van de Ven, *War and Nationalism in China*, 11–12.

20. Ch'i, *Jianbanuzhang de mengyou*, 47–53, 283.

21. December 3, 1941, diary entry, MacMorland Papers, box 1, Diary 1941–1942, USACMH.

22. Xiong, *Hai sang ji—Xiong Shihui de huiyi lu*, 332–34; Zhou, *Jiang Zhongzheng zongtong dang'an: Shilue gaoben*, 49:111.

23. Chiang Kai-shek to Song Ziwen, April 19, 1942, T.V. Soong Papers, box 36, folder 5, HIA.

24. Zhou, *Jiang Zhongzheng zongtong dang'an: Shilue gaoben*, 49:396–98.

25. Chiang Kai-shek to Song Ziwen, April 19, 1942, T.V. Soong Papers, box 36, folder 5, HIA.

26. Wertheim, *Tomorrow, the World*, 2–13, 81, 135–49.

27. Wertheim, *Tomorrow, the World*, 83–98.

28. Ch'i, *Jianbanuzhang de mengyou*, 83–85; Romanus and Sunderland, *Stilwell's Mission to China*, 71–72; White, *The Stilwell Papers*, 26–27.

29. Romanus and Sunderland, *Stilwell's Mission to China*, 94–95.

30. Zhonghua minguo zhongyao shiliao chu bian, *Zhanshi waijiao*, 559–66; Ch'i, *Jianbanuzhang de mengyou*, 94–95, 181, 242–43, 630–31.

31. Mitter, *Forgotten Ally*, 252. On prewar Sino-British tensions in Burma, see "Intelligence Reports on Chinese Activities," November 13, 1945; Series 1/1(A), accession no. 6280, file 491D(M), Intelligence Reports on Chinese Activities, MNA.

32. Ch'i, *Jianbanuzhang de mengyou*, 111–20, 179–80.

33. Van de Ven, *War and Nationalism in China*, 28–32.

34. Van de Ven, *War and Nationalism in China*, 32.

35. Taylor, *Generalissimo*, 204–5.

36. Taylor, *Generalissimo*, 204–5. Civil Affairs Staff, Subject: Chinese Infiltration, July 7, 1945, Series 1/1(A), accession no. 6284, file S-CHI, Chinese Affairs, MNA.

37. Summary of the Situation Regarding the Chinese 93rd Division Activities in Relation to Kengtung State, July 25, 1945, Series 1/1, accession no. 10161, F/N 20/CA-25, MNA; Ch'i, *Jianbanuzhang de Mengyou*, 134.

38. Ch'i, *Jianbanuzhang de Mengyou*, 162.

39. "General Stilwell," *Life*, June 15, 1942; van de Ven, "Stilwell in the Stocks," 248–49.

40. Van de Ven, *War and Nationalism in China*, 8–11, 32–33; Ch'i, *Jianbanuzhang de Mengyou*, 147–51.

41. White, *The Stilwell Papers*, 50–51.

42. White, *The Stilwell Papers*, 105.

43. White, *The Stilwell Papers*, 115–16.

44. Ch'i, *Jianbanuzhang de mengyou*, 178.

45. Van de Ven, "Stilwell in the Stocks," 249; Mitter, *Forgotten Ally*, 253; Romanus and Sunderland, *Stilwell's Mission to China*, 98.

46. Ch'i, *Jianbanuzhang de mengyou*, 139, 169–71, 177, 180–85.

47. Quoted in Paine, *Wars for Asia*, 198.

48. Ch'i, *Jianbanuzhang de mengyou*, 87–88, 630–35.

49. Van de Ven, "Stilwell in the Stocks," 247–48; van de Ven, *War and Nationalism in China*, 8–11.

50. Mitter, *Forgotten Ally*, 256.

51. Romanus and Sunderland, *Stilwell's Mission to China*, 14, 25–27.

52. Romanus and Sunderland, *Stilwell's Mission to China* 184–85, 192, 194. "Notes on Ramgarh (Cont'd)," undated, Haydon L. Boatner Papers, box 2, CBI Campaigns and Strategy, HIA. On Ramgarh's establishment, see Cao, "Establishing the Ramgarh Training Center," 1–10. Sun's division arrived at Ramgarh in late July, but the U.S. Army did not activate the training center until August 26. See Zhou, *Jiang Zhongzheng zongtong de dang'an: Shilue gaoben*, 50:459–60.

53. Tilman Durdin, "Stilwell's School in India a Success," *New York Times*, June 6, 1945.

54. Xue, *Sun Liren jiangjun zhuan*, 86; Ch'i, *Jianbanuzhang de mengou*, 311–14.

55. Zhou, *Jiang Zhongzheng zongtong de dang'an: Shilue gaoben*, 55:508–9.

56. "Zhong-Mei junguan zhijian moca qingxing," February 25, 1944, file no. 002-080103-00062-002-001a to 0072a, AHA.

57. Mitter, *Forgotten Ally*, 256. Haydon Boatner later wrote of Stilwell, "I know of no U.S. officer who, throughout his entire career, had so methodically collected such voluminous personal writing and photographs designed for his biographers and historians." See Boatner's statement on Tuchman's *Stilwell and the American Experience in China*, 16–17, Haydon L. Boatner Papers, box 1, Review of Tuchman's Biography, USACMH.

58. Sides, *Ghost Soldiers*, 20.

59. White, *The Stilwell Papers*, 143.

60. Romanus and Sunderland, *Stilwell's Mission to China*, 179, 192.

61. Franklin Roosevelt to Chiang Kai-shek, December 3, 1942, file no. 002-020300-00017-018, AHA. On MacArthur and the Philippine Army, see Capozzola, *Bound by War*, 133–46.

62. Brooks Atkinson, "Chinese Are Eager for War Training," *New York Times*, July 27, 1943, 7.

63. "Memorandum by the Second Secretary of the Embassy in China (Davies) to the Ambassador in China (Gauss), March 9, 1943, *FRUS: 1943, China*, 29.

64. Romanus and Sunderland, *Stilwell's Mission to China*, 216–17.

65. Xue, *Sun Liren jiangjun zhuan*, 90–91. Like Sun, Liao had graduated from a military academy abroad, Saint-Cyr in France. Zheng was a graduate from the first class (1924) of the Huangpu (Whampoa) Military Academy, where Chiang served as commandant.

66. Jiang Weiguo cheng Jiang Jieshi dian, September 24, 1942, file no. 020-040300-00002-016-001a, AHA.

67. Zhou, *Jiang Zhongzheng zongtong de dang'an: Shilue gaoben*, 55:508–9.

68. "Establishment of a Co-Operative Store," June 3, 1943, RG 493, UD-UP 218, box 15, PX and Other Company Exchanges, NARA.

69. Historians have argued that Stilwell forced Luo out of Ramgarh for attempted embezzlement, but Haydon Boatner insisted that Stilwell sacked Luo largely because Luo had told Stilwell he—not Stilwell—would command the CAI in Burma. See Boatner's statement on Tuchman, 4, Haydon L. Boatner Papers, box 1, Review of Tuchman's Biography USACMH; Romanus and Sunderland, *Stilwell's Mission to China*, 255.

70. Wen Mingjian cheng Jiang Jieshi dian, August 16, 1943, file no. 002-090105-00009-006-001a to 002a, AHA.

71. Zheng Dongguo cheng Jiang Jieshi dian, August 18, 1943, file no. 020-020300-00024-023, AHA.

72. Shu Shicun ji Sun Liren cheng Jiang Jieshi dian, August 16, 1943, file no. 002-090105-00006-047-001 to 003, AHA.

73. Romanus and Sunderland, *Time Runs Out in CBI*, 34.

74. "Chinese Comments and News," *Termite Hill Gazette*, vol. 1, edition 4, week of October 14, 1944, and "School Notes," *Termite Hill Gazette*, vol. 1, edition 3, week of October 7, 1944, Lewis Kemper William Papers, box 1, USAMHC.

75. Capozzola, *Bound by War*, 79–80.

76. White, *The Stilwell Diaries*, 137.

77. "The Chinese Division as a Combat Unit," June 22, 1944, RG 493, UD-UP 215, box 11, Organization of Units, NARA.

78. "Final Report of FATC," undated, RG 493, UD-UP 590, box 15, FATC Final Report, NARA.

79. Romanus and Sunderland, *Stilwell's Mission to China*, 184, 230–34, 292–300; "Final Report of FATC," undated, RG 493, UD-UP 590, box 15, Field Artillery Training Center Final Report, NARA.

80. Dorn to all personnel of Yoke Force, March 2, 1944, RG 493, UD-UP 300, box 650, INT-Directives-SOP, NARA.

81. "Will the Chinese Fight," January 4, 1944, Frank Dorn Papers, box 1, folder 30, HIA.

82. See, for example, Royal F. Wenke to Haydon Boatner, May 5, 1945; Maurice Metcalf to Haydon Boatner, April 18, 1945; Haydon Boatner to William Bergin, September 17, 1943, Haydon Boatner Papers, box 2, Supplementary Documents 2/4, USACMH.

83. Gallicchio, "Other China Hands," 46–58, 61–62; Ch'i, *Jianbanuzhang de mengyou*, 765–66.

84. Wakeman, *Spymaster*, 285–86, 291–93.

85. Miles, *Different Kind of War*, 111–14.

86. For promotions, see "Lieutenant Seth I. Morris," June 29, 1945, RG 38, box 5, Personnel S-1 folder 13; Miles to Purnell, September 9, 1944, RG 38, box 28, Morale; "Recommendation for the Promotion to Rank of Warrant Officer, Case of Gunnery

Sergeant Way Holland," February 15, 1945, RG 38, box 5, Personnel S-1 folder 7, NARA. On dismissals, see Miles to Metzel, September 15, 1944, RG 38, box 7, Dispatches Outgoing, folder 9; Irwin Byerly to Interior Control Board, December 25, 1944, RG 38, box 5, Personnel S-1 folder 5, NARA.

87. "School Notes," Lewis Kemper William Papers, box 1, USAMHC.

88. Guofang bu junshi qingbao ju, ed., *ZhongMei hezuo suo zhi*, 36, 122; Wakeman, *Spymaster*, 294. Approximately 2,300 American personnel were serving in SACO in China at the time of Japan's surrender. See "Recapitulation," August 31, 1945, RG 38, box 6, Personnel S-1, folder 17, NARA.

89. Wakeman, *Spymaster*, 295–96.

90. Stoddard, *Rising Tide of Color*, 29.

91. Stoddard, *Rising Tide of Color*, 29.

92. Wakeman, *Spymaster*, 500n9.

93. Wakeman, *Spymaster*, 299–301. In recruiting navy personnel, Miles insisted that they be willing to live under the same conditions as Chinese; in practice, this occurred mostly outside the training camps, when units were in the field. See Secret War Diary, September 1, 1943, RG 38, box 8, War Diaries 1943 folder 1, NARA.

94. Wakeman, *Spymaster*, 302–3.

95. Warnock, "Chinese American Composite Wing," 21–29.

96. Guo, *Feihu xinzhuan*, 195.

97. Guo, *Feihu xinzhuan*, 83–84, 99.

98. Warnock, "Chinese American Composite Wing," 21–23.

99. Van de Ven, *War and Nationalism in China*, 35, 37–38; Ch'i, *Jianbanuzhang de mengyou*, 189, 193–95; Mitter, *Forgotten Ally*, 301.

100. Jiang Jieshi ling Song Ziwen dian, May 8, 1943, file no. 002-060100-00176-008, AHA.

101. Quoted in Ch'i, *Jianbanuzhang de mengyou*, 218.

102. Mitter, *Forgotten Ally*, 300–303. The two Song sisters feared that if Stilwell were removed, it would threaten China's relationship with the United States at a time when Japanese forces still threatened to overwhelm the Nationalists.

103. Van de Ven, *War and Nationalism in China*, 42–44; Ch'i, *Jianbanuzhang de mengyou*, 414–24.

104. "The Cairo Communiqué," December 1, 1943, www.ndl.go.jp/constitution /e/shiryo/01/002_46shoshi.html.

105. Van de Ven, *War and Nationalism in China*, 45–50; Ch'i, *Jianbanuzhang de mengyou*, 432–33.

106. White, *The Stilwell Papers*, 262–63.

107. White, *The Stilwell Papers*, 266.

108. Ch'i, *Jianbanuzhang de mengyou*, 437–40.

109. Van de Ven, *War and Nationalism in China*, 46, 50–54; Mitter, *Forgotten Ally,* 317.

110. Van de Ven, *China at War*, 179–87; van de Ven, *War and Nationalism in China*, 51–55. Stilwell's diary mentions almost nothing about the military situation in China between April and August 1944. See White, *The Stilwell Papers*, 287–314.

111. Taylor, *Generalissimo*, 282.

112. Van de Ven, *China at War*, 185–90.

113. Romanus and Sunderland, *Stilwell's Command Problems*, 121.

114. Van de Ven, *War and Nationalism in China*, 48, 50–51.

115. Ch'i, *Jianbanuzhang de mengyou*, 475–76; Romanus and Sunderland, *Stilwell's Command Problems*, 188, 253.

116. Van de Ven, *War and Nationalism in China*, 51; Ch'i, *Jianbanuzhang de mengyou*, 522–23, 533–34.

117. Capozzola, *Bound by War*, 178–82; Wertheim, *Tomorrow, the World*, 135–49.

118. Ch'i, *Jianbanuzhang de mengyou*, 541–44.

119. Ch'i, *Jianbanuzhang de mengyou*, 565–73; Romanus and Sunderland, *Stilwell's Command Problems*, 422–29.

120. White, *The Stilwell Papers*, 329–31; Ch'i, *Jianbanuzhang de mengyou*, 573–74.

121. Van de Ven, *War and Nationalism in China,* 55–56; Ch'i, *Jianbanuzhang de mengyou*, 574–80.

122. Quoted in Romanus and Sunderland, *Stilwell's Command Problems*, 435–36.

123. White, *The Stilwell Papers*, 331.

124. President Roosevelt to Generalissimo Chiang Kai-shek, September 16, 1944, *FRUS: 1944, China*, 157–58.

125. Lohbeck, *Patrick J. Hurley*, 415–16.

126. White, *The Stilwell Papers*, 333.

127. Mitter, *Forgotten Ally*, 335–39.

128. Diary entry, September 19, 1944, Chiang Kai-shek Diaries, box 43, folder 21, HIA.

129. Ch'i, *Jianbanuzhang de mengyou*, 595–604.

130. Ch'i, *Jianbanuzhang de mengyou*, 610–12.

131. President Roosevelt to Generalissimo Chiang Kai-shek, October 5, 1944, *FRUS: 1944, China*, 165–66.

132. Ch'i, *Jianbanuzhang de mengyou*, 596, 598.

133. Wedemeyer, *Wedemeyer Reports!*, 278–82; Wang, "Weidemai yu zhanshi Zhongguo," 139–42, 147–48; Ch'i, *Jianbanuzhang de mengyou*, 668–75.

134. Van de Ven, *China at War*, 189–90; Romanus and Sunderland, *Time Runs Out in CBI*, 147–50.

135. Romanus and Sunderland, *Time Runs Out in CBI*, 134–41, 155–58, 238–46.

136. Ch'i, *Jianbanuzhang de mengyou*, 675.

137. "Efficiency Report on General Officer," January 25, 1945, Albert Wedemeyer Papers, box 87, Frank Dorn folder, HIA.

138. Dorn to Stilwell, September 22, 1944, Frank Dorn Papers, box 1, folder 45, HIA.

139. "History, Chinese Training Center, final report," October 1, 1945, RG 493, UD-UP 590, box 14, CTC HQ's Final Report, NARA. Centers opened in 1945 include the ITC, the Heavy Mortar Training Center, the Signal School, the Chinese Ord-

nance Training Center, the Interpreters Pool, and a Motor Transport School. The FATC opened in 1943, and the General Staff School opened in May 1944.

140. "Alpha Units Strength Report," July 31, 1945, RG 493, UD-UP 590, box 11, Chinese-American Combat Liaison, NARA; Setzekorn, *Rise and Fall of an Officer Corps*, 66–67; Romanus and Sunderland, *Time Runs Out in CBI*, 372.

141. "Evaluation of CCC Operations," September 1945; Annex No. III to the Formal Historical Record, Eastern Command, CCC, undated; RG 493, UD-UP 590, box 12, CCC and Assigned Units, Historical Reports to September 1945, NARA.

142. Liao Yaoxiang cheng Jiang Jieshi dian, March 30, 1944, file no. 002-020300-00026-040-001x, AHA. American commanders disagreed with Liao's assessment. They blamed the Eighteenth Division's escape on communication problems and Liao's excessive caution. See Romanus and Sunderland, *Stilwell's Command Problems*, 154–59.

143. "Non-Compliance with Orders," March 16, 1945, RG 493, UD-UP 215, box 7, Barred or Restricted Places, NARA.

144. Huang, *Guanyu Meiguo bing*, 49–53, 81–83, 93, 117–18.

145. "Final Report: Possible Black Market and Smuggling by Chinese Troops," March 22, 1945, RG 493, UD-UP 185, box 10, 000.5, Crimes 1945, NARA.

146. "Non-Compliance with Orders," March 16, 1945, RG 493, UD-UP 215, box 7, Barred or Restricted Places, NARA.

147. Boatner to Regional Office, Theater Provost Marshall, IBT, APO 689, April 10, 1945, RG 493, UD-UP 215, box 1, 000.51 Smuggling, NARA.

148. "Possible Black Market and Smuggling by Chinese Troops," March 22, 1945; Theatre Directive, April 29, 1944, RG 493, UD-UP 185, box 10, 000.5, Crimes 1945, NARA.

149. "Misbehavior of Chinese Personnel Traveling from India to China," March 26, 1945, RG 493, UD-UP 215, box 7, Morals and Conduct, NARA.

150. Wedemeyer to Chiang, May 19, 1945, RG 493, UD-UP 265, box 62, 000.5, April 5 to July 31, 1945, NARA.

151. "Punishment of Murder," February 20, 1945; "Shooting of Chinese Trespasser," March 7, 1945, RG 493, UD-UP 215, box 1, Murder, Shooting, Stabbing, NARA.

152. "Investigation of Shooting at the 14th Evacuation Hospital, March 11, 1945, RG 493, UD-UP 215, box 1, Murder, Shooting, Stabbing, NARA.

153. "Conduct of Allied Troops Towards Civilian Population," February 14, 1945, RG 493, UD-UP 215, box 2, Relations between Civil and Military Authorities, NARA.

154. ADV HQ ALFSEA, May 5, 1945, Series 1/1(A), accession no. 6284, file S-CHI, Chinese Affairs, MNA; CAS NCAC no. 66, Subject: Chinese Infiltration, June 23, 1945, Series 1/1(A), accession no. 6284, file S-CHI, Chinese Affairs, MNA. Desertions were common at Ramgarh, with deserters usually fleeing to Calcutta, where American military police assisted colonial authorities in identifying Chinese personnel and making arrests. See Boatner to Sultan, March 16, 1945; "Deserters in January 1945," undated, RG 493, UD-UP 215, box 8, Deserters and Desertions, NARA.

155. S. Y. Kao, "Report of Incident," May 13, 1945; Statement by Majors Sun and Ma, undated; Statement of Lt. F.W. Nollen, undated; RG 493, UD-UP 215, box 7, Incidents, NARA.

156. "Report of Investigation of Alleged Mishandling of Chinese Officers," May 12, 1945, RG 493, UD-UP 215, box 7, Incidents, NARA.

157. Wedemeyer to Chiang, August 5, 1945, RG 493, UD-UP 590, box 15, Contact Liaison with New First Army, NARA.

158. Aurand to Wedemeyer, August 13, 1945, RG 493, UD-UP 541, box 67, August 1 to December 31, 1945, NARA.

159. Wedemeyer to Chiang, August 5, 1945, RG 493, UD-UP 590, box 15, Contact Liaison with New First Army, NARA.

160. "Chinese-American Relations," August 10, 1945, RG 493, UD-UP 541, box 67, 000.5, Crimes folder from July 22, 1945, NARA.

161. On the Yunnan bandit holdups, see the following files: 020-050204-0012-0007x to 0179x, AHA; Aurand to Wedemeyer, August 13, 1945, RG 493, UD-UP 541, box 67, August 1 to December 31, 1945, NARA.

162. Wedemeyer to Marshall, September 8, 1945, RG 493, UD-UP 590, box 25, Military Advisory Group CT, NARA; "Panorama of China," undated, Earl M. Revell Collection, box 2, folder 15, USACMH.

163. Wedemeyer to Marshall, September 8, 1945, RG 493, UD-UP 590, box 25, Military Advisory Group CT, NARA.

164. The Ambassador in China (Hurley) to the Secretary of State, September 2, 1945, *FRUS: 1945, China*, 7:547.

165. The Ambassador in China (Hurley) to the Secretary of State, September 1, 1945, *FRUS: 1945, China*, 7:546.

166. Wedemeyer to Marshall, September 8, 1945, RG 493, UD-UP 590, box 25, Military Advisory Group CT, NARA.

167. Setzekorn, *Rise and Fall of an Officer Corps*, 86.

168. Wedemeyer to Marshall, September 8, 1945, RG 493, UD-UP 590, box 25, Military Advisory Group CT, NARA.

169. See, for example, "Report on the 2nd Honorable Division," August 26, 1945, RG 493, UD-UP 590, box 12, CCC and Assigned Units, Historical Report April to September 1945, NARA.

170. Wedemeyer to Marshall, September 8, 1945, RG 493, UD-UP 590, box 25, Military Advisory Group CT, NARA; Memorandum by the Secretary of State to President Truman, September 3, 1945, *FRUS: 1945*, 7:547–48.

171. Memorandum by the Director of the Office of Far Eastern Affairs (Vincent) to the Secretary of State, November 12, 1945, *FRUS: 1945, China*, 7:614–16.

172. Aide-mémoire from the headquarters of the Gissimo, October 9, 1944, *FRUS: 1944, China*, 6:169.

173. Mitter, *Forgotten Ally*, 261. The aircraft involved in the raid all crash-landed at various places in eastern China except for one B-25 that landed in Vladivostok, in the USSR. Japanese forces also destroyed all the airfields in Zhejiang that Chennault had built up while serving as Chiang's advisor before taking over the AVG.

174. See Kramer, *Blood of Government*, 305–6.

175. Ch'i, *Jianbanuzhang de mengyou*, 576.

176. "Historical Report of the Chinese Combat Command, period 8 January 1945 through 31 March 1945," August 31, 1945, RG 493, UD-UP 590, box 21, CCC History of Instructions to American Liaison Officers, NARA.

177. U.S. Army Service Forces, *Pocket Guide to China*, 2.

Chapter 4

1. John Matthew Gambardella Collection, AFC/2001/001/43532, VHP; U.S. Army Service Forces, *Pocket Guide to China*, 65–75.

2. Chennault, *Way of a Fighter*, 241–44.

3. Carl Kostol Collection, AFC/2001/001/56123, VHP. See also Milton McGee Collection, AFC/2001/001/37418, VHP.

4. Ralph Wilcox Memoir, MSS, box 562, folder 1, Ralph Wilcox Collection, AFC/2001/001/12418, VHP.

5. John Matthew Gambardella Collection, AFC/2001/001/43532, VHP.

6. Liu, *Erzhan shiqi Meiguo yuan Hua kongjun*, 196; Chennault, *Way of a Fighter*, 241–44.

7. "Jiang Jieshi ling Chongqing shi zhengfu dian," June 1939, file no. 53-29-230, pp. 19–19.1, CMA. The payment was 500 fabi for a Japanese colonel and 200 fabi for Chinese fliers and lower-ranked Japanese.

8. Yunnan sheng dang'an guan, *Nan wang feihudui*, 239.

9. Yujiang shi guan qu siling bu dai dian, August 28, 1942, file no. 81-4-1589, p. 14, CMA.

10. "Chennade jiangjun han Zhu De zong siling zhi xie," *Jiefang ribao*, August 30, 1944.

11. John Matthew Gambardella Collection, AFC/2001/001/43532, VHP.

12. Ford, *Flying Tigers*, 124–25.

13. Yunnan sheng dang'an guan, *Nan wang feihudui*, 235.

14. Wu Guozhen ling di shi qu zhang Xu Shu dian, May 12, 1942, file no. 61-15-3039, p. 122, CMA.

15. Van de Ven, *War and Nationalism in China*, 142–46.

16. Tengchong xianzhang cheng Yunnan sheng zhengfu dian, April 27, 1945, file no. 94-1-57, p. 65, YPA.

17. Yunnan sheng dang'an guan, *Nan wang feihudui*, 236.

18. "Jiuhu wo guo ji tongmeng guo kongjun pojiang renyuan jiangcheng banfa," May 1945, file no. 107-4-434, pp. 18–19, CMA.

19. He Yaozu ling Chongqing shi jingcha ju dian, July 11, 1944, file no. 61-1-29, pp. 75–77, CMA.

20. Jiang Jieshi ling Chongqing shi zhengfu dian, December 4, 1944, file no. 53-10-69, p. 34, CMA.

21. Tow, "Great Bombing of Chongqing," 258–63.

22. On the December 20 raid, see Ford, *Flying Tigers*, 100–107; on other raids, see Yunnan sheng dang'an guan, *Nan wang feihudui*, 86–97.

23. Chinese sources put the number at several million. See Yunnan sheng dang'an guan, *Nan wang Feihudui*, 221.

24. Romanus and Sunderland, *Stilwell's Command Problems*, 17, 77, 111–15; Cate, "Twentieth Air Force and Matterhorn," 68.

25. "Historical Report for Hsinching Airfield" and "Historical Report of Construction of Chanyi Airfield," RG 493, UD-UP 317, box 685, NARA. At least one airfield expansion project was completed entirely by a Chinese military unit stationed near the airfield.

26. Peck, *Two Kinds of Time*, 450.

27. "Historical Report of Construction of Laowhangping Airfield," RG 493, UD-UP 317, box 685, NARA.

28. "Historical Report of Construction of Loping Airfield," RG 493, UD-UP 317, box 685, NARA.

29. Watt, *Saving Lives in Wartime China*, 244.

30. FAB no. 2693, May 29, 1945, RG 493, Records of the Special Staff/Adjutant General, General Correspondence, box 95, 1944–1945, NARA; Kunming Police Headquarters to SOS Headquarters, November 10, 1943, RG 493, UD-UP 365, box 64, 250.1, Discipline, 1943–1944, NARA.

31. "Report of Investigation Regarding Misconduct of Captain James F. Byrne," June 29, 1945, RG 493, UD-UP 266, box 314, Morals and Conduct, October 1 to November 30, 1945, NARA.

32. "Captain James Bohlkin," June 14, 1945, RG 493, UD-UP 306, box 665, China Theater Report Misc., Jun-Aug 1945, NARA.

33. Junshi weiyuan hui waishi ju zhi waijiao bu dian, September 11, 1945, file no. 020-050210-0053-0061a to 0064a, AHA; "Fatal Shooting of a Chinese Civilian, Yu Pinghui," July 2, 1945, RG 493, UD-UP 309, box 670, June to October 1945 Investigation, NARA.

34. Chennault, *Way of a Tiger*, 240.

35. Cate, "Twentieth Air Force and Matterhorn," 70.

36. "Historical Report for Hsinching Airfield," RG 493, UD-UP 317, box 685; "Statement of James F. Byrne," June 15, 1945, RG 493, UD-UP 265, box 137, Investigation, 1945, NARA.

37. Cate, "Twentieth Air Force and Matterhorn," 170–71.

38. Hemingway, "Ernest Hemingway Tells How 100,000 Chinese Labored Day and Night to Build Huge Landing Field for Bombers," *PM*, June 18, 1941, 16–17.

39. Gerald Broida Collection, AFC/2001/001/60827, VHP; Chennault, *Way of a Fighter*, 238–39.

40. Warren Arnett to Martha Arnett, May 30, 1945, Warren Jefferson Arnett Collection, AFC/2001/001/11032, VHP.

41. Melvin Lees Collection, AFC/2001/001/75174, VHP.

42. Gerald Broida Collection, AFC/2001/001/60827, VHP.

43. Ford, *Flying Tigers*, 199–200; "Ben sheng jisi chu jinian san zhou nian," *Saodang bao*, December 9, 1944.

44. "Sammy Yuan," December 29, 1943, RG 493, UD-UP 306, box 664, China Theater AG Section Provost Marshal, Smuggling and Related Activities 1943, NARA.

45. "Sammy Yuan," December 29, 1943; Headquarters, Rear Echelon, to Wedemeyer, June 12, 1945, RG 493, UD-UP 266, box 314, China Theater AG, Section 250.1, NARA.

46. Scully, *Bargaining with the State from Afar*, 105–7, 193–94.

47. Roosevelt authorized Secretary of War Henry Stimson to establish a Judge Advocate General branch office in the CBI theater on June 19, but Stilwell was not vested and empowered to exercise all the powers pertaining to courts-martial until November 12. See "Courts-Martial Powers, Commanding General, USF, CBI Theater," November 12, 1942, RG 493, UD-UP 7, box 29, Courts Martial, May 15 to November 12, 1942, NARA.

48. "Madam Chu," March 12, 1945, RG 493, UD-UP 306, box 664, China Theater AG Section Provost Marshal, Black Market and Smuggling 1945, NARA; William Engel Milner Collection, AFC/2001/001/57101, VHP.

49. Wakeman, *Spymaster*, 320–29. Chiang relieved Dai of command over this office in July 1943 for exposing smuggling activities involving the children of Chiang's brother-in-law Kong Xiangxi.

50. Junshi weiyuan hui zhi Song Ziwen dian, December 20, 1942, file no. 020-011904-0021-0014z to 0021x, AHA.

51. "Orders Re Unauthorized Transportation of Goods," December 18, 1942, RG 493, UD-UP 7, box 28, 250 Discipline, December 31, 1943; "Anti-Smuggling Inspections," December 19, 1943, RG 493, UD-UP 365, box 53, 000.5, 1943–1944, NARA.

52. However, aircraft belonging to the China National Aviation Corporation (CNAC), a Chinese government–Pan Am Airlines joint venture, were subject to inspections by both Chinese customs and U.S. military authorities.

53. "Report on Trials and Punishments Arising from the Transportation of Articles for Sale in Airplanes or the Sale of Such Articles," November 26, 1943, RG 493, UD-UP 7, box 29, Charges, Proceedings, Trials 1943, NARA; "Statement of William M. Morris," September 15, 1944, RG 493, UD-UP 306, box 664, China Theater AG Section, Misc. Documents 1/45 to 9/45, NARA.

54. Craven and Cate, *Army Air Forces in World War II*, 6:567–68. CNAC's policy to fire people caught smuggling led to a shortage of qualified personnel. See W. H. Bond to T. H. Shen, April 21, 1945, RG 493, UD-UP 306, box 664, China Theater AG Section Provost Marshal, Black Market and Smuggling 1945, NARA.

55. Junshi weiyuan hui zhi Song Ziwen dian, December 20, 1942, file no. 020-011904-0021-0014x to 0021x, AHA.

56. Waijiao bu zhi Yunnan tepai yuan dian, January 10, 1943, file no. 020-011904-0021-0010x, AHA; "Chen Mengzhao Ge Zunxian toushui zousi chusi," *Guangxi ribao*, October 20, 1943.

57. "Report on Trials and Punishments Arising from the Transportation of Articles for Sale in Airplanes or the Sale of Such Articles," November 26, 1943, RG 493, UD-UP 7, box 29, Charges, Proceedings, Trials 1943, NARA.

58. See, for example, the following lengthy ROC Foreign Ministry files: 020-011903-0017-0015a to 0153a, 020-011908-0007-0005a to 0053a, 020-011903-0015-0171a to 0219a, AHA.

59. William Engel Milner Collection, AFC/2001/001/57101, VHP.

60. "With the Flying Tigers in China," unpublished memoir, 53–54, Arthur Perry Hauge Collection, AFC/2001/001/02877, VHP.

61. Whitney Greenberg Collection, AFC/2001/001/51147, VHP.

62. "Smuggling of Drugs," August 10, 1943, RG 493, UD-UP 306, box 664, China Theater AG Section Provost Marshal, Smuggling and Related Activities 1943, NARA.

63. "Final Report: Case No. 25.355CH," February 3, 1945; RG 493, Records of the Special Staff/Adjutant General, General Correspondence, box 95, 1944–1945, NARA.

64. "Black Market Activities," October 4, 1943, RG 493, UD-UP 365, box 64, 250 Discipline, 1943–1944 (second folder), NARA.

65. "Linnie Violet Fullerton, alias Jeanette Fullerton, May 10, 1944, RG 493, UD-UP 306, box 666, Lt. Col. Gilbert Stewart 1945, NARA.

66. "Black Market Activities," October 4, 1943, RG 493, UD-UP 365, box 64, 250 Discipline, 1943–1944 (second folder), NARA; Roy Farrell, undated letter passed by censor, RG 493, UD-UP 306, box 667, Investigation, CIC, APO 629 Dec. 1943 to Sept. 1944, NARA.

67. "Black Market Activities of the 14th Air Service Group, 14th Air Force," August 12, 1945, RG 493, UD-UP 309, box 670, Black Market Activities of the 14th Air Service Group, NARA.

68. "Suspected Black Market Activity," July 22, 1945, RG 493, UD-UP 306, box 663, Correspondence, June to August 1945, from Regional Offices, NARA.

69. See, for example, Joe Virgilio Collection, AFC/2001/001/68485 and John Salerno Collection, AFC/2001/001/47924, VHP; Headquarters, USF, China Theater, Subject: "Report of Alleged Illegal Activities of American Motor Vehicle Drivers," April 4, 1945; RG 493, Records of the Special Staff/Adjutant General, General Correspondence, box 98, Morals and Conduct, Dec. 1944 to May 15, 1945, NARA; "General Court Martial Orders Number 18," May 21, 1945, RG 493, UD-UP 541, box 85, 250 Discipline, 1945, NARA.

70. See, for example, "Sworn Statement Made by Ho Shet Yu," November 12, 1943, RG 493, UD-UP 306, box 665, China Theater HQ Intelligence Reports, October–November 1943, NARA; A. Duff to Colonel Ownby, July 25, 1945, RG 493, UD-UP 306, box 663, Correspondence, June to August 1945, from Regional Offices, NARA; "Statement of Private John Doe," May 23, 1945, RG 493, UD-UP 265, box 139, Investigations to August 1945, NARA; "Smuggling," December 27, 1943, RG 493, UD-UP 306, box 667, Investigation, CIC, APO 629, Dec. 1943 to Sept. 1944, NARA.

71. "Government Forbids Transportation and Transactions on Foreign Made Cigarettes," undated, RG 493, UD-UP 365, box 64, Morals and Conduct, 1943–1944, NARA.

72. "Jin shou Meijun yongpin," *Saodang bao*, October 2, 1944.

73. "Sigou Meijun yongpin jingju jihuo duoqi," *Saodang bao*, January 6, 1945.

74. "Long Yun shoushi wu dian ji zongling chuxi ge cai fangmian zhi yijian duiyu jinzhi maimai Meijun jun yongpin guiding zhixing banfa ba xiang," May 1945, RG 493, UD-UP 306, box 644, Correspondence File 1945, NARA. "Huge Quantity of U.S. Army Stores in Town Confiscated by American MP," *Zhongyang ribao*, June 14,

1945, OWI Kunming Branch Translation Service, no. 551, RG 208, OWI Overseas Branch, Information File on Asia, box 383, unmarked folder, NARA; "Huguo menkou you chahuo sishou Meijun yongpin," *Saodang bao*, July 5, 1945.

75. "Long Yun shoushi wu dian," May 1945, RG 493, UD-UP 306, box 644, Correspondence File, 1945, NARA; He Haoruo to Albert Wedemeyer, August 5, 1945, RG 493, Records of the Special Staff/Adjutant General, General Correspondence, box 98, Morals and Conduct, July 1 to September 30, 1945, NARA.

76. Wang Pingshun, "Prohibition of Dealing in G.I. Goods," *Grand View Mansion Weekly*, June 1945, OWI Kunming Branch Translation Service, no. 564, RG 208, OWI Overseas Branch, Information File on Asia, box 383, unmarked folder, NARA.

77. Earl Revell to Leona Revell, November 23, 1944, Earl Revell Collection, box 1, folder 11, USAMHC.

78. Warren Arnett to Martha Arnett, May 8, 1945, Warren Arnett Collection, AFC/2001/001/11032, VHP

79. Howard Rubin Collection, AFC/2001/001/50901, VHP.

80. Political Report for March 1945, April 16, 1945, RG 84, Kunming Consulate Classified General Records, 1944–1949, box 3, Classified Files, 1945, NARA; "Political Reports for April 1944 and December 1943, May 3, 1944, and January 11, 1944," RG 84, Kunming Consulate Classified General Records, 1944–1949, box 1, Kunming 1944, vol. 2, NARA. On profiteering, see also "Ben shi ji ying shezhi mengjun fuwu she," *Guangxi ribao*, December 18, 1943.

81. Theodore White via press wireless, April 7, 1945, box 58, folder 8, Theodore White Papers, HUA.

82. "Boen Nam Hioen, et al.," January 1, 1944, RG 493, SOS, UD-UP 365, box 64, Morals and Conduct, 1943–1944, NARA.

83. "Stolen Vehicles," February 28, 1944, RG 493, UD-UP 365, box 64, Morals and Conduct, 1943–1944, NARA. The only reporting on theft in the Chinese press emphasized either its decline or the success of detectives in solving cases. See "Meijun yong che shiqie shu jianshao," *Yunnan ribao*, October 3, 1944; "Meijun che beiqie, jingcha poan xunsu," *Yunnan ribao*, April 30, 1944.

84. "Fangzhi daoqie mengjun che," *Saodang bao*, June 7, 1944.

85. "Safeguarding Military Property," April 9, 1945, RG 493, UD-UP 265, box 62, 000.5, April 5 to July 31, 1945, NARA.

86. Headquarters, USF China Theater, Memorandum, June 20, 1945, RG 493, UD-UP 265, box 62, 000.5, April 5 to July 31, 1945, NARA.

87. Albert Wedemeyer to Chiang Kai-shek, June 18, 1945, RG 493, UD-UP 265, box 62, 000.5, April 5 to July 31, 1945, NARA.

88. Waijiao bu zhu Yunnan tepai yuan Wang Zhanqi cheng Song Ziwen dian, December 30, 1944, file no. 020-50204-0039-0077x to 0077a, AHA.

89. Junshi weiyuan hui zhi waijiao bu dian, March 2, 1945, file no. 020-050201-0053-0049x to 0050x, AHA.

90. Yunnan Special Delegate for Foreign Affairs to U.S. Consulate, Kunming, May 10, 1945, RG 84, Kunming Consulate, General Records 1938–1949, box 67, Kunming 1945, vol. 11, NARA.

91. Headquarters, 14th Air Force, June 26, 1945, RG 84, Kunming Consulate, General Records 1938–1949, box 67, Kunming 1945, vol. 11, NARA.

92. FAB no. 3076, July 23, 1945, RG 493, Records of the Special Staff, General Correspondence, box 98, Morals and Conduct, July 1 to September 30, 1945, NARA.

93. Attached Report on Theft of Building Material and Incidental Shooting," August 21, 1944, and "Investigation of Incident of 12th August," October 21, 1944, RG 493, UD-UP 491, box 244, Correspondence, 1944, NARA.

94. Headquarters, Fifth Route Air Force to Fourteenth Air Force, August 25, 1944, RG 493, UD-UP 419, box 244, Correspondence, 1944, NARA.

95. "Incidents of Shooting Chinese," June 19, 1945, RG 493, UD-UP 306, box 663, Correspondence with Chinese Authorities June to September 1945, NARA.

96. FAB no. 3702, January 16, 1945, RG 493, UD-UP 265, box 62, 000.5, Crimes, from Jan. 1, 1946, NARA.

97. "Shooting of Chinese Civilian, Mile 295 Ledo Road, Burma," March 10, 1945, RG 493, UD-UP 185, box 10, 000.5 Crimes 1945, NARA.

98. C. J. Zhou to Albert Wedemeyer, January 29, 1945, RG 493, UD-UP 265, box 62, 000.5, to March 30, 1945, NARA. The study analyzed 136 theft cases and found American servicemen responsible in 63.

99. Minutes of Conference Held at Chinese Supreme Commander's Headquarters, June 27, 1945, RG 493, UD-UP 541, box 68, Report of Pipeline Investigation, NARA.

100. Chongqing shi jingcha ju ling dishi fenju dian, May 27, 1942, file no. 61-15-40704, p. 85, and Chongqing shi jingcha ju diyi fenju cheng Chongqing shi jingcha ju dian, May 22, 1942, file no. 61-15-40704, p. 277, CMA.

101. Waijiao bu zhi Chongqing shi zhengfu dian, June 29, 1942, file no. 53-10-19, p. 7, CMA.

102. Junshi weiyuan hui dai dain 7275, October 21, 1944, file no. 61-15-1503, pp. 20–21, CMA.

103. Chongqing shi jingcha ju ling di'er fenju dian, April 26, 1945, file no. 61-15-1327, p. 48, CMA.

104. Waijiao bu zhu Yunnan tepai yuan zhi Mei zhu Dian zong siling guan, December 15, 1944, RG 84, Kunming Consulate, General Records 1938–1949, box 60, Kunming 1944, vol. 12, NARA.

105. "Note 188," August 7, 1945, RG 493, UD-UP 365, box 53, 000.5, file 2, 1945, NARA.

106. "Truck Accident of American Convoy," *Zhongyang ribao*, April 28, 1945, China Press Review no. 116; RG 208, OWI Overseas Branch, Information File on Asia, box 380, unmarked folder 3, NARA.

107. Shidiwei zhi Tang Yi dian, February 10, 1943, file no. 020-050204-0039-0014x to 0015x, AHA; "Speeding, Reckless Driving, and Lack of Military Courtesy and Discipline," August 12, 1944; RG 493, UD-UP 365, box 64, 250.1, Discipline 1943–1944, NARA.

108. "Speed Limits," February 22, 1945, RG 493, UD-UP 541, box 85, 250 Discipline, NARA.

109. Rear Echelon Headquarters, USF China Theater, Subject: "Uniform Punishments," May 15, 1945, RG 493, UD-UP 541, box 85, 250 Discipline, NARA.

110. Shidiwei zhi Tang Yi dian, February 10, 1943, file no. 020-050204-0039-0014x to 0015x, AHA; "Courts-Martial, 1 June to 30 June 1945," RG 493, UD-UP 419, box 246, Monthly Reports JAG, Aug. 1944 to Nov. 1945, NARA.

111. Jan Peeke to Anne Peeke, December 3, 1942, Alonzo Jan Peeke Collection, AFC/2001/001/01530, VHP.

112. Jan Peeke to Anne Peeke, October 23, 1942, Alonzo Jan Peeke Collection, AFC/2001/001/01530, VHP.

113. Arthur Perry Hauge, "With the Flying Tigers in China," unpublished memoir, 2, Arthur Perry Hauge Collection, AFC/2001/001/02877, VHP.

114. Norman Victor Key Collection, AFC/2001/001/01162, VHP.

115. Warren Arnett to Martha Arnett, May 11, 1945, Warren Jefferson Arnett Collection, AFC/2001/001/11032, VHP.

116. Circular no. 68, May 17, 1945, RG 493, Records of the Special Staff, General Correspondence Decimal File, box 95, Morals and Conduct, May 16 to June 30, 1945, NARA.

117. Zhongguo zhu Meiguo dashi guan guang cheng waijiao bu dian, May 6, 1944, file no. 020-050204-0039-0028a to 30a, AHA.

118. See, for example, FAB no. 2130, January 4, 1945, RG 493, Records of the Special Staff, General Correspondence Decimal File, box 95, 1943–1944, NARA; Chang Sing to Wedemeyer, April 25, 1945, RG 493, Records of the Special Staff, General Correspondence Decimal File, box 98, Morals and Conduct from Dec. 1944 to May 15, 1945, NARA; Fei Xiaodong to William Langdon, May 10, 1945; RG 84, Kunming Consulate, General Records 1938–1949, box 67, Kunming 1945, vol. 11, NARA.

119. Headquarters, USF China Theater, August 25, 1945; RG 493, Records of the Special Staff, General Correspondence Decimal File, box 98, Morals and Conduct, July 1 to September 30, 1945, NARA.

120. He Yingqin to Joseph Stilwell, September 27, 1944; RG 493, UD-UP 365, box 64, 250.1 Discipline 1943–1944, NARA; Yunnan Special Delegate for Foreign Affairs to U.S. Consulate, Kunming, August 7, 1944, RG 84, Kunming Consulate, General Records 1938–1949, box 60, Kunming 1944, vol. 12, NARA.

121. "Wire Sections Severed by Shooting," undated, RG 493, UD-UP 541, box 67, 000.5, Crimes, from July 22, 1945, NARA.

122. "Damage to Telephone Lines," undated, RG 493, UD-UP 541, box 67, 000.5, Crimes, from July 22, 1945, NARA.

123. Chongqing shi jingcha ju cheng Chongqing shi zhengfu dian, December 13, 1944, file no. 54-10-19, pp. 93–94, CMA.

124. According to He Haoruo, even high-ranking American officers violated the ban on indiscriminate shooting. FAB no. 3138, August 2, 1945, RG 493, Records of the Special Staff, General Correspondence Decimal File, box 98, Morals and Conduct, July 1 to September 30, 1945, NARA. For complaints from the Ministry of Military Administration, see "Report on Shooting Incident Caused by American Personnel," July 2, 1945, RG 493, UD-UP 365, box 53, 000.5, file 2, 1945, NARA. The two August 1945 convictions for wrongfully shooting civilians resulted in a $20 salary forfeiture for three months in one case, and seven days' confinement to base in the other. See General Court Martial Cases Competed (August 1945), RG 493, UD-UP 185, box 34,

250.4 Courts Martial; and Albert Wedemeyer to George Stratemeyer, August 25, 1945, RG 493, Records of the Special Staff, General Correspondence Decimal File, box 98, Morals and Conduct, July 1 to September 30, 1945, NARA.

125. See, for example, Chongqing shi zhengfu ling Chongqing shi jingcha ju dian, June 5, 1942, file no. 61-14-04091, p. 278, CMA.

126. Waijiao bu zhu Guangdong Guangxi tepai yuan cheng waijiao bu dian, December 20, 1943, file no. 020-050204-0039-0023 a to 0024x, AHA.

127. Waijia bu zhu Yunnan tepai yuan cheng waijiao bu dian, March 10, 1945, file no. 020-050204-0039-0067x, AHA.

128. Waijiao bu zhu Yunnan tepai yuan cheng Waijiao bu dian, December 15, 1944, RG 84, Kunming Consulate, General Records 1938–1949, box 60, Kunming 1944, vol. 12, NARA; Young, *China's Wartime Finance and Inflation*, 361.

129. Rittenberg and Bennett, *The Man Who Stayed Behind*, 19.

130. Albert Wedemeyer to He Haoruo, August 19, 1945, RG 493, Records of the Special Staff, General Correspondence, box 99, Courts Martial, Dec. 1944 to Dec. 1945, NARA.

131. Mayling Soong Chiang, "First Lady of the East Speaks to the West," *New York Times*, April 19, 1942; Ma, "The Invisible War between the United States and Japan over China," 93–111.

132. Memorandum of Conversation by the Chief of the Division of Far Eastern Affairs (Hamilton), October 9, 1942, *FRUS: 1942, China*, 307–8; "The Secretary of State to the Ambassador in China (Gauss), January 4, 1943, *FRUS: 1943, China*, 691–93.

133. Zheng, "Specter of Extraterritoriality," 17–44; George Atcheson to Wu Guozhen, May 21, 1943, file no. 53-10-19, pp. 60–68, CMA.

134. When vice foreign minister Wu Guozhen signed the agreement on May 21, he added a note stating that the ROC government had authorized him to do so because "of the provision for placing the said understanding on a reciprocal basis." See George Atcheson to Wu Guozhen, May 21, 1943, file no. 53-10-19, pp. 60–68, CMA.

135. Zheng, "Specter of Extraterritoriality," 30–31.

136. Sun Ke cheng Jiang Jieshi dian, September 17, 1945, file no. 0010120 37002059a-2066a, AHA; Albert Wedemeyer to He Haoruo, August 19, 1945, RG 493, Records of the Special Staff, General Correspondence, box 99, Courts Martial, Dec. 1944 to Dec. 1945, NARA.

137. Zheng, "Specter of Extraterritoriality," 30–31; on the Visiting Forces Act, see Reynolds, *Rich Relations*, 144–46; King, "Further Developments concerning Jurisdiction over Friendly Armed Forces," 262.

138. United States of America (Visiting Forces) Act, 1942, 5 & 6 Geo. 6, c. 31, www.legislation.gov.uk/ukpga/1942/31/pdfs/ukpga_19420031_en.pdf.

139. McKerrow, "Scenes from a Marriage of Necessity," 21–42, 265–324.

140. Ruskola, *Legal Orientalism*, 6.

141. H. S. Aurand to Lee Hung Mo, August 9, 1945, RG 493, Records of the Special Staff, General Correspondence, box 99, Courts Martial, Dec. 1944 to Dec. 1945, NARA.

142. Chongqing shi jingcha ju cheng Chongqing shi zhengfu dian, October 12, 1943, file no. 53-10-19, pp. 80–81, CMA; "Brewer, Jesse J.," May 3, 1944, RG 493, UD-UP 365, box 64, Morals and Conduct, 1943–1944, NARA.

143. "Sgt. Meade France," May 1, 1944, RG 493, UD-UP 365, box 64, Morals and Conduct, 1943–1944, NARA.

144. "Shooting of Chinese," June 12, 1944, and Headquarters Y-Force Operations Staff, September 4, 1944, RG 84, Kunming Consulate, General Records 1938–1949, box 60, Kunming 1944, vol. 12, NARA.

145. "Pfc. Norman Byrn," April 24, 1944, RG 493, UD-UP 365, box 64, Morals and Conduct, 1943–1944, NARA.

146. "James E. Gingell," May 3, 1944, RG 493 UD-UP 365, box 64, Morals and Conduct, 1943–1944, NARA.

147. Summary Courts-Marital for February 1945, February 28, 1945, RG 493, UD-UP 419, box 244, Correspondence, 1943–1945, NARA.

148. Court Martial no. 7, February 21, 1945, RG 493, UD-UP 541, box 85, 250 Discipline 1945, NARA; General Court Martial Cases, September 1945, RG 493, UD-UP 419, box 244, Correspondence, 1943–1945, NARA.

149. "Transfer of Military Personnel from China," September 29, 1944, RG 493, UD-UP 36, box 205, Morals and Conduct, July 1 to October 30, 1944, NARA.

150. McKerrow, "Scenes from a Marriage of Necessity," 268.

151. "Final Report: Death of Mrs. Zhang Zengshi 71 Years, Chinese Civilian," May 7, 1945, RG 493, UD-UP 309, box 669, Investigations China Theater, April, May 1945, NARA.

152. Yunnan Special Delegate for Foreign Affairs to U.S. Consulate, Kunming, June 1, 1945 and USF China Theater, July 19, 1945, RG 84, Kunming Consulate, General Records 1938–1949, box 67, Kunming 1945, vol. 11, NARA; "Final Report: Death of Mrs. Zhang Zengshi 71 Years, Chinese Civilian," May 7, 1945, RG 493, UD-UP 309, box 669, Investigations China Theater, April, May 1945, NARA; Report of Staff of Judge Advocate for the Month of June 1945, July 5, 1945; RG 493, UD-UP 419, box 244, Correspondence, 1943–1945, NARA.

153. "Mei bing ousi yi lao furen," *Sao dang bao*, July 16, 1945.

154. Political Report for December 1943; U.S. Consulate General, Kunming to U.S. Embassy, Chongqing, February 3, 1944; U.S. Consulate General, Kunming to U.S. Embassy, Chongqing, March 1, 1944, RG 84, Kunming Consulate, Classified General Records, 1944–1949, box 1, Kunming 1944, vol. 2, NARA.

155. Political Report for December 1943 and U.S. Consulate General, Kunming to U.S. Embassy, Chongqing, February 15, 1944, RG 84, Kunming Consulate, Classified General Records, 1944–1949, box 1, Kunming 1944, vol. 2, NARA.

156. Political Report for March 1944; and Special Yunnan Delegate of the Ministry of Foreign Affairs to Kunming Consulate General, April 13, 1944, RG 84, Kunming Consulate, Classified General Records, 1944–1949, box 1, Kunming 1944, vol. 2, NARA; Chinese Foreign Ministry to U.S. Embassy, Chongqing, April 11, 1944, RG 84, Kunming Consulate, Classified General Records, 1944–1949, box 58, Kunming 1944, vol. 9, NARA.

157. Memo for the American Consul General, April 23, 1944, RG 84, Kunming Consulate, Classified General Records, 1944–1949, box 58, Kunming 1944, vol. 9, NARA.

Chapter 5

1. Tang Yi cheng He Yaozu dian, April 14, 1945, file 53-10-19, pp. 99–101, CMA.

2. Theodore White, "GIs and Chungking Girls," June 2, 1945, box 58, folder 16, Theodore White Papers, HUA; "Chongqing 'Jipu nvlang' shijian shimo," *Meizhou yibao*, di 3 qi (1945), 41; "Guan yu qudi Zhongguo nvzi dazai Meijun renyuan Jipuche gei Chongqing shi zhengfu renshi chuli de xunling," file 53-2-179, p. 16, June 1945, CMA.

3. "Report of 'Mr. X' on Precarious Sino-American Relations in Chongqing," April 25, 1945, RG 493, UD-UP 266, box 314, Morals and Conduct, May 16 to June 30, 1945, NARA.

4. "Guan yu qudi Zhongguo nvzi dazai Meijun renyuan Jipuche gei Chongqing shi zhengfu renshi chuli de xunling," file 53-2-179, p. 16, June 1945, CMA; "Kunming ZhongMei nannv shejiao," *Xinwen tiandi*, June 20, 1945.

5. Hershatter, *Women and China's Revolution*; Hershatter, *Dangerous Pleasures*, 3–24; Duara, "Regime of Authenticity," 287–98.

6. Hershatter, *Dangerous Pleasures*, 3–4; Enloe, *Maneuvers*, 51–60.

7. This policy followed the U.S. military's pattern in the Philippines. See Kramer, "Shades of Sovereignty," 249–53.

8. Cornebise, *United States Army in China*, 85–92; McCarthy, *Papago Traveler*, 96. Marriage between Americans and ethnic Chinese women in China was actually more common before the Russian Revolution. The influx of Russian refugees led to a drop in interracial marriages among Americans in China. See Noble, *Eagle and the Dragon*, 129–30.

9. Reynolds, *Rich Relations*, 209–10.

10. Ludden to Tull, January 16, 1943, RG 84, Kunming Consulate Records, box 52, 1943, pt. 8, NARA.

11. Chennault biographer and former Fourteenth Air Force navigator Jack Samson wrote that Chennault felt guilty for cheating on his wife, Nell, with numerous Chinese women during the war. They divorced in 1945. See Samson, *Flying Tiger*, 346–47.

12. On Southeast Asia, see Stoler, *Carnal Knowledge and Imperial Power*, 1–21.

13. This policy derived from War Department Circular no. 307, issued on July 18, 1944. See "Marriage of Military and Naval Personnel," January 23, 1943, RG 127, box 73, III MAC War Diary January 1946, NARA.

14. Reynolds, *Rich Relations*, 210–14, 413, 420–22; Bioletti, *Yanks Are Coming*, 75; Barker and Jackson, *Fleeting Attraction*, 170–74.

15. "Kunming ZhongMei nannv shejiao," *Xinwen tiandi*, June 20, 1945.

16. On midcentury race-making, see Shibusawa, *America's Geisha Ally*, 55–83, 296. See also Kramer, *Blood of Government*.

17. U.S. Army Service Forces, *Short Guide to Britain*, 10–20; U.S. Army Service Forces, *Pocket Guide to Australia*, 12–32; U.S. Army Service Forces, *Pocket Guide to New Zealand*, 7–11.

18. U.S. Army Service Forces, *Pocket Guide to China*, 5.

19. Rittenberg and Bennett, *Man Who Stayed Behind*, 26.

20. Richard Bates Oral History, WVM.

21. Cornebise, *United States Army in China*, 87–93; G. B. Clark, *Treading Softly*, 105–6; Noble, *Eagle and the Dragon*, 125–34; Tolley, *Yangtze Patrol*, 91, 102, 209.

22. Headquarters, USF China Theater, January 22, 1945, RG 493, Records of the Special Staff, box 95, 1944–1945, NARA.

23. Meikong silingbu cheng Kunming xingying, August 3, 1942, file 1094-1-87, pp. 70–73, YPA.

24. SOS, "Operation of United Nations Club," May 29, 1944, RG 493, UD-UP 365, box 64, 250.2, barred or restricted areas, NARA; A. W. Clark, *Eyes of the Tiger*, 59–60.

25. John Hlavacek, *Letters Home*, 210–11.

26. Miles, *Different Kind of War*, 94, 138–39; SACO China no. 1, September 20, 1944, and "Report of Mr. 'X' on Precarious Sino-American Relations in Chongqing," April 24, 1945, RG 493, UD-UP 266, box 314, Morals and Conduct, May 16 to June 30, 1945, NARA.

27. Acting Theater Provost Marshal Harry Cooper to Wedemeyer, "Major Gerald E. Reed," January 26, 1945, RG 493, UD-UP 266, box 314, China Theater AG 250.1, NARA.

28. Diary entry, June 26, 1943, Paul LeRoy Jones Papers, box 1, folder 5, HI.

29. Chennault, *Way of a Fighter*, 201–6.

30. Henriot, *Prostitution and Sexuality in Shanghai*, 312–32.

31. Tanaka, *Japan's Comfort Women*, 84–109; Roberts, *What Soldiers Do*, 159–72.

32. Zeiger, *Entangling Alliances*, 72.

33. "Shidai fengcai nianzhong pan dian: 2004 nian Yunnan shi da xinwen jiaodian nvxing," *Shidai fengcai* [Modern elegance], 8–13.

34. The Truman administration awarded Tao the Medal of Freedom, Bronze Palm, for her work with American personnel. See Citation, Madame Chiang Monlin-lin, James B. Hinchcliff Collection, FSU. Tao was married to Chinese Red Cross director Jiang Menglin.

35. Theodore White, "GIs and Chungking Girls," June 2, 1945, box 58, folder 16, Theodore White Papers, HUA.

36. "Civilians and Dayrooms," *Shanghai Stars and Stripes*, December 15, 1945.

37. Peck, *Two Kinds of Time*, 518–50; Cheng Huina, "Jipu nvlang yan zhong de Meiguo bing," *Duzhe*, 57–58.

38. Dikötter, *Discourse of Race in Modern China*, 58; Ch'en, *China and the West*, 164–66.

39. Edwards, "Policing the Modern Woman in Republican China," 134–35; Ferlanti, "New Life Movement at War," 194, 198.

40. Theodore White, "GIs and Chungking Girls," June 2, 1945, box 58, folder 16, Theodore White Papers, HUA.

41. Zhu, *Wartime Culture in Guilin*, 167–96.

42. Peck, *Two Kinds of Time*, 520.

43. Peck, *Two Kinds of Time*, 537–40.

44. "Qudi bu zhengdang yule," *Guangxi ribao*, March 15, 1944. "New Woman" discourse was an attempt by male intellectuals to shore up their class's declining political influence by policing Chinese womanhood. See Edwards, "Policing the Modern Woman in Republican China," 115–43.

45. Mitter, *Forgotten Ally*, 318–26; Young, *China's Wartime Finance and Inflation*, 264–66.

46. "Political Reports for January and February 1945," RG 84, Kunming Consulate, Classified General Records 1944–1949, box 3, Classified Files 1945; and "Inflation and Countermeasures," undated, RG 493, UD-UP 243, box 16, Black Book China no. 5:2, NARA.

47. "Personnel Strength: China Theater," undated, RG 493, UD-UP 243, box 15, Black Book China no. 1, and "Personnel Strength Jan. 1945 to Jan. 1946," RG 493, UD-UP 590, box 11, Charts on Strength USFCT, NARA.

48. Chinese generals earned 20,000 fabi per month, or just over $6 at black market exchange rates in Chongqing. Chang, *Kangzhan shiqi de guojun renshi*, 91–99; U.S. War Department, *WAC Life*, 35–3.

49. Huang, *Guanyu Meiguo bing*, 38–39.

50. Huang, *Guanyu Meiguo bing*, 41–42. Hershatter, *Dangerous Pleasures*, 37–50; Henriot, *Prostitution and Sexuality in Shanghai*, 88–98. On camp-town prostitution, see Höhn and Mood, *Over There*, 1–77; Sturdevant and Stoltzfus, *Let the Good Times Roll*; Liao, "Yu jun Jinling yi jianwen," 63.

51. A. W. Clark, *Eyes of the Tiger*, 59–60.

52. Counter Intelligence Corps, "Jeep Girls," May 13, 1945, RG 493, UD-UP 266, box 314, Morals and Conduct, May 16 to June 30, 1945, NARA.

53. Huang, *Guanyu Meiguo bing*, 40.

54. Zhu, "Jeep Car yu Jeep Girl," *Xinwen tiandi*, March 20, 1945.

55. "Gei jipu xiaojiemen," *Zhongyang ribao* (Chengdu), May 2, 1945.

56. "The Jeep Girl," *Zhengyi bao*, May 3, 1945, cited in OWI Kunming Branch Translation Service, RG 208, entry 370, box 383, unmarked folder 3, NARA.

57. "So This Is Kunming," *Zhongyang ribao* (Kunming), May 16, 1945, cited in OWI Kunming Branch Translation Service, RG 208, entry 370, box 383, unmarked folder 3, NARA.

58. Theodore White, "This Week in Chungking," May 10, 1945, Theodore White Papers, HUA.

59. On the "modern girl," see Hershatter, *Women and China's Revolutions*, 129, 142–51.

60. Peck, *Two Kinds of Time*, 636. See also Bickers, *Out of China*, 269–70. Patriarchal nationalist movements elsewhere shared this trait. See Roberts, *What Soldiers Do*, 88–89; Enloe, *Maneuvers*, 51–99.

61. Shen Lusha, "Wo shi Jeep Girl," *Xinwen tiandi*, April 20, 1945.

62. Edwards, "Policing the Modern Woman in Republican China," 115–47.

63. Howard, "Politicization of Women Workers at War," 1892–93; Li, *Echoes of Chongqing*, 122–23. On the limited options besides prostitution available to impoverished women, see Hershatter, *Dangerous Pleasures*, 63, 195; Gronewald, *Beautiful Merchandise*, 76–77; Henriot, *Prostitution and Sexuality in Shanghai*, 126–29.

64. On the price of sex, see "Xianbing dui siling bu cheng Chongqing shi zhengfu dian," July 25, 1945, file 61-1-10, pp. 19–21, CMA.

65. This phenomenon was common throughout Asia. See Bayly and Harper, *Forgotten Armies*, 330.

66. This analysis borrows from Cynthia Enloe's insight about the Philippines. See Enloe, *Does Khaki Become You?*, 38–39.

67. This literature is too vast to describe here in detail. A representative example includes Roberts, *What Soldiers Do,* esp. 108–10, 198–99; Reynolds, *Rich Relations*; Blower, "V-J Day, 1945, Times Square"; Bailey and Farber, *First Strange Place*; Barker and Jackson, *Fleeting Attraction*; Bioletti, *Yanks Are Coming*; Tanaka, *Japan's Comfort Women*; Lilly, *Taken by Force*; Enloe, *Bananas, Beaches, and Bases*, esp. 1–13, 35.

68. Fourteenth Air Force Service Command, "Discipline," July 7, 1945, RG 493, Records of the Special Staff, box 98, Morals and Conduct, July 1 to 30 May 1945, NARA.

69. Tanaka, *Japan's Comfort Women*, 175–82; Blower, "V-J Day, Times Square," 10–11; Enloe, *Does Khaki Become You?*, 35.

70. Blower, "V-J Day, Times Square," 10.

71. Barker and Jackson, *Fleeting Attraction*, 120–36, 150–51.

72. Reynolds, *Rich Relations*, 183–99.

73. Roberts, *What Soldiers Do*, 57–73, 108.

74. Mary Krauss to Mrs. A. P. Krauss, May 10, 1944, folder 15, Mary Theresa Krauss Collection, FSU.

75. Enloe, *Does Khaki Become You?*, 38–39.

76. CCC, "Responsibility for U.S. Personnel," July 3, 1945, RG 493, Records of the Special Staff, box 98, Morals and Conduct, July 1 to September 30, 1945, NARA.

77. Reynolds, *Rich Relations,* 147–48; Potts, *Yanks Down Under*, 235.

78. Roberts, *What Soldiers Do*, 195.

79. Bioletti, *Yanks Are Coming*, 149–54; Barker and Jackson, *Fleeting Attraction*, 191–92; Roberts, *What Soldiers Do*, 75–77, 108.

80. Bickers, *Out of China*, 17, 185.

81. Sichuan sheng renmin zhengfu waishi qiaowu (Gang Ao) bangong shi, "Waiguo ren feifa, fanzui an de jiaoshe," www.scfao.gov.cn/info/detail.jsp?infoId=B000000650.

82. Zhipu Gang cheng Tang Yi dian, October 18, 1940, file 61-15-02080, CMA. On the *Tutuila*'s crew, see also Dong and Woerfugang, *Chongqing wangshi*, 59–61.

83. Zhang Wanli zhi Chongqing shi zhengfu dian, October 7, 1942, and FAB zhi Chongqing shi zhengfu dian, October 14, 1942, file 53-10-19, pp. 23–25, CMA.

84. Tang Yi cheng Chongqing shi zhengfu dian, December 13, 1944, file 53-10-19, pp. 93–94, CMA.

85. He Haoruo to Albert Wedemeyer, January 26, 1945, RG 493, Records of the Special Staff, box 95, 1944–1945, NARA.

86. Tang Yi cheng Chongqing shi zhengfu dian, December 13, 1944, file 53-10-19, pp. 93–94, CMA.

87. Commander, Naval Group China, September 21, 1944, RG 38, NHC-75, box 28, chap. 17.1 Morale, NARA.

88. Wang Shimin to US Army Headquarters, March 19, 1945, RG 493, Records of the Special Staff, box 98, Dec. 1944 to May 15, 1945, NARA.

89. Fourteenth Air Force, "Report of Investigation of Attack on Chinese Guard," March 20, 1945, RG 493, UD-UP 266, box 314, Dec. 10, 1944 to May 15, 1945; Courts Martial, May 1945, June 1, 1945, RG 493, UD-UP 419, box 244, Correspondence, 1943–45, NARA.

90. Fourteenth Air Force, "Report of Investigation Regarding Misconduct of Personnel," November 3, 1944, RG 493, UD-UP 266, box 325, Pat O'Brien Case, NARA.

91. Statements of George B. Gellas and Peter Smeicinski, May 12 and 13, 1945, RG 493, UD-UP 266, box 314, Morals and Conduct, May 16 to June 30, 1945, NARA.

92. He Haoruo to Albert Wedemeyer, February 21, 1945, RG 493, Records of the Special Staff, box 98, Morals and Conduct, Dec. 1944 to May 15, 1945, NARA.

93. Baoshan Area Command SOS, "Final Report of Case No. W96-88," January 25, 1945, RG 493, UD-UP 541, box 87, Special Court Martial, NARA.

94. "Statement of Mr. Chang Ching Dah," March 11, 1945, RG 493, UD-UP 309, box 670, CASC no. 627-17-84, NARA.

95. Rear Echelon Headquarters, "Rumor of Rape," June 26, 1945, RG 493, UD-UP 306, box 664, Rape/Sex Crimes, March to June 1945, NARA.

96. China Theater Headquarters "Report of Derelictions," April 5, 1945, RG 493, Records of the Special Staff, box 98, Morals and Conduct, December 1944 to May 15, 1945, NARA.

97. Regional Office, Theater Provost Marshal, Initial and Final Report, March 21, 1945; Statement of Mrs. Yang Zhengcai, March 6, 1945; Statement of Pvt. Harvey Miller, March 8, 1945; Statement of Private Harold Hughes, March 9, 1945; Statement of Pvt. Harvey Miller, March 17, 1945, RG 493, UD-UP 306, box 665, Investigations: Rape, March 1945, NARA. Hughes originally received a five-year sentence, but it was reduced to six months. Fourteenth AF Courts-Martial for the period of June 1, 1945, to July 1, 1945, RG 493, UD-UP 419, box 246, Monthly Reports JAG, Aug. 1944 to Nov. 1945, NARA.

98. U.S. Army Armed Forces, *Pocket Guide to China*, 2.

99. "Board of Review CM CBI 245," *Holdings and Opinions Board of Review: Branch Office of the Judge Advocate General, CBI and IBT* (vol. 2), 1–17.

100. Roberts, *What Soldiers Do*, 213–14.

101. Headquarters, Chinese American Composite Wing Kunming to Claire Chennault, February 22, 1945, RG 493, Records of the Special Staff, General Correspondence Decimal file, box 95, 1944–1945, NARA.

102. "Rumor of Rape," June 26, 1945, RG 493, UD-UP 306, box 664, Rape Sex Crimes, March to June 1945, NARA.

103. "Alleged Kidnapping and Rape," March 3, 1945, RG 493, UD-UP 309, box 670, 49a PA9-61, NARA.

104. Roberts, *What Soldiers Do*, 239–42.

105. "Tan Jipu nvlang," *Xiandai funv* 6, no. 1/2 (1945). On the *Modern Woman* biweekly, see Liu, "KangRi jiuwang houqi Zhongguo Gongchang dang lingdao de funv qikan: *Xiandai funv*," 56–59.

106. "Jeep Drivers Abducting Girls," May 14, 1945, RG 493, UD-UP 266, box 314, Morals and Conduct, May 16 to June 30, NARA.

107. Roberts, *What Soldiers Do*, 78–83.

108. "Report of 'Mr. X' on Precarious Sino-American Relations in Chongqing," April 25, 1945, RG 493, UD-UP 266, box 314, Morals and Conduct, May 16 to June 30, 1945, NARA.

109. "Chungking Rumors on Immorality of American Military Personnel," May 10, 1945, RG 493, UD-UP 266, box 314, Morals and Conduct, May 16 to June 30, 1945, NARA.

110. Tang Yi cheng He Yaozu dian, March 31, 1945, file 53-10-19, pp. 95–96, CMA.

111. See "Memorandum for the Officer in Charge," April 9, 20, and 22, 1945, RG 493, UD-UP 266, box 314, Morals and Conduct, May 16 to June 30, 1945, NARA.

112. "Behavior of U.S. Military Personnel, Chongqing Area," April 25, 1945, RG 493, UD-UP 266, box 314, Morals and Conduct, May 16 to June 30, 1945, NARA.

113. CIC, "Conduct of U.S. Military Personnel in Chongqing and Effect on Sino-American Relations," May 5, 1945, RG 493, UD-UP 266, box 314, Morals and Conduct, May 16 to June 30, 1945, NARA.

114. Shen Zui, *Juntong neimu*, 62–111; Wakeman, *Spymaster*, 331–36, 344.

115. Wakeman, *Strangers at the Gate*, 38–56; Dikötter, *Discourse of Race in Modern China*, 43–44, 158.

116. Wakeman, *Shanghai Badlands*, 22–23; Shen Zui, *Juntong neimu*, 72–73.

117. CIC, "Friction between U.S. Army Personnel and Chinese Civilians," April 27, 1945, RG 493, UD-UP 266, box 314, Morals and Conduct, May 16 to June 30, 1945, NARA.

118. Shen Zui, *Juntong neimu*, 71–72, 93–94; Wakeman, *Spymaster*, 336.

119. "Guan yu qudi Zhongguo nvzi dazai Meijun renyuan Jipuche gei Chongqing shi zhengfu renshi chuli de xunling," file 53-2-179, p. 16, June 1945, CMA; "Kunming ZhongMei nannv shejiao," *Xinwen tiandi*, June 20, 1945.

120. Wang Zhangqi cheng Song Ziwen dian, file 020-050204-0039-0105x to 106z, AHA.

121. SOS Baoshan Area, Office of the Provost Marshal, "Off Limits Area in the Town of Baoshan," April 28, 1945, RG 493, UD-UP 541, box 85, 250 Discipline, NARA.

122. He Haoruo to Wedemeyer, July 17, 1945, RG 493, Records of the Special Staff, box 98, Morals and Conduct, December 1944 to May 15, 1945, NARA.

123. CCC, "Discipline of US Troops in Huachi," May 12, 1945, RG 493, UD-UP 541, box 85, 250 Discipline, NARA.

124. CIC, "Attack on American Officer," May 14, 1945, RG 493, UD-UP 266, box 314, Morals and Conduct, May 16 to June 30, 1945, NARA.

125. Junshi weiyuan hui ling Chongqing shi zhengfu dian, May 27, 1945, file 53-10-142, pp. 270–71, CMA.

126. CIC, "Jeep Drivers Abducting Girls," May 14, 1945, RG 493, UD-UP 266, box 314, Morals and Conduct, May 16 to June 30, 1945, NARA.

127. Headquarters USF China Theater, "Safeguarding Chinese-American Relationships," May 16, 1945, RG 493, Records of the Special Staff, box 95, Morals and Conduct, May 16 to June 30, 1945, NARA.

128. Weidemai cheng Jiang Jieshi dian, May 18, 1945, file 53-10-142, pp. 235–37, CMA.

129. Ch'i, *Jianbanuzhang de mengyou*, 697.

130. Other U.S.-supported autocrats would find themselves in similar dilemmas after 1945. See McCoy, *In the Shadows of the American Century*, chap. 2.

131. Jiang Jieshi ling He Yaozu dian, May 31, 1945, file 53-10-142, p. 293, CMA.

132. Yi Ren, "Cong ZhongMei nannv shijiao tan guomin waijiao," *Funv qikan* 4, no. 4 (May 1945): 4–5; Hong Shen, "Guanyu Jipu nvlang," *Liang zhou pinglun* 1, no. 3–4; Nan Mo, "Jipu nvlang," *Xingqi zhoukan*, June 3, 1945.

133. Yu, *The Dragon's War*, 159–60.

134. "Yingxiang ZhongMei youyi de 'Jipu nvlang' shijian," *Liang zhou pinglun* 1, no. 3–4 (1945): 47–48.

135. Yan Jun, "ZhongMei nannv shejiao," *Xi feng* 79 (1945): 25–27.

136. Dong Shijin, "Guanyu Jipu nvlang," *Da gong bao*, May 25, 1945.

137. "He Haoruo jiang jun tan ZhongMei shejiao," *Shishi xin bao*, May 27, 1945.

138. He Haozu, "ZhongMei nannv shejiao guannian zhi chengqing," *Da gong bao*, May 27, 1945.

139. He Yaozu zhi Bao Huaguo dian," May 29, 1945, file 60-2-1932, p. 22, CMA.

140. Junshi weiyuan hui ling Chongqing shi zhengfu dian, May 29, 1945, file 53-10-142, pp. 270–80, CMA.

141. Tang Yi ling jingcha ju shi fenju dian, June 19, 1945, file 61-611-213, p. 9, CMA.

142. Chongqing shi zhengfu ge jiguan shangtao qiadai mengjun huiyi jilu, May 26, 1945, file 53-4-201, pp. 26–27, CMA.

143. "Miscellaneous News," *Xinmin wanbao*, May 28, 1945, Chinese Press Review #144, RG 208, OWI Informational File on Asia, box 381, unmarked folder; "New Measures concerning Public Order," *Guomin gongbao*, May 30, 1945, Chinese Press Review no. 145, RG 208, OWI Informational File on Asia, box 383, NARA; "Chongqing weishu zong siling bu bugao," May 31, 1945, file 61-1-29, p. 92, CMA.

144. Tang Yi ling jingcha ju dishiyi fenju dian, June 19, 1945, file 61-611-213, p. 9; Chongqing weishi zong siling bu bugao, June 11, 1945, file 85-1-29, p. 29, CMA.

145. "Weizuo xunling budui jiaqiang dui Meijun youyi," *Saodang bao*, May 28, 1945.

146. Ruhe zhidao guanbing yu mengjun xiangchu, June 18, 1945, file 53-10-142, pp. 312–15.108, CMA.

147. Chongqing shi ge jiguan shangtao qiadai mengjun huiyi jilu, May 26, 1945, file 53-4-201, pp. 26–27, CMA.

148. "Guanyu Jeep Girl Weidemai rushi shuo" and "Kunming nannv shejiao," *Xinwen tiandi*, June 20, 1945.

149. CCC, "Conduct of United States Military Personnel," June 7, 1945, RG 493, UD-UP 541, box 85, 250 Discipline, NARA.

150. SOS, "Discipline and Morale of Troops in China," May 12, 1945, RG 493, UD-UP 541, box 85, 250 Discipline, NARA.

151. CCC, "Report of Delinquency: Omer White," May 18, 1945, RG 493, UD-UP 541, box 82, 230.742, NARA.

152. CID, "Initial and Final Report, Case no. 627-232, September 5, 1945, RG 493, UD-UP 541, box 85, 250 Discipline, NARA.

153. CID, "Alleged Shooting of Chinese Civilians by American Personnel at Baise, Guangxi," September 13, 1945, RG 493, UD-UP 541, box 85, 250 Discipline, NARA.

154. SOS, "Report of Staff Judge Advocate for the Month of July 1945," August 5, 1945, RG 493, UD-UP 419, box 246, Monthly JAG Reports, NARA.

155. Zhao Tangshi zibai shu, undated, file no. 61-1-10, p. 46, CMA; "Report made by Mr. He Chi Ming," May 30, 1945, RG 493, UD-UP 266, box 314, Morals and Conduct, May 16 to June 30, 1945, NARA.

156. CCC "Display of Weapons by U.S. and Chinese Personnel," August 3, 1945, RG 493, UD-UP 265, box 63, 000.5, August 1 to December 31, 1945, NARA.

157. CID, "Murder and Robbery of American Soldiers at APO 430: Final Report," July 5, 1945, RG 493, UD-UP 306, box 666, Investigation, May 1945, NARA.

158. CID, "Altercation between American and Chinese Military Personnel," June 28, 1945, RG 493, UD-UP 541, box 68, 014.13, Relations with Civil and Military, NARA.

159. Provost Marshal, "Altercation between Chinese and American Personnel at Baoshan," July 28, 1945, RG 493, UD-UP 541, box 67, 000.5, Crimes folder, July 22, 1945, NARA.

160. Tang Yi ling dishi fenju dian, September 4, 1945, file 61-11-48, pp. 19–19.1 CMA; Wedemeyer to Chiang, August 11, 1945, RG 493, UD-UP 265, box 63, 00.5, August 1 to December 31, 1945, NARA.

161. Duara, "Regime of Authenticity," 287, 296–99.

162. Pickowicz, *China on Film*, 135–36.

163. Enloe, *Bananas, Beaches, and Bases*, 66–67.

Chapter 6

1. "Panorama of China," Earl M. Revell Collection, box 2, folder 15, USACMH.

2. On Chiang's and Mao's beliefs in the inevitability of civil war, see Westad, "Losses, Chances, and Myths," 105–6; van de Ven, *China at War*, 209–15; Tanner, *Battle for Manchuria and the Fate of China*, 36–39, 50–51.

3. Sledge, *China Marine*, 9.

4. Shaw, *United States Marines in North China*, 1; Westad, *Cold War and Revolution*, 99–103; Spector, *In the Ruins of Empire*, 48–53; III Amphibious Corps main landing at Dagu Bar took place on September 30, III Amphibious Corps War Diary, September 1 to September 30, 1945, *China Marine Scuttlebutt*, December 2003, John L. Haynes Collection, Center for the Study of World War II and the Human Experience, FSU. Marines were also stationed in Tangshan and Beidaihe.

5. WASC continued to operate sightseeing tours for U.S. personnel and run a hostel for the Army advisory group in Nanjing, but the Marine Corps took over all responsibility for housing and feeding its personnel in China. See Zhang Yan'e ling Weishengju dian, December 2, 1945, file no. J116-1-268, p. 14, TMA; Chen Chao ling nei wu qu fenju, November 11, 1945, file no. J183-2-38875, p. 1, BMA.

6. M. Johnson, "Anti-Imperialism as Strategy," 124–31.

7. Spector, *In the Ruins of Empire*, 29–36.

8. On looting and crimes committed by Soviet forces in Manchuria, see "Sulian jundui zai dongbei zhi baoxing," 1946, file no.020-021803-0022, 020-021803-0023, and 020-021803-0024, Foreign Ministry Files, AHA; Westad, *Cold War and Revolution*, 122.

9. On Soviet arms transfers in 1945 and 1946, see van de Ven, *China at War*, 232–33; Tanner, *Battle for Manchuria and the Fate of China*, 55–60.

10. Yang, *Dushi qiushi*, 3–38.

11. Tanner, *Battle for Manchuria and the Fate of China*, 218–20.

12. Marine Corps troop strength dropped nearly 70 percent in the six months after Marshall's departure. See "1st Marine Division Tientsin China Periodic G-1 Reports," February 6, 1947, and "1st Marine Division Tientsin China Periodic G-1 Reports," July 6, 1947, RG 127, FRC box 99, 1st Marine Division Periodic Reports, NARA; Tanner, *Where Chiang Kai-shek Lost China*, 97.

13. On the "Lost Chance" thesis, see Chen, "The Myth of America's 'Lost Chance' in China," 77–86; Garver, "Little Chance," 87–94; Sheng, "The Triumph of Internationalism," 95–104; Westad, "Losses, Chances, and Myths," 105–15.

14. Du, "Kangri zhanzheng shiqi JiangMei goujie yu maodun," 111–54; Chiang Kai-shek Diary, March 14, 1945, HIA.

15. Huabei junzheng xuanfu weiyuan hui ling Beiping shi jiaoyu ju dian, August 16, 1945, file no. J4-1-00706; "Beiping jingcha ju huanying mengjun dao Beiping banfa," December 11, 1945, file no. J181-24-217, pp. 1–3, BMA.

16. Luo Longji, "Tan Meijun deng JinGu," *Xi feng* 3 (1945): 86–90.

17. Sledge, *China Marine*, 16, 19–21. For more personal accounts, see Russel Fritz Collection, AFC/2001/001/11783, MSS box 525, VHP; Jack Whiteaker Collection, AFC/2001/001/71876, VHP; John B. Dillon: China Marine, unpublished memoir, 112–16, John B. Dillon Papers, box 1, McHC; Paul Hassett to Charlotte Hassett, October 10, 1945, Paul E. Hassett Collection, box 1, folder 8, WVM; Spector, *In the Ruins of Empire*, 51–52.

18. Spector, *In the Ruins of Empire*, 21.

19. Gallicchio, *Scramble for Asia*, 43; Glantz, *August Storm*, 42, 79–152.

20. Van de Ven, "Wartime Everydayness," 1–2; van de Ven, *China at War*, 198–202, 209–13.

21. Luo, "Tan Meijun deng JinGu," *Xi feng* 3 (1945): 86–90.

22. "Directive by President Truman to the Supreme Commander for the Allied Powers in Japan (MacArthur): Instruments for the Surrender of Japan, General Order No. 1," August 15, 1945, *FRUS: 1945, the Far East, China*, vol. 7. https://history.state.gov/historicaldocuments/frus1945v07/d390.

23. Spector, *In the Ruins of Empire*, 36–42.

24. On the surrender ceremonies, see van de Ven, *China at War*, 203–5; "Formal Surrender of the Senior Japanese Army and Military Force Commander in the Tsingtao Area," October 25, 1945, RG 127, China 370/D/1-3/2, box 17, A1-2, III Mac Japs Surrender Document China, NARA.

25. "A Chronological History of the Third Battalion, Seventh Regiment, First Marine Division," RG 127, China 370/D/1-3/2, box 18; G-5 Periodic Report, December 1, 1945, RG 127, China 370/D/1-3/2 box 17, NARA.

26. G-5 Periodic Report, February 1, 1946, RG 127, China 370/D/1-3/2, box 17, NARA.

27. Tanner, *Battle for Manchuria and the Fate of China*, 60–65.

28. Crimea (Yalta) Conference, 1945: Entry of Soviet Union into War against Japan, February 11, 1945, E.A.S. 498 (*Executive Agreement Series*).

29. Van de Ven, *China at War*, 230–31.

30. Kurtz-Phelan, *China Mission*, 11–14, 36, 44, 60.

31. Van de Ven, *China at War*, 231.

32. Tanner, *Battle for Manchuria and the Fate of China*, 76–105, 187–91.

33. Van de Ven, *China at War*, 232.

34. On the challenges Manchuria's terrain and infrastructure posed for Nationalist troops, see Tanner, *Battle for Manchuria and the Fate of China*, 216–17.

35. G-5 Periodic Report, July 1, 1946, RG 127, FRC box 99, 370/C/4/60, 1st Marine Division, Tientsin, NARA.

36. James W. Fackler Collection, unpublished memoir, 83, ACC #98.0161, Center for the Study of World War II and the Human Experience, FSU.

37. Spector, *In the Ruins of Empire*, 50.

38. Sledge, *China Marine*, 9, 15.

39. Sledge, *China Marine*, 16; Fackler, unpublished memoir, 84, FSU.

40. For wartime accounts, see Everett Deibler, January 21, 1946, Everett Deibler Collection, MSS box #1033, folder 2, VHP. For memoirs, oral histories, and veteran newsletter accounts, see George Fox Collection, AFC/2001/001/32107, VHP; Paul O'Neil Collection, AFC/2001/001/6874, VHP; Norman Hughes Collection AFC/2001/001/66389, VHP; Donald Foelker Collection, AFC/2001/001/11863, VHP; Sledge, *China Marine*, 48; Fackler, unpublished memoir, 84–86, FSU; *China Marine Scuttlebutt*, December 2003, March 2006, and September 2006, OH and News folder, John L. Haynes Collection, Center for the Study of World War II and the Human Experience, FSU.

41. Carl Johnson to Marion Bennett Johnson, December 24, 1945, Carl Emil and Marion Bennett Johnson Collection, box 7, folder 5, Center for the Study of World War II and the Human Experience, FSU.

42. Guo, "Paradise or Hell Hole?," 168.

43. On body discipline and civilization in imperial encounters, see Rotter, *Empires of the Senses*, 6–7, 17–20, 31–32, 168–76, 184–86.

44. Eugene Coplan Collection, AFC/2001/001/81963, VHP; George Fox Collection, AFC/2001/001/32107, AFC; Robert Eminger Collection, AFC/2001/001/45476, VHP; Guo, "Paradise or Hell Hole?," 168–70.

45. Walter Grzeskiewicz Collection, AFC/2001/001/66062, VHP.

46. Rotter, *Empires of the Senses*, 198–200.

47. "Epidemiology and Diseases of Naval Importance in China," undated, RG 52, Cancelled and Superseded Bureau of Medicine and Surgery Publications, box 3, NARA; Lee Kauffman Collection, AFC/2001/001/46485, VHP; Harry Rodenburg Collection, AFC/2001/001/2255, VHP.

48. Carl Johnson to Marion Bennett Johnson, January 13 and January 15, 1946, box 7, folders 7 and 8, FSU.

49. Sledge, *China Marine*, 27.

50. Tianjin shi zhaodai mengjun weiyuan hui zhi jingcha ju dian, December 15, 1945, file no. J219-3-28156, pp. 1–3, TMA.

51. Shao Shuixiong baogao, undated, file no. J219-3-28156, pp. 12–15, TMA.

52. Carl Johnson to Marion Bennett Johnson, December 25, 1945, box 7, folder 5, FSU.

53. See, for example, letters in the B-Bag section on November 9, 20, 24, 26, 27, and 28, and December 7, 1945, *Stars and Stripes*.

54. "Jingcha ju xunling benshi ge shangdian yin mengjun goumai wupin wangwang gaotai wujia yity baoli yang zhuyi qudi you," November 24, 1945, file no. J184-2-5903, pp. 1–2, and "Standard Ricksha and Tricycle Fare Table in Peiping," December 15, 1945, file no. J181-10-440, p. 14, BMA.

55. Diyi fenju zhang Liu Baozhang cheng jingcha ju juzhang Li Hanyuan dian, January 14, 1946, file no. J219-3-28156, pp. 17–18, TMA.

56. "Jubao you gongji haijun lu zhandui ji qi guyuan qingshi," January 29, 1946, file no. J184-2-43020, pp. 15–17, BMA; Frank Duesler, Oral History #54, WVM.

57. Sledge, *China Marine*, 17, 40.

58. Tanner, *Battle for Manchuria and the Fate of China*, 63; Gallicchio, *Scramble for Asia*, 110–11; Spector, *In the Ruins of Empire*, 52, 67–68; John Schottelkotte Collection, AFC/2001/001/15530, VHP; Thomas Maynard Collection, AFC/2001/001/52310, VHP; Benjamin Welles, "Chinese Attack U.S. Marines at Ammunition Depot Near Port," *New York Times*, October 5, 1946, A1.

59. G. B. Clark, *Treading Softly*, 144–45.

60. "Final Report on the Anping Incident," October 8, 1946, *FRUS: 1946, the Far East, China*, vol. 10, https://history.state.gov/historicaldocuments/frus1946v10/d168; Niu, *Cong Yan'an zouxiang shijie*, 283.

61. Paul Hassett to Charlotte Hassett, November 8, 1945, Paul E. Hassett Collection, box 1, folder 8, WVM.

62. Gallicchio, *Scramble for Asia*, 111; Spector, *In the Ruins of Empire*, 67.

63. "Zhonggong zhongyang guanyu dongyuan ge qunzhong tuanti yaoqiu Meiguo gaibian dui Hua zhengce de zhishi," *Zhonggong zhongyang wenjian xuanji*, di 16 juan, 216–17.

64. Yang, *Dushi qiushi*, 3–38.

65. John J. Pioster, "Chinese Policeman Shoots Americans in Racetrack Fray," *Stars and Stripes*, November 5, 1945; Wedemeyer to Shanghai Mayor Qian Dajun, April 2, 1946, RG 493, UD-UP 265, box 62, 000.5, Crimes, from January 1, 1946, NARA; "Incident Involving Chinese Soldiers," August 19, 1946, RG 493, box 96, 1946, NARA.

66. Wedemeyer to N. L. Liu, November 23, 1945, RG 493, UD-UP 265, box 63, 000.5, August 1 to December 31, 1945, NARA; "Conduct of Chinese Army Personnel," January 21, 1946, and "Discrimination against U.S. Armed Forces," January 22, 1946, RG 493, UD-UP 265, box 62, 000.5, Crimes, from January 1, 1946, NARA; He Haoruo to Wedemeyer, November 6, 1945, RG 493, UD-UP 265, box 63, 000.5, from August 1 to December 31, 1945, NARA; John J. Pioster, "Chinese Policeman Shoots Americans in Racetrack Fray."

67. Jiang Jieshi ling Huang Xuchu dian, November 2, 1945, file no.002-090103-00005-121-001a, waijiao bu dang'an, AHA.

68. "Shooting Incident of Schoolgirl," December 30, 1945, China Marines Association Collection: Individual Donations, Charles Haseltine folder, McHC.

69. See, for example, Shenxun bilu: Zhao Chongbai, November 26, 1946, J181-225-543, pp. 9–10; Zhencha dadui duizhang Li Lianfu cheng jingcha juzhang Tang Yongxian, November 13, 1946, file no. J181-27-2550, p. 1; ZhongMei jingxian lianluo shi guanyi yisong Liu Haonian deng huo qie Meijun cangku wuzi an de han, November 16, 1946, file no. J181-27-2526, p. 3, BMA.

70. Beiping shi difang fayuan xingshi panjue: Li Wenlong, June 21, 1947, file no. J191-2-9656, pp. 9–10; Beiping shi difang fayuan jiancha chu, November 27, 1946, file no. J65-12-1208, pp. 1, 16; Shenxun bilu: Xu Decheng, November 25, 1946, file no. J181-225-543, pp. 5–6, BMA.

71. "Missing Vehicles, Number Of," February 1, 1947, file no. J181-10-303, pp. 15–18, BMA.

72. Wedemeyer to Qian Dajun, April 2, 1946, RG 493, UD-UP 265, box 62, 000.5, Crimes, from January 1, 1946, NARA.

73. Fackler, unpublished memoir, 89, FSU.

74. Willie S. Harrison to Commanding Officers, Seventh Service Regiment, December 11, 1946, file no. J219-3-38684, pp. 7–8, TMA. Marines had other warehouses around the city, including three in the fifth precinct. See Tianjin shi jingcha ju diwu fenju cheng, January 28, 1946, file no. J219-3-38684, p. 27, TMA.

75. *North China Marine*, January 9, 1946, 1.

76. Qian Dajun cheng Jiang Jieshi dian, January 13, 1946, file no. 002-08020-00304-030-001a to 002, AHA. On demobilization protests, see Gallicchio, *Scramble for Asia*, 119–20.

77. "China 1945: You Served Your Hitch in Hell," Paul E. Hassett Collection, box 1, folder 11, WVM.

78. Sun Lianzhong cheng Jiang Jieshi dian, October 23, 1945, file no. J2-3-7260, p. 1, TMA.

79. See numerous reports in file no. J2-3-7260, pp. 1–19; J219-3-32783, pp. 1–4; J219-3-32784, pp. 1–10, TMA.

80. Ren Dongying cheng Li Hanyuan dian, December 26, 1946, Han Lixun cheng Tianjin jingcha ju dian, December 26, 1946, file no. J219-3-32767, pp. 2–5, TMA.

81. "Meijun zhaoshi anjian shangwei jieshu anzhe yi lan biao," undated, file no. J219-3-32773, pp. 2–3, TMA.

82. "Additional Reports of Reprehensible Acts of the U.S. Naval Personnel in the Vicinity of Hishito and Saie, Takao [Gaoxiong], Feburary 9, 1946, RG 493, Records of Special Staff, box 95, Morals and Conduct, December 1 to December 30, 1945, NARA.

83. Wedemeyer blamed the Shanghai police for permitting the sale of fireworks. See Wedemeyer to Shanghai Police Headquarters, November 20, 1945, RG 493, UD-UP 266, box 314, Morals and Conduct, October 1 to November 30, 1945, NARA; "Disciplinary Action Under 104th AW," October 9, 1945, RG 493, box 99, Courts Martial, December 1944 to December 1945, NARA.

84. "Report of Delinquency," November 22, 1945, RG 493, Records of Special Staff, box 97, Morals and Conduct, NARA.

85. "Nei qi fenju baogao mengjun renyi ouda jingcha qing paiyuan jiaoshe you," February 5, 1946, file no. J181-10-299, pp. 19–22, BMA.

86. "Feng Sun siling zhang guan dian yifeng weizuo dian xun Tianjin Meijun bufa qingshi dengyin zhuan ling chabao you," November 29, 1945, file no. J219-3-032790, pp. 1–2, TMA. On the attempted rape, see Di shi fenju zhang Ren Dongying cheng Li Hanyuan dian, November 30, 1945, file no. J219-3-32782, p. 2, TMA.

87. Guo, "Paradise or Hell Hole?," 182–83; Chen Chao to Thomas A. Henton, July 22, 1946, file no. J181-10-299, p. 74, BMA; Jiangsu sheng zhengfu cheng waijiao bu dian, June 8, 1946, file no. 020-050204-0039, 0123a to 126a, Foreign Ministry Archives, AHA; "Recommendation for Trial by Court Martial, case of Floyd W. Copley," June 20, 1946, RG 127, entry 46c, box 1, folder 6, NARA.

88. Guo, "Paradise or Hell Hole?," 182–83.

89. Chen Chao cheng Xiong Bin dian, December 14, 1945, and Wei Yunfeng cheng Xiong Bin dian, January 19, 1946, file no. J1-1-293, pp. 5–7, 12–14, BMA.

90. Di shi fenju juzhang Ren Dongying cheng Li Hanyuan dian, November 6, 1945, file no. J219-3-32780, p. 1, TMA.

91. Di shi fenju juzhang Ren Dongying cheng Li Hanyuan dian, December 7, 1945, file no. J219-3-32779, pp. 1–2, TMA.

92. Di liu fenju juzhang Zheng Guobin cheng Li Hanyuan dian, December 23, 1945, file no. J219-3-32765, p. 1, TMA.

93. Case no. PM-35, January 31, 1946, RG 493, Records of Special Staff, box 97, Morals and Conduct, February 18 to February 28, 1946, NARA.

94. "Tianjin shi zhengfu jingcha ju xingshi jingcha dui ba jiu yuefen Meijun zai shi nei fasheng bu fa shijian baogao biao," October 1, 1946, file no. J219-3-40697, pp. 51–53, TMA.

95. Several scholars have written about the killing of Zang. See Wilkinson, "American Military Misconduct in Shanghai and the Chinese Civil War," 146–74; H. Zhang, *America Perceived*, 34–35, 40, 88, 93. For Chinese Foreign Ministry files on the killing, see note no. Mei-36/13301, June 24, 1947, file no. 202-050204-0040-0106a to 109a, Foreign Ministry Files, AHA.

96. "Bao Hu Xiaomei bei Meijun touru hezhong yansi," September 25, 1946, file no. J219-3-38732, pp. 1–3, 15–17, TMA.

97. First Marine Police Company, RE Case #4481, September 24, 1946, file no. J219-3-38732, pp. 42–44, TMA.

98. "Zhao chao Hu Shenshi yuan cheng yi jian," October 4, 1946, file no. J219-3-38732, pp. 32–34, TMA.

99. "Meijun renyi sha ren!," *Renmin ribao*, October 5, 1946.

100. "Meibing jibi chefu," *Shen bao*, September 24, 1946, 4. On the *Shen bao*'s politics, see Chin, "The Historical Origins of the Nationalization of the Newspaper Industry in Modern China," *China Review*, 12–14.

101. "Renmin an ying yifa banli," *Shen bao*, October 4, 1946, 2.

102. "Bian zhe de hua," *Wenhui bao*, September 24, 1946.

103. Wilkinson, "American Military Misconduct in Shanghai and the Chinese Civil War," 152.

104. Guo, "Anticlimax of an Ill-Starred Sino-American Encounter," 229.

105. For example, according to the city police bureau, Tianjin's population increased by more than 200,000 in the fourteen months after Japan's surrender. See Jing cha ju juzhang Li Hanyuan cheng shichang Du Jianshi dian, December 12, 1946, file no. J2-3-2418-40, p. 120, TMA.

106. Jin, *Zhuanzhe niandai*, 64–65.

107. Ray J. Hawkins, "Safe Driving," *Stars and Stripes*, November 10, 1945, 4.

108. "Mei fang zhaoshi chuli baogao," October, November, and December 1945; January 1946, file no. J181-10-299, pp. 203–33, BMA.

109. Jingcha ju juzhang Li Hanyuan cheng shizhang Du Jianshe dian, December 12, 1946, file no. J2-3-2418-40, p. 120, TMA.

110. "Tianjin shi jingcha ju jiaotong gushi tongji biao qianlou buchong biao," file no. J219-3-30683, pp, 1–19, TMA.

111. Zhang et al., *Zhongguo xiandai shi*, 616.

112. Ling Hong, "Lun Meiguo ren suo shuo de hua," *Minzhu* di 12 qi, December 29, 1945. On *Minzhu*, see Zhao Yi, "*Minzhu* zhoukan wei minzhu fasheng," 72–74.

113. Cathcart, "Atrocities, Insults, and 'Jeep Girls,'" 146–47; Hung, "Fuming Image," 130–31.

114. This pattern holds in both Beijing and Tianjin. See "Meijun budui qiche zhaoshi tongji biao," January to August 1946, file no. J181-10-299, pp. 110–17, BMA; "Tianjin shi jingcha ju jiaotong shigu tongjibiao 1946 nian," file no. J219-3-30683, pp. 1–19, TMA.

115. See, for example, "Meifang zhaoshi chuli baogao 35 nian 10 yuefen," file no. J181-10-299, pp. 217–20, BMA; Baoan jingcha zongdui zhang Nie Bufei cheng jingcha juzhang Li Hanyuan dian, December 24, 1946, file no. J219-3-28738, pp. 1–2, TMA; Di yi fenjuzhang Zheng Guobin cheng jingcha juzhang Li Hanyuan dian, December 12, 1946, file no. J219-3-28810, p. 8, TMA. On the accident in Nanjing, see "Activities of Major Vincent Sexton," April 25, 1946, RG 493, Records of Special Staff, box 95, 1946 folder, NARA.

116. "Beiping renmin ziyou baozhang weiyuan hui han wei Meijun qiche zhaoshi weihai shimin shengming qing jiang chuli banfa," November 29, 1946, file no. J181-10-299, pp. 181–82, BMA.

117. Huang, "Guanyu Meiguo bing," *Zhoubao,* di 20 qi, January 19, 1946.

118. Jin, *Zhuanzhe niandai*, 64–65.

119. Chiang originally made October 1 the changeover date but postponed it to January 1 after Japan's surrender. See "Right-Hand Drive," August 4, 1945, RG 493, UD-UP 541, box 68, 010.8, Traffic Regulations, NARA; Cathcart, "Atrocities, Insults, and 'Jeep Girls,'" 147; Wedemeyer, *Wedemeyer Reports!*, 355–56; Campanella, *Concrete Dragon*, 227–28.

120. "Cheliang xingshi fasheng zhuangche weixian ji qita yiwai shijian," September 1945, file no. J183-2-33839, pp. 9–10, BMA.

121. Chen juzhang zhi wai wu fenju juzhang Chu Shenshen, April 23, 1946, file no. J184-2-44021, pp. 5–6, BMA.

122. Yang, "U.S. Marines in Qingdao: History, Public Memory, and Chinese Nationalism," 60.

123. "Yiding shu," October 4, 1946, file no. J181-10-299, pp. 189–190, BMA; Zhang, *America Perceived,* 42.

124. Jingcha ju juzhang Li Hanyuan cheng shizhang Du Jianshe dian, December 12, 1946, file no. J2-3-2418-40, p. 120, TMA.

125. "Cheliang xingshi fasheng zhuangche weixian ji qita yiwai shijian," September 1945, file no. J183-2-33839, pp. 9–10, BMA.

126. Local police and U.S. MPs still assisted in such cases, helping with translation and providing the release forms that Chinese had to sign indicating their satisfaction with the cash payment and forfeiting the right to further claims. See, for example, P. W. Davis to the Tianjin Police Bureau, February 2, 1947, file no. J219-3-208738, p. 122, TMA.

127. See the case of Li Qingfu in Tianjin, an impoverished laborer who needed two months of medical care after being hit by an American Jeep that fled the scene. The Tianjin Police Hospital had to find a charity hospital to care for Li because of limited funds. Di liu fenju zhang Meng Zhaopei cheng jingcha ju juzhang Li Hanyuan, April 18, 1947, file no. J219-3-28810, p. 201, TMA.

128. "Xinmin bao zhuanlai niming xin wei Meijun cheliang shichang zhaoguo wei dedao heli peichang deng," August 31, 1946, file no. J181-10-299, pp. 83–84, BMA. On the *Xinmin bao*, see Zhang, *America Perceived*, 80.

129. Yang, "U.S. Marines in Qingdao: History, Public Memory, and Chinese Nationalism," 62.

130. Tang Yongxian zhi Xinmin bao dian, September 19, 1946, file no. J181-10-299, pp. 95–98, BMA.

131. Di wu fenju daili fenju zhang Liu Xinyan cheng Li Hanyuan dian, January 17, 1947, file no. J219-3-28738, pp. 98–100, TMA.

132. S. L. Howard to Chi Tse-chin, March 3, 1947, file no. 020-050204-0039-0197a, AHA.

133. Report of Investigation by Joseph Brill, April 9, 1947, file no. J219-3-28810, p. 106, TMA.

134. On varying policies toward theft, see Guo, "Paradise or Hell Hole?," 179. On the August 1944 decision, see "Attached Report on Theft of Building Material and Incidental Shooting," August 21, 1944, RG 493, UD-UP, box 244, Correspondence 1944, NARA.

135. Yang, "U.S. Marines in Qingdao: History, Public Memory, and Chinese Nationalism," 62–63.

136. Spencer R. Allen, Officer of the Day, First Engineering Battalion Report, March 13, 1946, file no. J219-3-682, pp. 8–9, TMA.

137. On the unidentified boys, see Di wu fenju daili fenju zhang Liu Xinyan cheng Li Hanyuan dian, July 5, 1946, and Li Hanyuan zhiling waishi ke dian, July 19, 1946, file no. J219-3-812, pp. 8–10, 15, TMA. For other cases, including shootings of minors and adults, see Di yi fenju zhang Liu Baozhang cheng Li Hanyuan dian, December 17, 1945, file no. J219-3-32776, p. 1; Di wu fenju zhang Zhu Xuefang cheng Li Hanyuan dian, December 31, 1945, file no. J219-3-32778, pp. 1–2; daili di si

fenju zhang Wang Yixuan cheng Li Hanyuan dian, April 18 and 19, 1946; file no. J219-3-677, pp. 10–13; Zeng Zhaoyi cheng Li Hanyuan dian, April 24, 1946, file no. J219-3-6779, pp. 1–2, 7–8, TMA.

138. "Ducha yuan Dun Jun baogao xuesheng Cao Guiming yinzhe Meijun ku bei Mei xianbing yongqiang jishang," September 6, 1946, file no. J181-10-299, pp. 141–45, 150, BMA.

139. Quoted in Guo, "Paradise or Hell Hole?," 180–81.

140. Daili di shi fenju zhang Han Guirong cheng Li Hanyuan dian, August 28, 1946, "Tianjin shi jingcha ju di shi fenju zhi'an ji bao biao," August 26, 1946, and "Report of Incident," August 27, 1946, file no. J219-3-781, pp. 32, 34, 52–57, TMA.

141. Di yi fenju zhang Zheng Guobin cheng Li Hanyuan dian, October 2, 1946, file no. J219-3-40697, p. 47; "Report of Incident," August 27, 1946, file no. J219-3-781, p. 52, TMA.

142. Provost Marshal Willie S. Harrison to Commanding Officer, Seventh Service Regiment, December 11, 1946, file no. J219-3-38684, pp. 7–8, TMA.

143. Xingjing diwu fendui duifu Liu Wenhong cheng duizhang Xiao dian, December 19, 1946, file no. J219-3-38684, p. 19, TMA.

144. On the difficulty of rehabilitating shooting victims, see Yang, "U.S. Marines in Qingdao: History, Public Memory, and Chinese Nationalism," 63.

145. Shuishang fenju zhang Tong Xiangyin cheng Li Hanyuan dian, March 12, 1946, file no. J219-3-679, pp. 8–9; Daili di si fenju zhang Wang Yixuan cheng Li Hanyuan dian, April 12, 1946, file no. J219-3-788, p. 14, TMA.

146. Sears's sentence was reduced to fifteen years. See Daili di si fenju zhang Wang Yixuan cheng Li Hanhuan dian, September 7, 1946, file no. J219-3-787, pp. 9–10, TMA; "Report of an Incident Involving Private First Class Willard V. Sears," February 11, 1947, file no. 20-050204-0039-0217a, Foreign Ministry Files, AHA.

147. Daili di si fenju zhang Wang Yixuan cheng Li Hanyuan dian, September 7, 1946, file no. J219-3-787, pp. 9–10, TMA.

148. "Report of Investigation by Sergeant C. Moroukian, November 11, 1946, and Major General S. L. Howard to Li Hanyuan," January 4, 1947, file no. J219-3-038749, pp. 10–11, 24–25, TMA.

149. Guo, "Anticlimax of an Ill-Starred Sino-American Encounter," 228–29; "Martial Law Ends Shanghai Rioting," *North China Marine*, December 7, 1947.

150. Daili di yi fenju zhang Wang Luoceng cheng Li Hanyuan dian, August 2, 1946, file no. J219-3-681, pp. 18–19, TMA.

151. Pepper, *Civil War in China*, 16–28; Lary, *China's Civil War*, 45–48, 139.

152. On opium smuggling by American pilots flying between Shanghai and Beijing, see William Crawford to George Plotkin, March 16, 1946, RG 493, UD-UP 306, box 664, China Theater, Air Transport Command 12/45 to 4/46, NARA. On weapons smuggling, see William Morris Interrogation, undated, RG 493, UD-UP 306, box 664, Chinese Theater AG Section, Misc. Statements, NARA.

153. "Smuggling of Gold," April 26, 1945, RG 493, UD-UP 265, box 62, 000.5, April 5 to July 31, 1945, NARA.

154. Yang, "U.S. Marines in Qingdao: Military-Civilian Interaction, Nationalism, and China's Civil War," 126.

155. Bar Cards, Art Goetz folder, China Marines Association Collection, Individual Donations, box 9; Item #47, China Marines Association, box 6, McHC.

156. Carl Johnson to Marion Johnson, January 6, 1946, box 7, folder 7, FSU.

157. Fackler, unpublished memoir, 90, FSU; Robert Ravelle Collection, AFC/2001/001/54936, VHP.

158. One unit in Dagu recorded an annual rate of 818 per 1,000 men. "Health of Command 1st Marine Division (reinforced) for the Month of June 1946," July 9, 1946, RG 127, 370-C-4-60, FRC box 99, First Marine Division, Tientsin Periodic G-1 Reports, NARA.

159. "Jipu nvlang," *Heibai zhoubao*, 1946 nian, di 2 qi, 10.

160. Chen Er, "Beiping Meijun de yihan?," *Qiri tan*, 1946 nian di 5 qi, 11.

161. Hui Feng, "Jipu nvlang de mingyun!," *Qiri tan*, 1946 nian, di 11 qi, 2.

162. Feng Chun, "Chen Lu Qingdao zuo Jipu nvlang!," *Hai yan*, 1946 nian, di 2 qi, 7; Wei Tuo, "Bai Guang: zuo Jipu nvlang," *Xin Shanghai*, 1946 nian di 12 qi, 1; "Ye Baobao lun wei Jipu nvlang," *Hai jing*, 1946 nian, di 41 qi, 8.

163. See, for example, "Tianjin shi zhengfu jingcha ji xingshi jingdui ba jiu fen Meijun zai shimie fasheng bu fa shijian baogao biao," October 1, 1945, file no. J219-3-40697, pp. 51–52, TMA; Yang, "U.S. Marines in Qingdao: Military-Civilian interaction, Nationalism, and China's Civil War," 161–63.

164. "Recommendation for trial by general court-martial," June 20, 1946, RG 127, Entry 46c, box 1, folder 6, NARA.

165. "Nei liu qu baogao wei Meijun jiuzui ouda jingshi qingxing," February 3, 1946, file no. J181-10-299, pp. 16–18, BMA.

166. See Goeede, *GIs and Germans*, 84–86; Kovner, 49–56. On crimes committed by Soviet forces in Manchuria, see "Sulian jundui zai dongbei zhi baoxing," 1946, file no. 020-021803-0022, 020-021803-0023, and 020-021803-0024, Foreign Ministry Files, AHA.

167. Zhang, *America Perceived*, 97.

168. F. J. Dau to Mayor K. C. Wu, September 19, 1946, RG 493, box 98, Correction Punishment, NARA.

169. Omar T. Pfieffer interview transcript, Marine Corps History Project, 1968, 410–11.

170. Huebner, "Chinese Anti-Americanism," 121.

171. Jin, *Zhuanzhe niandai*, 70.

172. Zhang, *America Perceived*, 63–69, 97.

173. Kurtz-Phelan, *China Mission*, 287–88.

174. Zhang, *America Perceived,* 68–69.

175. "Alleged Rape of Miss Shen Chung by Corporal William G. Pierson, Investigation of," December 28, 1946, file no. 020-050204-0001-0067a to 0085a, Foreign Ministry Files, AHA.

176. Zhang, *America Perceived*, 80–91.

177. As Arne Westad has shown, the incident's symbolic meaning and the CCP's admission in 1950 that Shen was already an underground party member by Christmas 1946 have added to the difficulty of piecing together what happened. How-

ever, Shen herself later claimed that she joined the party in 1956. See Westad, *Decisive Encounters*, 101, 140, 354n61.

178. Jin, *Zhuanzhe niandai*, 74–75, 78–80; an anonymous writer, claiming to be a student at Tsinghua, also accused Shen of being a Communist agent in a letter to the U.S. consul general in Beijing. See anonymous letter, January 6, 1947, RG 84, Peiping Consulate General Record 1945–1950, box 15, 1947, vol. 10, 830 USMC Assault Case, NARA.

179. "Wei dian bao ben shi fasheng Meibing wuru Zhongguo nvsheng shijian jiaoshe jingguo qing cha zhao you," January 3, 1947, file no. 020-050204-0001-0048x to 0050a, Foreign Ministry Files, AHA.

180. Jin, *Zhuanzhe niandai*, 77.

181. Yu Diqing, "Huiyi Beiping dixia dang xuewei lingdao de xuesheng yundong," *Beiping dixia dang douzheng shiliao*, 274–75.

182. Jin, *Zhuanzhe niandai*, 77–80.

183. They worked with students from Tianjin's Beiyang University. "Jin xuesheng youxing jieguo yuanman," *Yishi bao*, January 2, 1946, file no. 020-050204-0001-0056x, Foreign Ministry Files, AHA; Jin, *Zhuanzhe niandai*, 82.

184. "'Don't Know Much,' N'king Students Tell Newsman at Confab," *Shanghai Evening Post and Mercury*, January 4, 1947, file no.020-050204-0002-0009x, Foreign Ministry Files, AHA.

185. Zhonggong Beijing shiwei dangshi yanjiu shi, *Kangyi Meijun zhuHua baoxing yundong ziliao huibian* [hereafter KYMJZHBX], 210–343; Jin, *Zhuanzhe niandai*, 78–85; Zhongguo minzhu tongmeng zhongyang weiyuan hui, *Zhongguo minzhu tongmeng lishi wenxian, 1941–1949*, 284.

186. "Zhongyang guanyu zai ge da chengshi zuzhi qunzhong xiangying Beiping xuesheng yundong de zhishi," KYMJZHBX, 3–4.

187. Zhang, *America Perceived*, 97–98.

188. "Zhongyang guanyu liyong PingJinJingHu xue yun chengji kuoda wo dang huodong de zhishi," KYMJZHBX, 7–8.

189. Jin, *Zhuanzhe niandai*, 86–87.

190. Westad, *Decisive Encounters*, 101; Jin, *Zhuanzhe niandai*, 81.

191. Zhang, *America Perceived*, 94–96.

192. Zheng, "Specter of Extraterritoriality," 21, 39–41.

193. Jin, *Zhuanzhe niandai*, 87.

194. Tanner, *Where Chiang Kai-shek Lost China*, 67–83.

195. Van de Ven, *China at War*, 232–36; Tanner, *Where Chiang Kai-shek Lost China*, 142–49.

196. Van de Ven, *China at War*, 252–53; Pepper, *Civil War in China*, 109–12; Lary, *China's Civil War*, 89–91; Westad, *Decisive Encounters*, 86–89.

197. "Case of William G. Pierson, Corporal U.S. Marine Corps," January 17–22, 1947, RG 59, 250/37/06/02, box 4663, 811.32/1-147 to 811.32/11-3048, NARA.

198. "Kangbao yundong bu hui zhongzhi," *Xinhua ribao*, January 29, 1947, in KYMJZHBX, 36–38.

199. Jin, *Zhuanzhe niandai*, 83.

200. Tanner, *Where Chiang Kai-shek Lost China*, 167.

201. "Report of Investigation Conducted by Ernest A. LeBlanc," February 6, 1947, file no. J219-3-038759, p. 9; Di wu daili fenju zhang Liu Xinyan cheng Li Hanyuan dian, February 6, 1947, file no. J219-3-038765, p. 6; Di wu daili fenju zhang Liu Xinyan cheng Li Hanyuan dian, February 8, 1947, file no. J219-3-038786, pp. 18–19, TMA.

202. "Li Wenzhong zhengci"; "Qing Zhongsheng zhengci"; "Chen Dedi zhengci"; "Zhang Guoshan zhengci"; Hu Junqing zhengci"; February 7, 1947, file no. J219-3-38786, pp. 7–8, 11–14, 28, 37, 40, 43, 47, TMA.

203. "Statement of Mr. C. C. Hsiao [Xiao Zhichun]," February 12, 1947, file no. J219-3-38786, p. 29, TMA.

204. Chen Zecheng cheng Tang Yongxian dian, March 17, 1947; "Bai Mashi zhengci," "Wang Chaoshan Zhengci," Weisi Leide zhengci," March 19, 1947, file no. J65-1-353, pp. 4–9, 63–70, BMA.

205. General Court-Martial Order Number 12, April 20, 1947, file no. 020-050204-0040-0214a, Foreign Ministry Files, AHA; "Meijun zai Jin zhaoshi wei jie anjian diaocha biao," September 20, 1947, file no. J219-3-38754, pp. 6–9, TMA; F. L. Wieseman to Du Jianshi, July 21, 1947, file no. J219-3-38786, p. 62, TMA.

206. Admiral Charles M. Cooke to Li Xianliang, August 6, 1947; "Anti-US Move Breaks Out in Tsingtao," *Shanghai Evening Post and Mercury*, April 14, 1947, file no. 020-050204-0041-0059a, 0008a, Foreign Ministry Files, AHA.

207. Shaffer, "Rape in Beijing," 59–62.

208. "Meijun qiangjian fan jing wu zui," *Qunzhong*, August 21, 1947, in KYM-JZHBX, 653–54.

209. Tanner, *Where Chiang Kai-shek Lost China*, 85–96; Westad, *Decisive Encounters*, 89; Shaffer, "Rape in Beijing," 60.

210. See, for example, "'Ting hao' sheng zhong liang ren mie ting," *Nanjing Xinmin bao*, August 3, 1947; "Zhonghe qiao Meibing xing xiong," *Heping ribao*, August 3, 1947; "Zhonghe qiao an diaocha wanjun, Meifang biaoshi zhunqi gong shen," *Zhongyang ribao*, August 13, 1947; "Zhonghe qiao an zhaoshi Meibing Meijun fating jinri gong shen," *Zhongyang ribao*, August 15, 1947, file nos. 020-050204-0042-0109a to 0111a, 0174x, and 0176x, Foreign Ministry Files, AHA. The corporal in question, Frank Aldrich, was convicted of murder and sentenced to life in prison. The army's judge advocate general upheld the sentence. See U.S. Embassy, Nanjing to Chinese Foreign Ministry, February 10, 1948, file no.020-050204-0042-0251a to 0254a, Foreign Ministry Files, AHA.

211. The Consul at Tsingtao (Strong) to the Secretary of State," May 26, 1949, *FRUS: 1949, the Far East, China*; Yang, "U.S. Marines in Qingdao: Military-Civilian Interaction, Nationalism, and China's Civil War," 281–85.

212. On the Liao-Shen campaign and Communist victories in 1949, see Tanner, *Where Chiang Kai-shek Lost China*; Westad, *Decisive Encounters*, 181–293; Bjorge, *Moving the Enemy*; Jay Taylor, *Generalissimo*, 393–408, 416–19.

213. Tanner, *Battle for Manchuria and the Fate of China*, 60–68, 213–21.

214. Tanner, *Where Chiang Kai-shek Lost China*, 261.

215. Shaffer, "Rape in Beijing," 49–56.

216. Jin, *Zhuanzhe niandai*, 59.

217. Tanner, *Where Chiang Kai-shek Lost China*, 168–71, 275–80.

Epilogue

1. See, for example, Harold Hinton, "White Paper Blunt: Stresses That Chinese Nationalists Failed to Utilize Past Help," *New York Times*, August 6, 1949; "Solon Critics Reblast at China Policy," *Atlanta Constitution*, August 6, 1949; "China Whitewash," *Wall Street Journal*, August 8, 1949.

2. Peraino, *Force So Swift*, 155–57, 168–70.

3. Acheson, "Letter of Transmittal," in U.S. State Department, *China White Paper*, XVI.

4. Acheson, "Letter of Transmittal," III.

5. Lin, *Accidental State*, 107–9, 113–14, 127–29; Peraino, *Force So Swift*, 217–32.

6. McCarthy, "Enemies from Within," https://liberalarts.utexas.edu/coretexts /_files/resources/texts/1950%20McCarthy%20Enemies.pdf.

7. Mao, "'Friendship' or Aggression," August 30, 1945, reprinted in Arkush and Lee, *Land without Ghosts*, 243–45.

8. On the origins of the Korean War and China's decision to intervene, see van de Ven, *China at War*, 256–64; Masuda, *Cold War Crucible*, 132–39.

9. For overviews of the campaign, see Kuech, "Imagining 'America' in Communist and Nationalist China," 59–94; Rawnsley, "Great Movement to Resist America and Assist Korea," 285–315; He, "Xin Zhongguo minzhong dui Meiguo de renzhi ji qi bianhua," 47–62; Hou, "KangMei yuanChao yundong yu minzhong shehui xintai yanjiu," 19–28.

10. Wu, *Meiguo—Yi ge sha ren he xue de guojia*, 129–35; Zhongguo renmin baowei shijie heping fandui Meiguo qinlue zhe weiyuan hui Guangzhou fen hui, *Bu gong dai tian de chou hen*, 1–10. The Shanghai and Nanjing municipal libraries house the largest collections of published Resist America and Aid Korea propaganda materials. For the most extensive accounts on violence and accidents involving U.S. forces in China during the 1940s, see Cai et al., *Meidi baoxing*, 9–10, 12, 20–23, 26–28, 33–34, 37; Qing nian bao, *Wo kong su!*, 1–11, 14, 16, 18–19, 21, 24, 29–35, 41, 44; Lv, *Meidi de xuehzai*, 1–7, 11–24, 43; Renmin chu ban she, *Meijun zhu Hua shiqi de xuezhai*; Wei ren chu ban she, *Meiguo bing zai xinan*; Sunan wenlian chou wei hui, *Meidi baoxing jishi*, 1–6, 23, 28, 31–35, 37, 42–45, 50–54; Laodong chu ban she, *Kong su de xue*, 27–97.

11. Liu, *Meidi qin Hua shi*, 40–41; Zhuang, *Meijun zai Zhongguo de baoxing*. On comic exhibitions, see "Gaoqiao qu kangMei yuanChao baojia weiguo xuanchuan huodong gongzuo zongjie," December 29, 1950, file no. A71-2-883, SMA.

12. KangMei yuanChao zhuanji, *Zang da erzi*, 22–23.

13. Beijing shi zong gong hui, "Beijing shi gongren kangMei yuanChao baojia weiguo yundong xuanchuan jiaoyu gongzuo zongjie," March 16, 1951, in "Beijing shi yu kangMei yuanChao," Beijing shi dang'an guan yanjiu shi ed., 417.

14. "Gaoqiao qu kangMei yuanChao baojia weiguo xuanchuan huodong gongzuo zongjie," December 29, 1950, file no. A71-2-883; "Shanghai shi kangMei yuanChao yundong de qingkuang," undated (summer 1951), file no. A22-1-17, pp. 90–101, SMA.

15. Liao, "Wei shen me yao kai kongsu hui?," 16–17.

16. Qingnian tuan Beijing shi weiyuan hui bangong shi, "Guanyu yanjiu shimin sixiang jinxing KangMei yuanChao xuanchuan de jingyan baogao,"

March 7, 1951, in "Beijing shi yu kangMei yuanChao," Beijing shi dang'an guan yanjiu shi ed., 419.

17. "Shanghai shi kangMei yuanChao yundong de qingkuang," undated (summer 1951), file no. A22-1-17, pp. 100–101, SMA.

18. "Gaoqiao qu kangMei yuanChao baojia weiguo xuanchuan huodong gongzuo zongjie," December 29, 1950, file no. A71-2-883, SMA.

19. Beijing shi zong gong hui, "Beijing shi gongren kangMei yuanChao baojia weiguo yundong xuanchuan jiaoyu gongzuo zongjie," March 16, 1951, in "Beijing shi yu kangMei yuanChao," Beijing shi dang'an guan yanjiu shi ed., 415.

20. On evangelical conversion experiences, see McLoughlin, *Revivals, Awakening and Reform*, 19, 65.

21. Qingnian tuan Beijing shi weiyuan hui bangong shi, "KangMei yuanChao yundong zhong zhong xuesheng de sixiang qingkuang," December 26, 1950, in "Beijing shi yu kangMei yuanChao," Beijing shi dang'an guan yanjiu shi ed., 406–7.

22. Li, ed., "Meijun zai chuanxi liuxia de xuezhai," in *Meiguo bing zai xinan* [hereafter MGBZXN], wei ren chu ban she ed., 22–23.

23. "Guanghan jintang gejie renmin de kongsu," in MGBZXN, 36.

24. "Yizu tongbao fennu kongsu Meijun shouxing," in MGBZXN, 54–56.

25. "Ranshao zai Liangshan renmin xinli de xin chou jiu hen," in MGBZXN, 14.

26. "Xue zhai xue huan! Da duan Meidi qinlue zhe de mo shou!" in MGBZXN, 45–46.

27. "Kongsu Meijun baoxing jianjue kangMei yuanChao," "Meiguo bing zai Yunnan de zuixing, longxing," and "Xue zhai xue huan! Da duan Meidi qinlue zhe de mo shou!," in MGBZXN, 27, 4, 48–49.

28. Xia, "Meijun zai Zhanyi de xuexing tusha," in MGBZXN, 51–54.

29. Li, "Meiguo bing zai Chongqing tuwan he huangsha xi de baoxing," in MGBZXN, 1–3.

30. Van de Ven, *China at War*, 259–60; Masuda, "Public Reactions and the Shaping of 'Reality' in the Communist State," 9–12, 15–16.

31. Hou, "KangMei yuanChao yundong yu minzhong shehui xintai yanjiu," 21–22.

32. Van de Ven, *China at War*, 261; Chen, *China's Road to the Korean War*, 215; Pomfret, *Beautiful Country and the Middle Kingdom*, 384–88; Masuda, *Cold War Crucible*, 140–43; Kuech, "Imagining 'America' in Communist and Nationalist China," 86.

33. On false allegations against missionaries, see Pomfret, *Beautiful Country and the Middle Kingdom*, 383–84.

34. Craft, *American Justice in Taiwan*, 12, 35–46.

35. Craft, *American Justice in Taiwan*, 7–9, 60–91, 101–47, 181–93, 197.

36. Vine, *Base Nation*, 74–75, 78; Moon, *Sex among Allies*, 17.

37. Moon, *Sex among Allies*, 1. See also Enloe, *Bananas, Beaches, and Bases*, 1–2, 66–67, 81–87; Enloe, *Maneuvers*, 51–52, 91–96, 112–14; J. M. Miller, *Cold War Democracy*, 164–66; Takeuchi, "'Pan-Pan Girls' Performing and Resisting Neocolonialism(s) in the Pacific Theater," 78–108.

38. Scholars have illustrated how the power differential between host countries and the United States influences the degree of restrictions on the U.S. military in each SOFA, but race clearly influences SOFAs as well. See Craft, *American Justice in Taiwan*, 148–63; Vine, *United States of War*, 291–92; Höhn and Moon, *Over There*, 14–16.

39. S. Moon, "Camptown Prostitution and the Imperial SOFA," 354.

40. J. M. Miller, *Cold War Democracy*, 166.

41. Moon, *Sex among Allies*, 31; S. Moon, "Camptown Prostitution and the Imperial SOFA," 355.

42. Enloe, *Maneuvers*, 96.

43. Angst, "Sacrifice of a Schoolgirl," 243–66; Peter Landers, "Security Issues Loom as Hashimoto Makes First U.S. Trip," *AP News*, February 23, 1996.

44. Vine, *Base Nation*, 265; Simbulan, "People's Movement Responses to Evolving U.S. Military Activities in the Philippines," 157–58; Man, *Soldiering through Empire*, 74.

45. Mitchell, "U.S. Marine Corps Sexual Violence on Okinawa," 2–5.

46. Kovner, "Soundproofed Superpower," 87–109.

47. Enloe, *Bananas, Beaches, and Bases*, 66.

48. Höhn and Moon, *Over There*, 17. After 2003, protesters have demonstrated against noise, construction, and the role of bases in U.S. military operations. See Vine, *Base Nation*, 277–87.

49. Man, *Soldiering through Empire*, 6–10.

50. Fredman, "Specter of an Expansionist China," 111–36.

51. Man, *Soldiering through Empire*, 11–14.

52. On this process, see E. G. Miller, *Misalliance,* 6–7, 16–17, 214–77.

53. E. G. Miller, *Misalliance*, 290–94, 311–18. On Stilwell and Dorn plotting Chiang's removal, see van de Ven, *War and Nationalism in China*, 44.

54. Dallek, *Flawed Giant*, 99–100.

55. Watson Institute for International and Public Affairs, "Human and Budgetary Costs to Date of the U.S. War in Afghanistan, 2001–2022," https://watson.brown.edu /costsofwar/figures/2021/human-and-budgetary-costs-date-us-war-afghanistan -2001-2022.

56. On corruption, civilian casualties, and bigotry, see Gopal, *No Good Men among the Living*, 198, 273–76; Edstrom, *Un-American*, 2–8, 58, 123–29, 138–39, 143, 146–50, 162–64, 177–83, 198, 210–13.

57. On this pattern in Afghanistan, see Andrew Bacevich, "Why We Lost in Afghanistan," *Nation*, August 23, 2021.

Bibliography

Archives and Abbreviations

Mainland China

BMA	*Beijing shi dang'an guan*, Beijing Municipal Archives, Beijing
CMA	*Chongqing shi dang'an guan*, Chongqing Municipal Archives, Chongqing
SHAC	*Di er lishi dang'an guan*, Second Historical Archives of China, Nanjing
SMA	*Shanghai shi dang'an guan*, Shanghai Municipal Archives, Shanghai
TMA	*Tianjin shi dang'an guan*, Tianjin Municipal Archives, Tianjin
YPA	*Yunnan sheng dang'an guan*, Yunnan Provincial Archives, Kunming

Myanmar

MNA	National Archives Department of Myanmar, Yangon

Taiwan

AHA	*Guoshiguan*, Academia Historica Archives, Taipei
IMHA	*Wajiaobu dang'an*, Academia Sinica, Institute of Modern History Archives, Taipei

United Kingdom

CAC	The Churchill Archives Centre, Cambridge

United States

FSU	Center for the Study of World War II and the Human Experience, Florida State University, Tallahassee, Florida
HIA	Hoover Institution Archives, Palo Alto, California
HUA	Harvard University Archives, Cambridge, Massachusetts
McHD	Archives Branch, Marine Corps History Division, Quantico, Virginia
NARA	National Archives II, College Park, Maryland
USACMH	U.S. Army Center for Military History, Carlisle Barracks, Pennsylvania
VHP	Veterans History Project, Library of Congress, Washington, DC
WVM	Wisconsin Veterans Museum, Madison, Wisconsin

Online Archives and Sources

Annual Reports of the Department of the Navy, Gale Archives Unbound: Political, Economic, and Military Conditions in China.

Marxists Internet Archive.

Sichuan sheng renmin zhengfu waishi qiaowu (Gang Ao) bangong shi [Sichuan Provincial Foreign and Overseas Chinese (Hong Kong and Macao) Affairs Office].

Published Primary Sources and Memoirs

Beijing shi dang'an guan yanjiu shi, ed. "Beijing yu kangMei yuanChao" [Beijing and the Resist America and Aid Korea campaign]. *Lengzhan guoji shi yanjiu* 2 (2006): 392–466.

Cai Tong, ed. *Meidi baoxing* [American imperialist violence]. Beijing: Bei xin shu ju, 1951.

Chengdu tiyu xueyuan tiyushi yanjiusuo, ed. *Zhongguo jindai tiyushi ziliao* [Historical materials on the history of sport in Modern China]. Chengdu: Sichuan jiaoyu chubanshe, 1988.

Chennault, Claire. *Way of a Fighter: The Memoirs of Claire Lee Chennault.* New York: G. P. Putnam's Sons, 1949.

Chiang Kai-shek. *Xian zongtong Jiang gong sixiang yanlun ji (di 21 juan)* [Collected speeches and thoughts of President Chiang Kai-shek, vol. 21]. Edited by Qin Xiaoyi. Taipei: Zhongguo Guomindang zhongyang weiyuan hui dangshi weiyuan hui, 1984.

Chiang Kai-shek, and Philip Jaffe. *China's Destiny and Chinese Economic Theory.* Leiden: Brill, 2011. First published 1947 by Roy Publishers (New York).

Dong Jingxuan and Woerfugang. *Chongqing wangshi: Yige youtairen de wannian huiyi, 1940–1951* [Looking back on Chongqing: One Jewish man's memoirs, 1940–1951]. Xi'an: Shanxi chu ban she, 2014.

Dorn, Frank. *The Sino-Japanese War, 1937–1941: From Marco Polo Bridge to Pearl Harbor.* New York: Macmillan, 1974.

——. *Walkout: With Stilwell in Burma.* New York: Crowell, 1971.

Du Jianshi. "KangRi zhanzheng shiqi JiangMei goujie yu maodun" [Contradictions and collaboration between Chiang Kai-shek and the United States during the war of resistance]. *Wenshi ziliao* [Historical Materials] 57 (1978): 111–54.

Eskelund, Karl. *My Chinese Wife.* Garden City, NY: Doubleday, 1945.

Fu Shuti. "Mianbei zhanchang wubai tian—yige suijun yiyuan de huiyi" [Five hundred days on the Northern Burma front: Memoirs of a military interpreter]. *Beijing wenshi ziliao* [Beijing historical materials] 52 (1995): 68–77.

Guo Guanlin, ed. *Feihu xinzhuan: Zhong-Mei hunhe tuan koushu lishi* [The immortal Flying Tigers: An oral history of the Chinese American Composite Wing]. Taipei: Guofang bu shizheng bianyi shi, 2009.

Guo Guanqiu. "Liangci zhengdiao zai Meijun zhaodai suo." In *Guoli xinan lianhe daxue babai xuezi congjun huiyi* [Memoirs of the 800 Southwest associated university students who joined the military], edited by Xinan Lianda, 19–20. Beijing: Xinan Lianda 1944 ji, 2003.

Guofang bu junshi qingbao ju. *ZhongMei hezuo suo zhi* [Annals of the Sino-American Cooperative Organization]. Taipei: Guofang bu junshi qingbao ju, 2011.

Huang, J. L. *The Memoirs of J.L. Huang.* Taipei: Ying Chung chu ban she, 1984.

Huang Shang. *Guanyu Meiguo bing* [On American soldiers]. Shanghai: Shanghai chu ban she gongsi, 1946.

Jin Chongji. *Zhuanzhe niandai: Zhongguo de 1947 nian* [Turning point: China's 1947]. Beijing: Xinhua shu dian, 2002.

KangMei yuanChao zhuanji, ed. *Zang da erzi* [Zang Da Erzi]. Shanghai: Qunzhong shu dian, 1950.

King, Archibald. "Jurisdiction over Friendly Armed Forces." *American Journal of International Law* 36, no. 4 (October 1942): 539–67.

Kunming shi zhengxie wenshi xuexi weiyuan hui. *Kunming wenshi ziliao (KangRi zhanzheng-wujia)* [Kunming historical materials: Prices during the War of Resistance]. Kunming: Kunming shizhi bianzuan bangong shi, 1989.

Kwan, Stanley S. K. *The Dragon and the Crown: Hong Kong Memoirs.* With the collaboration and assistance of Nicole Kwan. Hong Kong: Hong Kong University Press, 2009.

Laodong chu ban she, ed. *Kong su de xue: Mei guo qiangdao zai Hua bao xing* [Denunciation: Violent behavior of American bandits in China]. Shanghai: Laodong chu ban she, 1950.

Letcher, John Seymour. *Goodbye to Old Peking: The Wartime Letters of U.S. Marine Captain John Seymour Letcher, 1937–1939.* Athens: Ohio University Press, 1998.

Li Shengting. "KangRi shengzhan wo zuo fanyi san nian yu" [Over three years of interpreter service in the righteous war of resistance]. *Zhuanji wenxue* 27, no. 7 (1975): 54–61.

Liao Gailong. "Wei shen me yao kai kongsu hui?" [Why do we need to hold denunciation meetings?]. In *Jixu shenru fadong qunzhong guanxhe kangMei yuanChao yu zhenya geming yundong* [Continue carrying out the Resist American and Suppress Counterrevolutionary campaigns], edited by Xinxiang shi kangMei yuanChao fen hui, 1951, 16–17. Xinxiang: Xinxiang shi kangMei yuanChao fen hui, 1951.

Liao Zuoqi. "Yu jun Jinling jianwen" [Reminiscences of Jinling, Yujun]. *Zhuanji wenxue* 78, no. 6 (2000).

Liu Danian. *Meidi qin Hua shi* [The history of American imperialist aggression in China]. Shanghai: Jiaoyu chu ban she, 1950.

Lv Yan. *Meidi de xuezhai* [The blood debt of American imperialism]. Shanghai: Bei xin shu ju, 1951.

McCarthy, James. *A Papago Traveler: The Memories of James McCarthy.* Tucson: University of Arizona Press, 1985.

Mei Zuyan. *Wannian suibi* [Writings from my later years]. Beijing: Qinghua daxue chu ban she, 2004.

Miles, Milton. *A Different Kind of War.* New York: Doubleday, 1967.

Office of the Under Secretary of Defense (Comptroller)/Chief Financial Officer. *Operation and Maintenance Overview: Fiscal Year 2020 Budget Estimates.* March 2019. https://comptroller.defense.gov/Portals/45/Documents/defbudget /fy2020/fy2020_OM_Overview.pdf.

Peck, Graham. *Two Kinds of Time.* Seattle: University of Washington Press, 2008.

Qing nian bao, ed. *Wo kong su!* [I denounce!]. Shanghai: Qing nian chu ban she, 1950.

Renmin chu ban she, ed. *Meijun zhu Hua shiqi de xuezhai* [The U.S. military's blood debt in China]. Beijing: Ren min chu ban she, 1950.

Rittenberg, Sidney, and Amanda Bennett. *The Man Who Stayed Behind.* New York: Simon and Schuster, 1993.

Shen Keqin. *Sun Liren zhuan* [Biography of Sun Liren]. Taipei: Xuesheng shuju youxian gongsi, 2005.

Shen Zui. *Shen Zui huyi lu: Juntong neimu, yige juntong tewu de chanhui lu* [Memoirs of Shen Zui: Inside story of the Bureau of Investigation and Statistics, a secret agent's confession]. Beijing: Zhongguo wenshi chu ban she, 2016.

Sledge, E. B. *China Marine: An Infantryman's Life after World War II.* Oxford: Oxford University Press, 2002.

Stoddard, Lothrop. *The Rising Tide of Color against White World-Supremacy.* New York: Charles Scribner's Sons, 1920.

Sun Ke. "Zhankai 'mengjun zhiyou' yundong" [Launch the "Friends of the Allied Forces" Movement]. *Xinyun daobao* [New Life Guide] 11, no. 2 (1944): 39–41.

Sunan wenlian chou wei hui, ed. *Meidi baoxing jishi* [Documentary record of American imperialist violence]. Nanjing: Sunan wenlian chou wei hui, 1951.

Tsu, Andrew Yu Yue. *Friend of Fisherman.* Atlanta: Trinity Press, 1951.

Tunner, William. *Over the Hump.* New York: Duell, Sloan, and Pearce, 1964.

U.S. Army, Branch Office of the Judge Advocate General. *Holdings and Opinions Board of Review: Branch Office of the Judge Advocate General, CBI and IBT.* 2 vols. Washington, DC: Office of the Judge Advocate General, 1946.

U.S. Army Service Forces. *A Pocket Guide to Australia.* Washington, DC: War and Navy Departments, 1942.

——. *A Pocket Guide to China.* Washington, DC: War and Navy Departments, 1943.

——. *A Short Guide to Britain.* Washington, DC: War and Navy Departments, 1942.

——. *A Short Guide to New Zealand.* Washington, DC: War and Navy Departments, 1942.

U.S. Department of State. *The China White Paper, August 1949.* Stanford, CA: Stanford University Press, 1967.

——. *Executive Agreement Series.* Washington, DC: Government Printing Office, 1937–.

——. *Foreign Relations of the United States: Diplomatic Papers, 1945, the Far East, China.* Washington, DC: Government Printing Office, 1969.

——. *Foreign Relations of the United States: Diplomatic Papers, 1944, China.* Washington, DC: Government Printing Office, 1967.

——. *Foreign Relations of the United States: Diplomatic Papers, 1946, the Far East, China.* Washington, DC: Government Printing Office, 1972.

——. *Foreign Relations of the United States: Diplomatic Papers, 1943, China.* Washington, DC: Government Printing Office, 1965.

——. *Foreign Relations of the United States: Diplomatic Papers, 1942, China.* Washington, DC: Government Printing Office, 1956.

U.S. War Department. *WAC Life* (War Department Pamphlet 35-3). Washington, DC: War Department, 1945.

Wang Demao. "Wo zuo Meijun fanyi guan de rizi" [My days as an interpreting officer with the US Army]. In collaboration with Wang Liexian. *Wenshi tiandi* [Literature and history world] 8 (2015): 77.

Wedemeyer, Albert. *Wedemeyer Reports!* New York: Henry Holt, 1958.

Wei ren chu ban she, ed. *Meiguo bing zai xinan* [American servicemen in Southwest China]. Chongqing: Wei ren chu ban she, 1951.

Weng Xinjun. "Nan wang de junshi yiyuan shenghuo" [Unforgettable military interpreter life]. *Beijing wenshi ziliao* [Beijing historical materials] 52 (1995): 1–47.

White, Theodore, ed. *The Stilwell Papers*. New York: W. Sloane, 1948.

White, Theodore, and Annalee Jacoby. *Thunder Out of China.* New York: W. Sloane, 1946.

Wu Fu, ed. *Meiguo—Yi ge sha ren he xue de guojia* [America: A murderous blood-drinking country]. Beijing: Xin hu shu dian, 1951.

Xinan Lianda. *Guoli xinan lianhe daxue babai xuezi congjun huiyi* [Memoirs of the 800 Southwest Associated University students who joined the military]. Beijing: Xinan Lianda, 1944 ji, 2003.

Xiong Shihui. *Hai sang ji—Xiong Shihui de huiyi lu* [An Insider's account of modern Chinese history: Memoirs of Governor and General Xiong Shihui, 1907–1949]. Taipei: Mingjing chu ban she, 2008.

Yang Baoguang. "Wo wei Meijun dang fanyi" [I served as an interpreter for the U.S. Army]. *Zongheng* [Sweep over] 5 (1995): 56–60.

Yang Yuxiang, ed. *Erzhan Zhong-Yin-Mian zhanchang Zhongguo yiyuan* [Chinese interpreters in the CBI theater during World War II]. Kunming: Feihudui yanjiu yuan, 2008.

Yao Baohuang. "Wo wei Meijun dang yiyuan" [I served as an interpreter for the U.S. military]. *Zongheng* [Sweep over] 5 (1995): 55–56.

Yunnan sheng dang'an guan, ed. *Nan wang feihudui* [Unforgettable Flying Tigers]. Kunming: Yunnan renmin chu ban she, 2011.

Zhang Airong, and Guo Jianrong, eds. *Guoli xinan lianhe daxue shiliao (er) huiyi jilu juan* [Southwest Associated University historical materials. Vol. 2, Meeting records]. Kunming: Yunnan jiaoyu chu ban she, 1998.

Zhonggong Beijing shiwei dangshi yanjiu shi, ed. *Kangyi Meijun zhuhua baoxing yundong ziliao huibian* [Collected materials on the Anti-American Brutality Movement]. Beijing: Beijing daxue chu ban she, 1989.

Zhongguo Guomindang zhongyang weiyuan hui. *Xian zongtong Jiang gong sixiang yanlun zongji* [The thoughts and speeches of President Chiang Kai-shek], Vol. 32. Taipei: Zhongguo Guomindang zhongyang dangshi weiyuan hui, 1984.

Zhongguo minzhu tongmeng zhonguang weiyuan hui. *Zhongguo minzhu tongmeng lishi wenxian, 1941–1949* [Historical documents of the China Democratic League, 1941–1949]. Beijing: Zhongguo shehui kexue chu ban she, 1983.

Zhongguo renmin baowei shijie heping fandui Meiguo qinlue zhe weiyuan hui Guangzhou fen hui, ed. *Bu gong dai tian de chou hen* [Inveterate hatred]. Guangzhou: Xin xing yin shu guan, 1950.

Zhongguo renmin zhengzhi xieshang huiyi Beijing shi weiyuan hui wenshi ziliao yanjiu weiyuan hui. *Beiping dixia dang douzheng shiliao* [Historical materials on the Chinese Communist Party's underground struggles in Beiping]. Beijing: Beijing chu ban she, 1988.

Zhonghua minguo zhongyao shiliao chu bian. *DuiRi kangzhan shiqi disan bian: Zhanshi waijiao* [War of resistance. Vol. 3, Wartime foreign relations]. Taipei: Zhongguo guomindang zhongyang weiyuan hui dangshi weiyuan hui, 1981.

Zhou, Meihua, ed. *Jiang Zhongzheng zongtong de dang'an: Shilue gaoben* (Archives of President Chiang Kai-shek: Biographical sketch). Taipei: Guo shi guan, 2011–.

Zhuang, Long. *Meijun zai Zhongguo de baoxing* [The U.S. military's violence in China]. Shanghai: Da dong shu ju, 1951.

Periodicals

CBI Roundup
China Lantern
China Marine Scuttlebutt
Da gong bao [L'impartial]
Dongfang zazhi [Eastern miscellany]
Duzhi [Reader]
Funv qikan [Women's magazine]
Guangxi ribao [Guangxi daily]
Guoli zhongyang daxue xiaokan [National Central University journal]
Guomin gongbao [National bulletin]
Haijing zhoubao [Haijing weekly]
Haiyan [Petrel]
Heibai zhoubao [Black and white weekly]
Heping ribao [Peace daily]
Information Pamphlets on China
Liangzhou pinglun [Fortnightly news]
Life
Meizhou yibao [Weekly translated news]
Minzhu zhoukan [Democracy weekly]
Nanjing Xinmin bao [The Nanjing New People's paper]
New York Times
North China Marine
PM Magazine
Renmin ribao [People's daily]
Qiri tan [Heptaméron]
Qunzhong [The masses]
Saodang bao [Sweeping away]
Shanghai Evening Post and Mercury
Shanghai Stars and Stripes
Shen bao [Shanghai news]
Shidai fengcai [Modern elegance]
Shidai xuesheng [Student times]
Shishi xinbao [China times]
Tsinghua xiaoyou tongxun [Tsinghua alumni newsletter]
Wenhui bao [Wenhui daily]
Xi feng [West wind]
Xiandai funv [Modern woman]
Xin Shanghai [New Shanghai]
Xingqi zhoukan [Weekly newsweekly]
Xinwen tiandi [News universe]
Xinxin xinwen [Latest news]
Xinyun dao bao [New life guide]
Yank: The Army Weekly
Yenching News
Yishi bao [Social welfare]
Yixun xunkan [Interpreter dispatch] (ten-day periodical)
Yunnan ribao [Yunnan daily]
Zhengyi bao [Justice]
Zhongyang ribao [Central daily news]
Zhoubao [Weekly news]

Secondary Sources

Alexander, Bevin. *The Strange Connection: U.S. Intervention in China, 1944–1972.* New York: Greenwood Press, 1992.

Allen, Roy George Douglas. "Mutual Aid between the U.S. and the British Empire, 1941–1945." *Journal of the Royal Statistical Society* 109, no. 3 (1946): 243–71.

Alvah, Donna. "U.S. Military Personnel and Families Abroad: Gender, Sexuality, Race, and Power in the U.S. Military's Relations with Foreign Nations and Local Inhabitants during Wartime." In *The Routledge History of Gender, War, and the U.S. Military,* edited by Kara D. Vuic, 247–86. New York: Routledge, 2018.

Angst, Linda Isako. "The Sacrifice of a Schoolgirl: The 1995 Rape Case, Discourses of Power, and Women's Lives in Okinawa." *Critical Asian Studies* 33, no. 2 (2001): 243–66.

Arkush, R. David, and Leo O. Lee. *Land without Ghosts: Chinese Impressions of American from the Mid-Nineteenth Century to the Present.* Berkeley: University of California Press, 1989.

Arrighi, Giovanni, Po-keung Hui, Ho-fung Hung, and Mark Selden. "Historical Capitalism, East and West." In *The Resurgence of East Asia: 500, 150 and 50 Year Perspectives,* edited by Giovanni Arrighi, Takeshi Hamashita, and Mark Selden, 259–333. London: Routledge, 2003.

Babb, Geoff. "The Harmony of Yin and Yank: The American Military Advisory Effort in China, 1941–1945." PhD diss., University of Kansas, 2012.

Bacevich, Andrew J. *American Empire: The Realities and Consequences of U.S. Diplomacy.* Cambridge, MA: Harvard University Press, 2002.

———. *America's War for the Greater Middle East: A Military History.* New York: Random House, 2016.

Bailey, Beth L., and David Farber. *The First Strange Place: Race and Sex in World War II Hawaii.* Baltimore: Johns Hopkins University Press, 1992.

Baker, Anni P. *American Soldiers Overseas: The Global Military Presence.* Westport, CT: Praeger, 2004.

Baker, Mona. "Interpreters and Translators in the War Zone." *Translator* 16, no. 2 (2010): 197–222.

Barker, Anthony J., and Lisa Jackson. *Fleeting Attraction: A Social History of American Servicemen in Western Australia during the Second World War.* Nedlands: University of Western Australia Press, 1996.

Bayly, Christopher, and Tim Harper. *Forgotten Armies: The Fall of British Asia, 1941–1945.* Cambridge, MA: Belknap Press of Harvard University Press, 2005.

Bays, Michael H., and Ellen Widmer, eds. *China's Christian Colleges: Cross-Cultural Connections, 1900–1950.* Stanford, CA: Stanford University Press, 2009.

Bederman, Gail. *Manliness and Civilization: A Cultural History of Gender and Race in the United States, 1880–1917.* Chicago: University of Chicago Press, 1995.

Bender, Daniel E., and Jana K. Lipman, eds. *Making the Empire Work: Labor and United States Imperialism.* New York: New York University Press, 2015.

Bickers, Robert. *Out of China: How the Chinese Ended the Era of Western Domination.* Cambridge, MA: Harvard University Press, 2017.

Bieler, Stacey. *"Patriots" or "Traitors"? A History of American-Educated Chinese Students.* London: Routledge, 2003.

Bioletti, Harry. *The Yanks Are Coming: The American Invasion of New Zealand, 1942–1944.* London: Century Hutchinson, 1989.

Bjorge, Gary J. *Moving the Enemy: Operational Art in the Chinese PLA's Huai Hai Campaign.* Leavenworth, KS: Military Bookshop, 2010.

Blower, Brooke. "Nation of Outposts: Forts, Factories, Bases, and the Making of American Power." *Diplomatic History* 41 no. 3 (2017): 439–59.

———. "V-J Day, 1945, Times Square." In *The Familiar Made Strange: American Icons and Artefacts after the Transnational Turn,* edited by Brooke L. Blower and Mark Philip Bradley, 70–87. Ithaca, NY: Cornell University Press, 2015.

Bradley, James. *The China Mirage: The Hidden History of American Disaster in Asia.* Boston: Little, Brown, 2015.

Bradley, Mark Philip. *Imagining America and Vietnam: The Making of Postcolonial Vietnam, 1919–1950.* Chapel Hill: University of North Carolina Press, 2000.

Brady, Anne-Marie. *Making the Foreign Serve China: Managing Foreigners in the People's Republic.* Lanham, MD: Rowman and Littlefield, 2003.

Braisted, William R. *Diplomats in Blue: U.S. Naval Officers in China, 1922–1933.* Gainesville: University Press of Florida, 2009.

Briggs, Laura. *Reproducing Empire: Race, Sex, Science, and U.S. Imperialism in Puerto Rico.* Berkeley: University of California Press, 2002.

Bristow, Nancy. *Making Men Moral: Social Engineering during the Great War.* New York: New York University Press, 1997.

Brooks, Charlotte. *American Exodus: Second-Generation Chinese Americans in China, 1901–1949.* Oakland: University of California Press, 2019.

Callahan, William A. *China: The Pessoptimist Nation.* Oxford: Oxford University Press, 2010.

———. "National Insecurities: Humiliation, Salvation, and Chinese Nationalism." *Alternatives* 29 (2004): 199–218.

Campanella, Thomas J. *The Concrete Dragon: China's Urban Revolution and What It Means for the World.* Princeton, NJ: Princeton Architectural Press, 2008.

Cao, Yin. "Establishing the Ramgarh Training Center: The Burma Campaign, the Colonial Internment Camp, and the Wartime Sino-British Relations." *TRaNS: Trans-Regional and National Studies of Southeast Asia* 9, no. 1 (2020): 1–10.

Capozzola, Christopher. *Bound by War: How the United States and the Philippines Built America's First Pacific Century.* New York: Basic Books, 2020.

Carruthers, Susan L. *The Good Occupation: American Soldiers and the Hazards of Peace.* Cambridge, MA: Harvard University Press, 2016.

Cate, James Lea. "The Twentieth Air Force and Matterhorn." In *The Army Air Forces in World War II.* Vol. 5, *The Pacific: Matterhorn to Nagasaki, June 1944 to August 1945,* edited by Wesley Frank Craven and James Lea Cate, 3–175. Washington, DC: Government Printing Office, 1953.

Cathcart, Adam. "Atrocities, Insults, and 'Jeep Girls': Depictions of the US Military in China." *International Journal of Comic Art* 10, no. 1 (2008): 140–54.

Chang Jui-te. *Kangzhan shiqi de guojun renshi* [Anatomy of the Nationalist Army during the War of Resistance]. Taibei: Zhongyang yanjiu yuan, 1993.

———. "The Nationalist Army on the Eve of the War." In *The Battle for China: Essays on the Military History of the Sino-Japanese War of 1937–1945*, edited by Mark Peattie, Edward Drea, and Hans van de Ven, 83–104. Stanford, CA: Stanford University Press, 2010.

Chen, Jian. "The Myth of America's 'Lost Chance' in China: A Chinese Perspective in Light of New Evidence." *Diplomatic History* 21, no. 1 (1997): 77–86.

Ch'en, Jerome. *China and the West: Society and Culture, 1815–1937*. Bloomington: Indiana University Press, 1979.

Cheng, Sealing. *On the Move for Love: Migrant Entertainers and the U.S. Military in South Korea*. Philadelphia: University of Pennsylvania Press, 2011.

Cheng, Yinghong. "From Campus Racism to Cyber Racism: Discourse of Race and Chinese Nationalism." *China Quarterly* 207 (September 2011): 561–79.

Ch'i Hsi-sheng. *Jianbanuzhang de mengyou: Taiping yang zhanzheng shiqi de ZhongMei junshi hezuo guanxi, 1941–1945* [Allies at loggerheads: Chinese-American military cooperation during the Pacific War]. Beijing: Shehui kexue wenxian chu ban she, 2012.

———. *Nationalist China at War: Military Defeats and Political Collapse, 1937–1945*. Ann Arbor: University of Michigan Press, 1982.

Chin, Sei Jeong. "The Historical Origins of the Nationalization of the Newspaper Industry in Modern China: A Case Study of the Shanghai Newspaper Industry, 1937–1953." *China Review* 13, no. 2 (2013): 1–34.

Chor, So Wai. "The Making of the Guomindang's Japan Policy, 1932–1937: The Roles of Chiang Kai-shek and Wang Jingwei." *Modern China* 28, no. 2 (2002): 213–52.

Chung, Yuehtsen Juliette. "Better Science and Better Race? Social Darwinism and Chinese Eugenics." *Isis* 105, no. 4 (2014): 793–802.

Clark, Arthur W. *Eyes of the Tiger: China 1944–1945*. Chapel Hill, NC: Arthur W. Clark, 2015.

Clark, George B. *Treading Softly: U.S. Marines in China, 1819–1949*. Westport, CT: Greenwood Press, 2001.

Coats, K. S., and W. R. Morrison. *The Alaska Highway in World War II: The U.S. Army Occupation of Canada's Northwest*. Norman: University of Oklahoma Press, 1992.

Coble, Parks M. *China's War Reporters: The Legacy of Resistance against Japan*. Cambridge, MA: Harvard University Press, 2015.

———. *The Shanghai Capitalists and the Nationalist Government, 1927–1937*. Cambridge, MA: Harvard University Press, 1986.

Coffman, Edward M. "The American 15th Infantry Regiment in China, 1912–1938: A Vignette in Social History." *Journal of Military History* 58, no. 1 (1994): 57–74.

Cohen, Paul A. *China Unbound: Evolving Perspectives on the Chinese Past.* London: Routledge, 2003.

———. *Discovering History in China: American Writing on the Recent Chinese Past.* 1984. Reissue, New York: Columbia University Press, 2010.

———. *History in Three Keys: The Boxers as Event, Experience, and Myth.* New York: Columbia University Press, 1998.

———. "Remembering and Forgetting National Humiliation in Twentieth-Century China." *Twentieth-Century China* 27, no. 2 (2002): 1–39.

Cohen, Warren I. *The Chinese Connection: Roger S. Greene, Thomas W. Lamont, George E. Sokolsky, and American-East Asian Relations.* New York: Columbia University Press, 1978.

Cong, Xiaoping. *Teachers' Schools and the Making of the Modern Chinese Nation-State, 1897–1937.* Vancouver: University of British Columbia Press, 2011.

Converse, Elliot V., Daniel K. Gibran, John A. Cash, Robert K. Griffith, and Richard H. Kohn. *The Exclusion of Black Soldiers from the Medal of Honor in World War II.* Jefferson, NC: McFarland, 1997.

Cooley, Alexander. *Base Politics: Democratic Change and the U.S. Military Overseas.* Ithaca, NY: Cornell University Press, 2008.

Cornebise, Alfred Emile. *The United States Army in China, 1900–1938.* Jefferson, NC: McFarland, 2015.

———. *The United States 15th Infantry Regiment in China, 1912–1938.* Jefferson, NC: McFarland, 2004.

Craft, Stephen G. *American Justice in Taiwan: The 1957 Riots and Cold War Foreign Policy.* Lexington: University of Kentucky Press, 2016.

Craven, Wesley F., and James L. Cate, eds. *The Army Air Forces in World War II.* Vol. 6, *Men and Planes.* Washington, DC: Office of Air Force History, 1984.

Daggett, Stephen. "Costs of Major U.S. Wars." *Library of Congress Congressional Research Service*, June 29, 2010.

Dallek, Robert. *Flawed Giant: Lyndon Johnson and His Times.* New York: Oxford University Press, 1998.

Daugherty, Leo J., III. *The Allied Resupply Effort in the China-Burma-India Theater during World War II.* Jefferson, NC: McFarland, 2008.

Dikötter, Frank. *The Age of Openness: China before Mao.* Berkeley: University of California Press, 2008.

———. "Culture, 'Race,' and Nation: The Formation of National Identity in Twentieth Century China." *Journal of Interdisciplinary Affairs* 49, no. 2 (1996): 590–605.

———. *The Discourse of Race in Modern China.* Oxford: Oxford University Press, 1992.

———. "Racial Identities in China: Context and Meaning." *China Quarterly* 138 (1994): 404–12.

Donoghue, Michael. *Borderland on the Isthmus: Race, Culture, and the Struggle for the Canal Zone.* Durham, NC: Duke University Press, 2014.

Dower, John. *Embracing Defeat: Japan in the Wake of World War II.* New York: W. W. Norton, 1999.

Dreyer, Edward R. *China at War, 1901–1949.* New York: Longman, 1995.

Duara, Prasenjit. "The Chinese World Order in Historical Perspective: The Imperialism of Nation-States or Soft Power." *China and the World: Ancient and Modern Silk Road* 2, no. 4 (2019): 1–33.

———. "The Cold War as a Historical Period: An Interpretive Essay." *Journal of Global History* 6, no. 3 (2011): 457–80.

———. "De-Constructing the Chinese Nation: How Recent Is It?" In *The Global and Regional in China's Nation Formation*, edited by Prasenjit Duara, 97–116. London: Routledge, 2009.

———. "The Regime of Authenticity: Timelessness, Gender, and National History in Modern China." *History and Theory* 37, no. 3 (1998): 287–308.

———. *Rescuing History from the Nation: Questioning Narratives of Modern China.* Chicago: University of Chicago Press, 1996.

Eastman, Lloyd. "Nationalist China during the Sino-Japanese War, 1937–1945." In *The Nationalist Era in China, 1927–1949*, edited by Lloyd E. Eastman, Jerome Ch'en, Suzanne Pepper, and Lyman P. Van Slyke, 115–76. Cambridge: Cambridge University Press, 1991.

———. *Seeds of Destruction: Nationalist China in War and Revolution, 1937–1945.* Stanford, CA: Stanford University Press, 1984.

Edstrom, Erik. *Un-American: A Soldier's Reckoning of Our Longest War.* New York: Bloomsbury, 2020.

Edwards, Louise. "Policing the Modern Woman in Republican China." *Modern China* 26, no. 2 (2000): 115–47.

Ehrman, James M. "Ways of War and the American Experience in the China-Burma-India Theater, 1942–1945." PhD diss., Kansas State University, 2006.

Ekbladh, David. *The Great American Mission: Modernization and the Construction of an American World Order.* Princeton, NJ: Princeton University Press, 2009.

Enloe, Cynthia. *Bananas, Beaches, and Bases: Making Feminist Sense of International Politics.* Berkeley: University of California Press, 1990.

———. *Does Khaki Become You? The Militarization of Women's Lives.* Boston: South End Press, 1983.

———. *Maneuvers: The International Politics of Militarizing Women's Lives.* Berkeley: University of California Press, 2000.

Erksine, Kristopher. "Frank W. Price, 1895–1974: The Role of an American Missionary in Sino-US Relations." PhD diss., University of Hong Kong, 2013.

Fang Rennian, ed. *Wen Yiduo zai Meiguo* [Wen Yiduo in the United States]. Shanghai: Huadong shifan daxue chu ban she, 1985.

Ferlanti, Federica. "The New Life Movement at War: Wartime Mobilisation and State Control in Chongqing and Chengdu, 1938–1942." *European Journal of East Asian Studies* 11, no. 2 (2012): 187–212.

Footitt, Hilary, and Simona Tobia. *War Talk: Foreign Languages and the British War Effort in Europe.* London: Palgrave Macmillan, 2013.

Ford, Daniel. *Flying Tigers: Claire Chennault and His American Volunteers, 1941–1942.* New York: Smithsonian Books, 2007.

Foster, Anne. *Projections of Power: The United States and Europe in Colonial Southeast Asia, 1919–1941.* Durham, NC: Duke University Press, 2010.

Fredman, Zach. "Lofty Expectations and Bitter Reality: Chinese Interpreters for the US Army during the Second World War, 1941–1945." *Frontiers of History in China* 12, no. 4 (2017): 566–98.

———. "The Longer History of Imperial Incidents on the Yangtze." *Modern American History* 3, no. 1 (2020): 87–91.

———. "Military Occupations and Overseas Bases in Twentieth-Century U.S. Foreign Relations." In *A Companion to U.S. Foreign Relations: Colonial Era to the Present*, edited by Christopher R. W. Dietrich, 596–612. Hoboken, NJ: Wiley, 2020.

———. "The Specter of an Expansionist China: Kennedy Administration Assessments of Chinese Intentions in Vietnam." *Diplomatic History* 38, no. 1 (2014): 111–36.

Fussell, Paul. *Wartime: Understanding Behavior in the Second World War.* New York: Oxford University Press, 1989.

Gallicchio, Marc. "The Other China Hands: U.S. Army Officers and America's Failure in China, 1941–1950." *Journal of American-East Asian Relations* 4, no. 1 (1995): 49–72.

———. *The Scramble for Asia: U.S. Military Power in the Aftermath of the Pacific War.* Lanham, MD: Rowman and Littlefield, 2008.

Garver, John W. "Little Chance: Revolutions and Ideologies." *Diplomatic History* 21, no. 1 (1997): 87–94.

Gillem, Mark L. *America Town: Building the Outposts of Empire.* Minneapolis: University of Minnesota Press, 2007.

Glantz, David. *August Storm: The Soviet Strategic Offensive in Manchuria, 1945.* Fort Leavenworth, KS: Combat Studies Institute, U.S. Army Command and General Staff College, 1983.

Go, Julian, and Anne L. Foster, eds. *The American Colonial State in the Philippines: Global Perspectives.* Durham, NC: Duke University Press, 2003.

Gobat, Michael. *Confronting the American Dream: Nicaragua Under U.S. Imperial Rule.* Durham, NC: Duke University Press, 2005.

Goedde, Petra. *GIs and Germans: Culture, Gender, and Foreign Relations.* New Haven, CT: Yale University Press, 2003.

Gopal, Anand. *No Good Men among the Living: America, the Taliban, and the War through Afghan Eyes.* New York: Metropolitan Books, 2014.

Gou Kunming. "Huang Renlin yu Lizhe shi" [Huang Renlin and the Officers' Moral Endeavor Association]. *Minguo Chunqiu* [Republican annals] 1 (1998): 20–22.

Grieve, William George. "Belated Endeavor: The American Military Mission to China (AMMISCA), 1941–1942." PhD diss., University of Illinois at Urbana-Champaign, 1979.

Gronewald, Sue. *Beautiful Merchandise: Prostitution in China, 1860–1936.* London: Routledge, 1985.

Guldin, Gregory Eliyu. *The Saga of Anthropology in China: From Malinowski to Moscow to Mao.* London: Routledge, 1994.

Guo, Ting. *Surviving in Violent Conflicts: Chinese Interpreters in the Second Sino-Japanese War, 1931–45.* London: Palgrave, 2016.

Guo, Xixiao. "The Anticlimax of an Ill-Starred Sino-American Encounter." *Modern Asian Studies* 35, no. 1 (2001): 217–44.

———. "Paradise or Hell Hole? U.S. Marines in Post–World War II China." *Journal of American-East Asian Relations* 7, no. 3–4 (1998): 157–85.

Harmsen, Peter. *Shanghai 1937: Stalingrad on the Yangtze.* Philadelphia: Casemate, 2013.

Harrison, Henrietta. *China: Inventing the Nation.* London: Arnold, 2001.

He Hui. "Xin Zhongguo minzhong dui Meiguo de renzhi ji qi bianhua" [Changes in the public perception of the United States in new China]. *Lengzhan guoji shi yanjiu* [International Cold War History Research] 2 (2012): 47–62.

Henriot, Christian. *Prostitution and Sexuality in Shanghai: A Social History, 1849–1949.* Cambridge: Cambridge University Press, 2001.

Hershatter, Gail. *Dangerous Pleasures: Prostitution and Modernity in Twentieth-Century Shanghai.* Berkeley: University of California Press, 1997.

———. *Women and China's Revolutions.* Lanham, MD: Rowman and Littlefield, 2018.

Herzstein, Robert E. *Henry R. Luce, "Time," and the American Crusade in Asia.* Cambridge: Cambridge University Press, 2005.

Hiltner, Aaron. *Taking Leave, Taking Liberties: American Troops on the World War II Home Front.* Chicago: University of Chicago Press, 2020.

Hlavacek, John. *Letters Home: An American in China: 1939–1944.* Omaha, NE: Hlucky Books, 2004.

Hobsbawm, Eric. *The Age of Extremes: A History of the World, 1914–1991.* New York: Vintage, 1994.

Hoganson, Kristin L. *Fighting for American Manhood: How Gender Politics Provoked the Spanish-American and Philippine-American Wars.* New Haven, CT: Yale University Press, 1998.

Höhn, Maria. *GIs and Fräuleins: The German-American Encounter in 1950s West Germany.* Chapel Hill: University of North Carolina Press, 2002.

Höhn, Maria, and Seugsook Moon, eds. *Over There: Living with the US Military Empire from World War II to the Present.* Durham, NC: Duke University Press, 2011.

Hou Songtao. "KangMei yuanChao yundong yu minzhong shehui xintai yanjiu" [Social attitudes of the Chinese populace during the war to resist America and aid Korea]. *Zhonggong dangshi yanjiu* [Party history research] 2 (2005): 19–29.

Howard, Joshua H. "The Politicization of Women Workers at War: Labour in Chongqing's Cotton Mills during the Anti-Japanese War." *Modern Asian Studies* 47, no. 6 (2013): 1888–1940.

Hsu, Madeline Y. *The Good Immigrants: How the Yellow Peril Became the Model Minority.* Princeton, NJ: Princeton University Press, 2015.

Hsuing, James, and Steven I. Levine, eds. *China's Bitter Victory: War with Japan, 1937–1945.* London: Routledge, 1992.

Huebner, Jon W. "Chinese Anti-Americanism, 1946–1948." *Australian Journal of Chinese Affairs* 17 (1987): 115–25.

Hung, Chang-Tai. "The Fuming Image: Cartoons and Public Opinion in Late Republican China, 945–1949." *Comparative Studies in Society and History* 36, no. 1 (1994): 122–45.

Hunt, Michael. "The Forgotten Occupation: Peking, 1900–1901." *Pacific Historical Review* 48, no. 4 (1979): 501–29.

———. *The Making of a Special Relationship: China and the United States to 1914.* New York: Columbia University Press, 1985.

Immerwahr, Daniel. *How to Hide an Empire: A History of the Greater United States.* New York: Farrar, Straus and Giroux, 2019.

———. *Thinking Small: The United States and the Lure of Community Development.* Cambridge, MA: Harvard University Press, 2015.

———. "The Ugly American: Peeling the Onion of an Iconic Cold War Text." *Journal of American-East Asian Relations* 26, no. 1 (2019): 7–20.

Inghilleri, Moira. "Translators in War Zones: Ethics under Fire in Iraq." In *Globalization, Political Violence and Translation*, edited by Esperanza Bielsa and Christopher Hughes, 207–21. London: Palgrave Macmillan, 2009.

Israel, John. *Lianda: A Chinese University in War and Revolution.* Stanford, CA: Stanford University Press, 1998.

———. *Student Nationalism in China, 1927–1937.* Stanford, CA: Stanford University Press, 1966.

Jacobson, Matthew Frye. *Barbarian Virtues: The United States Encounters Foreign Peoples at Home and Abroad, 1876–1917.* New York: Hill and Wang, 2000.

Jespersen, T. Christopher. *American Images of China, 1931–1949.* Stanford, CA: Stanford University Press, 1996.

Johnson, Akemi. *Night in the American Village: Women in the Shadow of U.S. Military Bases in Okinawa.* New York: New Press, 2019.

Johnson, Chalmers. *Blowback: The Costs and Consequences of American Empire.* New York: Metropolitan Books, 2000.

———. *The Sorrows of Empire: Militarism, Secrecy, and the End of the Republic.* New York: Metropolitan Books, 2004.

———. "Three Rapes: The Status of Forces Agreement and Okinawa." *Asia Pacific Journal: Japan Focus* 1, no. 4 (2004): 1–19.

Johnson, Clare Torrey. *Ambassador to Three Cultures: The Life of Dr. R.A. Torrey Jr.* Phoenix: Jesus Abbey, 1990.

Johnson, Matthew. "Anti-Imperialism as Strategy: Masking the Edges of Foreign Entanglements in Civil War-Era China, 1945–1948." In *Overcoming Empire in Post-Imperial East Asia: Repatriation, Redress, and Rebuilding*, edited by Barak Kushner and Serzod Muminov, 123–45. London: Bloomsbury, 2019.

Juvinall, Ben. "Heaven or Hell: The Plight of Former Wartime Interpreters of the Iraq and Afghanistan Conflicts Living in the U.S." *Michigan State University International Law Review* 205 (2013): 205–27.

Karl, Rebecca E. *Staging the World: Chinese Nationalism and the Turn of the Twentieth Century.* Durham, NC: Duke University Press, 2002.

Karlin, Mara. "Why Military Assistance Programs Disappoint: Minor Tools Can't Solve Major Problems." *Foreign Affairs* 96, no. 6 (Nov./Dec. 2017): 111–20.

Kendi, Ibram X. *How to Be an Antiracist.* New York: One World, 2019.

——. *Stamped from the Beginning: The Definitive History of Racist Ideas in America.* New York: Bold Type Books, 2016.

Kim, Han Sang. "*My Car* Modernity: What the U.S. Army Brought to South Korean Cinematic Imagination about Modern Mobility." *Journal of Asian Studies* 75, no. 1 (2016): 63–85.

Kim, Phil Ho, and Hyunjoon Shin. "The Birth of 'Rok': Cultural Imperialism, Nationalism, and the Glocalization of Rock Music in South Korea, 1964–1975." *Positions* 18, no. 1 (2010): 199–230.

King, Archibald. "Further Developments concerning Jurisdiction over Friendly Foreign Armed Forces." *American Journal of International Law* 40, no. 2 (1946): 257–79.

Kovner, Sarah. *Occupying Power: Sex Workers and Servicemen in Postwar Japan.* Stanford, CA: Stanford University Press, 2012.

——. "The Soundproofed Superpower: American Bases and Japanese Communities, 1945–1972." *Journal of Asian Studies* 75, no. 1 (2016): 87–109.

Kramer, Paul A. *Blood of Government: Race, Empire, the United States, and the Philippines.* Chapel Hill: University of North Carolina Press, 2006.

——. "Power and Connection: Imperial Historians of the United States in the World." *American Historical Review* 116, no. 5 (2011): 1348–91.

——. "Race-Making and Colonial Violence in the U.S. Empire: The Philippine-American War as Race War." *Diplomatic History* 30, no. 2 (2006): 169–210.

——. "Shades of Sovereignty: Racialized Power, the United States in the World." In *Explaining the History of American Foreign Relations*, edited by Frank Costigliola and Michael J. Hogan, 245–70. Cambridge: Cambridge University Press, 2016.

Kramm, Robert. *Sanitized Sex: Regulating Prostitution, Venereal Disease, and Intimacy in Occupied Japan, 1945–1952.* Berkeley: University of California Press, 2017.

Kraus, Teresa L. *China Offensive: The U.S. Army Campaigns of World War II.* Washington, DC: U.S. Army Military History Institute, 1996.

Kuech, Andrew. "Imagining 'America' in Communist and Nationalist China, 1949–1965." PhD diss., New School for Social Research, 2019.

Kurtz-Phelan, Daniel. *The China Mission: George Marshall's Unfinished War, 1945–1947.* New York: W. W. Norton, 2018.

Kush, Linda. *The Rice Paddy Navy: U.S. Sailors Undercover in China.* Oxford: Osprey, 2012.

Lary, Diana. *China's Civil War: A Social History, 1945–1949.* Cambridge: Cambridge University Press, 2015.

——. *The Chinese People at War: Human Suffering and Social Transformation, 1937–1945.* Cambridge: Cambridge University Press, 2010.

Lee, Keith K. *A Chinese in the A.V.G.: The Story of Ng Bak Lim in the American Volunteer Group, the China Air Task Force, the US Army Fourteenth Air Force and the United States Air Force.* AVG Legacy, 2011.

Lei, Sean Hsiang-lin. *Neither Donkey nor Horse: Medicine in the Struggle over China's Modernity*. Chicago: University of Chicago Press, 2014.

Leong, Karen J. *The China Mystique: Pearl S. Buck, Anna May Wong, Mayling Soong, and the Transformation of American Orientalism*. Berkeley: University of California Press, 2005.

Li, Danke. *Echoes of Chongqing: Women in Wartime China*. Champaign: University of Illinois Press, 2010.

Lilly, Robert J. *Taken by Force: Rape and American GIs in Europe during World War II*. London: Palgrave Macmillan, 2007.

Lin, Hsiao-ting. *Accidental State: Chiang Kai-shek, the United States, and the Making of Taiwan*. Cambridge, MA: Harvard University Press, 2016.

Lipman, Jana K. *Guantanamo: A Working-Class History between Empire and Revolution*. Berkeley: University of California Press, 2009.

Liu Hongyi, ed. *Erzhan shiqi Meijun yuan Hua kongjun* [American airmen in China during World War II]. Beijing: World Flight Journal, 2005.

Liu Renfeng. "KangRi jiuwang houqi Zhongguo gongchang dang lingdao xia de funü qikan: *Xiandai funuv*" [Women's periodicals under Chinese Communist Party leadership in the late stages of the Resistance War: The modern woman]. *Zhonghua nüzi xueyuan* [Women's Academy at Shandong] 4, no. 92 (2008): 56–59.

Liu Xiaodong. *Tuofeng hangxian: Kangzhan Zhongguo de yi tiao zhengming tongdao* [Flying the Hump]. Guilin: Guangxi shifan da xue chu ban she, 2015.

Liu, Xiaoyuan. *A Partnership for Disorder: China, the United States, and Their Policies for the Postwar Disposition of the Japanese Empire, 1941–1945*. New York: Cambridge University Press, 1996.

Lohbeck, Don. *Patrick J. Hurley*. Self-published, Arcole, 2017. Kindle.

Lu, Zhouxiang, "Sport, Nationalism, and the Building of the Modern Chinese Nation-State (1912–1949)." *International Journal of the History of Sport* 28, no. 7 (2011): 1030–54.

Luo Tian. "Dian-Mian zhanyi zhong de junshi fanyi" [Military interpreters in the Burma and Salween campaigns]. In *Fanyi shi yanjiu* [Research on the history of translation studies], edited by Wang Hongzhi, 229–43. Shanghai: Fudan daxue chu ban she, 2011.

———. "Kangzhan shiqi Chongqing de junshi kouyi huodong" [The military interpreter program in Chongqing during the War of Resistance]. *Yiyuan xintan* [New perspectives in translation studies] 1 (2012): 280–97.

Lutz, Catherine, ed. *The Bases of Empire: The Global Struggle against U.S. Military Posts*. New York: New York University Press, 2011.

Ma, Xiaohua. "The Invisible War between the United States and Japan over China: A Study of the Abolition of Extraterritoriality." *Journal of American and Canadian Studies (Japan)* 15 (March 1998): 99–111.

Madsen, Grant. *Sovereign Soldiers: How the U.S. Military Transformed the Global Economy after World War II*. Philadelphia: University of Pennsylvania Press, 2018.

Man, Simeon. *Soldiering through Empire: Race and the Making of the Decolonizing Pacific*. Berkeley: University of California Press, 2018.

Manela, Erez. "The Fourth Policeman: Franklin Roosevelt's Vision for China's Global Role." In *Kailuo xuanyan de yiyi yu yingxiang* [The significance and impact of the Cairo Declaration], edited by Wu Sihua, Fangshang Lü, and Yongle Lin, 213–35. Taipei: Zheng da chu ban she, 2014.

———. *The Wilsonian Moment: Self-Determination and the International Origins of Anticolonial Nationalism.* Oxford: Oxford University Press, 2007.

Masuda, Hajimu. *Cold War Crucible: The Korean Conflict and the Postwar World.* Cambridge, MA: Harvard University Press, 2015.

———. "The Korean War through the Prism of Chinese Society: Public Reactions and the Shaping of 'Reality' in the Communist State, October–December 1950." *Journal of Cold War Studies* 14, no. 3 (2012): 3–38.

McCoy, Alfred. *In the Shadows of the American Century: The Rise and Decline of U.S. Global Power.* Boston: Haymarket Books, 2017.

McCoy, Alfred, and Francisco A. Scarano, eds. *Colonial Crucible: Empire in the Making of the Modern American State.* Madison: University of Wisconsin Press, 2009.

McKerrow, John. "Scenes from a Marriage of Necessity: Social Relations during the American Occupation of Australia, 1941–1945." PhD diss., McMaster University, 2009.

McLelland, Mark. *Love, Sex, and Democracy in Japan during the American Occupation.* New York: Palgrave Macmillan, 2012.

McLoughlin, William G. *Revivals, Awakening, and Reform.* Chicago: University of Chicago Press, 1978.

McPherson, Alan. *The Invaded: How Latin Americans and Their Allies Fought and Ended U.S. Occupations.* New York: Oxford University Press, 2014.

———. "The Irony of Legal Pluralism in U.S. Occupations." *American Historical Review* 117, no. 4 (2012): 1149–72.

Miller, Edward G. *Misalliance: Ngo Dinh Diem, the United States, and the Fate of South Vietnam.* Cambridge, MA: Harvard University Press, 2013.

Miller, Jennifer M. *Cold War Democracy: The United States and Japan.* Cambridge, MA: Harvard University Press, 2019.

Mitchell, Jon. "U.S. Marine Corps Sexual Violence on Okinawa." *Asia Pacific Journal: Japan Focus* 16, no. 3 (2018): 1–8.

Mitter, Rana. *Forgotten Ally: China's World War II, 1937–1945.* Boston: Houghton Mifflin, 2013.

Moon, Katherine H. S. *Sex among Allies: Military Prostitution in U.S.-Korea Relations.* New York: Columbia University Press, 1997.

Moon, Seugsook. "Camptown Prostitution and the Imperial SOFA." In *Over There: Living with the US Military Empire from World War II to the Present*, edited by Maria Höhn and Seugsook Moon, 337–65. Durham, NC: Duke University Press, 2011.

Moore, John Hammond. *Over-Sexed, Over-Paid, and Over Here: Americans in Australia, 1941–1945.* Brisbane, University of Queensland Press, 1981.

Morden, Bettie J. *The Women's Army Corps, 1945–1978.* Washington, DC: U.S. Government Printing Office, 1990.

Morris, Andrew D. *Marrow of the Nation: A History of Sport and Physical Culture in Republican China.* Berkeley: University of California Press, 2004.

Moser, Don. *China-Burma-India.* New York: Time-Life Books, 1978.

Mosher, Steven W. *China Misperceived: American Illusions and Chinese Reality.* New York: Basic Books, 1990.

Neptune, Harvey. *Caliban and the Yankees: Trinidad and the United States Occupation.* Chapel Hill: University of North Carolina Press, 2007.

Niu Jun. *Cong Yan'an zouxiang shijie: Zhongguo gongchan dang dui wai guanxi de qiyuan* [From Yan'an to the world: The origins of Chinese communist foreign policy]. Xiamen: Fujian renmin chu ban she, 1992.

Noble, Denis L. *The Eagle and the Dragon: The United States Military in China, 1901–1937.* Westport, CT: Greenwood Press, 1990.

Oldstone-Moore, Jennifer Lee. "The New Life Movement of Nationalist China: Confucianism, State Authority and Moral Formation." PhD diss., University of Chicago, 2000.

Oyen, Meredith. *The Diplomacy of Migration: Transnational Lives and the Making of U.S.-Chinese Relations in the Cold War.* Ithaca, NY: Cornell University Press, 2016.

Paine, S. C. M. *The Wars for Asia, 1911–1949.* Cambridge: Cambridge University Press, 2012.

Peattie, Mark, Edward Drea, and Hans van de Ven, eds. *The Battle for China: Essays on the Military History of the Sino-Japanese War, 1937–1945.* Stanford, CA: Stanford University Press, 2011.

Pepper, Suzanne. *Civil War in China: The Political Struggle, 1945–1949.* Berkeley: University of California Press, 1978.

Peraino, Kevin. *A Force So Swift: Mao, Truman, and the Birth of Modern China, 1949.* New York: Crown, 2017.

Perdue, Peter. *China Marches West: The Qing Conquest of Central Asia.* Cambridge, MA: Belknap Press of Harvard University Press, 2005.

Pickowicz, Paul G. *China on Film: A Century of Exploration, Confrontation and Controversy.* Lanham, MD: Rowman and Littlefield, 2011.

Plating, John D. *The Hump: American Strategy for Keeping China in World War II.* College Station: Texas A&M University Press, 2011.

Pomfret, John. *The Beautiful Country and the Middle Kingdom: American and China, 1776 to the Present.* New York: Henry Holt, 2016.

Potts, E. Daniel, and Annette Potts. *Yanks Down Under, 1941–1945: The American Impact on Australia.* Melbourne: Oxford University Press, 1985.

Preston, Andrew. *Sword of the Spirit, Shield of Faith: Religion in American War and Diplomacy.* New York: Alfred A. Knopf, 2012.

Rafael, Vicente L. "Translation in Wartime." *Public Culture* 19, no. 2 (2007): 239–46.

Rawnsley, Gary D. "'The Great Movement to Resist America and Assist Korea': How Beijing Sold the Korean War." *Media, War and Conflict* 2, no. 3 (2009): 285–315.

Reilly, Brett. "The Sovereign States of Vietnam, 1945–1955." *Journal of Vietnamese Studies* 11, no. 3–4 (2016): 103–39.

Renda, Mary. *Taking Haiti: Military Occupation and the Culture of U.S. Imperialism, 1915–1940.* Chapel Hill: University of North Carolina Press, 2001.

Reynolds, David. *Rich Relations: The American Occupation of Britain, 1942–1945.* New York: Random House, 1995.

Roberson, James E. "'Doin' Our Thing': Identity and Colonial Modernity in Okinawan Rock Music." *Popular Music and Society* 34, no. 5 (2011): 593–620.

Roberts, Mary Louise. *What Soldiers Do: Sex and the American GI in World War II France.* Chicago: University of Chicago Press, 2013.

Romanus, Charles, and Riley Sunderland. *Stilwell's Command Problems.* Washington, DC: Department of the Army, 1956.

———. *Stilwell's Mission to China.* Washington, DC: Department of the Army, 1953.

———. *Time Runs Out in CBI.* Washington, DC: Department of the Army, 1959.

Rotter, Andrew J. *Empires of the Senses: Bodily Encounters in Imperial India and the Philippines.* Oxford: Oxford University Press, 2019.

———. "Empires of the Senses: How Seeing, Hearing, Smelling, Tasting, and Touching Shaped Imperial Encounters." *Diplomatic History* 35, no. 1 (2011): 3–19.

———. "Saidism without Said: *Orientalism* and U.S. Diplomatic History." *American Historical Review* 105, no. 4 (2000): 1205–17.

Rozman, Gilbert, ed. *East Asian National Identities: Common Roots and Chinese Exceptionalism.* Stanford, CA: Stanford University Press, 2012.

Ruskola, Teemu. "Canton Is Not Boston: The Invention of American Imperial Sovereignty." *American Quarterly* 57, no. 3 (September 2005): 859–84.

———. *Legal Orientalism: China, the United States, and Modern Law.* Cambridge, MA: Harvard University Press, 2013.

Ryan, Kyla. "Left Behind: The Afghan Translators Who Served with the U.S. Military." *Diplomat*, January 8, 2015.

Salama-Carr, Myriam, ed. *Translating and Interpreting Conflict.* Amsterdam: Rodopi, 2007.

Samson, Jack. *Flying Tiger: The True Story of General Claire Chennault and the US 14th Air Force in China.* Lanham, MD: Rowman and Littlefield, 2011.

Sandars, C. T. *America's Overseas Garrisons: The Leasehold Empire.* Oxford: Oxford University Press, 2000.

Schaller, Michael. *The U.S. Crusade in China, 1938–1945.* New York: Columbia University Press, 1978.

Scully, Eileen. *Bargaining with the State from Afar: American Citizenship in Treaty Port China, 1844–1942.* New York: Columbia University Press, 2001.

Setzekorn, Eric. *The Rise and Fall of an Officer Corps: The Republic of China Military, 1942–1945.* Norman: University of Oklahoma Press, 2018.

Shaffer, Robert. "A Rape in Beijing: December 1946, GIs, Nationalist Protestors, and US Foreign Policy." *Pacific Historical Review* 69, no. 1 (2000): 31–64.

Shaw, Henry I. *The United States Marines in North China, 1945–1949.* Washington, DC: Historical Branch, G-3 Division Headquarters, U.S. Marine Corps, 1968.

Sheehan, James J. "The Problem of Sovereignty in European History." *American Historical Review* 111, no. 1 (2006): 1–15.

Shen, Yu. "SACO: An Ambivalent Experience of Sino-American Cooperation during World War II." PhD diss., University of Illinois at Urbana-Champaign, 1995.

Sheng, Michael. "The Triumph of Internationalism: CCP-Moscow Relations before 1949." *Diplomatic History* 21, no. 1 (1997): 95–104.

Shibusawa, Naoko. *America's Geisha Ally: Reimagining the Japanese Enemy.* Cambridge, MA: Harvard University Press, 2006.

"Shidai fengcai nianzhong pan dian: 2004 nian Yunnan shi da xinwen jiaodian nüxing" [Modern elegance's year-end list: Ten women who made the news in Kunming in 2004]. *Shidai fengcai* [Modern elegance], December 2012, 8–13.

Sides, Hampton. *Ghost Soldiers: The Epic Account of World War II's Greatest Rescue Mission.* New York: Anchor Books, 2001.

Sigley, Gary. "*Suzhi*, the Body, and the Fortunes of Technoscientific Reasoning in Contemporary China." *positions: East Asia Cultures Critique* 17, no. 3 (2009): 537–66.

Sihn, Kyu-hwan. "Eugenics Discourse and Racial Improvement in Republican China, 1911–1949." *Korean Journal of Medical History* 19, no. 2 (2010): 459–85.

Simbulan, Roland G. "People's Movement Responses to Evolving U.S. Military Activities in the Philippines." In *The Bases of Empire: The Global Struggle against U.S. Military Posts*, edited by Catherine Lutz, 145–80. New York: New York University Press, 2009.

Song, Mingwei. *Young China: National Rejuvenation and the Bildungsroman, 1900–1959.* Cambridge, MA: Harvard University Press, 2015.

Song, Xiaoping. *Teachers' Schools and the Making of the Modern Chinese Nation-State, 1897–1937.* Vancouver: UBC Press, 2007.

Spector, Ronald. *In the Ruins of Empire: The Japanese Surrender and the Battle for Postwar Asia.* New York: Random House, 2008.

Spence, Jonathan D. *To Change China: Western Advisors in China, 1620–1960.* Boston: Little, Brown, 1969.

Stoler, Ann Laura. *Carnal Knowledge and Imperial Power: Race and the Intimate in Colonial Rule.* Berkeley: University of California Press, 2010.

Sturdevant, Saundra, and Brenda Stoltzfus. *Let the Good Times Roll: Prostitution and the U.S. Military in Asia.* New York: New Press, 1993.

Sun Xiangmei. "Minguo shiqi de guochi jinianri" [National Humiliation Day in the Republican era]. *Zhongshan fengyu* (Zhong Shan storm) 4 (2007): 16–19.

Takeuchi, Michiko. "'Pan Pan Girls': Performing and Resisting Neocolonialism(s) in the Pacific Theater." In *Over There: Living with the US Military Empire from World War II to the Present*, edited by Maria Höhn and Seugsook Moon, 78–108. Durham, NC: Duke University Press, 2011.

Tanaka, Yuki. *Japan's Comfort Women: Sexual Slavery and Prostitution during World War II and the US Occupation.* London: Routledge, 2002.

Tang Xinyu. "KangRi zhansheng shiqi ZhongMei hezuo yu jiaoliu zhong de yishi huodong" [The role of communication and translation activities in Sino-American cooperation during the War of Resistance]. *Waiguo yuwen* (Foreign language) 31, no. 3 (2015): 129–35.

Tanner, Harold M. *The Battle for Manchuria and the Fate of China: Siping, 1946.* Bloomington: Indiana University Press, 2013.

———. *Where Chiang Kai-shek Lost China: The Liao-Shen Campaign, 1948.* Bloomington: Indiana University Press, 2015.

Taylor, Jay. *The Generalissimo: Chiang Kai-shek and the Struggle for Modern China.* Cambridge, MA: Belknap Press of Harvard University Press, 2009.

Taylor, Jeremy. "The Production of the Chiang Kai-shek Personality Cult, 1929–1975." *China Quarterly* 185, no. 1 (2006): 96–110.

Thomson, James C., Jr. *When China Faced West: American Reformers in Nationalist China, 1928–1937.* Cambridge, MA: Harvard University Press, 1969.

Tillman, Ellen D. *Dollar Diplomacy by Force: Nation-Building and Resistance in the Dominican Republic.* Chapel Hill: University of North Carolina Press, 2016.

Tolley, Kemp. *Yangtze Patrol: The U.S. Navy in China.* Annapolis, MD: Naval Institute Press, 2013.

Tow, Edna. "The Great Bombing of Chongqing and the Anti-Japanese War, 1937–1945." In *The Battle for China: Essays on the Military History of the Sino-Japanese War of 1937–1945*, edited by Mark Peattie, Edward Drea, and Hans van de Ven, 256–82. Stanford, CA: Stanford University Press, 2010.

Tsu, Jing. *Failure, Nationalism, and Literature: The Making of Modern Chinese Identity, 1895–1937.* Stanford, CA: Stanford University Press, 2005.

Tsui, Brian. "Clock Time, National Space, and the Limits of Guomindang Anti-imperialism." *positions: East Asia Cultures and Critique* 24, no. 4 (2013): 921–45.

Tuchman, Barbara. *Stilwell and the American Experience in China.* New York: Grove Press, 1972.

Utset, Marial Iglesias. *A Cultural History of Cuba during the U.S. Occupation, 1898–1902.* Chapel Hill: University of North Carolina Press, 2011.

Van de Ven, Hans. *China at War: Triumph and Tragedy in the Emergence of the New China.* Cambridge, MA: Harvard University Press, 2018.

———. "Stilwell in the Stocks: The Chinese Nationalists and the Allied Powers in the Second World War." *Asian Affairs* 34, no. 3 (2003): 243–59.

———. *War and Nationalism in China, 1925–1945.* London: Routledge, 2003.

———. "Wartime Everydayness: Beyond the Battlefield in China's Second World War." *Journal of Modern Chinese History* 13, no. 1 (2019): 1–23.

Vine, David. *Base Nation: How U.S. Military Bases Abroad Harm America and the World.* New York: Metropolitan Books, 2015.

———. *The United States of War: A Global History of America's Endless Conflicts, from Columbus to the Islamic State.* Oakland: University of California Press, 2020.

Von Eschen, Penny. *Race against Empire: Black Americans and Anticolonialism, 1937–1957.* Ithaca, NY: Cornell University Press, 2014.

Wakeman, Frederic. *The Shanghai Badlands: Wartime Terrorism and Urban Crime, 1937–1941.* Cambridge: Cambridge University Press, 2002.

———. *Spymaster: Dai Li and the Chinese Secret Service.* Berkeley: University of California Press, 2003.

———. *Strangers at the Gate: Social Disorder in South China, 1839–1861.* Berkeley: University of California Press, 1997.

Wang, Dong. "The Discourse of Unequal Treaties in Modern China." *Pacific Affairs* 76, no. 3 (Fall 2003): 399–425.

Wang Chengmian. "Weidemai yu zhanshi Zhongguo (1944 nian 10 yue–1945 nian 8 yue)" [Wedemeyer and wartime China, October 1944 to August 1945]. *Zhonghua junshi xuehui huikan* [Journal of the Chinese Society of Military History] 13 (2008): 121–50.

Wang Lixin. "Zai long de yingchen xia: Dui Zhongguo de xiangxiang yu Meiguo guojia shenfen de jiangou" [In comparison with the dragon: Imagining China and constructing America's national identity]. *Zhongguo shehui kexue* [Social sciences in China] 3 (2008): 156–73.

Warnock, A. Timothy. "The Chinese American Composite Wing: A Case Study of the Versatility of the Composite Concept. *Air Power History* 39, no. 3 (Fall 1992): 21–30.

Wasserstrom, Jeffrey N. "Chinese Students and Anti-Japanese Protests, Past and Present." *World Policy Journal* 22, no. 2 (2005): 59–65.

Watt, John R. *Saving Lives in Wartime China: How Medical Reformers Built Modern Healthcare Systems amid War and Epidemics.* Leiden: Brill, 2013.

Wen Liming. "Guanyu Xinan lianhe daxue zhanshi congjun yundong de kaocha" [Investigation into the wartime movement to join the army at Southwest Associated University]. *KangRi zhanzheng yanjiu* [Journal of studies of China's Resistance War against Japan] 3 (2010): 5–18.

Wertheim, Stephen. *Tomorrow, the World: The Birth of U.S. Global Supremacy.* Cambridge, MA: Belknap Press of Harvard University Press, 2020.

Westad, Odd Arne. *Cold War and Revolution: Soviet-American Rivalry and the Origins of the Chinese Civil War, 1944–1946.* New York: Columbia University Press, 1993.

———. *Decisive Encounters: The Chinese Civil War: 1946–1950.* Stanford, CA: Stanford University Press, 2003.

———. "Losses, Chances, and Myths: The United States and the Creation of the Sino-Soviet Alliance, 1945–1950." *Diplomatic History* 21, no. 1 (1997): 105–15.

———. *Restless Empire: China and the World since 1750.* New York: Basic Books, 2012.

Whitlock, Craig. "Unguarded Nation: Built to Fail." *Washington Post,* December 14, 2019.

Wilkinson, Mark. "American Military Misconduct in Shanghai and the Chinese Civil War: The Case of Zang Da Yaozi." *Journal of American-East Asian Relations* 17, no. 2 (2010): 146–73.

Willoughby, John. *Remaking the Conquering Heroes: The Social and Geopolitical Impact of the Post-War Occupation of Germany.* New York: Palgrave Macmillan, 2001.

Wong, Kevin Scott. *Americans First: Chinese Americans and the Second World War.* Cambridge, MA: Harvard University Press, 2009.

Wong, Lawrence Wang-chi. "Translators and Interpreters during the Opium War between Britain and China (1839–1842)." In *Translating and Interpreting Conflict*, edited by Myriam Salama-Carr, 41–57. Amsterdam: Rodopi, 2007.

Worthing, Peter. *General He Yingqin: The Rise and Fall of Nationalist China*. Cambridge: Cambridge University Press, 2016.

Wu, Tien-wei. "Contending Political Forces during the War of Resistance." In *China's Bitter Victory: The War with Japan, 1937–1945*, edited by James Hsuing and Steven I. Levine, 51–78. London: Routledge, 1992.

Wu Su-feng. "Kangzhan shiqi Jiang Jieshi de 'yiyuan' renzhi ji peiyu" [Chiang Kai-shek's understanding and cultivating of interpreters during the War of Resistance]. In *Jindaishi shilun: duoyuan sikao yu tansuo* [Explaining modern history: Pluralistic reflections and explorations], edited by Li Dazha, 291–307. Taipei: Donghua shuju, 2017.

Xie Benshu. *Long Yun zhuan* [Biography of Long Yun]. Kunming: Renmin chu ban she, 2011.

Xu, Guangqiu. "The Chinese Air Force with American Wings." *War and Society* 16, no. 1 (1998): 61–81.

Xu, Guoqi. *Chinese and Americans: A Shared History*. Cambridge, MA: Harvard University Press, 2014.

Xu Kangming. *ZhongMianYin zhancchang kangRi zhanzheng shi* [A history of the War of Resistance in the CBI theater]. Beijing: Jiefangjun chu ban she, 2007.

Xu, Xiaoguang. "A Southern Methodist Mission to China: Soochow University." PhD diss., Middle Tennessee State University, 1993.

Xue Qingyu. *Sun Liren Jiangjun chuan: Di erci shijie dazhan Zhongguo zhuYin jun xin yi jun YinMian kangRi zhanzheng shilu* [A biography of General Sun Liren: The New First Army of the Chinese Army in India in World War II]. Hohhot: Nei menggu da xue chu ban she, 2000.

Yang Jui-sung. *Bingfu, huanghuo yu shuishi: [Xifang] shiye de Zhongguo xingxiang yu jindai Zhongguo guozu lunshu xiangxiang* [Sick man, yellow peril, and sleeping tiger: "Western" Images of China and the discourse of national identity in modern China]. Taipei: zhengda chu ban she, 2010.

——. "Xiangxiang minzu chiru: Jindai Zhongguo sixiang wenhua de 'Dongya bingfu'" [Imagining national humiliation: "The sick man of Asia in modern Chinese culture and thought]. *Chengchi daxue xueli xuebao* [Journal of the Department of History of National Chengchi University] 23 (2005): 1–42.

Yang Kuisong. *Dushi qiushi: Zhongguo xiandai shi dushi zhaji* [Seeking truth from reading history: Notes on contemporary Chinese history]. Hanghzou: Zhejiang daxue chu ban she, 2011.

——. "Wei minzu xuming: Pan Guangdan yu ta de shidai" [To save the race: Pan Guangdan and his era]. *Tsinghua shehui xue pinglun* [Qingua sociology review] 11, no. 1 (2019): 1–7.

Yang Tianshi. *Xunzhao zhenshi de Jiang Jieshi: Jiang Jieshi riji jiedu* [Searching for the deal Chiang Kai-shek: Interpreting Chiang's Diary]. Hong Kong: Sanlian shu dian, 2011.

Yang, Zhiguo. "U.S. Marines in Qingdao: History, Public Memory, and Chinese Nationalism." In *Exploring Nationalisms of China: Themes and Conflicts*, edited by C. X. George Wei and Xiaoyuan Liu, 57–75. Westport, CT: Greenwood Press, 2002.

———. "U.S. Marines in Qingdao: Military-Civilian Interaction, Nationalism, and China's Civil War, 1945–1949." PhD diss., University of Maryland, 1988.

Ye, Weili. *Seeking Modernity in China's Name: Chinese Students in the United States, 1900–1927*. Stanford, CA: Stanford University Press, 2001.

Yeo, Andrew. *Activists, Alliances, and Anti-U.S. Base Protests*. Cambridge: Cambridge University Press, 2011.

Yin, Xinzhong. "The Treatment of Night Soil and Waste in Modern China." In *Health and Hygiene in Chinese East Asia: Policies and Publics in the Long Twentieth Century*, edited by Angela Ki Che Leung, and Charlotte Furth, 51–72. Duke, NC: Durham University Press, 2010.

Young, Arthur N. *China's Wartime Finance and Inflation, 1937–1945*. Cambridge, MA: Harvard University Press, 1965.

Yu, Maochun. *The Dragon's War: Allied Operations and the Fate of China, 1937–1947*. Annapolis, MD: Naval Institute Press, 2013.

———. *OSS in China: Prelude to Cold War*. New Haven, CT: Yale University Press, 1996.

Yuh, Ji-Yeon. *Beyond the Shadow of Camptown: Korean Military Brides in America*. New York: New York University Press, 2002.

Zarrow, Peter. *Educating China: Knowledge, Society, and Textbooks in a Modernizing World, 1902–1937*. Cambridge: Cambridge University Press, 2015.

Zeiger, Susan. *Entangling Alliances: Foreign War Brides and American Soldiers in the Twentieth Century*. New York: New York University Press, 2010.

Zhang, Baijia. "China's Quest for Foreign Military Aid." In *The Battle for China: Essays on the Military History of the Sino-Japanese War of 1937–1945*, edited by Mark Peattie, Edward Drea, and Hans van de Ven, 283–307. Stanford, CA: Stanford University Press, 2010.

Zhang, Hong. *America Perceived: The Making of Chinese Images of the United States*. Westport, CT: Greenwood Press, 2002.

Zhang Mochao. *Zhongguo xiandai shi* [Modern Chinese history]. Chongqing: Chongqing daxue chu ban she, 1996.

Zhang, Yufa. "Returned Chinese Students from America and the Chinese Leadership (1846–1949)." *Chinese Studies in History* 35, no. 3 (Spring 2002): 52–86.

Zhang Zhenli. "Cong Minguo dang'an kan 1944 nian zhu Dian Meijun roulei gongying fengbo" [Using Republican archives to examine problems with meat supplies for U.S. forces in Yunnan during 1944]. *Yunnan dang'an* [Yunnan archives] 12 (2011): 20–22.

Zhao Mei. "Qingmo yilai Zhongguo zhongxue lishi jiaocai zhong de Meiguo xingxiang" [The image of America in Chinese middle school history textbooks since the late Qing]. *Meiguo yanjiu* [American studies] 20, no. 4 (2006): 51–71.

Zhao, Suisheng. "Chinese Nationalism and Its International Orientations." *Political Science Quarterly* 115, no. 1 (2000): 1–33.

———. *A Nation-State by Construction: Dynamics of Modern Chinese Nationalism*. Stanford, CA: Stanford University Press, 2004.

Zhao Yi. "*Minzhu* zhoukan wei minzhu fasheng" [*Democracy Weekly*: A voice for democracy]. *Hongyan Chunqiu* [Annals of the Red Crag] 8 (2014): 72–74.

Zheng, Yanqiu. "A Specter of Extraterritoriality: The Legal Status of US Troops in China." *Journal of American-East Asian Relations* 22, no. 1 (2015): 17–44.

Zhu, Pingchao. *Wartime Culture in Guilin, 1938–1944: A City at War.* Lanham, MD: Lexington Books, 2015.

Zuo Ping. "Kangzhan shiqi mengjun zhong de Zhongguo yiyuan" [Chinese interpreters in the Allied Army during the War of Resistance]. *Shehui kexue yanjiu* [CASS Research] 1 (2013): 167–72.

Index

Page numbers in *italics* refer to illustrations.

accidents, by U.S. military personnel, 8, 133, 160, 168, 176, 196, 198, 200; compensation for, 181–84; lenient response to, 127–28, 134, 183; from military exercises and maneuvers, 17, 115; by off-duty GIs, 18, 127; postwar documenting of, 19; vehicular, 124–26, 128, 158, 167, 178–82, 195

Acheson, Dean, xxiv, 196, 197, 206

Afghanistan, 9, 205–6

airfield construction, 113–16

Allan, David, 40

Allison, John R., 36

ALPHA Force, xxi, 105

American Military Mission to China (AMMISCA), 36, 82–83, 84, 104

American Volunteer Group (AVG): Flying Tigers, 6, 24, 51, 109–12, 129, 189; dissolution of, xviii, 39; formation of, xvii, 4; hostel program and, 21, 27–29, 53; impunity of, 117; interpreter program and, 53, 76, 78; smuggling linked to, 116

Anti-Brutality Movement, 19, 189–92, 195

Army Nurse Corps, 5

Arnett, Warren, 32, 121, 127

Assam-Burma-China Ferry Command, xviii

Atkinson, Brooks, 88–89

Atlantic Charter (1941), 10

Australia, 18, 130, 131, 134, 137, 146

Bai Guang, 186–87

baojia system, 111

Battle of Leyte Gulf (1944), xxi

Beijing, 194; American brutality in, 176, 178; Communist protests in, 168; prewar Marine presence in, 14; sexual assaults and misconduct in, xxiii, 19; theft and corruption in, 173, 175

Belitz, Raymond, 158

Berthaine, Frank, 119

Bickers, Robert, 147

Black GIs, 5, 69, 73, 160

black marketeering, 8, 38, 40, 116–21, 141, 185, 191, 196–97

Boatner, Haydon, xv, 72, 79–80, 81, 90, 102, 158

Bohlkin, James, 114–15

Bolden, Frank, 73

Boxer Uprising (1901), 13

Brennan, John, 132

Brill, Joseph, 182

Brochon, James, 32

Buck, Pearl, 13, 30

Bulger, C. F., 37–38

Bureau of Investigation and Statistics (Juntong), xix, 18, 22, 53, 92–93, 152–53, 156–57

Burma, xix, xx, 71, 79, 80; Black GIs in, 5, 73; Chiang's strategy in, 84–85, 87–88, 94, 98–99, 106; interpreter training in, 76; Japanese attack on, 82, 84–85, 116; reconquest planning for, 94–100

Burma Road, 13, 28

Byrn, Norman, 131

Byrne, James F., 114

Byrnes, James, 105
Byroade, Henry, xx

Cairo Conference (1943), xix, 30, 94, 97
Cai Zukang, 70, 71
Cao Guiming, 182–84
Carney, Boatner, 116, 137
Carney, Rose Mok, 116–17, 139
Ceder, Melvin, 37–38
Central News Daily (newspaper), 126, 143, 151, 156
Central University, 56, 59, 190
Chang, James H. S., 114
Chang Chun, 63
Chen Chao, 180–81
Chen Cheng, 92
Chen Futian, 51
Chen Jinzhang, 177
Chen Lifu, 60
Chen Lu, 186
Chen Mengzhao, 118
Chennault, Claire, xv, xvi, xvii, xviii, xxii, 42, 93, 97, 137; airfield construction viewed by, 115; as AVG commander, 24; Chinese air force forged by, 27–28; hostel workers viewed by, 37–38; policing under, 117, 131; prostitution rumors and, 139; rescues of U.S. airmen viewed by, 109, 111; rickshaw ban by, 184; as soldiers' soldier, 70–71; theft decried by, 121, 122
Cheves, Gilbert, 158, 228n173
Chiang, Lucy (Tao Zigu), 140
Chiang Kai-shek, xvi, xvii, 1, 25, 80, 91, 107, 129; anti-Americanism directed at, 18, 157–58, 167; anti-crime campaigns of, 133, 155, 156; Black GIs banned by, 5, 73; Burma strategy of, 84–88, 94, 98–99, 106; at Cairo Conference, xix, 94–95; Chinese capital moved by, xv; combat command experience of, 88; Communists underestimated by, 170; defeat and exile of, xxiv, 2, 20, 194, 203;

"gunboat policy" denounced by, 15; hostel program and, 6, 22, 23, 24, 27, 41–46; interpreter program and, 48, 50, 52–55, 58, 62, 64–65, 75; after Japanese surrender, 165; kidnapping of, 12–13; opposition suppressed by, 9; personality cult of, 26; physical education rhetoric of, 52; postwar advisory mission backed by, 81, 84; postwar criminality and, 175, 176; rescue instructions from, 110, 112; Sino-American military cooperation viewed by, 7; Stilwell and, xviii, xx, 3, 7, 13, 17, 81, 87–88, 94–96, 98–100; traffic accidents and, 124, 180; Truman's disaffection with, 196; U.S. dismissiveness toward, 82–83; U.S. military demands accepted by, 20; Wedemeyer and, 100, 104, 105, 155, 157–58, 161–62
Chiang Weiguo, 90
Ch'i Hsi-sheng, 3, 87, 96
China Air Task Force, xviii, 39
China-Burma-India (CBI) theater, xvii, 15, 110
China White Paper, xxiv, 196–97, 206
Chinese-American Composite Wing (CACW), 81, 93–94
Chinese Army in India (CAI, X-Force), xviii, xxi, 88–91, 94–98
Chinese Civil War, 1, 9, 75, 196, 201
Chinese Combat Command (CCC), xxi, 100–101, 107, 124
Chinese Communist Party (CCP), xxiii, xxiv, 9, 162; anti-Americanism exploited by, 19, 167, 168, 174, 178, 179, 187, 201; North China offensive by, 170, 174; Sino-American Commercial Treaty denounced by, 188; student groups controlled by, 189–91; victory of, 193–94
Chinese Exclusion Act (1882), xix, 2, 13, 137
Chinese Expeditionary Force, xvii–xviii, 84–85, 87, 105

Chinese Training Center (CTC), xxi, 64, 100–101

Chongqing: as capital, xv, 2; guerrilla training in, xix; Japanese bombing of, xvi, 2, 27, 109, 112; riots in, 18, 22; soil collection in, 32, 33; weather in, 34

Chu Anping, 188

Churchill, Winston, 94; at Cairo Conference, xix; "Europe-first" strategy and, xvii; Iron Curtain speech by, xxiii; at Yalta Conference, 171

Clark, Arthur, 143

Clark, Gerald, 115

Clinton, Bill, 204

Colclough, O. S., 193

Commission on Aeronautical Affairs, 28, 53, 58, 61, 112, 123

Communist Youth League, 200

Cooke, Charles M., Jr., 182

Cooper, James, 132

courts martial, 40, 114, 126, 127, 132, 158, 193

Coverdale, Garrison, 72

Currie, Laughlin, 83

Cushing, Caleb, 129

Daffin, James, 149

Da gong bao (newspaper), 44, 48, 64, 183

Dai Anlan, 85

Dai Li, xix, 58, 92, 93, 117, 152–53

Dai Shiguang, 65, 70

Dai Zhaoran, 68, 70

Davies, John Paton, 90

DiBaggis, John, 73

Diltz, Joseph, 159

Dong Shijin, 156

Dong Xianguang (Hollington Tong), 58

Doolittle Raid, 106

Dorn, Frank, xv, xxi, 82–83, 190, 205; anti-banditry campaign praised by, 133; dismissal of, 100; Guomindang forces denigrated by, 14; interpreter program and, 57, 70, 72, 77; as Y-Force commander, xviii, xix, 59–60, 91–92

drinking, 26, 66, 83, 154, 187; sexual misconduct linked to, 145, 147, 148, 168, 181, 200; traffic accidents linked to, 124, 126, 158, 179–80; violent incidents fueled by, 130–32, 135, 149, 152, 176, 177, 193

Duara, Prasenjit, 10

Du Jianshi, 169, 182

Du Jun, 182–83

Du Yuming, 171, 191–94

Eggers, Fred, 70

Enloe, Cynthia, 162

Etris, Samuel, 34

Evans, William, 185

Export-Import Bank, xvi

extraterritoriality, 40, 128–29, 203, 206; Britain and, xviii, 18, 129–32, 134, 147; Chinese opposition to, 18, 161–62; United States and, xviii, xix, 2, 12, 147

Fackler, James, 172, 175

Falkenberg, Jinx, 148

Fan Jichang, 51, 62

Fei Xiaotong, 29

Field Artillery Training Center (FATC), 65, 91–92

Fifteenth Infantry Regiment, 14–15

Filipino People (periodical), 30

First Opium War (1839–42), 13, 153

First Sino-Japanese War (1894–95), 52

Fisken, A. D., 60–61

Flying Tigers. *See* American Volunteer Group (AVG)

Foreign Affairs Bureau (FAB), 44, 51, 53, 58–64, 72, 76, 127, 146

Foreign Claims Act (1942), 128

Fourth Marine Regiment, 14

France, xix, 139, 146, 151

Friends of the Allied Forces, 44

Fudan University, 56

Gallagher (lieutenant), 76

Gambardella, John, 108, 109

Gatheval, Roland, 181–82
Gauss, Clarence, 43, 62
Ge Liang, 72
Germany: advisors to Chinese military from, 15–16; Poland invaded by, xvi; postwar U.S. military presence in, 204; U.S. occupation of, 11
Ge Zunxian, 118
Gingell, James, 131
Gluckman, Arcadi, 91
gold trafficking, 117–19, 185
Goodrich, Charlie, 131
Great Britain, 137; Asian colonies of, 10, 31, 106, 118; in Burma campaign, 84, 87, 94–98, 103; extraterritoriality and, xviii, 18, 129–32, 134, 147; in postwar planning, 16, 84; sexual assault in, 146; U.S. forces in, 146, 204; X-Force backed by, xx
Greenberg, Whitney, 34, 118
Grzeskiewicz, Walter, 173
Guancha (periodical), 188
Guangdan, Pan, 50–51
Gu Hanling, 183
Guilin Infantry Training Center, xix
Guo Darong, 181–82
Guo Erfu, 181–82
Guomindang (GMD). See Nationalist Party
Guo Yushou, 54, 63, 64
Guo Zenling, 183
Gu Yuxiu, 67

Hague Regulations (1907), 1
Haiti, 17
Hanson, Perry, 65, 66, 68–70, 74–75
Hardwick, Tom, 34–35
Hashimoto, Ryutaro, 204
Hassett, Paul, 32
Hasty, Raymond, 116
He Haoruo: GIs' misconduct and, 120, 122, 128, 147, 149, 150, 156, 159; interpreter program and, 62–63, 64, 72–73, 75–76
Hemingway, Ernest, 115

He Wanshun, 184
He Yaozu, 155, 156, 157
He Yingqin, 39, 42, 54, 57, 73, 99, 128
Hiroshima bombing (1945), xxii, 80
Hirtz, Rafael, 34
Hlavacek, John, 139
hostel program, 2, 4, 6, 16–17, 21–47, 163; cost of, 21, 23, 38–39, 43–45; failures of, 23, 24, 45–47, 135; food provided by, 23, 30–31, 32, 42, 46; interpreter program's frictions with, 68; launch of, 27–29; as nation-building project, 22–23, 38; racist stereotypes and, 23, 30, 35–38, 39–41, 45, 47; sanitation lacking in, 32, 34; Yunnan autonomy in tension with, 42
Hsu, Madeline, 52
Huang Jiade, 141
Huang Qixiang, 124, 133
Huang Renlin, xvii, 6, 21–22, 24–30, 82, 83, 146; American background of, 24–26, 52; at Cairo Conference, 30–31; hostel program and, 32, 35, 38–39, 41, 44, 45–46, 163; interpreter program and, 48, 50, 56, 58, 66, 67, 75
Huang Shang, 53, 67, 68, 69, 142, 143, 180
Hua Sanhuan, 184
Hughes, Harold, 149
Hu Guohua, 118
Hull, Cordell, 43
Humphries, James, 131
Hurley, Patrick, 98, 99, 104–5, 171
Hu Xiaomei, 177–78
Hu Yimei, 73

Ichigo offensive, xx, xxi, 8, 21, 68, 96–97, 106, 147
Immerwahr, Daniel, 10
India, xviii, 2, 5, 42, 139, 150; poverty in, 31; training centers in, 56, 76, 88–91
inflation, 21–22, 39, 42, 43, 135, 141, 142, 173; black-marketeering linked to,

120–21; civilian laborers and professionals hurt by, 113, 115, 133; hostel program linked to, 23; interpreter program threatened by, 57, 67; Nationalist government weakened by, 183, 192, 193

intermarriage: in China, 141, 156; in United States, 137–38

interpreter program, 4, 6–7, 16–17, 48–78; conflicts within, 57–58, 60, 61, 64, 65, 69; dissolution of, 75–76; failures of, 76–78; goals of, 48–49, 50, 54–56; hostel program's frictions with, 68; morale problems in, 64, 67, 72; physical conditioning in, 51–52; partial U.S. takeover of, 62–63, 71; pedestrian duties in, 65–66; political indoctrination in, 53; racial segregation in, 73–74; recruitment shortfalls in, 56–61; slights and humiliation in, 70–72, 135; U.S. imperialism foreshadowed by, 75

Iraq, 9

Isaacs, Harold, 73

Italy, xvi, 139

Janzen, Francis, 187

Japan: Burma attacked and blockaded by, 82, 84–85, 116; China blockaded by, 2, 22, 42; Chinese cities bombed by, 2, 27; Chinese territory gained by, xx, xxi; espionage by, 58; Ichigo offensive by, xx, xxi, 8, 21, 68, 96–97, 106, 147; Nanjing Massacre (1937) by, xv; postwar recovery of, 19; postwar U.S. military presence in, 204; Rangoon seized by, xvii–xviii; Soviet neutrality pact with, 27; surrender by, xxii, 4, 104, 170; U.S. occupation of, 11; U.S. oil sales to, xvii; Western colonies conquered by, 10

"Jeep girls," 8–9, 136, 160, 162, 186; in prostitution narrative, 137–45; in rape victim narrative, 145–51, 162, 201

Jia Yuhui, 79

Jiefang ribao (newspaper), 183, 191

Jin Chongji, 180, 195

Johnson, Carl, 172, 185

Johnson, Lyndon, 205

Johnson, Marion, 173

Johnson, Nelson, xv

Joint Office of Sino-American Police (JOSAP), 181

Juntong (Bureau of Investigation and Statistics), xix, 18, 22, 53, 92–93, 152–53, 156–57

Kang Shihao, 40

Kang Youwei, 74

Kao, S. Y., 103

Karzai, Hamid, 205

Kelling, William, 118

Kennedy, John F., 204

Key, Norman, 127

Kong Qingnian, 177

Kong Xiangxi (H. H. Kung), 26, 43, 44, 99

Korean War, 201, 202

Kostol, Carl, 32, 109

Krauss, Mary, 34, 146

Kunming, 142; complaints about, 34–35; hostels near, 21, 28, 34, 43; inflation in, 22, 32, 42, 141; interpreter training in, 51, 53, 55–61, 63, 64, 67, 72–73, 76, 78; lawlessness and mayhem in, 104, 116, 118–19, 121–22, 124, 126, 132, 139–40, 148, 153, 158, 200, 201; military justice in, 41, 73; as military target, 100, 112, 134; racism in, 36; sexual relations in, 138–39, 148; weapons training in, 68, 91; weather in, 31–32, 34

Lakin, Charles, 57

Langdon, William, 62

League of Nations, 27

Leavell, Lewis, 79–80, 81, 103–4

Lee, Andrew, 151–52

Lees, Melvin, 116

Lei Haizong, 29

Lei Zhilin, 127

lend-lease, xvi, xvii, xix, 27, 88, 95, 98, 99; as leverage, 82, 92, 96; reverse, 23, 42, 43, 44, 46; small scale of, 2, 16, 92

Lianda (Southwest Associated University), 190; hostel program and, 29; interpreter program and, 50–51, 52, 55–62, 77–78

Liang Jiayou, 71

Liang Nan, 131

Liao Gailong, 200

Liao Yaoxiang, 88, 90, 101

Li Benmao, 128

Li Ceji, 200

Li Fengshi, 127

Li Fuyou, 192

Li Hong, 80, 102

Li Huangtun, 57

Li Longhui, 201

Lin Biao, xxiv, 192, 194

Ling Hong, 179

Lin Sheng, 131

Li Shengting, 51

Li Songnian, 73

Liu Dongshi, 128

Liu Enhua, 176–77

Liu Junying, 190

Liu Kaiqi, 123

Liu Maochun, 73

Liu Yalou, 192

Liu Ziran, 202

Li Wenling, 175

Long Yun, 24, 42, 116, 122, 133, 139, 143; black market targeted by, 120; Chiang's frictions with, 28

Lowe, Pardee, 151–52

Luce, Henry, 13, 134

Ludden, Raymond, 137

Luo Daren, 71

Luo Guangru, 159

Luo Longji, 169, 170

Luo Zhuoying, 90

Lu Zhicheng, 41

Lytton Commission, 27

MacArthur, Douglas, 89, 106

MacMorland, Edward, 36, 82–83

Magruder, John, xv, xvii, 36, 87, 92, 197; AMMISCA led by, 82–84; hostel program disparaged by, 38, 46

Manchuria, 95; Nationalist offensive and defeat in, 168–71, 194; Soviet occupation of, 1, 9, 19, 165, 167, 171

Mao Bangchu, xvi

Mao Zedong, xxiv, 165, 197, 201; anti-Americanism exploited by, 3, 15, 167

Mariana Islands, xx, 115

Markle, Kenneth, 203–4

Marshall, George C., 15, 195; interwar China service of, 14; lend-lease pressure by, 82, 96; Magruder and Stilwell unchallenged by, 36, 88, 97–98, 105–6; mediation attempted by, xviii, xxiv, 168, 188, 192; as special envoy to China, 171; Stilwell and, 88, 96, 98–99

Ma Shagwan, 150

Mason, Fred, 148

Ma Weihan, 150

Ma Yuehan, 51–52

McAleenan, Harry, 148–49

McCabe, Frederick, 25

McCarthy, Joseph, 197

McDonald, Lieutenant, 41

McKinley, William, 91

McNeill, Norman, 68

Mei Yiqi, 51, 55, 58–59, 140

Merrill, Frank, 95, 97, 101

Middleton, John, 49, 64

Miles, Milton, xix, 92–93, 148

Military Advisory Group (MAG), xxiii, xxiv

Military Assistance and Advisory Group (MAAG), 202–3

military-to-military relations, 79–107; during Burma campaign, 94–99; fragility of, 81; origins of, 82; under Wedemeyer, 100–107

Miller, Earl, 116

Miller, Harvey, 149
Miller, Jennifer, 203
Millner, William, 35, 118
Minzhu bao (newspaper), 179
Minzhu zhoukan (magazine), 179
missionaries, 6, 23, 40, 49, 56, 134
missionary colleges, 56, 59, 60, 63
Mitter, Rana, 3, 88
Moon Katharine, 203
Morgenthau, Hans, 43, 44
Morris, William, 119
Mountbatten of Burman, Louis, Earl, 98
Moy, Ernest K., 29, 40–41
Mydans, Carl, 27

Nagasaki bombing (1945), xxii
Nanjing Massacre (1937), xv
Nationalist Party (Guomindang, GMD), xvi, 1; anti-Americanism directed at, 9; collapse of, 194; covert U.S. aid to, 197; declining legitimacy of, 17; extraterritoriality tolerated by, 18; GIs' clashes with, 174–75; GIs' misconduct ignored by, 8; interpreter program and, 7; postwar press freedom under, 167; in repatriation of Japanese troops, 170, 172; secret police of, xix, 18, 22, 53, 92–93, 152–53, 156–57; in war against Japan, 3, 14
National Military Council, 21, 44, 51, 53, 54, 59, 113, 157
National Security (Allied Forces) Regulations (NSR), 129–30
NATO (North Atlantic Treaty Organization), 202, 203
Neal, Jack, 31
New First Army, 79–80, 90
New Life Movement, 26, 29, 139, 141, 143
New Zealand, 137
Ngo Dinh Diem, 205
Normandy invasion (1944), xx, 11, 146
North Korea, 194, 197

Office of Secret Services (OSS), 155
Office of War Information (OWI), 36, 65

Officers' Moral Endeavor Association (OMEA), 26–27, 29
Operation Beleaguer (1945), 165, 167
Operation Matterhorn (1944), xx, 113, 115
opium trafficking, 185

"Panorama of China," 163–65
Patton, George S., 145
Pearl Harbor attack (1941), xvii, 30, 110
Peck, DeWitt, 174
Peck, Graham, 36, 113, 141, 143
Peeke, Anne, 32
Peeke, Jan, 32, 34, 35, 57, 126–27
People's Liberation Army (PLA), 193–94
Pfieffer, Omar, 188
Philippines, 11, 81, 142, 203; MacArthur in, 89, 106; as U.S. colony, 12, 14, 17, 72, 91, 96, 173; U.S. bases evicted from, 204
Philipps, Charles, 40
Pierson, William, xxiii, xxiv, 188–89, 191, 192, 193
Pocket Guide to China, 16, 17, 24, 37, 107, 108, 138, 149
Poland, xvi
Price, Frank, xix, xxi, 45, 65
Pritchard, Warren, xxiii, 188–89, 191
profiteering, 121–24
prostitution, 9–10, 18, 26, 137–45

Quezon, Manuel, 30, 106

racism, 2–3, 5, 13, 126–27, 196–97; toward Chinese officers, 83; in Chinese textbooks, 73–74; toward Chinese trainees, 91, 92–93; colonialism linked to, 106; in hostel program, 23, 30, 35–38, 39–41, 45, 47; in interpreter program, 7, 72, 73, 77; Japanese propaganda focused on, 16, 107; among marines in North China, 172–73, 175; nationalist regime undermined by, 169; military justice weakened by, 146–47; sexism linked to, 145, 146

Radford, Arthur, 202
Rafael, Vicente L., 69
Ramgarh training center, xviii, xxii, 79; in Burma campaign planning, 94; Chiang's visit to, 25, 88; interpreter training at, 56–57, 64, 69, 71, 77; racism at, 73, 91; Stilwell's control of, 88–89, 90; Y-Force training contrasted with, 92
Reed, Gerald, 139, 148
rescues, by civilians, 108–12
Resist America and Aid Korea Campaign, 198, 200, 201–2
Revell, Earl, 35, 36, 47, 121, 163, 195
Reynolds, Robert G., 202
The Rising Tide of Color (Stoddard), 93
Rittenberg, Sidney, 128, 138
Rock, Paul, 40
Roosevelt, Franklin D., xvi, xvii, xx, 43, 83, 94, 96, 98; airlifts authorized by, xviii; at Cairo Conference, xix, 30–31, 95; Chinese partnership viewed by, 2, 16; Doolittle Raid authorized by, 106; "Europe-first" strategy and, xvii; lend-lease to China authorized by, 27; extraterritoriality relinquished by, 129; Stilwell removed by, xxi, 7; Stilwell's command effort backed by, 99; universalist rhetoric of, 24; at Yalta Conference, 171
Roosevelt, Theodore, 117
Rosser, Harold, 34
Ruvo, Angelo, 31

Salween campaign (1944), xx, xxi, 95–100
Sears, William V., 184
Second Sino-Japanese War (Resistance War, 1937–45), xv, 27
Services of Supply (SOS), 38–39, 44, 100
sexual relations, 8, 135–62, 168, 185–87, 203–4
Shanghai: Communist takeover of, 194; complaints about, 172, 173; crime in,

174–75, 177, 178, 198–99; Japanese occupation of, xv, 117; protests in, 191; rickshaw ban in, 184; traffic accidents in, 179
Shang Zhen, 56, 58, 59
Shen bao (newspaper), 178
Shen Chong, xxiii, 168, 188–92, 197, 198
Sheng, Colonel, 77
Shen Lusha, 144
Shen Youkang, 69, 73
Shen Zui, 152
Shi, Peter, 37–38
Sichuan province: conservative mores in, 141; GIs' misconduct in, 149, 154; interpreter program's recruitment from, 56, 76; Operation Matterhorn's recruitment from, 113, 115
Sichuan University, 56
Sino-American Commercial Treaty (1946), xxiii, 188
Sino-American Cooperative Organization (SACO), xix, 7, 53, 92–93
Sino-American New Equal Treaty (1943), xix, 129–30
Sino-Soviet Treaty of Friendship (1945), 171
Sledge, E. B., 172, 173, 174
Slim, William, 95
Smith, Harry, 72
Smitty, P. B., 154, 156
smuggling, 8, 101–2, 116–21, 185
Song Ailing, 94
Song Meiling, xv, 94, 129
Song Ziwen, xvi, 43, 88, 94, 96, 99, 117
South China Patrol, 13
South East Asia Command (SEAC), 98
South Korea, 203, 204
Southwest Associated University (Lianda), 190; hostel program and, 29; interpreter program and, 50–51, 52, 55–62, 77–78
Soviet Union, 194; advisors to Chinese military from, 15; Chinese postwar security role opposed by, 16; Japanese cease-fire with, xvi; Japanese

neutrality pact with, 27; Manchuria occupied by, 1, 9, 19, 165, 167, 171; postwar U.S. policy toward, 171
Spanish-American War (1898), 13
Stalin, Joseph, xx, 95, 167, 171
Stars and Stripes, 173, 179
status of forces agreements (SOFAs), 10, 202, 203
Stewart, Leslie, 76
Stilwell, Joseph, xv, xvi, 82–83, 126, 128, 134, 197, 205; in Burma campaign, 95–98, 105–6; as CAI commander, 89–91, 94, 95; as CBI commander, xvii, 17, 84–85, 87, 160; Chiang and, xviii, xx, 3, 7, 13, 17, 81, 87–88, 94–96, 98–100; Chinese military viewed by, 79, 85; command of Chinese military sought by, 12, 81, 84, 65, 84, 87, 95, 99–100, 106; early career of, 14; hostel program and, 38–39, 42, 46; interpreter program and, 56–57, 58, 59, 77; military courts' jurisdiction backed by, 129; myth surrounding, 168; prostitution viewed by, 139; Roosevelt's removal of, xxi, 7; shortcomings of, 88; smuggling tolerated by, 117; as soldiers' soldier, 70–71; Y-Force training under, xviii, xix, 92
Stimson, Henry, 84
Stoddard, Lothrop, 73, 93
Stone, Robert, 182
Stuart, J. Leighton, 190
Sullivan, John, 193
Sultan, Daniel, 103
Sun Lianzhong, 176
Sun Liren, 79–80, 88, 90, 91, 102, 107
Sun Rutian, 177
Sun Yat-sen, 29, 53
Sun Yugui, 184

Taiwan, 95, 176
Taliban, 205–6
Tanaka, Shinichi, 101
Tang Yi, 126, 147–48, 161

Tang Yongxian, 181
Tanner, Harold, 167
Tao Zigu (Lucy Chiang), 140
Tehran Conference (1943), 95
Thompson, Loren B., 58, 61–63, 65
Three Principles of the People Youth League, 52, 189
timeline, xv–xxiv
Tong, Hollington (Dong Xianguang), 58, 60–61
Torrey, Reuben, 45
Treaty of Wangxia (1844), 129
Trent, Joseph, 77
Trident Conference (1943), 94
Tripartite Pact (1940), xvi
Truman, Harry S., xxiv, 165, 168, 170, 171, 188, 195–96
Tull, J. E., 137

United China Relief, 30
United Nations, 169
United States of America (Visiting Forces) Act (1942), 129, 130
U.S. Court for China, 117
U.S. Foreign Claims Commission, 181, 182, 184
USS *Hornet*, 106
USS *Luzon*, xv
USS *Panay*, xv
USS *Tutuila*, xv, 147

van de Ven, Hans, 3
V-E Day (1945), xxii
Vietnam War, 204–5
Vincent, John Carter, 105
V-J Day (1945), 4

Wang (interpreting officer), 48, 49, 64, 65, 69
Wang, Y. D., 40–41
Wang Anlin, 149
Wang Chonghui, 129
Wang Fengxi, 193, 198
Wang Haotang, 40
Wang Jingwei, xvi, xxi, 106

Wang Pingshun, 120–21
Wang Shijie, 99
Wang Shimin, 58, 148
Wang Songjin, 94
Wang Yabo, 137–38
Wang Yumao, 53–54
War and Nationalism in China
  (van de Ven), 3
War Area Service Corps (WASC), xvii,
  6; hostel program administered by,
  21, 27–28, 31, 35, 36, 39, 43–44, 47,
  76; interpreter program and, 51, 53,
  56, 61, 66
Ward, Angus, xxiv
Wavell, Archibald, 84
Wedemeyer, Albert, xv, xxi, 7, 17, 73, 76,
  80–81, 100–107, 122, 128, 175, 197;
  Chiang's position undermined by,
  157–58, 161–62; after Japanese
  surrender, 165; postwar advisory
  mission backed by, 81; postwar
  setbacks foreseen by, 169; sexual
  misconduct combated by, 9, 139,
  147–50, 152, 154–55, 156, 187, 189,
  201; traffic reforms attempted by,
  180, 181
Wei Lihuang, 96
Welles, Sumner, 16
Weng Xinjun, 67
Wenhui bao (newspaper), 178, 188
Wen Mingjing, 90–91, 94
Wen Yiduo, 51
Wertheim, Stephen, 83
West, Lloyd, 193
Wheeler, Raymond, 39, 41, 148
White, Omar, 158
White, Theodore, 87, 91, 135
Wilcox, Ralph, 109
Wingate, Orde, 95
With the Old Breed (Sledge), 172
Women's Army Corps, 5
Wood, Orlando, 34
Wright, Peter, 140
Wu Cunya, 70
Wuhan University, 56

Wu Liuxiao, 183
Wu Zelin, 51, 63, 73

X-Force (Chinese Army in India), xviii,
  xx, xxi, 88–91, 95, 96–98
Xi'an Incident (1936), 12–13
Xia Yu, 201
Xie Chuwen, 41
Xi feng (magazine), 156
Xinhua ribao (newspaper), 191
Xinmin bao (newspaper), 181
Xinwen tiandi (magazine), 138
Xiong Shihui, 83, 88, 99, 107
Xu Boxin, 179
Xu Decheng, 175

Yacavone, Gene, 119
Yalta Conference (1945), xxii, 171
Yang Chenren, 122
Yangtze Patrol, xv, xvii, 13
Yang Xianjian, 65–67
Yang Zhengcai, 149
Yao Baobao, 187
Yao Guanshun, 73
Yao Kai, 57
Yavelak, William, 65
Y-Force, xviii, 60, 64, 91–92, 106;
  consolidation of, xix; in Salween
  campaign, xx, xxi, 95–100
Yin Erwu, 182
Yixun xunkan (Interpreting dispatch),
  64, 65
YMCA, 26
Yu Diqing, 189–90
Yun Geum-i, 203–4
Yunnan province, xviii; airfield
  construction in, *114*, 115, 200; banditry
  in, 104, 111; hostels in, 6, 24, 28, 34, 40,
  42; inflation in, 23, 42; Japanese
  occupation of, xx, 64, 95, 96; physical
  beauty of, 32; sexual relations in, 149,
  153, 158, 159; theft and smuggling in,
  120, 122, 123–24; training programs
  in, xviii, xix, 57, 60, 72, 91
Yu Pinghui, 115

Zang Da Erzi (Zang Yaocheng), xxiii, 177–78, 183, 184, 190
Zha Hailun, 138
Zhang Ding, 179
Zhang Guoqing, 132
Zhang Guoshui, 132, 201
Zhang Guqing, 41
Zhang Mingsheng, 109–10
Zhang Shaosong, 177
Zhang Shaoxun, 70
Zhang Wanli, 147
Zhang Zhiliang, 71

Zhang Zhizhong, 99
Zhejiang University, 56
Zheng Dongguo, 90
Zhen Lin, 200
Zhou Enlai, 188, 191
Zhou Erbao, 184
Zhou Mingheng, 64
Zhou Zihuan, 41
Zhu Junle, 143
Zhu Youyu, 51
Zong Yongyu, 147
Zou Jiacai, 41

CPSIA information can be obtained
at www.ICGtesting.com
Printed in the USA
LVHW101909240822
726781LV00005B/292